Fors Clavigera

LETTERS

TO THE WORKMEN AND LABOURERS OF GREAT BRITAIN

BY

JOHN RUSKIN

VOLUME III.

GREENWOOD PRESS, PUBLISHERS
NEW YORK   1968

Originally published in 1886 by
FRANK F. LOVELL AND COMPANY

First Greenwood reprinting, 1968
LIBRARY OF CONGRESS catalogue card number: 68-55326

PRINTED IN THE UNITED STATES OF AMERICA

FORS CLAVIGERA.

LETTER LVI.

I BELIEVE my readers will scarcely thank me for printing, this month, instead of the continuation of the letter from Wakefield, a theological essay by Mr. Lyttel. But it is my first business, in *Fors*, to be just,—and only my second or third to be entertaining ; so that any person who conceives himself to have been misrepresented must always have my types at his command. On the other side, I must point out, before entering further into controversy of any kind, the constant habit in my antagonists of misrepresenting *me*. For instance ; in an article forwarded to me from a local paper, urging what it can in defence of the arrangements noticed by me as offensive, at Kirby Lonsdale and Clapham, I find this sentence :

" The squire's house does not escape, though one can see no reason for the remark unless it be that Mr. Ruskin dislikes lords, squires, and clergymen."

Now I have good reason for supposing this article to have been written by a gentleman ;—and even an amiable gentleman,—who, feeling himself hurt, and not at all wishing to hurt anybody, very naturally cries out : and thinks it monstrous in me to hurt *him ;* or his own pet lord, or squire. But he never thinks what wrong there may be in printing his own momentary impression of the character of a man who has been thirty years before the public, without taking the smallest pains to ascertain whether his notion be true or false.

It happens, by Fors' appointment, that the piece of my
early life which I have already written for this month's letter, sufficiently answers the imputation of my dislike to
lords and squires. But I will preface it, in order to illustrate my dislike of clergymen, by a later bit of biography ;
which, at the rate of my present progress in giving account
of myself, I should otherwise, as nearly as I can calculate,
reach only about the year 1975.

Last summer, in Rome, I lodged at the Hotel de Russie ;
and, in the archway of the courtyard of that mansion, waited
usually, in the mornings, a Capuchin friar, begging for his
monastery.

Now, though I greatly object to any clergyman's coming
and taking me by the throat, and saying ' Pay me that
thou owest,' I never pass a begging friar without giving him
sixpence, or the equivalent fivepence of foreign coin ;—extending the charity even occasionally as far as tenpence, if
no fivepenny-bit chance to be in my purse. And this particular begging friar having a gentle face, and a long white
beard, and a beautiful cloak, like a blanket ; and being altogether the pleasantest sight, next to Sandro Botticelli's Zip-
porah, I was like to see in Rome in the course of the day, I
always gave him the extra fivepence for looking so nice ;
which generosity so worked on his mind,—(the more usual
English religious sentiment in Rome expending itself rather in
buying poetical pictures of monks than in filling their bellies),
—that, after some six or seven doles of tenpences, he must
needs take my hand one day, and try to kiss it. Which being only just able to prevent, I took him round the neck
and kissed his lips instead : and this, it seems, was more to
him than the tenpences, for, next day, he brought me a little
reliquary, with a certificated fibre in it of St. Francis' cloak,
(the hair one, now preserved at Assisi) ; and when afterwards I showed my friend Fra Antonio, the Assisi sac-
ristan, what I had got, it was a pleasure to see him open his
eyes, wider than Monsieur the Syndic at Hansli's fifty thousand crowns. He thought I must have come by it dishon-
estly ; but not I, a whit,—for I most carefully explained to

the Capuchin, when he brought it to me, that I was more a Turk than a Catholic ;—but he said I might keep the reliquary, for all that.

Contenting myself, for the moment, with this illustration of my present dislike of clergymen, I return to earlier days.

But for the reader's better understanding of such further progress of my poor little life as I may trespass on his patience in describing, it is now needful that I give some account of my father's mercantile position in London.

The firm of which he was head-partner may be yet remembered by some of the older city houses, as carrying on their business in a small counting-house on the first floor of narrow premises, in as narrow a thoroughfare of East London, —Billiter Street, the principal traverse from Leadenhall Street into Fenchurch Street.

The names of the three partners were given in full on their brass plate under the counting-house bell,—Ruskin, Telford, and Domecq.

Mr. Domecq's name should have been the first, by rights, for my father and Mr. Telford were only his agents. He was the sole proprietor of the estate which was the main capital of the firm,—the vineyard of Macharnudo, the most precious hillside, for growth of white wine, in the Spanish peninsula. The quality of the Macharnudo vintage essentially fixed the standard of Xeres 'sack,' or 'dry '—secco—sherris, or sherry, from the days of Henry the Fifth to our own ;—the unalterable and unrivalled chalk-marl of it putting a strength into the grape which age can only enrich and darken,—never impair.

Mr. Peter Domecq was, I believe, Spanish born ; and partly French, partly English bred : a man of strictest honour, and kindly disposition ; how descended, I do not know ; how he became possessor of his vineyard, I do not know ; what position he held, when young, in the firm of Gordon, Murphy, and Company, I do not know ; but in their house he watched their head-clerk, my father, during his nine years of duty, and when the house broke up, asked him to be his own agent in England. My father saw that he could

fully trust Mr. Domecq's honour, and feeling ;—but not so
fully either his sense, or his industry : and insisted, though
taking only his agent's commission, on being both nominally, and practically, the head-partner of the firm.

Mr. Domecq lived chiefly in Paris ; rarely visiting his
Spanish estate, but having perfect knowledge of the proper
processes of its cultivation, and authority over its labourers
almost like a chief's over his clan. He kept the wines at the
highest possible standard ; and allowed my father to manage
all matters concerning their sale, as he thought best. The
second partner, Mr. Henry Telford, brought into the business what capital was necessary for its London branch. The
premises in Billiter Street belonged to him ; and he had a
pleasant country house at Widmore, near Bromley ; a quite
far-away Kentish village in those days.

He was a perfect type of an English country gentleman
of moderate fortune ;—unmarried, living with three unmarried sisters—who, in the refinement of their highly educated,
unpretending, benevolent, and felicitous lives, remain in my
memory more like the figures in a beautiful story than
realities. Neither in story, nor in reality, have I ever again
heard of, or seen, anything like Mr. Henry Telford ;—so gentle, so humble, so affectionate, so clear in common sense, so
fond of horses,—and so entirely incapable of doing, thinking, or saying, anything that had the slightest taint in it of
the racecourse or the stable.

Yet I believe he never missed any great race ; passed the
greater part of his life on horseback ; and hunted during
the whole Leicestershire season ;—but never made a·bet,
never had a serious fall, and never hurt a horse. Between
him and my father there was absolute confidence, and the
utmost friendship that could exist without community of
pursuit. My father was greatly proud of Mr. Telford's
standing among the country gentlemen ; and Mr. Telford
was affectionately respectful to my father's steady industry
and infallible commercial instinct. Mr. Telford's actual part
in the conduct of the business was limited to attendance in
the counting-house during two months at Midsummer, when

my father took his holiday, and sometimes for a month at
the beginning of the year, when he travelled for orders. At
these times Mr. Telford rode into London daily from Widmore, signed what letters and bills needed signature, read
the papers, and rode home again : any matters needing deliberation were referred to my father, or awaited his return.
All the family at Widmore would have been limitlessly kind
to my mother and me, if they had been permitted any opportunity; but my mother always felt, in cultivated society,
—and was too proud to feel with patience,—the defects of
her own early education, and therefore (which was the true
and fatal sign of such defect) never familiarly visited any
one whom she did not feel to be, in some sort, her inferior.

Nevertheless, Mr. Telford had a singularly important influence in my education. By, I believe, his sister's advice,
he gave me, as soon as it was published, the illustrated
edition of Rogers' *Italy.* This book was the first means
I had of looking carefully at Turner's work : and I might,
not without some appearance of reason, attribute to the gift
the entire direction of my life's energies. But it is the great
error of thoughtless biographers to attribute to the accident
which introduces some new phase of character, all the circumstances of character which gave the accident importance.
The essential point to be noted, and accounted for, was that
I could understand Turner's work when I saw it ; not by
what chance or in what year it was first seen.

Poor Mr. Telford, nevertheless, was always held by papa
and mamma primarily responsible for my Turner insanities.

In a more direct, though less intended way, his help to me
was important. For, before my father thought it right to
hire a carriage for the above mentioned Midsummer holiday,
Mr. Telford always lent us his own travelling chariot.

Now the old English chariot is the most luxurious of travelling carriages, for two persons, or even for two persons and
so much of third personage as I possessed at three years
old. The one in question was hung high, so that we could
see well over stone dykes and average hedges out of it ; such
elevation being attained by the old-fashioned folding-steps,

with a lovely padded cushion fitting into the recess of the door,—steps which it was one of my chief travelling delights to see the hostlers fold up and down ; though my delight was painfully alloyed by envious ambition to be allowed to do it myself :—but I never was,—lest I should pinch my fingers.

The ' dickey,'—(to think that I should never till this moment have asked myself the derivation of that word, and now be unable to get at it !)—being, typically, that commanding seat in her Majesty's mail, occupied by the Guard ; and classical, even in modern literature, as the scene of Mr. Bob Sawyer's arrangements with Sam,—was thrown far back in Mr. Telford's chariot, so as to give perfectly comfortable room for the legs, (if one chose to travel outside on fine days), and to afford beneath it spacious area to the boot, a storehouse of rearward miscellaneous luggage. Over which—with all the rest of forward and superficial luggage—my nurse Anne presided, both as guard and packer ; unrivalled, she, in the flatness and precision of her in-laying of dresses, as in turning of pancakes ; the fine precision, observe, meaning also the easy wit and invention of her art; for, no more in packing a trunk than commanding a campaign, is precision possible without foresight.

Posting, in those days, being universal, so that at the leading inns in every country town, the cry " Horses out ! " down the yard, as one drove up, was answered, often instantly, always within five minutes, by the merry trot through the archway of the booted and bright-jacketed rider, with his caparisoned pair,—there was no driver's seat in front : and the four large, admirably fitting and sliding windows, admitting no drop of rain when they were up, and never sticking as they were let down, formed one large moving oriel, out of which one saw the country round, to the full half of the horizon. My own prospect was more extended still, for my seat was the little box containing my clothes, strongly made, with a cushion on one end of it ; set upright in front (and well forward), between my father and mother. I was thus not the least in their way, and my horizon of sight the widest possible. When no object of particular interest presented itself, I trotted, keeping time with the postboy—on my trunk cushion for a saddle, and whipped my father's legs for horses ; at first theoretically only, with dextrous motion of wrist ; but ultimately in a quite practical and efficient manner, my father having presented me with a silver-mounted postilion's whip.

The Midsummer holiday, for better enjoyment of which Mr. Telford provided us with these luxuries, began usually on the fifteenth of May, or thereabouts ;—my father's birthday was on the tenth ; on that day I was always allowed to gather the gooseberries for his first gooseberry pie of the year, from the tree between the buttresses on the north wall of the Herne Hill garden ; so that we could not leave before that *festa*. The holiday itself consisted in a tour for orders through half the English counties ; and a visit (if the counties lay northward) to my aunt in Scotland.

The mode of journeying was as fixed as that of our home life. We went from forty to fifty miles a day, starting always early enough in the morning to arrive comfortably to four-o'clock dinner. Generally, therefore, getting off at six o'clock, a stage or two were done before breakfast, with the dew on the grass, and first scent from the hawthorns : if in the course of the midday drive there were any gentleman's house to be seen,—or, better still, a lord's—or, best of all, a duke's, my father baited the horses, and took my mother and me reverently through the state rooms ; always speaking a little under our breath to the housekeeper, major domo, or other authority in charge ; and gleaning worshipfully what fragmentary illustrations of the history and domestic ways of the family might fall from their lips. My father had a quite infallible natural judgment in painting ; and though it had never been cultivated so as to enable him to understand the Italian schools, his sense of the power of the nobler masters in northern work was as true and passionate as the most accomplished artist's. He never, when I was old enough to care for what he himself delighted in, allowed me to look for an instant at a bad picture ; and if there were a Reynolds, Velasquez, Vandyck, or Rembrandt in the rooms, he would pay the surliest housekeepers into patience until he had seen it to heart's content ; if none of these, I was allowed to look at Guido, Carlo Dolce—or the more skilful masters of the Dutch school—Cuyp, Teniers, Hobbima, Wouvermans ; but never any second-rate or doubtful examples.

I wonder how many of the lower middle class are now capable of going through a nobleman's house, with judgment of this kind ; and yet with entirely unenvious and reverent delight in the splendour of the abode of the supreme and beneficent being who allows them thus to enter his paradise ?

If there were no nobleman's house to be seen, there was certainly, in the course of the day's journey, some ruined castle or abbey ; some celebrated village church, or stately cathedral. We had always unstinted time for these ; and if I was at disadvantage because neither my father nor mother could tell me enough history to make the buildings authoritatively interesting, I had at least leisure and liberty to animate them with romance in my own fashion.

I am speaking, however, now, of matters relating to a more advanced age than that to which I have yet brought myself :—age in which all these sights were only a pleasant amazement to me, and panoramic apocalypse of a lovely world.

Up to that age, at least, I cannot but hope that my readers will agree with me in thinking the tenour of my life happy, and the modes of my education, on the whole, salutary.

Admitting them to have been so, I would now question farther ; and, I imagine, such question cannot but occur to my readers' minds, also,—how far education, and felicities, of the same kind, may be attainable for young people in general.

Let us consider, then, how many conditions must meet ; and how much labour must have been gone through, both by servile and noble persons, before this little jaunty figure, seated on its box of clothes, can trot through its peaceful day of mental development.

I. A certain number of labourers in Spain, living on dry bread and onions, must have pruned and trodden grapes ;— cask-makers, cellarmen, and other functionaries attending on them.

II. Rough sailors must have brought the wine into the London Docks.

III. My father and his clerks must have done a great deal of arithmetical and epistolary work, before my father could have profit enough from the wine to pay for our horses, and our dinner.

IV. The tailor must have given his life to the dull business of making clothes—the wheelwright and carriage-maker to their woodwork—the smith to his buckles and springs—the postilion to his riding—the horse-breeder and breaker to the cattle in his field and stable,—before I could make progress in this pleasant manner, even for a single stage.

V. Sundry English Kings and Barons must have passed their lives in military exercises, and gone to their deaths in military practices, to provide me with my forenoons' entertainments in ruined castles ; or founded the great families whose servants were to be my hosts.

VI. Vandyck and Velasquez, and many a painter before them, must have spent their lives in learning and practising their laborious businesses.

VII. Various monks and abbots must have passed their lives in pain, with fasting and prayer ; and a large company of stonemasons occupied themselves in their continual service, in order to provide me, in defect of castles and noblemen's seats, with amusement in the way of abbeys and cathedrals.

How far, then, it remains to be asked, supposing my education, in any wise exemplary, can all these advantages be supplied by the modern school board, to every little boy born in the prosperous England of this day ?   And much more in that glorious England of the future ; in which there will be no abbeys, (all having been shaken down, as my own sweet Furness is fast being, by the luggage trains) ; no castles, except such as may have been spared to be turned into gaols, like that of " time-honoured Lancaster," also in my own neighbourhood ; no parks, because Lord Derby's patent steam agriculture will have cut down all the trees ; no lords, nor dukes, because modern civilization won't be Lorded over, nor Led anywhere ; no gentlemen's seats, except in the Kirby Lonsdale style ; and no roads anywhere, except trams and rails?

Before, however, entering into debate as to the methods of education to be adopted in these .coming times, let me examine a little, in next letter, with help from my readers of aristocratic tendencies, what the real product of this olden method of education was intended to be ; and whether it was worth the cost.

For the impression on the aristocratic mind of the day was always (especially supposing I had been a squire's or a lord's son, instead of a merchant's) that such little jaunty figure, trotting in its easy chariot, was, as it were, a living diamond, without which the watch of the world could not possibly go; or even, that the diminutive darling was a kind of Almighty Providence in its first breeches, by whose tiny hands and infant fiat the blessings of food and raiment were continually provided for God's Spanish labourers in His literal vineyard; for God's English sailors, seeing His wonders in the deep ; for God's tailors' men, sitting in attitude of Chinese Josh for ever ; for the divinely appointed wheelwrights, carpenters, horses and riders, hostlers and Gaius-mine-hosts, necessary to my triumphal progress ; and for my nurse behind in the dickey. And it never once entered the head of any aristocratic person,—nor would ever have entered mine, I suppose, unless I had "the most analytical mind in Europe,"—that in verity it was not I who fed my nurse, but my nurse me ; and that a great part of the world had been literally put behind me as a dickey,—and all the aforesaid inhabitants of it, somehow, appointed to be nothing but my nurses : the beautiful product intended, by papa and mamma, being—a Bishop, who should graciously overlook these tribes of inferior beings, and instruct their ignorance in the way of their souls' salvation.

As the Master of the St. George's Company, I request their permission to convey their thanks to Mr. Plimsoll, for his Christian, knightly, and valiant stand, made against the recreant English Commons, on Thursday, 22nd July, 1875.

NOTES AND CORRESPONDENCE.

I HAVE thankfully received this month, from the first donor of land to the St. George's Company, Mrs. Talbot, £11 0s. 4d., rent of cottages on said land, at Barmouth, North Wales; and I have become responsible, as the Master of the Company, for rent or purchase of a room at Sheffield, in which I propose to place some books and minerals, as the germ of a museum arranged first for workers in iron, and extended into illustration of the natural history of the neighbourhood of Sheffield, and more especially of the geology and flora of Derbyshire. The following two letters respecting the neighbouring town of Leeds will be found interesting in connection with this first opening of St. George's work:—

" LEEDS, *June 21st*, 1875.

" Dear Sir,—Being more or less intimately mixed up with the young of the working classes, in night schools and similar works, I am anxious to know what I can do to counteract two or three growths, which seem likely to be productive of very disastrous results, in the young men from seventeen to twenty-five, who are many of them earning from 20s. to 35s. per week,—the almost morbid craving for drink, and the excitement which is to be found in modern French dramas of very questionable morality, concert halls and singing rooms, where appeal is principally made to their animal passions and lusts—whose chief notion of enjoyment seems to be in getting drunk. Then the young women of similar ages, and earning from 14s. to 20s., who are in a chronic state of unrest, ever eager for novelty and sensationalism, though not quite so much given to drink as the men, yet treading a similar course. They have no pleasure in going to the country, to see flowers, birds, and fish, or to the seaside to see the sea; if there be no fireworks, no prize band, no dancing on the green, or something of the sort, they will not attempt to go. Now, where is all this to end? Nature has no charms for them; music little attraction, except in the form of *dance ;* pictures nothing: what remains? And yet something should, and must be done, and that speedily,—otherwise what will become of the poor things?

" Then, in your *Elements of Drawing*, you lay down certain books to be studied, etc.

" Now, suppose a woman or man has been brought up to have a kind of contempt for *Grimm's Goblins, Arabian Nights*, etc., as childish and frivolous,—and on account of the Calvinistic tendency of relatives, has been precluded from reading *books*,—how should a healthy tendency be brought about? For the mind is not a blank, to receive impressions like a child, but has all sorts of preconceived notions and prejudices in the way,—Shakespeare looked upon as immoral, or childish, and the rest treated in an equally cavalier manner by people who probably never looked inside the books."

I should like to answer the above letter at some length ; but have, to-day, no time. The sum of answer is—Nothing *can* be done, but what I am trying to form this St. George's Company to do. I am sorry to omit the 'thoughts' to which my second correspondent refers, in the opening of this following letter, but she gave me no permission to publish them :—

' These thoughts made me settle in Leeds (being free from family obligations), in order to see for myself what I could do for these towns, and what their state really was. The Borough Surveyor of Leeds (who had been six months only in office, and was perhaps new to commercial life,) said to me, ' There is nothing in Leeds but jobbery, and trickery.' Almsgiving (for the law of supply and demand cannot do it) in the shape of decent houses, was the first thing to be done, I found.

" The late Canon Kingsley, in his tract on the ' Application of Associative Principles and Methods to Agriculture ' (1851), confounds justice and almsgiving together. They are surely distinct,* but you cannot give alms till you have paid just debts.

" You say nothing in *Fors* of the custom which rules that rich capitalists and landowners † shall leave each of, say five or six daughters, (I am eldest of six,) a fortune large enough to enable her to live in idleness, and more or less luxury, for life. This custom is, I believe, at the root of much extortion and avarice on the part of fathers, and leads to marriages for money ‡ on the part of younger men. I deny the claim of women to political power; but I think, with Lord Salisbury, that every girl (no matter what her rank) has a moral right to be educated for self-maintenance, and proper rational feminine self-reliance.—and not mainly for society, or, in other words, for marriage.

" Believing § that, in the abstract, men are morally, mentally, and physically superior to women, I yet believe that the perfect relative independence and indifferent dignity of mental attitude which rightly trained and educated women should possess before matrimony (an attitude which is, to say the least, now often wanting) is essential to the proper influence women should exercise over men. It is essential to the vantage ground on which unmarried women should stand, and from which they should draw men up to their standard, not bend themselves down to men's.

" An article (one of a series on ' French Home Life ') in *Blackwood,* some years ago, says (nearly in these words)—' Supply will follow demand : if men prefer a virtuous type of womanhood, good and well ; if otherwise, young ladies and their mothers will recognize the demand

---

* Very surely.

† Because I entirely ignore rich capitalists and landowners,—or look on them only as the claws of my Dragon.

‡ Every unmarried woman should have enough left her by her father to keep herself, and a pet dog—but not, also, an idle man.

§ On what grounds? I don't understand a word of this paragraph : least of all why either men or women should be considered ' in the abstract'; and, in the concrete, I can't make out why men are the higher, at the beginning of the sentence, and women at the end of it.

and will meet it.' ! ! ! That an old-established magazine, much read by the aristocracy, should give utterance to a sentiment like this (whether or not it be true) strikes me as a sign of the times, as bad as most you have quoted in *Fors.* [Assuredly.]

"Apart from the *élite* of the women of the genuine aristocracy, who, with long inherited noble instincts of all kinds, are always charming, and full of noble influence, over those who come within its sphere,—there is the vast mass of English middle-class women who make up the nation, women whose inherited instincts are perhaps ignoble, or at best indefinite. The right education of these is surely an important point in social reform, and yet is still a practically unsolved problem. I have done parish work for thirteen years and more, and know the existing relations between rich and poor experimentally. The root of the matter seems to be this. Modern Christianity professes and attempts to practise the moral code of the New Testament *—mercy, while ignoring, or trampling under foot, the moral code of the Old—justice, which must come. It is thus that so much Christianity, in all sects, is (unconsciously often) sham Christianity. I agree with what you say of the clergy in many things ; they do not know if Christianity in our days means peace, or the sword. Saying to their rich parishioners ' Thou art the man' would often be an ending to the peace and comfort of their own lives : subscriptions would be stopped, on which they rely for almsgiving, and by means of which almsgiving they try to draw the poor to church, and so to heaven.

"Again, who in this day has quite clean hands with regard to money ? I know a clergyman who worked for many years in a parish, and improved the morality of the people by his work. Among other things, he caused (by persuasion, and substitution of a reading-room) a public-house to be shut up—the squire co-operating with him. This selfsame squire wants to sell the property ; is told it will sell better with a public-house. He rebuilds one in the village before he sells it !

"Broadly speaking, the creed of young men of the richer classes is self-indulgence, that of young women, self-sacrifice, (shown in mistaken ways, no doubt). To thinking and well-disposed women of all classes, church or chapel going is a necessity. The life of most of them is only made endurable by the hope of another world than this.

"For the past six years I have been wandering about more or less, investigating, and experiencing personally, to some extent, and at the cost of much suffering, the various forms of distress in the various classes. I look back on my years of parish work as on one long monotonous day—so hopeless is such work, unless regarded, from the ecclesiastical point of view, as a self-preparation for Heaven. Seeing, as I did, and do, how entirely preventible half of the misery is, which is coolly accepted by religious and charitable people as the ordained Will of God, I stopped short (among other reasons), and gave my mind and my time to investigate and analyse the causes of the miseries, and how far it was practicable to cut at the roots of them—not snip off the blossoms, merely. Will you bear with a word as to the position of women ? I agree with you : it is a futile discussion, that of equality or inequality. But as unhappily I have had to think, see, and judge for myself, in a way that, in a right order of things, ought not to be required of a

---

* My dear lady, it attempts nothing of the sort. It supposes the New Testament to be an announcement of universal pardon and speedy promotion to rascals.

woman, I wish to disclaim all sympathy with the women of the women's rights party. They are well-intentioned, but mistaken. It is dread of being identified with their views that prevents the best and most influential women of the aristocracy from doing what they might do. I trust you will secure the co-operation of such women for your St. George's Company."

I wish I could! It will be a curious point in the story of the founding of the St. George's Company, that at any rate during five years, only one woman of the upper classes gave me any help.

I hope, however, that the fact (perhaps less universally true than formerly) that "to thoughtful and well-disposed women of all classes, church-going is a necessity," may be accounted for otherwise than by the misery of their earthly lives. For the sake, however, of my female, and theological, readers, I print the next following letter :—

"THE PARSONAGE, WERRINGTON, PETERBOROUGH, *July* 7, 1875.

"MY DEAR SIR,—In your comment on a former letter of mine you acknowledged, (*a*) that the Gospel which I endeavour to preach—Be persuaded by the Lord Jesus Christ; let His life rule your lives—is eternally true and salutary, but, because I have joined with you in condemning a doctrine opposed to this, you have rather hastily assumed (*b*) that I have 'eagerly repudiated the doctrine of the Eleventh Article of the Church of England,' to which Article I have given, and not withdrawn, my public assent.

"You have of course taken for granted (*c*) that the Eleventh Article teaches the 'pleasant and supremely false gospel'—Let His life be instead of your lives; you may be saved by faith without righteousness. But does it?

The Article says:

"'*We are accounted righteous before God, only for the merit of our Lord and Saviour Jesus Christ, by Faith, and not for our own works or deservings: Wherefore, that we are justified by Faith only is a most wholesome doctrine, and very full of comfort, as more largely is expressed in the Homily of Justification.*'

"This teaches, in simple English enough, that there is but one righteousness in God's sight—the righteousness of Christ; and that this righteousness becomes ours by faith: so that faith alone sets us right with God.

"Before the court of public opinion (*d*) men may be accounted righteous for 'works and deservings' of their own, like those which were so eminently satisfactory to the Pharisee who went up to the Temple to pray; but before God, whose judgments are true, the only merit for which any man is accounted righteous is the merit of Jesus Christ. The Publican 'went down to his house justified' because of that faith in God which led him to hunger and thirst after a righteousness higher than his own, and in due time to be filled with it.

"A man is 'justified by faith only' because by faith only he accepts the righteousness of Christ, not instead of, but *for*, (*e*) his own. He is therefore accounted righteous before God because, in His sight, who sees the end from the beginning, he *is* righteous.

" But, while the righteousness is verily his own, he confesses that, in the deepest sense, it is not his own, for the source and efficient cause of it is Christ—the merit is His.

" From all this it will appear that what I repudiate is not the Eleventh Article, but the eternally false and damnatory doctrine which has seemed to you to be set forth therein.

" I cannot think that the Article was intended to teach that a man can be accounted righteous before God without righteousness—that faith will serve as a substitute for it, since I read in the Homily in which the doctrine of the Article is 'more largely expressed' such words as the following :

" ' *This true Christian faith neither any devil hath, nor yet any man who, in the outward profession of his mouth, and his outward receiving of the Sacraments, in coming to the Church, and in all other outward appearances, seemeth to be a Christian man, and yet in his living and deeds sheweth the contrary.*'

" I am, my dear Sir,

" Very faithfully yours,

" JOHN RUSKIN, Esq.   " EDWARD Z. LYTTEL."

(*a*) My correspondent cannot quit himself of the idea that I am his antagonist. If he preaches what is true, I say so—if what is false, I say so. I congratulate him in the one case, and am sorry for him in the other ; but have nothing to 'acknowledge' in either case.

(*b*) and (*c*) "You have rather hastily assumed." "You have of course taken for granted." Compare Mr. Headlam's "I fancy that, on consideration, you would like to withdraw," Vol. II., p. 435. These clerical gentlemen, who habitually and necessarily write *without* consideration, and as habitually and necessarily ' take for granted' the entire grounds of their profession, are quaintly unable to enter into the mind of a man who for twenty years has not written a word without testing it syllable by syllable ; nor taking for granted one principle or fact, in art, science, or history,—having somewhat wide work in all three.

In the present case, I am very sorry to have to tell my correspondent that the last thing I should ' take for granted ' would be the completeness and accuracy of his own account of himself. What his words actually mean, my twenty years' study of English enables me to tell him with authority ;—but what he means by them, *he* only knows !

(*d*) Who is talking of public opinion? Does my correspondent suppose that in any—even among the rudest or most ignorant – debates on this subject ' righteousness ' was ever supposed to mean wordly credit? The question is, was, and will be—simply how men escape being damned—if they do.

(*e*) It is no part of my duty in *Fors* to occupy myself in exposing the verbal, or probing the mental, sophistries by which the aerial ingenuity of divines may guide itself in gossamer over the inconveniently furrowed ground of religious dogma. There are briefly two, and two only, forms of possible Christian, Pagan, or any other gospel, or 'good message': one, that men are saved by themselves doing what is right; and the other that they are saved by believing that somebody else did right instead of them. The first of these Gospels is eternally true, and holy; the other eternally false, damnable, and damning. Which of them Mr. Lyttel preaches, matters much to himself and his parishioners; but, to the world, considerably less than he seems to suppose. That the eleventh Article of the Church of England teaches the second, "in very simple English," is as certain as Johnson's dictionary can make it: and that it (the said sweet message) is currently preached with unction, and received with gladness, over the whole of England, and of Protestant France, Switzerland, and Italy, by the most active and influential members of the Protestant church, I take upon me to assert, on the grounds of an experience gained, (while Mr. Lyttel was, by his own account, "occupied from day to day in stuffy rooms among ignorant and immoral people") by the carefullest study of the best Protestant divines, and the hearing of sermons by the most eloquent pastors, in every important city of evangelical Europe. Finally, I must beg Mr. Lyttel to observe that I only printed his first letter because it expressed some degree of doubt, and discomfort, which I hoped to relieve. His succeeding letters show him, on the contrary, to be supremely confident and comfortable;—in which enviable state I must here take leave of him. For my challenge (as yet unanswered) was to his Bishop, and not to the clergy of the diocese; nor, if it had been, has Mr. Lyttel offered any evidence that he is their accredited champion.

I think I do Mr. Lyttel more justice by printing his kind and graceful last words on my impatient comments, than I should by disarranging my types, and altering my letter; which, indeed, I have no time to do.

"MY DEAR SIR,—It is both my fault and misfortune that you have taken parts of my letters 'clean from the purpose of the words themselves;' and I write at once in hope that you may be able to erase two unserviceable paragraphs, which my want of simple English, or some other misdirection, has produced.

"1. If you will allow me to substitute the word 'said' for 'acknowledged' in my letter, it will save paragraph (*a*).

"2. Then I should like to assure you that the feeling which called forth my first letter also produced the rest, and no one who knows me well would think of attributing to me 'supreme confidence and comfort.' Moreover, I have throughout spoken for myself alone, and have not for one moment pretended to be the 'accredited champion' of any one. So that if you can spare the latter part of paragraph (*e*), beginning with 'Finally,' I think neither you nor I would lose anything by the omission.

" Other parts of your comment I am sorry for, but I have not the same reason to object to them as I have to those I have specified.

" I am most faithfully yours,

"EDWARD Z. LYTTEL."

Some slips of newspaper have been forwarded to me, containing an abstract of a sermon by the Bishop of Manchester, in which some reference was made to *Fors :* but of course I cannot take any notice of expressions thus accidentally conveyed to me, and probably reported with inaccuracy. The postscript to the following interesting letter of Mr. Sillar's may perhaps receive from the Bishop of Manchester more honourable attention :—

"KINGSWOOD LODGE, LEE GREEN, S.E., 13*th January,* 1875.

" MY DEAR MR. RUSKIN,—I have great sympathy with your lady correspondent, and, for the life of me, I cannot tell what you would have me to do. I am not a landed proprietor, nor a country gentleman, though I am the son of one, a retired physician, and brought up in the blessed green fields, and among streams that were as clear as crystal, and full of trout ; but coal-pits appeared on the horizon, and gradually drove us out. I well remember the first vile red shaft that appeared within about a mile of our windows, and how the beastly smoke reconciled my mother to leave one of the loveliest country seats in Lancashire, which she had adorned with roses and laurels, I was going to say with her own hands, and I am not sure that it would be wrong to say so, for she saw every one (and the grounds were seven or eight acres in extent) planted with her own eyes, and superintended the doing of it.

" Living there in the country, and under a tutor, my education has not been that of an ordinary country gentleman ; I early learned to work with my hands as well as with my head, and though I must confess that personally I never had much taste for gardening, I had plenty of work to do in the open air. You tell me our education has to begin —yours as well as mine ; and expect me to say that I cannot make a brick or a tile, or build a rude dwelling. Singularly enough, I helped to do so when a boy, and it will be long before any of us forget the miniature cottage we built, and thatched, complete, with window, door, and fireplace, and with a cellar moreover, with wine of our own making, and beer of our own brewing made from treacle ; for we did everything ourselves, even to grooming our own ponies.

" In later life, my lot was cast in Liverpool, and after six or seven years spent in China, where I have seen the horrors of war, and where a cannon shot came through our roof, as we sat at tiffin, I found myself in London.

" My old business of a merchant I cannot carry on ; though I have capital sufficient for fair trade, I cannot carry it on in the face of the fierce competition by unprincipled men on borrowed money :

' Where man competes with man like foe with foe,
Till death that thins them scarce seems public woe '—

my business as a banker and bullion broker is sealed to me as iniquitous.

"At present, therefore, I am free to act; I fret because I am in a state of inactivity. I feel that I have health and strength, and that in a thousand ways I could be useful, but wherever I turn I am stopped. I am a good rough joiner; I can do small work in iron and brass; and I am a good practical chemist : my laboratory was recommended as an example of how a laboratory should be kept, by the editor of the *Chemical News* and an F.R.S.

"Now allow me to ask you seriously, would you have me to go out alone into the wilderness, and live like a Robinson Crusoe till I see an opening? The point is, the opening might come directly, or it might not come for years, and meantime I am standing in the market-place, such as it is (why is there not a real one?). It is this uncertainty that distresses me, for I must work for my living, and my substance is gradually melting away.

"Believe me, my dear Mr. Ruskin, ever yours affectionately,
"ROB. G. SILLAR.

"P. S.—I am glad to see you have challenged Dr. Fraser. I had a correspondence with him some years ago. I saw in one of Carlyle's works, that I might do some good, if I had two fingers and a pen ; so, after getting no answer from my own clergyman, and the secretary of the Society for Promoting Christian Knowledge, relative to the leaving out of a verse in the fifteenth Psalm in our collection, I appealed to the bishop. He was very polite, and corresponded with me till he felt it dangerous to go on, and then informed me that he really had no time to examine into the lawfulness of interest.

"I confess I don't like an officer who has no time to read and examine his standing orders, but who yet retains the command of the regiment ; so as you told me in *Sheepfolds* * that in our army the King was beside every one of us to appeal to in case of doubt, I ended by telling his lordship, as he had no time to hear me, I must leave it in other hands, *videat Altissimus*, and our correspondence closed."

* I am reprinting this pamphlet word for word as it was first issued from the press. Mr. Allen will have it ready for distribution by the first of September.

[I am honoured in the charge given me, without dissent, by the present members of the St. George's Company, to convey their thanks to MR. SAMUEL PLIMSOLL, *in the terms stated at the close of my last letter.]*

LETTER LVII.

I HAVE received, from the author, M. Émile de Lavelaye, his pamphlet,—" Protestantism and Catholicism in their bearing upon the Liberty and Prosperity of Nations, with an introductory letter by Mr. Gladstone." I do not know why M. de Lavelaye sent me this pamphlet. I thank him for the courtesy ; but he has evidently read none of my books, or must have been aware that he could not have written anything more contrary to the positions which I am politically maintaining. On the other hand, I have read none of *his* books, and I gather from passages in his pamphlet that there may be much in them to which I should be able to express entire adhesion.

But of the pamphlet in question, and its preface, he will, I trust, pardon my speaking in the same frank terms which I should have used had it accidentally come under my notice, instead of by the author's gift. The pamphlet is especially displeasing to me, because it speaks of 'Liberty' under the common assumption of its desirableness ; whereas my own teaching has been, and is, that Liberty, whether in the body, soul, or political estate of men, is only another word for Death, and the final issue of Death, putrefaction : the body, spirit, and political estate being alike healthy only by their bonds and laws ; and by Liberty being instantly disengaged into mephitic vapour.

But the matter of this pamphlet, no less than the assumption it is based on, is hateful to me ; reviving, as it does, the

miserable question of the schism between Catholic and Protestant, which is entirely ridiculous and immaterial; and
taking no note whatever of the true and eternal schism,
cloven by the very sword of Michael, between him that serveth
God, and him that serveth Him not.

In furtherance of which contempt of the only vital question in religious matters, I find, in the preface to this
pamphlet, the man, who was so long a favourite Prime
Minister of England, speaking of the "indifferentism, scep-
ticism, materialism, and pantheism, *which for the moment
are so fashionable*" only as "negative systems." He himself being, in fact, nothing else than a negative system,
hundred-tongued to his own confusion; the 'fashionable'
hairdresser, as it were, and Minister of extreme unction in
the manner of pomade, to the scald and moribund English
pates that still wear their religion decoratively, as a bob-wig
with a pigtail, (carefully also anointing and powdering the
remains of its native growth on the heads of their flunkies,)
and from under such contracted and loose-sitting substitute
for the Cavalier locks of their forefathers, look upon the
round heads of the European cropped populace, only as "for
the moment so fashionable,"—little thinking in what prison
discipline the Newgate cut has its origin with the most of
them, or in what hardship of war, and pressure of helmet on
weary brows, for others. The fact being that I am, at this
central time of my life's work, at pause because I cannot set
down any form of religious creed so simple, but that the re-
quirement of its faithful signature by persons desiring to
become Companions of St. George, would exclude some of
the noblest champions of justice and charity now labouring
for men; while, on the other hand, I cannot set down the
first principles of children's noble education without finding
myself in collision with an almost resistless infidel mob;
which, (I know not whether, in Mr. Gladstone's estimate,
fashionably or vulgarly,) is incapable of conceiving,—how
much less of obeying,—the first laws of human decency,
order, and honour. So that indeed I am fain to ask, with
my Leeds correspondent, in last *Fors*, page 13, what is to

be done for young folks to whom "music has little attraction, except in the form of dance, and pictures are nothing"?

With her pardon, pictures are much, to this class of young people. The woodcuts of halfpenny novels representing scenes of fashionable life,—those representing men murdering their wives, in the *Police News*,—and, finally, those which are to be bought only in the back-shop,—have enormous educational influence on the young British public : which its clergymen, alike ignorant of human nature and human art, think to counteract—by decorating their own churches, forsooth,— and by coloured prints of the story of Joseph ; while the lower tribes of them—Moodys and Sankeys—think to turn modern musical taste to account by fitting negro melodies to hymns.

And yet, my correspondent may be thankful that some remnant of delight *is* still taken in dance-music. It is the last protest of the human spirit, in the poor fallen creatures, against the reign of the absolute Devil, Pandemonium with Mammon on the throne, instead of Lucifer,—the Son of the Earth, Lord of Hell, instead of the Son of the Morning.

Let her stand in the midst of the main railroad station at Birmingham ; and think—what music, or dancing, or other entertainment fit for prodigal sons, could be possible in that pious and little prodigal locality.* Let her read the account of our modern pastoral music, at page 66 of my fifth letter, —of modern Venetian "Barcarolle," page 256 of Letter XIX. and 266 of Letter XX.,—and of our modern Campanile, and Muezzin call to prayer, at page 31 of this *Fors*.

" Work is prayer "—thinks your Wakefield Mahometan ;— his vociferous minaret, in the name, and by the name, of the Devil, shall summon English votaries to such worship for five miles round ; that is to say, over one hundred square miles of English land, the Pandemoniacal voice of the Archangel- trumpet thus arouses men out of their sleep ; and Wakefield becomes Wakeful-field, over that blessed space of acre-age.

Yes ; my correspondent may be thankful that still some

* Compare my Birmingham correspondent's opinion of David's " twangling on the harp," page 78, Letter VI.

feeble lust for dancing on the green ;—still some dim acknowledgment, by besotted and stupified brains, of the laws of
tune and time known to their fathers and mothers—remains
possible to the poor wretches discharged by the excursion
trains for a gasp of breath, and a gleam of light, amidst what
is left to them and us, of English earth and heaven. Waltzing,
drunk, in the country roads by our villages ; yet innocently
drunk, and sleepy at sunset ; not, like their born masters and
teachers, dancing, wilfully, the cancan of hell, with harlots,
at seven in the morning.*

Music, and dancing ! They are quite the two primal instruments of education. Make them licentious ; let Mr. John
Stuart Mill have the dis-ordering of them, so that—(see page
166 of Letter XII.)—" no one shall be guided, or governed, or
directed in the way they should go,"—and they sink to lower
and lower depth—till the dance becomes Death's ; and the
music—a shriek of death by strychnine. But let Miriam and
David, and the Virgins of Israel, have the ordering of them,
and the music becomes at last the Eternal choir ; and the
Dance, the Karol-dance of Christmas, evermore.†

Virgins of Israel, or of England, richly clad by your kings,
and " rejoicing in the dance," how is it you do not divide this
sacred,—*if* sacred,—joy of yours with the poor ? If it can
ever be said of you, as birds of God,

> " Oh beauteous birds, methinks ye measure
> Your movements to some heavenly tune,"

can you not show wherein the heavenliness of it consists, to
—suppose—your Sunday-school classes ? At present, you
keep the dancing to yourselves, and graciously teach *them*
the catechism. Suppose you were to try, for a little while,
learning the catechism yourselves ; and teaching *them*—to
dance ?

---

* *Sesame and Lilies*, page 61.

† Compare Letter XXIV., page 336 ; and Dante, *Paradiso*, xxiv. 16

> " Cosi, quelle carole differente—
> Mente danzando, della sua ricchezza
> Mi si facean stimar, veloci e lente."

Howbeit, in St. George's schools, this, the most 'decorous,' rightly taught, of all exercises, shall not fail of its due discipline to any class whatsoever :—reading, writing, and accounts may all be spared where pupils show no turn to any of those scholarships, but music and dancing, never.* Generally, however, it will be the best singers and dancers who ask for teaching also in literature and art ; for all, there shall at least be the way open to these ; and for none, danger or corruption possible in these. For in their libraries there shall be none but noble books, and in their sight none but noble art.

There is no real difficulty or occasion for dispute in choosing these. Admit the principle of selection, and the practice is easy enough ; only, like all practical matters, the work must be done by one man, sufficiently qualified for it ; and not by a council. If he err, the error may be represented by any one cognizant of it, and by council corrected. But the main work must be done single-handed.

Thus, for the use of the St. George's Company, I shall myself, if my life is spared, write out a list of books which without any question will be found serviceable in their libraries ; †—a system of art instruction which will be secure so far as it reaches ; and a list of purchaseable works of art, which it will be desirable to place in the national schools and museums of the company. With this list of purchaseable works, I shall name, as I have time, those in the museums of Europe which ought to be studied, to the exclusion of those on which time would be wasted.

I have no doubt that this work, though done at first for the St. George's Company, will be found generally useful, and especially that the system of drawing arranged for them will in many respects supersede that of Kensington. I had intended to write it separately, for the use of schools ; but after repeated endeavours to arrange it in a popular form, find that it will not so shape itself availably, but must consist of such broad statements of principle as my now enlarged

* Compare Letter VIII., p. 110; and Letter IX., p. 121.

† This will be added to by future Masters of the Company, with the farther means of specification indicated in page 275 of Letter XXI.

experience enables me to make ; with references to the parts of my other books in which they are defended or illustrated : and of directions for practice given as I can get illustrations of them prepared ; leaving the systematization of them to be made by the master of each drawing school, according to the requirements of his scholars. (See page 123 of Letter IX.)

For example of the impossibility of publishing on a system. It happens to be now fine weather here in Lancashire ;—I am able, therefore, to draw out of doors ; and am painting a piece of foreground vegetation, which I don't want to be used by students till after at least fifty other exercises have been gone through. But I must do this one while light and life serve ; and not wait till I am sixty, to do work which my eyes are not good enough for at fifty-five.

And if the readers of *Fors* think my letters too desultory, let them consider what this chief work, specified in page 123 of Letter IX., involves. No one has the least notion of the quantity of manual labour I have to go through, to discharge my duty as a teacher of Art. Look at the frontispiece to Letter XX., which is photographed from one of my architectural sketches ; and if you can draw, copy a bit of it ;—try merely the bead moulding with its dentils, in the flat arch over the three small ones, lowest on the left. Then examine those three small ones themselves. You think I have drawn them distorted, carelessly, I suppose. No. That distortion is essential to the Gothic of the Pisan school ; and I measured every one of the curves of those cusps on the spot, to the tenth of an inch ; and I ought to be engraving and publishing those drawings, by rights ; but, meantime, your Pisan Republicans dash the chapel down, for a job in rebuilding it ;—and the French Emperor dashes every cathedral in France to pieces, to find his masons work,—and gets, for result, Reuter's telegram, (page 85 of Letter VI.) ; and I, with my eyes full of dust and driven smoke, am obliged to leave my own work, and write *Fors,* more and more necessarily becoming principal, as I find all my other work rendered vain.

Nevertheless, in the course of *Fors* itself, I shall try to give, as aforesaid, art instruction enough for all need, if any one cares to obey it. How little any one is likely to care, the closing paragraphs of the letter from Wakefield show so clearly that I think it desirable to print them here consecutively, as part of the text of *Fors* itself.

"Yet people tell me that those were very benighted Tory days I am regretting. Wakefield was always held to be a Tory place, given up hand and foot to the magnates who owned the great estate round. I know how, when a small thing in frilled slops, but with my bosom full of patriotic pride in our town, I used to feel bitterly depressed at hearing a rising Radical Leeds clothier, who came to see us sometimes, denounce Wakefield as a 'one-eyed hoil,' his emphatic way of indicating our want of sweep of vision. I remember he generally capped his arguments by demanding, in sonorous tones, if any men worthy of the name of Britons would put up with that 'obsolete monopoly' of the (soke)* mills.

To tell truth, I am afraid that we felt a good deal of mean-spirited admiration for the neighbouring squires and lords on the occasions when they showed themselves and their handsome carriages in our streets : but at least the Wentworths and Pilkingtons and Squire Waterton were gentlemen and scholars ; our new magnates have nothing to boast but their money. It seems to me better that people should boast of the old oaks of Walton, and the old pictures of ———— Priory, than tell how many thousands an iron lord made by the last rise in iron : and that is what they talk of now. And if the iron kings have supplanted the landlords, they are not any more free. The old farmers might vote blindly out of blind respect for the old landlords ; but is it not better than the newly-enfranchised puddlers and strikers selling votes openly for the price of a gallon of whisky ? We have lost a good deal, although we are long rid of the soke monopoly, which used to be a standing re-

* I don't know what this word means, and may have mistaken the reading of it.

proach to us. I think that the town bought off the soke
just after the Corn Law agitation, when the great railways
began to enclose the wide meadows about the town with
their ugly ramparts and arches, where the trains keep up a
continual scream.

But the wool and corn magnates of the place held to their
old traditions long after that ; and when Titus Salt asked
for a footing in the town that he might build there his great
alpaca factories, he was rejected. I had gone abroad then,
but my heart was in the old place, and I caught up eagerly
all concerning it. Sometimes I heard doleful accounts of
its decadence—how the big houses were empty altogether,
how the inns were closed, the coaches stopped, the river
traffic diminished, and the great corn warehouses by the
bridge falling to ruin. There was no trace left of the gaie-
ties that once gave the town the name of ' Merrie Wakefield.' All the smart young men were leaving it to push
their way in Leeds or Manchester, and the girls left behind
were growing up into a population of old maids.

So the doleful story went on for many a year. But in-
sensibly the key changed. Mills were springing up, and
shops ; and the houses had gone up in rent. The sleepy
streets were thronged with workers ; in short, the town
seemed new-born altogether. And the G——s—I knew the
G——s,—nobody would have thought it, such a simple kind
of man as old G—— seemed ; yet the tale ran that he could
buy up all Wakefield, and young Ned was going to live in
Heath Hall ! ! Young Ned in Heath Hall ! one of the
most sacred spots my memory cherished.

I remembered him well,—an audacious boy, with a gift for
wry faces, and always up to some street prank. I remembered the well-worn jacket and battered cap that his father's
thrift imposed on him. And he was to be one of the new
rulers of the bright new time ! and lord it in those ven-
erable oaken chambers sacred to Lady B——'s ghost ! It
seemed incredible ; but twenty years had changed everything. Old G——, the father—a man of the true old English
grain, had, in my young days, a foundry at the lower end

of the town, and was said even then to be worth a 'mint
of money.' Worthy folks were he and his; but still people of whom the loftier town's-folk took no cognizance so-
cially, for was not the wife's father old Robin the Pedlar?
A good old soul he was, who peddled to frugal farm wives
the best thread and needles that could be got,—and took no
alms from his kinsfolk, and lived and died in blameless humble honesty. And his grandson now rules in the hall where
old Robin, perchance, took a humble bit and sup at the back
door. He has a Scotch estate besides, and only failed of
Parliament last year because he bribed his way a little too
openly. My enlightened friends look upon his rise as one of
the grandest signs of the grand new time ; but I cannot rejoice with them. When I see how he and his like are doing
their worst to foul the air and blacken the fields about the
town, I cannot help wishing the squires back in Heath
Hall.

Men say, too, that he is a stronger Tory than the bluest of
the old squires. He has forgotten old Robin of the bobbins,*
and rules the people from whom he sprang, with an iron
hand, as such often do. Naturally, his success has attracted
others, and the town will soon be surrounded with forges.
On the once green Calder bank, where I used to see garlands
of brown pears ripening in the sweet sunshine, there is a
desert of dross and ashes, and twenty black throats vomiting
fire and fumes into the summer sky ; and under the big sheds
you see hundreds of the liberated Britons of these improved
days, toiling, half-naked, in sweltering heat and din, from
morning to evening. This, however, is 'the activity and spread
of the iron trade,' which our local paper tells us 'are the most
satisfactory pledge of the future progress and prosperity of
our town.'

I wish that I could believe it ; but it vexes me beyond
comfort to see the first landscape I knew and loved blighted

---

* A favourite nursery-rhyme of my nurse Annie's comes musically
back to my ears, from fifty years afar,

"Robin-a-bobbin, a bilberry hen—
He ate more victuals than threescore men."

by the smoke of the forges, and to find one sweet association after another swept away.

Even Sunday brings no respite to the eye. The forges are fired up shortly after noonday, and many of the long chimneys follow suit. And in the town the noise is so constant, you can scarcely hear the church chimes unless you are close to the tower.

Did you ever hear Wakefield chimes? We were very proud of them in the old time. They had a round of pleasant sleepy tunes, that never failed us through summer suns and winter frost; and came to be bound up indelibly with the early memories of us children. How I loved to hear them as I bounded, full of morning gladness, across the green Vicar's Croft to school; or at night when lying an unwilling prisoner in bed, before the warm summer evening was ended.

To my childish fancy there was a strange wizardry bound up with that dark church steeple, frosted and crumbling with age, which would break out overhead into mysterious music when I was far afield, but expecting it.

Years after, when poor and lonely in a great foreign city, I came, one bitter winter's day, upon an obscure cloister church standing by a frozen river. It was a city without bells, and I had often longed for the familiar sound. I was dreadfully homesick that day, and stood upon the bridge, hapless, and listless; looking at the strange spire, the strange houses and frozen-up boats, in a kind of dream. Suddenly the cloister tower struck the hour,—four o'clock of a dark December day, and presently it broke into a chime.

It was a very simple ditty; but what a passion of longing it wakened for England and the old chimes of that little English town! I felt as if my heart could bear no more. I *must* go home; I *must* see the old places again, cost what it might. But morning brought fresh counsels, and many a year passed before I revisited the old place.

At last I was there again, after many disappointments, and laid my head to rest once more beneath the shadow of the old steeple.

I woke with an expectant heart. It was a bright May day, such as I remembered twenty years before. The big church bell tolled nine : then came a pause, and my thirsty ears were strained to catch the first sounds of the dear old chimes. 'Ding' went a treble bell high in the air, the first note of 'Tara's Halls,' and then !—a hideous sound I cannot describe, a prolonged malignant yell, broke from the sky and seemed to fill the earth. I stopped my ears and ran indoors, but the sound followed to the innermost chambers. It gathered strength and malignancy every moment, and seemed to blast all within its reach. It lasted near two minutes, and ended with a kind of spasm and howl that made every nerve shudder. I do not exaggerate. I cannot adequately describe the hideous sound. When I had recovered my wits, I asked the meaning of this horrible noise. My informant, a rising young townsman of the new stamp, told me that it was the new steam-whistle at the foundry, commonly called the 'American Devil ;' that it was the most powerful in the West Riding, and could be heard five miles off.

It was only at half-power then, calling the workmen from breakfast ; but at six in the morning I could hear it in double force. I asked if it was possible that people would quietly put up with such a hideous disturbance. He owned that the old inhabitants did not like it ; but then, he said, they were a sleepy set, and wanted stirring up.

Indeed, I actually found that the town was infected by four other similar whistles, profaning dawn and eve with their heaven-defying screech.

The nuisance has been abolished since, I hear. They say it actually killed one old lady by starting her up just at the only moment when it was possible for her weary nerves to get sleep. She happened to have a relation in the town council : a stir was made about it, and the whistles were suppressed.

But the peaceful, half town, half rural life of Wakefield is gone for ever, I fear.

Silk-mills and dye-works are encroaching on the corn-fields and pastures ; rows of jerry-built cottages are creeping up

Pinder's Fields, where I used to pull orchises ; greasy mill-girls elbow ladies in the Westgate, and laugh and jeer at passing young men in a way that would have horrified the old inhabitants. And everywhere there is an indescribable smokiness and dirtiness more demoralizing than any tongue can tell, or mind conceive.

Well, it is the ' march of the times.' It will go on, I suppose, as in other quiet pleasant English towns, until all the sweet Calder valley is swallowed up in the smoke of Tophet. They will cut the snowdrop wood down, and cover Heath Common with cheap villas, and make the old hall into an ' institution.' You know how it will be. A river black with filth and stagnant with foulness, a wilderness of toiling suburbs such as you saw at Bradford ; and where the cow-slips and the corn grew, the earth will be thick with ' institutions.' There will be a Blind Institution, and an Eye and Ear Institution, an Orthopædic Institution, and a Magdalen Institution, and Mechanics' Institutions ; and we shall hear a great deal of the liberality and beneficence of the cotton and iron kings of the place. But will all this compensate one little child for robbing it of its God-given birthright of earth and sky ?

I cannot believe it.

Poor little martyrs ! There will be no 'swallow twittering from the straw-built shed' for them,—only the American Devil calling father to his hot, hard day's labour. What can they make of it all ? What kind of outlook will *they* have in coming years from the bridge of my early recollections ? What I saw on the Medlock yesterday—such a hideous sight !—yet my husband remembers catching fish there. The gases would kill a fish like a lightning-stroke, now.

And the poor children ! It makes me so sad, having some of my own, to think of those who will be born there, with hearts as hungry for nature and truth as mine was ; who will never see God's heaven, save through grimy panes and smoke ; who will have no sweet cowslip-fields to walk in,— only the defiled pavement ; who will grow hard and sour before childhood is over, with the riddle of their joyless lives.

How I have drifted on.

Your allusion to Wakefield Bridge in the *Fors* of February (?) unloosed a flood of long-buried recollections.

This is what you draw on yourself by opening your heart to others. Pray forgive the trespass on your time.

Yours gratefully,

E. L."

NOTES AND CORRESPONDENCE.

THE following two paragraphs have been sent me by correspondents, from country papers. I do not answer for the facts stated in them; but however mythic either may be, they form part of the current history of the day, and are worth preserving; the latter especially in illustration of what I meant by the phrase "roseate repose of domestic felicity," in the *Fors* of July, this year; p. 440.

JOHN HOPPER.—On Tuesday week, July 6th, passed away from our midst the pioneer of Co-operation in Sunderland, John Hopper, shipwright, aged forty-seven on the 22nd April last, after a lingering illness of six weeks' duration, of paralysis of the right side, and the breaking of a blood-vessel in the brain. This was caused by his constant and unremitting study and writing on all questions relating to the progress of his fellow-workmen. More especially had he devoted his time and money to publishing several pamphlets on Co-operation. He also ably advocated the cause of Working Men's Unions and Trade Arbitration Councils instead of strikes. He looked forward to Co-operation for the solution of all the great questions in dispute between the employer and employed, and lived to see some portion of his ideas carried out with great success in the organization of a co-operative store in our own town, which now possesses two branch establishments and does a very large, extensive, and profitable business, and possesses also two libraries. The organization and successful carrying out of this store was largely due to his own exertions. As its first secretary he gave his arduous labours free to it for several years. Though frequently offered superior situations in his own trade as a shipwright, he conscientiously refused all such offers, preferring to cast his lot amongst the working classes, and with them finish his days, toiling on side by side with them, as an example of honesty, toil, and love of his trade, before all other things; for *work* indeed to him was truly *worship.* He scorned to earn his bread by any other means than by his own trade. He often lamented over men of superior talent who deserted their class for wealth and gain, and did not stay by their fellow-men, and by so doing try to elevate them by their example. He had been ailing some fifteen months, but kept at his work until quite exhausted, some six weeks before he died. He worked in the yard of Mr. Oswald, of Pallion, for many years, and also at Mr. J. Laing's, at Deptford. With the latter gentleman he served his apprenticeship as a shipwright. He leaves a widow and seven children unprovided for. The eldest is now serving his apprenticeship to his father's trade with Mr. Oswald. Simple and retired he lived, despite all their praise—content to live and die a working man. Often after a hard day's toil he was too ill to walk all the way home, and had to lay himself down to rest by the roadside for awhile. The following is a list of his pamphlets, eight in number :—Causes of Distress ; History of the Sunderland Co-operative Store ; Organization of Labour ; Co-operative Store System ; The Commercial Reformer's Bookkeeper ; the Workman's Path to Independence ; The Rights of Working Men ; and, Elections, Trades Unions, and the Irish Church.

MARRIAGE OF MISS VENABLES, FORMERLY OF LEICESTER.—From the Yarmouth papers, we learn that on Wednesday week Miss Eveline Mary Venables, the only daughter of the Rev. George Venables, vicar of Great Yarmouth, and formerly vicar of St. Matthew's, Leicester, was married at the parish church, Great Yarmouth, in the presence of 4,000 spectators, to the Rev. E. Manners Sanderson, M.A., vicar of Weston St. Mary's, Lincolnshire. The bridegroom was formerly curate of Great Yarmouth. Very extensive preparations, we are told, were made for the wedding festivities, both in the church and at the vicarage. A number of lady friends of the bride undertook to decorate the nave and chancel of the fine old church, and for several days they worked assiduously at this labour of love. Nearly the whole length of the chancel was tastefully decorated with a choice assortment of flowers, plants, mosses, and ferns, the gas standards being also similarly clothed, while along the communion rails were placed leaves of ferns, intermingled with roses and water-lilies. Within the communion rails were displays of cut flowers and plants, which gave a most pleasing effect to that portion of the church. The reredos was beautifully dressed in wreaths and flowers, and above the communion table were the words in white letters on a scarlet ground, "Jesus was called to the marriage." The effect of all these magnificent decorations was beautiful, and presented such a picture as our grand old church probably never before exhibited. The nave and chancel were converted into an avenue of flowers, and as the richly dressed bridal procession wended its way from the south porch, the scene was one of the most imposing and affecting nature. It was understood that the marriage would take place immediately after the usual morning service, and long before that service commenced (eleven o'clock), several hundreds of people had congregated in front of the church gates, and when they were thrown open, they flocked into the church, and soon every available space in the church was filled with thousands of people. A number of seats near and in the chancel were set apart for the bridal party and friends, and these were kept vacant until the arrival of the ladies and gentlemen for whom they were reserved, and who were admitted for the most part by ticket at the east door. The morning service concluded about half-past eleven, and the clergymen who were to take part in the ceremony, and who had been waiting in the vestry, then walked in procession down the chancel, taking up their position under the tower, where they awaited the arrival of the bridal party. Their names were as follows, besides the Vicar: Rev. E. Venables (canon of Lincoln), Rev. Dr. J. J. Raven (master of the Grammar School), Rev. Bowyer Vaux (minister of St. Peter's church), Rev. A. J. Spencer, Rev. F. G. Wilson (vicar of Rudham), Rev. G. Merriman, Rev. A. B. M. Ley, Rev. R. H. Irvine, Rev. F. C. Villiers, and Rev. R. J. Tacon (Rollesby). The first to arrive was the bridegroom, accompanied by his bestman, the Rev. R. V. Barker, who were shortly afterwards followed by the bridesmaids and other ladies and gentlemen constituting the bridal party, who entered by the south door and awaited the arrival of the bride. The bridesmaids were most elegantly attired in bleu de ciel silk dresses, with long trains, trimmed en tablier, with Mousseline d'Indienne, pink briar roses and white heath, wreaths to match, and long tulle veils. Their names were as follows : Miss Rose Venables, Miss Sanderson, Miss L. Sanderson, Miss M. Sanderson, Miss Wilson, Miss Ruth Venables, and Miss Mander. Each bridesmaid carried a bouquet of white roses, pink geraniums, and forget-me-nots, the gift of the bestman, the Rev. R. V. Barker. The last to arrive was the bride, who wore a dress of superb white satin, with a very long train, garnie en tulle et fleurs d'orange ; the corsage corresponding. The veil tulle de Bruxelles, brodé en soie ; the trailing wreath clematis, myrtle, and orange blossoms ; and a necklet of sprays of silver ivy leaves (the gift of Mr. Percy Sanderson). Her magnificent bouquet was composed of orange flowers, stephanotis, Cape jasmine, white roses, and ferns, and was the gift of the bridegroom. The bride was supported by her brother, Mr. E. Venables, and was received at the south porch of the church by her bridesmaids, who accompanied her up the nave to the chancel, where they were received by the vicar and clergymen. The choir were stationed in the triforium, and Mr. H. Stonex presided at the organ, which was used on this the first occasion since its removal, although the repairs are not yet complete. While the bridal party were entering the church, Mr. Stonex performed "The Wedding March" composed by Sir George Elvey on the occasion of the marriage of Princess Louise (Marchioness of Lorne). The bridal party took their places under the tower, and the marriage service began, the Vicar being assisted in his office by Canon Venables, and the bride being given away by her elder brother, Mr. Gilbert Venables. After singing the hymn, "The voice that breathed o'er Eden," to the tune St. Alphege, Canon Venables read the first address of the Marriage Service. The Vicar has just printed this service with a few explanatory remarks, and about a thousand copies were distributed on the occasion. After that portion of the Marriage Service ordered to be performed in the body of the church was completed, the clergy, bride and bridegroom, and bridesmaids proceeded up the choir to the chancel, the singers and congregation chanting the 128th Psalm. The clergy having taken their positions, the bride and bridegroom, with the bridesmaids and the Rev. R. V. Barker, knelt at the communion rails ; the service was continued, and a short sermon read by the Vicar, from the text, "Heirs together of the grace of life; that your prayers be not hindered." The service concluded with the benediction, and as the party left the church, Mr. Stonex performed Mendelssohn's "Wedding March," in a very skilful manner. The bride's trousseau was entirely supplied from Yarmouth, and the wedding cake, which weighed 100 lb., was manufactured by Mr. Wright, of King Street, Yarmouth. After the marriage, the bridal party assembled at the Vicarage, where the register was signed, and then sat down to a récherché breakfast, the management of which was placed in the hands of Mr. and Mrs. Franklin, of the Crown and Anchor Hotel. The following is a list of those who were present at the wedding breakfast : the Vicar and Mrs. Venables, the Honourable and Mrs. Sanderson, T. H. Sanderson, Esq., Lord Hastings, Chas. Venables, Esq. (Taplow, Bucks), and Mrs. C. Venables, Miss Sanderson, Miss Lucy

Sanderson, Miss Maud Sanderson, Canon Venables (Lincoln) and Mrs. Venables, Miss Ruth Venables (Lincoln), Miss Rose Venables (London), Gilbert Venables, Esq., B.A. (Lower Norwood), and Mrs. Gilbert Venables, Rev. F. G. Wilson (Vicar of Rudham) and Mrs. and Miss Wilson, Rev. J. J. Raven, D.D. (Yarmouth), and Mrs. Raven, Rev R. V Barker, M.A. (Yarmouth), Edward Venables, Esq. (Emmanuel College, Cambridge), and Mrs. Edward Venables, Rev. Bowyer Vaux, M.A., and Mrs. Vaux, Rev. R. H. Irvine, and Mrs. Irvine, Mrs. Palgrave (Yarmouth), Mrs. Woollnough, Rev. F. C. Villiers. M.A., and the Misses Villiers, E. Villiers, Esq. (Galway), Rev. A. B. M. Ley, M.A. (Yarmouth), Rev. G. Merriman, M.A., Rev. A. J. Spencer, B.A., Miss Mander (Tettenhall Wood), Mrs. Palmer, Rev. R. J. Tacon, M.A. (rector of Rollesby), Mr. Stonex. The presents to the bride were very numerous, and among the donors we find the names of Mr. and Mrs. T. North, of Leicester, a bread platter and knife; and Mr. and Mrs. Burbidge Hambly, of Mountsorrel, a dessert service. The honeymoon is being spent at Sans Souci, Dorsetshire.

LETTER LVIII.

"Deus, a quo sancta desideria, recta consilia, et justa sunt opera, da servis tuis illam quam mundus dare non potest pacem, ut et corda nostra mandatis tuis, et, hostium sublata formidine, tempora, sint tuâ protectione tranquilla."

"God, from whom are all holy desires, right counsels, and just works, give to Thy servants that peace which the world cannot, that both our hearts, in Thy commandments, and our times, the fear of enemies being taken away, may be calm under Thy guard."

THE adulteration of this great Catholic prayer in our English church-service, (as needless as it was senseless, since the pure form of it contains nothing but absolutely Christian prayer, and is as fit for the most stammering Protestant lips as for Dante's), destroyed all the definite meaning of it,* and left merely the vague expression of desire for peace, on quite unregarded terms. For of the millions of people who utter the prayer at least weekly, there is not one in a thousand who is ever taught, or can for themselves find out, either what a holy desire means, or a right counsel means, or a just work means,—or what the world is, or what the peace is which it cannot give. And half an hour after they have insulted God by praying to Him in this deadest of all dead languages, not understanded of the people, they leave the church, themselves pacified in their perennial determination to put no check on their natural covetousness ; to act on their own opinions, be they right or wrong ; to do

---

* Missing, in the phrase 'that our hearts may be set to obey' the entire sense of the balanced clause in the original,—namely, that the Law of God is *given* to be the shield and comfort of the soul against spiritual enemies, as the merciful angels encamp round us against earthly ones.

whatever they can make money by, be it just or unjust; and to thrust themselves, with the utmost of their soul and strength, to the highest, by them attainable, pinnacle of the most bedrummed and betrumpeted booth in the Fair of the World.

The prayer, in its pure text, is essentially, indeed, a monastic one; but it is written for the great Monastery of the Servants of God, whom the world hates. It cannot be uttered with honesty but by these; nor can it ever be answered but with the peace bequeathed to these, 'not as the world giveth.'

Of which peace, the nature is not to be without war, but undisturbed in the midst of war; and not without enemies, but without fear of them. It is a peace without pain, because desiring only what is holy; without anxiety, because it thinks only what is right; without disappointment, because a just work is always successful; without sorrow, because 'great peace have they which love Thy Law, and nothing shall offend them;' and without terror, because the God of all battles is its Guard.

So far as any living souls in the England of this day can use, understandingly, the words of this collect, they are already, consciously or not, companions of all good labourers in the vineyard of God. For those who use it reverently, yet have never set themselves to find out what the commandments of God are, nor how loveable they are, nor how far, instead of those commandments, the laws of the world are the only code they care for, nor how far they still think their own thoughts and speak their own words, it is assuredly time to search out these things. And I believe that, after having searched them out, no sincerely good and religious person would find, whatever his own particular form of belief might be, anything which he could reasonably refuse, or which he ought in anywise to fear to profess before all men, in the following statement of creed and resolution, which must be written with their own hand, and signed, with the solemnity of a vow, by every person received into the St George's Company.

I. I trust in the Living God, Father Almighty, Maker of heaven and earth, and of all things and creatures visible and invisible.

I trust in the kindness of His law, and the goodness of His work.

And I will strive to love Him, and keep His law, and see His work, while I live.

II. I trust in the nobleness of human nature, in the majesty of its faculties, the fulness of its mercy, and the joy of its love.

And I will strive to love my neighbour as myself, and, even when I cannot, will act as if I did.

III. I will labour, with such strength and opportunity as God gives me, for my own daily bread ; and all that my hand finds to do, I will do with my might.

IV. I will not deceive, or cause to be deceived, any human being for my gain or pleasure ; nor hurt, or cause to be hurt, any human being for my gain or pleasure ; nor rob, or cause to be robbed, any human being for my gain or pleasure.

V. I will not kill nor hurt any living creature needlessly, nor destroy any beautiful thing, but will strive to save and comfort all gentle life, and guard and perfect all natural beauty, upon the earth.

VI. I will strive to raise my own body and soul daily into higher powers of duty and happiness ; not in rivalship or contention with others, but for the help, delight, and honour of others, and for the joy and peace of my own life.

VII. I will obey all the laws of my country faithfully ; and the orders of its monarch, and of all persons appointed to be in authority under its monarch, so far as such laws or commands are consistent with what I suppose to be the law of God ; and when they are not, or seem in anywise to need change, I will oppose them loyally and deliberately, not with malicious, concealed, or disorderly violence.

VIII. And with the same faithfulness, and under the limits of the same obedience, which I render to the laws of my country, and the commands of its rulers, I will obey the laws of the Society called of St. George, into which I am this day received ; and the orders of its masters, and of all persons appointed to be in authority under its masters, so long as I remain a Companion, called of St. George.

I will not enter in the present letter on any notice of the terms of this creed and vow ; nor of the grounds which many persons whose help I sincerely desire, may perceive for hesitation in signing it. Further definitions of its meaning will be given as occasion comes ; nor shall I ever ask any one to sign it whom I do not know to be capable of understanding and holding it in the sense in which it is meant. I proceed at once to define more explicitly those laws of the Company of St. George to which it refers, and which must, at least in their power, be known before they can be vowed fealty to.

The object of the Society, it has been stated again and again, is to buy land in England ; and thereon to train into the healthiest and most refined life possible, as many Englishmen, Englishwomen, and English children, as the land we possess can maintain in comfort ; to establish, for them and their descendants, a national store of continually augmenting wealth ; and to organize the government of the persons, and administration of the properties, under laws which shall be just to all, and secure in their inviolable foundation on the Law of God.

"To buy land," I repeat, or beg it ; but by no means to steal it, or trespass on it, as I perceive the present holders of the most part of it are too ready to do, finding any bits of road or common which they can pilfer unobserved. Are they quite mad, then ; and do they think the monster mob, gaining every day in force and knowledge, will let their park walls stand much longer, on those dishonest terms ? Doubtful enough their standing is, even on any terms !

But our St. George's walls will be more securely founded, on this wise. The rents of our lands, though they will be required from the tenantry as strictly as those of any other estates, will differ from common rents primarily in being lowered, instead of raised, in proportion to every improvement made by the tenant ; secondly, in that they will be entirely used for the benefit of the tenantry themselves, or better culture of the estates, no money being ever taken by the landlords unless they earn it by their own personal labour.

For the benefit of the tenantry, I say ; but by no means, always, for benefit of which they can be immediately conscious. The rents of any particular farmer will seldom be returned to him in work on his own fields, or investment in undertakings which promote his interest. The rents of a rich estate in one shire of England may be spent on a poor one in another, or in the purchase of wild ground, anywhere, on which years of labour must be sunk before it can yield return ; or in minerals, or Greek vases, for the parish school. Therefore with the use made of the rents paid, the tenantry will have no practical concern whatever ; they will only recognise gradually that the use has been wise, in finding the prices of all serviceable articles diminishing, and all the terms and circumstances of their lives indicative of increased abundance. They will have no more right, or disposition, to ask their landlord what he is doing with the rents, than they have now to ask him how many race-horses he keeps—or how much he has lost on them. But the difference between landlords who live in Piccadilly, and spend their rents at Epsom and Ascot, and landlords who live on the ground they are lords of, and spend their rents in bettering it, will not be long in manifesting itself to the simplest minded tenantry ; nor, I believe, to the outside and antagonist world.

Sundry questions lately asked me by intelligent correspondents as to the intended relations of the tenantry to the Society, may best be answered by saying simply what I shall do, if ever the collected wealth of the Company enables me to buy an estate for it as large as I could have bought for myself, if I had been a railroad contractor.

Of course I could not touch the terms of the existing leases. The only immediate difference would be, the definitely serviceable application of all the rents, as above stated. But as the leases fell in, I should offer renewal of them to the farmers I liked, on the single condition of their complying with the great vital law of the St. George's Company,— " no use of steam power,—nor of any machines where arms will serve " ; allowing such reduction of rent as should fully compensate them for any disadvantage or loss which they could prove they incurred under these conditions. I should give strict orders for the preservation of the existing timber; see that the streams were not wantonly polluted, and interfere in nothing else.

Such farms as were thrown up by their tenants, rather than submit to these conditions, I should be in no haste to re-let; but put land agents on them to cultivate them for the Society in the best manner, and sell their produce;—as soon as any well recommended tenant offered for them, submitting to our laws, he should have them for fixed rent. Thus I should give room for development of whatever personal faculty and energy I could find, and set, if successful, more easily followed example. Meantime my schools and museums, always small and instantly serviceable, would be multiplying among the villages,—youth after youth being instructed in the proper laws of justice, patriotism, and domestic happiness;—those of the Companions who could reside on the lands would, each on their own farm, establish entirely strict obedience to the ultimate laws determined upon as necessary:—if these laws are indeed, as I do not doubt but that sincere care can make them, pleasantly tenable by honest humanity,* they will be gradually accepted voluntarily by the free tenants; and the system is as certain to extend itself, on all sides, once seen to be right, as the branches of an oak sapling.

While, therefore, I am perfectly content, for a beginning, with our acre of rocky land given us by Mrs. Talbot, and am so little impatient for any increase that I have been quietly drawing ragged-robin leaves in Malham cove, instead of going to see another twenty acres promised in Worcestershire,—I am yet thinking out my system on a scale which shall be fit for wide European work. Of course the single Master. of the Company cannot manage all its concerns as it extends. He must have, for his help, men holding the same relation to him which the Marshals of an army do to its General;—

---

* Most of these will be merely old English laws revived; and the rest. Florentine or Roman. None will be instituted but such as have already been in force among great nations.

bearing, that is to say, his own authority where he is not present ; and I believe no better name than ' Marshal' can be found for these. Beneath whom, there will again be the landlords, resident each in his own district ; under these, the land agents, tenantry, tradesmen, and hired labourers, some of whom will be Companions, others Retainers, and others free tenants : and outside all this there will be of course an irregular cavalry, so to speak, of more or less helpful friends, who, without sharing in the work, will be glad to further it more or less, as they would any other benevolent institution.

The law that a Companion shall derive no profit from his companionship does not touch the results of his own work. A Companion farmer will have the produce of his farm as much as a free tenant ; but he will pay no dividends to the Companions who are *not* farmers.

The landlords will in general be men of independent fortune, who, having gifts and ingenuity, choose to devote such gifts to the service of the Society ; the first condition of their appointment to a lordship will be that they can work as much better than their labourers at all rural labour as a good knight was wont to be a better workman than his soldiers in war. There is no rule of supremacy that can ever supersede this eternal, natural, and divine one. Higher by the head, broader in the shoulders, and heartier in the will, the lord of lands and lives must for ever be, than those he rules ; and must work daily at their head, as Richard at the trenches of Acre.

And what am I, myself then, infirm and old, who take, or claim, leadership even of these lords ? God forbid that I should claim it ; it is thrust and compelled on me—utterly against my will, utterly to my distress, utterly, in many things, to my shame. But I have found no other man in England, none in Europe, ready to receive it,—or even desiring to make himself capable of receiving it. Such as I am, to my own amazement, I stand—so far as I can discern —alone in conviction, in hope, and in resolution, in the wilderness of this modern world. Bred in luxury, which I

perceive to have been unjust to others, and destructive to
myself ; vacillating, foolish, and miserably failing in all my
own conduct in life—and blown about hopelessly by storms
of passion—I, a man clothed in soft raiment,—I, a reed
shaken with the wind, have yet this Message to all men
again entrusted to me : " Behold, the axe is laid to the root
of the trees. Whatsoever tree therefore bringeth not forth
good fruit, shall be hewn down and cast into the fire."

This message, yet once more ; and, more than message, the
beginning of the acts that must fulfil it. For, long since, I
have said all that needs to be said,—all that it was my proper
charge and duty to say. In the one volume of *Sesame and
Lilies*—nay, in the last forty pages of its central address to
Englishwomen—everything is told that I know of vital truth,
everything urged that I see to be needful of vital act ;—but
no creature answers me with any faith or any deed. They
read the words, and say they are pretty, and go on in their
own ways. And the day has come for me therefore to cease
speaking, and begin doing, as best I may ; though I know
not whether shall prosper, either this or that.

And truly to all wholesome deed here in England, the
chances of prosperity are few, and the distinctness of adversity only conquerable by fixed imagination and exhaustless
patience—' Adversis rerum immersabilis undis.' The wisest
men join with the fools, and the best men with the villains,
to prevent, if they may, any good thing being done permanently—nay, to provoke and applaud the doing of consistently
evil things permanently. To establish a National debt, and
in the most legal terms—how easy ! To establish a National
store, under any legal or moral conditions of perpetuity—
how difficult ! Every one calls me mad for so much as
hoping to do so. ' This looks like a charity, this educating
of peasants,' said the good lawyer, who drew up the already
published conditional form of association. ' You must not
establish a fund for charity ; it is sure to lead to all sorts of
abuses, and get into wrong hands.'

Well, yes—it in merely human probability may. I do
verily perceive and admit, in convinced sorrow, that I live in

the midst of a nation of thieves and murderers ; * that every. body rou·,d me is trying to rob everybody else ; and that, not bravely and strongly, but in the most cowardly and loathsome ways of lying trade ; that ' Englishman ' is now merely another word for blackleg and swindler ; and English honour and courtesy changed to the sneaking and the smiles of a whipped pedlar, an inarticulate Autolycus, with a steam hurdy-gurdy instead of a voice. Be this all so ; be it so to the heart's content—or liver and gall's content—of every modern economist and philosopher. I yet do verily trust that out of this festering mass of scum of the earth, and miserable coagulation of frog-spawn soaked in ditch-water, I can here and there pluck up some drowned honour by the locks, and leave written orders for wholesome deed, and collected moneys for the doing thereof, which will be obeyed and guarded after I am gone ; and will by no means fall into the power of the mendicant tribe who, too cowardly and heartless to beg from the face of the living, steal the alms of the dead, and unite the apparently inconsistent characters of beggar and thief, seasoning the compound with sacrilege.

Little by little, if my life is spared to me, therefore, (and if I die, there will I doubt not be raised up some one else in my room)—little by little, I or they, will get moneys and lands together ; handful gleaned after handful ; field joined to field, and landmarks set which no man shall dare hereafter remove. And over those fields of ours the winds of Heaven shall be pure ; and upon them, the work of men shall be done in honour and truth.

In such vague promise, I have for the most part hitherto spoken, not because my own plans were unfixed, but because I knew they would only be mocked at, until by some years of persistence the scheme had run the course of the public talk, and until I had publicly challenged the denial of its principles in their abstract statement, long enough to show them to be invincible. Of these abstract principles, the fifteenth, sixteenth, twentieth, twenty-second and twenty-third letters in *Time and Tide*, express all that is needful ,

* See first note in the Correspondence.

only, in the years that have passed since they were written, the ' difficulties ' stated in the seventeenth chapter have been under constant review by me ; and of the ways in which I mean to deal with them it is now time to speak.

Let us understand then, in the outset, the moral difference between a national debt and a national store.

A national debt, like any other, may be honestly incurred in case of need, and honestly paid in due time. But if a man should be ashamed to borrow, much more should a people : and if a father holds it his honour to provide for his children, and would be ashamed to borrow from them, and leave, with his blessing, his note of hand, for his grandchildren to pay, much more should a nation be ashamed to borrow, in any case, or in any manner ; and if it borrow at all, it is at least in honour bound to borrow from living men, and not indebt itself to its own unborn brats. If it can't provide for them, at least let it not send their cradles to the pawn-broker, and pick the pockets of their first breeches.

A national debt, then, is a foul disgrace, at the best. But it is, as now constituted, also a foul crime. National debts paying interest are simply the purchase, by the rich, of power to tax the poor. Read carefully the analysis given of them above, Letter VIII., p. 104.

The financial operations of the St. George's Company will be the direct reverse of these hitherto approved arrange-ments. They will consist in the accumulation of national wealth and store, and therefore in distribution to the poor, instead of taxation of them ; and the fathers will provide for, and nobly endow, not steal from, their children, and children's children.

My readers, however, will even yet, I am well aware, how-ever often I have reiterated the statement to them, be un-able to grasp the idea of a National Store, as an existing possession. They can conceive nothing but a debt ;—nay, there are many of them who have a confused notion that a debt *is* a store !

The store of the St. George's Company, then, is to be primarily of food ; next of materials for clothing and covert ;

next of books and works of art,—food, clothes, books, and works of art being all good, and every poisonous condition of any of them destroyed. The food will not be purveyed by the Borgia, nor the clothing dyed by Deianira, nor the scriptures written under dictation of the Devil instead of God.

The most simply measurable part of the store of food and clothing will be the basis of the currency, which will be thus constituted.

The standard of value will be a given weight or measure of grain, wine, wool, silk, flax, wood, and marble ; all answered for by the government as of fine and pure quality, variable only within narrow limits.

The grain will be either wheat, oats, barley, rice, or maize ; the wine of pure vintage, and not less than ten years old ;* the wool, silk, and flax of such standard as can be secured in constancy ; the wood, seasoned oak and pine ; and for fuel in log and faggot, with finest wood and marble for sculpture. The penny's worth, florin's worth, ducat's worth, and hundred ducat's worth of each of these articles will be a given weight or measure of them, (the penny roll of our present breakfast table furnishing some notion of what, practically, the grain standard will become). Into the question of equivalent value I do not enter here ; it will be at once determined practically as soon as the system is in work. Of these articles the government will always have in its possession as much as may meet the entire demand of its currency in circulation. That is to say, when it has a million in circulation, the million's worth of solid property must be in its storehouses : as much more as it can gather, of course ; but never less. So that, not only, for his penny, florin, ducat, or hundred-ducat note, a man may always be certain of having his pound, or ton, or pint, or cask, of the thing he chooses to ask for, from the government storehouses, but if the holders of the million of currency came in one day to ask for their money's worth, it would be found ready for

* Thus excluding all inferior kinds : wine which will keep ten years will keep fifty.

them in one or other form of those substantial articles. Consequently, the sum of the circulating currency being known, the minimum quantity of store will be known. The sum of the entire currency, in and out of circulation, will be given annually on every note issued (no issues of currency being made but on the first day of the year), and in each district, every morning, the quantities of the currency in and out of circulation in that district will be placarded at the doors of the government district bank.

The metallic currency will be of absolutely pure gold and silver, and of those metals only ; the ducat and half-ducat in gold, the florin, penny, halfpenny, and one-fifth of penny in silver ; the smaller coins being beat thin and pierced, the half-penny with two, the one-fifth of penny with five, apertures.* I believe this double-centime will be as fine a divisor as I shall need. The florin will be worth tenpence ; the ducat, twenty florins.

The weight of the ducat will be a little greater than that of the standard English sovereign, and, being in absolutely pure gold, it will be worth at least five-and-twenty shillings of our present coinage. On one of its sides it will bear the figure of the archangel Michael ; on the reverse, a branch of Alpine rose : above the rose-branch, the words 'Sit splen-dor' ; † above the Michael, 'Fiat voluntas' ; under the rose-branch, 'sicut in cœlo' ; under the Michael, 'et in terra,' with the year of the coinage : and round the edge of the coin, 'Domini.'

The half-ducat will bear the same stamp, except that while on the ducat the St. Michael will be represented standing on the dragon, on the half-ducat he will be simply armed, and bearing St. George's shield.

* I shall use this delicate coinage as a means of education in fineness of touch, and care of small things, and for practical lessons in arithme-tic, to the younger children, in whose hands it will principally be. It will never be wanted for alms ; and for small purchases, as no wares will be offered at elevenpence three-farthings for a shilling, or ninepence four-fifths for a florin, there will be no unreasonable trouble. The chil-dren shall buy their own toys, and have none till they are able to do so.

† The beginning of the last verse of the prayer of Moses, Psalm xc.

On the florin, the St. George's shield only ; the Alpine rose on all three.

On the penny, St. George's shield on one side and the English daisy on the other, without inscription. The pierced fractional coins will only bear a chased wreathen fillet, with the required apertures in its interstices.

There will be considerable loss by wear on a coinage of this pure metal ; but nothing is so materially conducive to the honour of a state in all financial function as the purity of its coinage ; and the loss will never, on the whole currency, equal annually the tenth part of the value of the gunpowder spent at present in salutes or fireworks ; and, if a nation can afford to pay for loyal noise, and fancies in fire, it may also, and much more rationally, for loyal truth and beauty in its circulating signs of wealth. Nor do I doubt that a currency thus constituted will gradually enter into European commerce, and become everywhere recognised and exemplary.

Supposing any Continental extension of the Company itself took place, its coinage would remain the same for the ducat, but the shield of the State or Province would be substituted for St. George's on the minor coins.

There will be no ultimate difficulty in obtaining the bullion necessary for this coinage, for the State will have no use for the precious metals, except for its currency or its art. An Englishman, as he is at present educated, takes pride in eating out of a silver plate ; and in helping, out of a silver tureen, the richest swindlers he can ask to dinner. The companions of St. George may drink out of pewter, and eat off delft, but they will have no knaves for guests, though often beggars ; and they will be always perfectly well able to afford to buy five or ten pounds' worth of gold and silver for their pocket change ; and even think it no overwhelming fiscal calamity if as much even as ten shillings should be actually lost in a year, by the wear of it ; seeing that the wear of their dinner napkins will be considerably greater in the same time. I suppose that ten pounds' worth of bullion for the head of each family will amply supply the necessary quantity for circulation ; but if it should be found convenient to have fifteen—twenty—or fifty pounds in such form, the national store will assuredly in time accumulate to such desirable level. But it will always be a matter of absolute financial indifference, what part of the currency is in gold and what in paper; its power being simply that of a government receipt for goods received, giving claim to their return on demand. The holder of the receipt may have it, if he likes, written on gold instead of paper, provided he bring the gold for it to be written on; but he may no more have a bar of gold made into money than a roll of foolscap, unless he brings the goods for which the currency is the receipt. And it will therefore, by St. George's law, be as much forgery to imitate the national coin in gold, as in paper.

Next to this store, which is the basis of its currency, the government will attend to the increase of store of animal food—not mummy food, in tins, but living, on land and sea; keeping under strictest overseership its breeders of cattle, and fishermen, and having always at its command such supply of animal food as may enable it to secure absolute consistency of price in the main markets. In cases when, by any disease or accident, the supply of any given animal food becomes difficult, its price will not be raised, but its sale stopped. There can be no evasion of such prohibition, because every tradesman in food will be merely the salaried servant of the company, and there will be no temptation to it, because his salary will be the same, whether he sells or not. Of all articles of general consumption, the government will furnish its own priced standard; any man will be allowed to sell what he can produce above that standard, at what price he can get for it; but all goods below the government standard will be marked and priced as of such inferior quality;—and all bad food, cloth, or other article of service, destroyed. And the supervision will be rendered simple by the fewness of the articles permitted to be sold at all; for the dress being in all classes as determined as the heraldry of coronets, and for the most part also rigorously simple; and all luxurious living disgraceful, the entire means of domestic life will be within easy definition.

Of course the idea of regulating dress generally will be looked upon by the existing British public as ridiculous. But it has become ridiculous because masters and mistresses attempt it solely for their own pride. Even with that entirely selfish end, the natural instinct of human creatures for obedience, when in any wholesome relations with their superiors, has enabled the masters to powder their coachmen's wigs, and polish their footmen's legs with silk stockings, and the mistresses to limit their lady's maids, when in attendance, to certain styles of cap.

Now as the dress regulations of the St. George's Company will be quite as much for the pride of the maid as the mistress, and of the man as the master, I have no fear but they will be found acceptable, and require no strictness of enforcement. The children of peasants, though able to maintain their own families, will be required to be as clean as if they were charity-boys or girls ; nobody will be allowed to wear the cast clothes of other people, to sell or pawn their own, or to appear on duty, agricultural or whatever other it may be, in rags, any more than the Horse Guards or the Queen's dairy-maids are now ; also on certain occasions, and within such limits as are needful for good fellowship, they will be urged to as much various splendour as they can contrive. The wealth of the peasant women will be chiefly in hereditary golden ornaments of the finest workmanship ; and in jewellery of uncut gems,—agates only, or other stones of magnitude, being allowed to be cut, and gems of large size, which are worth the pains, for their beauty ; but these will be chiefly used in decorative architecture or furniture, not in dress. The dress of the officers of the company will be on all occasions plainer than that of its peasants ; but hereditary nobles will retain all the insignia of their rank, the one only condition of change required on their entering the St. George's Company being the use of uncut jewels, and therefore—seldom of diamonds.*

---

* I never saw a rough diamond worth setting, until the Bishop of Natal gave me a sharply crystallized one from the African fields. Perhaps a star or two of cut ones may be permitted to the house-mistresses on great occasions.

The next main staple of the Company's store will be its literature.

A chosen series of classical books will be placed in every village library, in number of copies enough to supply all readers ; these classics will be perfectly printed and perfectly bound, and all in one size of volume, unless where engravings need larger space : besides these village libraries, there will be a museum in every district, containing all good ancient books obtainable : gradually, as the design expands itself, and as time passes on, absorbing, by gift, or purchase, the contents of private libraries, and connecting themselves with similarly expanding museums of natural history. In all schools, the books necessary for their work will be given to the pupils ; and one of their earliest lessons will be the keeping them clean and orderly.

By ordering of Fors, I went only this last month to see the school in which Wordsworth was educated. It remains, as it was then, a school for peasant lads only ; and the doors of its little library, therefore, hang loose on their decayed hinges ; and one side of the schoolroom is utterly dark—the window on that side having been long ago walled up, either 'because of the window-tax, or perhaps it had got broken,' suggested the guardian of the place.

Now it is true that this state of things cannot last long ; but the cure will be worse than the disease. A fit of reactionary vanity and folly is sure to seize the village authorities ; that old schoolroom, with its sacred associations, will be swept from the hillside, and a grand piece of Birmingham Gothic put up, with a master from Kensington, and enforced weekly competitive examination in Sanscrit, and the Binomial Theorem.

All that the school wants is, hinges to its library doors as good as every shop in the street has to its shutters ; the window knocked through again where it was originally ; the books whose bindings are worn out, rebound, and a few given (in addition to those on the subjects of arithmetic and grammar), which the boys may rather ask leave to read, than take opportunity to throw into corners.

But the ten or twenty pounds needed for this simple rε⁻. ormation could, I suppose, at present, by no persuasion noı argument be extracted from the united pockets of the gentlemen of the neighbourhood. Meantime, while the library doors flap useless on their hinges, the old country churchyard is grim with parallelograms of iron palisade, enforced partly to get some sacred market for the wares of the rich ironmongers who are buying up the country; and partly to protect their valuable carcases in their putrifying pride. Of such iron stores the men of St. George's Company, dead, will need none, and living, permit none. But they will strictly enforce the proper complement of hinges to their school-library doors.

The resuscitation of the, at present extinct, art of writing being insisted upon in the school exercises of the higher classes, the libraries will be gradually enriched with manuscripts of extreme preciousness. A well-written book is as much pleasanter and more beautiful than a printed one as a picture is than an engraving; and there are many forms of the art of illumination which were only in their infancy at the time when the wooden blocks of Germany abolished the art of scripture, and of which the revival will be a necessary result of a proper study of natural history.

In next *Fors*, I shall occupy myself wholly with the subject of our Art education and property; and in that for December, I hope to publish the legal form of our constitution revised and complete. The terminal clauses respecting the Companions' right of possession in the lands will be found modified, or in great part omitted, in the recast deed; but I am neither careful nor fearful respecting the terms of this instrument, which is to be regarded merely as a mechanical means of presently getting to work and having land legally secured to us. The ultimate success or failure of the design will not in the least depend on the terms of our constitution, but on the quantity of living honesty and pity which can be found, to be constituted. If there is not material enough out of which to choose Companions, or energy enough in the Companions chosen to fill the chain-mail of all terms and forms with living power, the scheme will be choked by its first practical difficulties ; and it matters little what becomes of the very small property its promoters are ever likely to handle. If, on the contrary, as I believe, there be yet honesty and sense enough left in England to nourish the effort, from its narrow source there will soon develop itself a vast Policy, of which neither I nor any one else can foresee the issue, far less verbally or legally limit it ; but in which, broadly, by the carrying out of the primally accepted laws of Obedience and Economy, the Master and Marshals will become the Ministry of the State, answerable for the employment of its revenues, for its relations with external powers, and for such change of its laws as from time to time may be found needful : the Landlords will be the resident administrators of its lands, and immediate directors of all labour,—its captains in war, and magistrates in peace : the tenants will constitute its agricultural and military force, having such domestic and acquisitive independence as may be consistent with patriotic and kindly fellowship : and the artists, schoolmen, tradesmen, and inferior labourers, will form a body of honourably paid retainers, undisturbed in their duty by any chance or care relating to their means of subsistence.

NOTES AND CORRESPONDENCE.

Mem. for Professor Ruskin.

The following is taken from the *Edinburgh Courant* of 2nd inst.:—

"The *Nautical Magazine* leads off with a bold and original article, the second of a series, on the somewhat startling subject of 'The Commercial Value of Human Life,' in which it states that human life has its commercial value, and that 'those who bring forward its sacredness as a plea for protective legislation of any and every kind are assuming not only a false position, but a position that is likely to work a serious injury upon the country at large.' An elaborate discussion of 'The Plimsoll Protest,' and a description of the 'Inman Line' of steamers, with the usual technical matter, make up an unusually interesting number."

"What can this mean? Does it point to something still more brutal than the ' carnivorous teeth ' theory ? *

"Submitted, with much respect, to Mr. Ruskin, for the *Notes and Correspondence* in *Fors*—if deemed admissible.

"4*th September,* 1875.   J. M."

A peculiarly sad instance of death from lead-poisoning was investigated this week before Dr. Hardwicke, at an inquest held in London. The deceased, Mary Ann Wilson, only three weeks ago went to work at a white-lead factory. After being there two or three days she felt the effects of lead-poisoning, which turned her lips blue. Subsequently the neighbours found her lying on the floor in convulsions, and in a dying state; and the next day she died from congestion of the brain, and disease of the chest organs, consequent on the evil effects of her employment. The coroner recommended that persons who followed this employment should drink diluted sulphuric acid, to counteract the action of the poison.—*Birmingham Daily Post,* Sept. 2, 1875.

* Yes, certainly. It points to teeth which shall have no meat (eat but only the lead of coffins, and to tongues which shall have no water to drink, but only the burnt sulphur of hell. See, for example, succeeding article.

LETTER LIX.

Herne Hill, *3rd October*, 1875.

The day before yesterday I went with a young English
girl to see her nurse ; who was sick of a lingering illness,
during which, with kindliest intent, and sufficient success,
(as she told me,) in pleasing her, books had been chosen for
her from the circulating library, by those of her pious friends
whose age and experience qualified them for such a task.

One of these volumes chancing to lie on the table near me,
I looked into it, and found it to be *Stepping Heavenward ;*—
as far as I could make out, a somewhat long, but not unintelligent, sermon on the text of Wordsworth's *Stepping Westward.* In the five minutes during which I strayed between
the leaves of it, and left the talk of my friend with her nurse
to its own liberty, I found that the first chapters described
the conversion of an idle and careless young lady of sixteen
to a solemn view of her duties in life, which she thus expresses
at the end of an advanced chapter : " I am resolved never to
read worldly books any more ; and my music and drawing I
have laid aside for ever." *

. The spiritually walled cloister to which this charming child
of modern enlightenment thus expresses her determination to
retire, differs, it would appear, from the materially walled
monastic shades of the Dark Ages, first, by the breadth and
magnanimity of an Index Expurgatorius rising to interdic-
tion of all uninspired books whatsoever, except Baxter's
Saint's Rest, and other classics of evangelical theology ;
and, secondly, by its holy abhorrence of the arts of picture

* I quote from memory, and may be out in a word or two ; not in the
sense : but I don't know if the young lady is really approved by the
author, and held up as an example to others ; or meant, as I have taken
her, for a warning. The method of error, at all events, is accurately
and clearly shown.

and song, which waste so much precious time, and give so much disagreeable trouble to learn ; and which also, when learned, are too likely to be used in the service of idols ; while the skills which our modern gospel substitutes for both, of steam-whistle, namely, and photograph, supply, with all that they need of terrestrial pleasure, the ears which God has redeemed from spiritual deafness, and the eyes which He has turned from darkness to light.

My readers are already, I hope, well enough acquainted with the Institutes of the St. George's Company to fear no monastic restrictions of enjoyment, nor imperative choice of their books, carried to this celestially Utopian strictness. And yet, understanding the terms of the sentence with true and scholarly accuracy, I must, in educational legislation, insist on the daughters of my Companions fulfilling this resolution to the letter : " I am resolved never to read worldly books any more, and *my* music and drawing I have laid aside for ever."

" Wórldly books " ? Yes ; very certainly, when you know which they are ; for I will have you to abjure, with World, Flesh, and Devil, the literature of all the three :—and *your* music and drawing,—that is to say, all music and drawing which you have learned only for your own glory or amusement, and respecting which you have no idea that it may ever become, in a far truer sense, other people's music and drawing.

For all the arts of mankind, and womankind, are only rightly learned, or practised, when they are so with the definite purpose of pleasing or teaching others. A child dancing for its own delight,—a lamb leaping,—or a fawn at play, are happy and holy creatures ; but they are not artists. An artist is—and recollect this definition, (put in capitals for quick reference,)—A PERSON WHO HAS SUBMITTED TO A LAW WHICH IT WAS PAINFUL TO OBEY, THAT HE MAY BESTOW A DELIGHT WHICH IT IS GRACIOUS TO BESTOW.*

* To make the definition by itself complete, the words ' in his work ' should be added after ' submitted ' and ' by his work ' after ' bestow ' ; but it is easier to learn without these phrases, which are of course to be understood.

" A painful law," I say ; yet full of pain not in the sense
of torture, but of stringency, or constraint ; and labour,
increasing, it may be, sometimes into aching of limbs, and
panting of breasts ; but these stronger yet, for every ache,
and broader for every pant ; and farther and farther strengthened from danger of rheumatic ache, and consumptive pant.

This, so far as the Arts are concerned, is ' entering in at the
Strait gate,' of which entrance, and its porter's lodge, you
will find farther account given in my fourth morning in
Florence, which I should like you to read, as a preparation
for the work more explicitly now to be directed under St.
George. The immediate gist of it, for those who do not care
to read of Florence, I must be irksome enough again to give
here ; namely, that the word Strait, applied to the entrance
into Life, and the word Narrow, applied to the road of Life,
do not mean that the road is so fenced that few can travel it,
however much they wish, (like the entrance to the pit of a
theatre),* but that, for each person, it is at first so stringent,
so difficult, and so dull, being between close hedges, that few
will enter it, though all *may*. In a second sense, and an
equally vital one, it is not merely a Strait, or narrow, but a
straight, or right road ; only, in this rightness of it, not at
all traced by hedges, wall, or telegraph wire, or even marked
by posts higher than winter's snow ; but, on the contrary,
often difficult to trace among morasses and mounds of desert,
even by skilful sight ; and by blind persons, entirely unten-
able, unless by help of a guide, director, rector, or rex : which
you may conjecture to be the reason why, when St. Paul's
eyes were to be opened, out of the darkness which meant
only the consciousness of utter mistake, to seeing what way
he should go, his director was ordered to come to him in the
" street which is called Straight."

Now, bringing these universal and eternal facts down to
this narrow, straight, and present piece of business we have
in hand ; the first thing we have to learn to draw is an extremely narrow, and an extremely direct, line. Only, observe,

---

* The ' few there be that find it' is added, as an actual fact ; a fact
consequent not on the way's being narrow, but on its being disagreeable.

true and vital direction does not mean that, without any de flection or warp by antagonist force, we can fly, or walk, or creep at once to our mark ; but that, whatever the antagonist force may be, we so know and mean our mark, that we shall at last precisely arrive at it, just as surely, and it may be in some cases more quickly, than if we had been unaffected by lateral or opposing force. And this higher order of contend-ing and victorious rightness, which in our present business is best represented by the track of an arrow, or rifle-shot, affected in its course both by gravity and the wind, is the more beautiful rightness or directness of the two, and the one which all fine art sets itself principally to achieve. But its quite first step must nevertheless be in the simple produc-tion of the mathematical Right line, as far as the hand can draw it ; joining two points, that is to say, with a straight visible track, which shall as nearly as possible fulfil the mathe-matical definition of a line, "length without breadth."

And the two points had better at first be placed at the small distance of an inch from each other, both because it is easy to draw so short a line, and because it is well for us to know, early in life, the look of the length of an inch. And when we have learned the look of our own English inch, we will proceed to learn the look of that which will probably be our currency measure of length, the French inch, for that is a better standard than ours, for European acceptance.

Here, I had made arrangements for the production of a plate, and woodcut, to illustrate the first steps of elementary design ; but the black-plague of cloud already more than once spoken of (as connected probably with the diminution of snow on the Alps), has rendered it impossible for my assistants to finish their work in time. This disappointment I accept thankfully as the ordinance of my careful and prudent mistress, Atropos,—the third Fors ; and am indeed quickly enough apprehensive of her lesson in it. She wishes me, I doubt not, to recognise that I was foolish in designing the intrusion of technical advice into my political letters ; and to understand that the giving of clear and separate direc-tions for elementary art-practice is now an imperative duty

for me, and that these art-lessons must be in companionship
with my other school books on the Earth and its Flowers.

I must needs do her bidding ; and as I gather my past
work on rocks and plants together, so I must, day by day,
gather what I now know to be right of my past work on art
together ; and, not in sudden thought, but in the resumption
of purpose which I humbly and sincerely entreat my mistress
to pardon me for having abandoned under pressure of extreme fatigue, I will publish, in the same form as the geology
and botany, what I desire to ratify, and fasten with nails in
a sure place, with instant applicability to school and university exercises, of my former writings on art.*

But this, I beg my readers to observe, will be the seventh
large book I have actually at this time passing through the
press ; † besides having written and published four volumes
of university lectures ‡ in the last six years ; every word of
them weighed with care. This is what I observe the *Daily
Telegraph* calls giving 'utterances few and far between.'
But it is as much certainly as I am able at present to manage;
and I must beg my correspondents, therefore, to have
generally patience with me when I don't answer their letters
by return of post ; and above all things, to write them clear,
and in a round hand, with all the *m*s and *n*s well distinguished from *u*s.

The woodcut, indeed, prepared for this *Fors* was to have
been a lesson in writing ; but that must wait till next year,

---

* Namely, *Modern Painters, Stones of Venice, Seven Lamps,* and
Elements of Drawing. I cut these books to pieces, because in the three
first, all the religious notions are narrow, and many false ; and in the
fourth, there is a vital mistake about outline, doing great damage to all
the rest.

† *Fors, Ariadne, Love's Meinie, Proserpina, Deucalion, Mornings in
Florence*—and this : and four of these require the careful preparation
of drawings for them by my own hand, and one of these drawings alone,
for *Proserpina,* this last June, took me a good ten days' work, and that
hard.

‡ *Inaugural Lectures, Aratra Pentelici, Val d' Arno,* and *Eagle's Nest ;*
besides a course on Florentine Sculpture, given last year, and not yet
printed, the substance of it being in re-modification for *Mornings in
Florence.*

now ; meantime you may best prepare yourself for that, and all other lessons to be given in my new edition of the *Elements of Drawing*, by beginning to form your own cherished and orderly treasures of beautiful art. For although the greatest treasury in that kind, belonging to St. George's Company, will be as often aforesaid public property, in our museums, every householder of any standing whatever among us will also have his own domestic treasury, becoming hereditary as accumulative ; and accurately catalogued, so that others may know what peculiar or separate good things are to be found in his house, and have graciously permitted use of them if true necessity be.

The basis, however, of such domestic treasury will of course be common to all ; every household having its proper books for religious and economic service, and its classic authors, and engravings.

With the last we must at present class, and largely use, the more perishable treasure of good photographs ; these, however, I do not doubt but that modern science will succeed, (if it has not already done so,) in rendering permanent ; and, at all events, permanent copies of many may soon be placed in all our schools. Of such domestic treasure we will begin with a photograph of the picture by Fra Filippo Lippi, representing the Madonna ; which picture last year had its place over the door of the inner room of the Uffizi of Florence, beyond the Tribune. This photograph can of course eventually be procured in any numbers ; and, assuming that my readers will get one, I shall endeavour in this and future numbers of *Fors*, to make it useful to them, and therefore a treasure.*

The first thing you are to observe in it is that the figures are represented as projecting in front of a frame or window-sill. The picture belongs, therefore, to the class meant to be, as far as possible, deceptively like reality ; and is in this respect entirely companionable with one long known in our

---

* Mr. W. Ward, 2, Church Terrace, Richmond, Surrey, will give any necessary information about this or other photographs referred to in *Fors ;* and generally have them on sale ; but see terminal Note.

picture-shops, and greatly popular with the British innkeeper, of a smuggler on the look-out, with his hand and pistol projecting over the window-sill. The only differences in purpose between the painter of this Anglican subject and the Florentine's, are, first, that the Florentine wishes to give the impression, not of a smuggler's being in the same room with you, but of the Virgin and Child's being so ; and, secondly, that in this representation he wishes not *merely* to attain deceptive reality ; but to concentrate all the skill and thought that his hand and mind possess, in making that reality noble.

Next, you are to observe that with this unusually positive realism of representation, there is also an unusually mystic spiritualism of conception. Nearly all the Madonnas, even of the most strictly devotional schools, themselves support the child, either on their knees or in their arms. But here, the Christ is miraculously borne by an angel ;—the Madonna, though seated on her throne, worships with both hands lifted.

Thirdly, you will at first be pained by the decision of line, and, in the children at least, uncomeliness of feature, which are characteristic, the first, of purely-descended Etruscan work ; the second, of the Florentine school headed afterwards by Donatello. But it is absolutely necessary, for right progress in knowledge, that you begin by observing and tracing decisive lines ; and that you consider dignity and simplicity of expression more than beauty of feature. Remember also that a photograph necessarily loses the most subtle beauty of all things, because it cannot represent blue or grey colours,* and darkens red ones ; so that all glowing and warm shadows become too dark. Be assured, nevertheless, that you have, in this photograph, imperfect as it is, a most precious shadow and image of one of the greatest works ever produced by hand of man : and begin the study of it piece by piece. If you fancy yourself able to draw at all, you may begin by practice over and over again the little

* The transparent part of the veil which descends from the point of the cap is entirely lost, for instance, in this Madonna.

angular band on the forehead, with its studs, and the connected chain of pearls.   There are seven pearls and fourteen
studs ; the fifteenth, a little larger, at the angle of the
transparent cap ; and four more, retiring.   They are to be
drawn with a fine brush and sepia, measuring the exact
length of the band first ; then marking its double curve,
depressed in the centre, and rising over the hair, and then
the studs and pearls in their various magnitudes.   If you
can't manage these, try the spiral of the chair ; if not that,
buy a penny's worth of marbles and draw them in a row,
and pick up a snail shell, and meditate upon it, if you have
any time for meditation.   And in my Christmas *Fors* I will
tell you something about marbles, and beads, and coral, and
pearls, and shells ; and in time—it is quite possible—you
may be able to draw a boy's marble and a snail's shell ; and
a sea urchin ; and a Doric capital ; and an Ionic capital ;
and a Parthenon, and a Virgin in it ; and a Solomon's Temple, and a Spirit of Wisdom in it ; and a Nehemiah's temple, and a Madonna in it.

This photograph, then, is to be our first domestic possession in works of art ; if any difficulty or improper cost occur
in attaining it, I will name another to answer its purpose ;
but this will be No. 1 in our household catalogue of reference : which will never be altered, so that the pieces may
always be referred to merely by their numbers.

Of public, or museum property in art, I have this month
laid also the minute foundation, by the purchase, for our
schools, of the engravings named in the annexed printseller's
account.*

And respecting the general operation of these schools,
and of the museums connected with them, the conclusion,
which I am happy to announce, of the purchase of a piece
of ground for the first of them, for six hundred pounds, requires some small special commentary.

Of such science, art, and literature as are properly connected with husbandry, (see Note *a*, p. 456 of Vol. II.,)
St. George primarily acknowledges the art which provides

* Last but one article in the Notes.

him with a ploughshare,—and if need still be for those more savage instruments,—with spear, sword, and armour.

Therefore, it is fitting that of his schools " for the workmen and labourers of England," the first should be placed in Sheffield : (I suppose, originally Sheaf-field ; but do not at all rest on that etymology, having had no time to inquire into it.)

Besides this merely systematic and poetical fitness, there is the farther practical reason for our first action being among this order of craftsmen in England ; that, in cutler's ironwork, we have, at this actual epoch of our history, the best in its kind done by English hands, unsurpassable, I presume, when the workman chooses to do all he knows, by that of any living nation.

For these two principal reasons, (and not without further direction from *Fors* of a very distinct nature,) I expressed, some time since, my purpose to place the first museum of the St. George's Company at Sheffield.

Whereupon, I received a letter, very well and kindly meant, from Mr. Bragge, offering me space in the existing Sheffield museum for whatever I chose to put there : Mr. Bragge very naturally supposing that this would be the simplest mode of operation for me ; and the most immediately advantageous to the town. To that (as I supposed private) communication I replied, in what I meant to be a private letter ; which letter Mr. Bragge, without asking my permission, read at a public dinner, with public comment on what he imagined to be the state of my health.

Now, I never wrote a letter in my life which all the world are not welcome to read, if they will : and as Fors would have it so, I am glad this letter *was* read aloud, and widely circulated : only, I beg Mr. Bragge and the other gentlemen who have kindly interested themselves in the existing Sheffield museum to understand that, had I intended the letter for publicity, it would have been couched in more courteous terms, and extended into clearer explanation of my singular and apparently perverse conduct in what I observe the Sheffield press, since it has had possession of the letter in question, characterizes as " setting up an opposition museum at Walkley."

I am glad to find the Sheffield branch of English journalism reprobating, in one instance at least, the—I had imagined now by all acclamation, divine—principle of Competition. But surely, the very retirement to the ˙solitude of Walkley of which the same journalist complains, might have vindicated St. George's first quiet effort in his own work, from this unexpected accusation,—especially since, in so far as I can assert or understand the objects of either of the supposedly antagonist showmen, neither Mr. Bragge nor St. George intend taking shillings at the doors.

Nevertheless, the impression on the mind of the Sheffield journalist that museums are to be opened as lively places of entertainment, rivals for public patronage, and that their most proper position is therefore in a public thoroughfare, deserves on St. George's part some careful answer. A museum is, be it first observed, primarily, not at all a place of entertainment, but a place of Education. And a museum is, be it secondly observed, not a place for elementary education, but for that of already far-advanced scholars. And it is by no means the same thing as a parish school, or a Sunday school, or a day school, or even—the Brighton Aquarium.

Be it observed, in the third place, that the word ' School' means ' Leisure,' and that the word ' Museum' means ' Belonging to the Muses ;' and that all schools and museums whatsoever, can only be, what they claim to be, and ought to be, places of noble instruction, when the persons who have a mind to use them can obtain so much relief from the work, or exert so much abstinence from the dissipation, of the outside world, as may enable them to devote a certain portion of secluded, laborious, and reverent life to the attainment of the Divine Wisdom, which the Greeks supposed to be the gift of Apollo, or of the Sun ; and which the Christian knows to be the gift of Christ. Now, I hear it continually alleged against me, when I advocate the raising of working men's wages, that already many of them have wages so high that they work only three days a week, and spend

the other three days in drinking. And I have not the least
doubt that under St. George's rule, when none but useful
work is done, and when all classes are compelled to share in
it, wages may indeed be so high, or which amounts to the
same thing as far as our present object is concerned, time so
short, that at least two, if not three days out of every week,
(or an equivalent portion of time taken out of each day,)
may be devoted by some British workmen—no more to the
alehouse, but to, what British clergymen ought to mean, if
they don't, by the 'concerns of their immortal souls,' that is
to say, to the contemplation and study of the works of
God, and the learning that complete code of Natural history
which, beginning with the life and death of the Hyssop on
the wall, rises to the knowledge of the life and death of the
recorded generations of mankind, and of the visible starry
Dynasties of Heaven.

The workmen who have leisure to enter on this course of
study will also, I believe, have leisure to walk to Walkley.
The museum has been set there, not by me, but by the second
Fors, (Lachesis,) on the top of a high and steep hill,—with
only my most admiring concurrence in her apparent intention
that the approach to it may be at once symbolically instruct-
ive, and practically sanitary.

NOTES AND CORRESPONDENCE.

I. The following communication was sent to me on a post-card, with-out the writer's name; but it is worth notice :—

"'Ut et corda nostra mandatis tuis *dedita*.' If some manuscript Breviary has omitted 'dedita,' it must be by a slip of the pen. The sense surely is this : that while there is either war or only an evil and deceitful peace within, self-surrender to the Divine commandments above and freedom from terror of foes around are alike impossible.

"In the English Prayer-book 'set' has the same meaning as in Psalm lxxviii. ver. 9 (*sic*: the writer means ver. 8) ; and the context shows the 'rest and quietness' desired to be rest and quietness of spirit."

The 'context' cannot show anything of the sort, for the sentence is an entirely independent one : and the MS. I use is not a Breviary, but the most perfect Psalter and full service, including all the hymns quoted by Dante, that I have seen in English thirteenth-century writing. The omission of the word 'dedita' makes not the smallest difference to the point at issue—which is not the mistranslation of a word, but the break-ing of a clause. The mistranslation nevertheless exists also ; precisely *because*, in the English Prayer-book, 'set' *has* the same meaning as in Psalm lxxviii. ; where the Latin word is 'direxit,' not 'dedit' ; and where discipline is meant, not surrender.

I must reserve my comments on the two most important letters next following, for large type and more leisure.

II. "I hope that you will live to see *Fors* and everything printed without steam : it's the very curse and unmaking of us. I can see it dreadfully in every workman that I come across. Since I have been so happily mixed up with you these eighteen years, great changes have taken place in workmen. It was beginning fearfully when I last worked as a journeyman. One instance among many :—The head foreman came to me at Messrs. Bakers', and threatened discharge if he caught me using a hand bow-saw to cut a little circular disc, which I could have done in ten minutes. I then had to go and wait my turn at the endless steam saw—or as commonly called, a band saw. I had to wait an hour and a half to take my turn : the steam saw did it in perhaps three minutes ; but the head foreman said, 'We've gone to great ex-pense for steam machinery, and what is the use if we don't employ it?' This little occurrence was by no means uncommon. What workpeople have been brought to is beyond conception, in tone of feeling and char-acter. Here, as I have told you, we do all we can ourselves, indoors and out; have no servant, but make the children do : and because we are living in a tidy-sized house, and a good piece of ground, the labouring people make a dead set against us because we are not dependent upon them, and have even combined to defeat us in getting a charwoman now and then. We ought, I suppose, to employ two servants, whether we can pay for them or not, or even obtain them (which we couldn't). They have been picking hops here next our hedge : this is done by people in the neighbourhood, not imported pickers ; and their children called over the hedge to ours, and said, ' Your mother is not a lady ; she don't keep a servant, but does the work herself.' I name this little incident because it seems so deep."

III. " My dear Mr. Ruskin,—I write to ask leave to come and enter my name on the Roll of Companions of the Company of St. George.* I have seen enough and read enough of the pace at which we are going, more especially in business matters, to make me long to see some effort made to win back some of the honesty and simplicity of our fathers. And although I am afraid I can be but of very little use to the Company, I would gladly do anything that lay within my power ; and it would be a great help to feel oneself associated with others, however feebly, in a *practical* work.

"I am trying to carry out what you have taught me in business, where I *can* do it. Our trade is dressing and buying and selling leather, etc., and making leather belting, hose, and boots. I am trying to the utmost to make everything as good as it can be made, then to ask a fair price for it, and resist all attempts to cheapen or depreciate it in any way. First, because the best thing is, as far as I know, invariably the ' best value '; secondly, because shoe manufacturing. as now carried on, is, through the division of labour, a largely mechanical work (though far less so than many trades),—and I believe the surest way of diminishing, as it is surely our duty to do, the amount of all such work, is to spend no labour, nor allow of its being spent, on any but the *best thing for wear* that can be made ; and thirdly, because workmen employed even somewhat mechanically are, I think, far less degraded by their employment when their work and materials are good enough to become the subjects of honest pride. You will understand that, being only in the position of manager of the business, I can only carry out these ideas to a certain point. Still I have been able to reduce the amount of what is called ' fancy stitching' on parts of boots, on the stated ground of the injury the work ultimately causes to the operator's eyesight. And in the dressing of some descriptions of leather, where we used to print by machinery an artificial grain on the skin or hide, we have dispensed with the process, and work up the natural grain by hand-power.

"And this brings me to the point I want to put to you about the permitted use of the sewing machine (see *Fors* XXXIV., p. 97).† It may

* The writer is now an accepted Companion.
† I am only too happy to be justified in withdrawing it. But my errors will, I trust, always be found rather in the relaxation than the unnecessary enforcement, even of favourite principles ; and I did not see what line I could draw between the spinning-wheel, which I knew to be necessary, and the sewing machine, which I suspected to be mischievous, and gave therefore *permission* only to use ; while I shall earnestly urge the use of the spinning-wheel. I will give the reason for distinction, (so far as my correspondent's most interesting letter leaves me anything more to say,) in a future letter,

seem unreasonable, when our firm employs so many. But it seems to me that the *admission* of machinery at all is unwise in principle. Machinery, especially the sewing machine, has demoralized the shoe trade, —the same I think you would find in all other trades,—notably in piece-goods for ladies' dresses—which, owing to the cheapness with which they can be made up, are far more in number than they *could* have been if no sewing machine had been used. And a manufacturer told me, only the other day, that common piece-goods, both woollen and others, take *as much* and generally *more* labour in making than the best. If all work required to supply clothing to the race were to be done by *hand*, it would be worth no one's while to make rubbish of any kind,—the work would be done by fewer people, and all raw material would be cheapened.

"In your advice to a young lady, printed at page 97, Letter XXXIV., in the second volume of *Fors Clavigera*, you give her permission to use a sewing machine. I hope that, on fuller consideration of the subject, you will advise all who set the weal of their country above their own convenience, to discontinue its use wherever it can possibly be dispensed with.

"For the effect of the sewing machine upon the great industries connected with clothing has been most disastrous.

"Given a certain quantity of cloth, or calico, or leather; and, before it can be made available as clothing, it must be joined or stitched together in certain shapes.

"Now so long as this stitching was, of necessity, all done by hand, it was never worth while, supposing the labour to be paid for at a just rate, to use any but good materials. A print dress at three-halfpence per yard, which might wear a week, would cost as much to make as a dress that would wear a year; and, except for the rich and luxurious, all extravagance of trimming, and all sewing useless for wear, were unattainable.

"But with the introduction of the sewing machine a great change took place. It would be impossible within the limits of a letter to follow it out in every trade which has felt its influence. But briefly,—when it was found that the stitching process could be got through, though less solidly, at a very much reduced cost, it became possible for all classes to have dresses, clothes, and shoes in far greater number, and to embody in all kinds of clothing a larger amount of useless and elaborate work.

"And then arose among manufacturers generally a vigorous competition,—each one striving, not to make the most enduring and sound fabric (*the best value*), but that which, retaining some appearance of goodness, should be saleable at the lowest price and at the largest apparent profit.

"The Statutes of the old Trade Guilds of England constantly provide for the purity of their several manufactures; as did Richard Cœur de Lion, in his law for the cloth makers, (*Fors*, Letter III., p. 38)—on this thoroughly wise and just ground: namely, that the best cloth, leather, etc., producible, being accurately the cheapest to the consumer,—the man who used his knowledge of his trade to make other than the best, was guilty of fraud. Compare this view of the duty of a manufacturer with modern practice!

"It may be said that the customer is not cheated; since he knows, when he buys what is called a cheap thing, that it is not the best. I reply that the consumer never knows to the full what bad value, or unvalue, the common article is. And whose fault is it that he buys any but the best value?

"The answer involves a consideration of the duty and position of the retailer or middleman, and must be given, if at all, hereafter.

"One might multiply instances to show how this kind of competition has lowered the standard of our manufactures: but here most readers will be able to fall back upon their own experience.

"Then these common fabrics require for their production always a larger amount of labour in proportion to their value,—often actually as much, and sometimes more, than would suffice to make an equal quantity of material of the best value. So that, roughly, when we demand two common coats where one good one would serve, we simply require certain of our fellow-creatures to spend double the necessary time working for us in a mill. That is, supposing we get the full value out of our two common coats when we have them : the evil is greater if we fail to do so, and, to gratify our selfishness or caprice, require three instead of two. And the question arises,—Is it *kind* or *just* to require from others double the needful quantity of such labour as we would not choose to undergo ourselves? That it is not *Christian* so to do, may be learned by any one who will think out the far-reaching consequences the words of our Lord : 'Therefore ALL THINGS WHATSOEVER ye would that men should do to you, do ye even so to them.'

"Now the use of the sewing machine has been all in favour of the 'three-coat' system, indefinitely multiplied and variously recommended ; and the consequent absorption, year by year, of larger numbers of persons in mechanical toil ; toil of the hands only—numbing to the brain, and blighting to the heart, or maddening to both.

"So far as the question of clothing is concerned, I would venture to sum up our duty under present circumstances, broadly, as follows." [It can't possibly be done better.—J. R.]

"Always demand the best materials, and use no more of them than is necessary to dress yourself neatly or handsomely, according to your station in society. Then have these materials made up by hand, if possible under your own supervision, paying a just price for the labour. For such ornament as you need to add, remember that it must be the expression, first of your delight in some work of God's, and then of the human skill that wrought it. That will save you from ever tampering with the lifeless machine-work ; and though you have little ornament, it will soon be lovely and right.

"Above all, never buy cheap ready-made clothing of any kind whatsoever ; it is most of it stained with blood, if you could see it aright. It is true you may now buy a 'lady's costume,' made up and trimmed by the sewing machine (guided by a human one), for the sum of two shillings and fourpence (wholesale), *but you had a great deal better wear a sack with a hole in it.* [Italics mine.—J. R.] It may be worth while hereafter to define with some precision what is the best value in various kinds of goods. Meantime, should it be suggested that machine-sewing is good enough for common materials, or for clothes that you intend to wear only a few times, and then throw aside, remember you have no business to buy any but good materials, nor to waste when you have bought them; and that it is worth while to put solid hand work into such."

(" I use the word 'value' for the strength or 'availing of a thing towards life.' See *Munera Pulveris*, p. 25.")

IV. With respect to the next following letter—one which I am heartily glad to receive—I must beg my readers henceforward, and conclusively, to understand, that whether I print my correspondence in large type, or small, and with praise of it, or dispraise, I give absolutely no sanction or ratification whatever to any correspondent's statements of fact, unless by express indication. I am responsible for my own assertions, and for none other; but I hold myself bound to hear, and no less bound to publish, all complaints and accusations made by persons supposing themselves injured, of those who injure them, which I have no definite reason for supposing to be false or malicious, and which relate to circumstances affecting St. George's work. I have no other means of determining their truth, than by permitting the parties principally concerned to hear them, and contradict them, according to their ability; and the wish with which my present correspondent's letter closes, to be delivered from evil speaking and slandering, (she seems not quite clearly to understand that the prayer in the Litany is to be delivered from the guilt of these,—not from their effects,) may, so far as these affect her own family, be much more perfectly accomplished by her own statement of their true history, than by any investigation possible to me of the facts in question. But, as far as respects the appeal made by her to myself, my answer is simply, that whether made by patents, ingenuities, or forges, all fortunes whatever, rapidly acquired, are, necessarily, *ill* acquired : and exemplary of universal ill to all men. No man is ever paid largely for ingenuity; he can only be paid largely by a tax on the promulgation of that ingenuity.

Of actual ingenuities, now active in Europe, none are so utterly deadly, and destructive to all the beauty of nature and the art of man, as that of the engineer.

And with respect to what my correspondent too truly urges—the shame of our ancient races in leaving their houses abandoned—it does not make me look with more comfort or complacency on their inhabitation by men of other names, that there will soon be left few homes in England whose splendour will not be a monument at once of the guilt of her nobles, and the misery of her people.

" Dear Mr. Ruskin,—We have only just read the September number of *Fors Clavigera*. My husband is the Ned G—— referred to in the letter you quote from E. L. Said he, ' It (*i.e.* the letter) is not worth notice.' I replied, ' In itself perhaps not; but I have known Mr. Ruskin in his writings many years, and I shall write him to put before him the actual facts, and request him to withdraw these misstatements.'

The whole letter is written on the supposition that Mr. Green is an *iron king,* or *iron lord.* No such thing: he is an *engineer*—quite a different affair; the maker of a patent which is known all over the world as the 'Fuel Economiser.' He consequently never had a forge, and is indebted to the use of his intellect and the very clever mechanical genius of his father for their rise in life, and not merely to *toiling half-naked Britons,* as stated. The picture of the forge, with its *foul smoke and sweltering heat and din,* is drawn from some other place, and is utterly unlike the real workshops of E. Green and Son—costly, airy, convenient, and erected to ensure the comfort of the workpeople, having a handsome front and lofty interior.

" As to smoke, the whole concern makes no more than, if as much as, an ordinary dwelling-house; while we suffer too much at Heath from the town smoke to add to the dense volumes. We have no whistle—some other place is meant; we were never possessed of a 'devil,' American or English, of any sort. Mr. Green derives no pecuniary benefit from Wakefield, and but for the attachment of his father and himself to their birthplace, would long ago have conducted his operations in a more central spot.

"Several other grave charges are brought against Mr. Green—one so serious that I am surprised to see it printed: viz., *that he rules his people with an iron hand.* That may go with the rest of the ' iron tale.' Your correspondent is either very ignorant or wilfully false. No such assertion can be for a moment sustained, after inquiry is made among our people ; nor by any one in the town could an instance of such be proved.

" As to the Scotch estate, Mr. Green does not possess one.

"The history of *Robin the Pedlar* is equally a work of E. L.'s imagination, although no false shame as to a humble descent has ever been shown or felt. What! you taunt a man because he and his father have risen above the state in which they were born by use of the intellect God gives them ? Fie! What sort of encouragement do you give to the working men to whom you address these letters, when you insinuate that *one sprung from the people* has no right to dwell in a hall or drive a carriage; and broadly hint he is no *gentleman,* no *scholar,* and *has nothing to boast of but his money?* Come here, and see if Ned G—— is the sort of man you picture; see the refinement visible in his idea of art, and which he has tried to impress on others by his example, and then ask yourself whether you have done well to lend the sanction of your name to decry, as a mere vulgar parvenu, one who has done his best to keep a high standard before him.

" As to living at Heath Hall, I ask, Is it a crime to spend your money in preserving to posterity a beautiful specimen of the house of the smaller gentry in Queen Elizabeth's time, which you only enjoy during a few years' lease? A little longer neglect, and this fine old house would have become a ruin : when we took it, ivy grew inside, and owls made their nests in what are now guest-chambers.

" No *squire* has lived here for a century and a quarter; and the last descendant of the *venerated Lady B——,* (Dame Mary Bolles, that is,) utterly refused to reside near so dull a town as Wakefield—preferring Bath, then at the height of its glory and Beau Nash's; even before his time the hereditary squires despised and deserted the lovely place, letting it to any who would take it. Now it is repaired and restored, and well worth a visit even from Mr. Ruskin—who, if he is what I believe him, will withdraw the false imputations whic ı must cause pain to us and surprise to those who know us. That last little stroke about bribery betrays E. L.'s disgust, not at the successful man, but at the Blue Tory. Well! from envy, malice, and all uncharitableness, from evil-speaking and slandering: Good Lord deliver us!

"Yours very truly,
"MARY GREEN."

(I make no comments on this letter till the relations of Dame Mary Bolles have had time to read it, and E. L. to reply.)

V. The following account, with which I have pleasure in printing the accompanying acknowledgment of the receipt, contains particulars of the first actual expenditure of St. George's moneys made by me, to the extent of twenty-nine pounds ten shillings, for ten engravings * now the property of the Company. The other prints named in the account are bought with my own money, to be given or not given as I think right. The last five engravings—all by Durer—are bought at present for my proposed school at Sheffield, with the Melancholia, which I have already; but if finer impressions of them are some day given me, as is not unlikely, I should of course withdraw these, and substitute the better examples—retaining always the right of being myself the ultimate donor of the two St. Georges, in their finest state, from my own collection. But these must at present remain in Oxford.

London, October 5th, 1875.

JOHN RUSKIN, ESQ.

			£	s.	d.
St. G. 1.	..	Apollo and the Python, by Master of the Die	1	0	0
,, 2.	..	Raglan Castle	3	10	0
,, 3.	..	Solway Moss	4	0	0
,, 4.	..	Hind Head Hill	1	10	0
,, 5, *a, b, c,*		Three impressions of Falls of the Clyde (£2 each)	6	0	0
,, 6.	..	Hindoo Worship	2	0	0
,, 7.	..	Dumblane Abbey	3	10	0
,, 8.	..	Pembury Mill			
,, 9.	..	Etching of the Severn and Wye	2	10	0
,, 10.	..	Tenth Plague (of Egypt) ..	2	0	0
,, 11.	..	Æsacus and Hesperie	3	10	0
			29	10	0

(The above Prints sold at an unusually low price, for Mr. Ruskin's school.)

* The printseller obligingly giving an eleventh, "Pembury Mill,"—Fors thus directing that the first art gift bestowed on the Company shall be Turner's etching of a flour mill.

				£	s.	d.
		Brought forward		29	10	0
J. R.	1.	..	Sir John Cust	0	10	0
,,	2.	..	Lady Derby	5	0	0
,,	3, 4.	..	Two etchings of Æsacus and Hes-			
			perie (£4 each)	8	0	0
,,	5, 6.	..	Two Holy Islands (£2 6s. each)	4	12	0
,,	7.	..	Etching of Procris	4	4	0
,,	8.	..	Holy Island	2	6	0
,,	9.	..	The Crypt	4	4	0
,,	10.	..	The Arveron	8	8	0
,,	11.	..	Raglan Castle	7	0	0
,,	12.	..	,, ,, ...	6	0	0
,,	13.	..	,, ,, ...	6	0	0
,,	14.	..	Woman at the Tank	7	17	6
,,	15.	..	Grande Chartreuse	8	8	0
				101	19	6
		Discount (15 per cent.)		10	1	0

				£	s.	d.
				91	18	6
St. G.	16.	..	Knight and Death..	18	0	0
,,	17.	..	St. George on Horseback	3	10	0
,,	18.	..	,, ,, Foot	7	0	0
,,	19.	..	Pilate	2	0	0
,,	20.	..	Caiaphas	3	0	0
				125	8	6

"My dear Sir,—It is delightful to do business with you. How I wish that all my customers were imbued with your principles ; I enclose the receipt, with best thanks, and am

Yours very sincerely and obliged.

JOHN RUSKIN, ESQ.

Of course, original accounts, with all other vouchers, will be kept with the Company's registers at Oxford. I do not think it expedient always to print names ; which would look like advertisement.

Respecting the picture by Filippo Lippi, I find more difficulty than I expected. On inquiring of various dealers, I am asked three shillings each for these photographs. But as I on principle never use any artifice in dealing, most tradesmen think me a simpleton, and think it also their first duty, as men of business, to take all the advantage in their power of this my supposed simplicity ; these photographs are therefore, I suppose, worth actually unmounted, about a shilling each ; and I believe that eventually, my own assistant, Mr. Ward, will be able to supply them, of good impression, carefully chosen, with due payment for his time and trouble, at eighteenpence each ; or mounted, examined by me, and sealed with my seal, for two shillings and six-pence each. I don't promise this, because it depends upon whether the government at Florence will entertain my request, made officially as Slade Professor at Oxford, to have leave to photograph from the picture.

At present holding it of more importance not to violate confidence * than to sell photographs cheap, I do not even publish what I have ascertained, since this note was half written, to be the (actual) trade price, and I must simply leave the thing in the beautiful complexity of competition and secretiveness called British Trade; only, at Oxford, I have so much personal influence with Mr. Davis, in Exeter Street, as may, I think, secure his obtaining the photographs, for which, as a dealer combined with other dealers, he must ask three shillings, of good quality; to him, therefore, at Oxford, for general business my readers may address themselves; or in London, to Miss Bertolacci, 7, Edith Grove, Kensington; and, for impressions certified by me, to Mr. Ward, at Richmond, (address as above.) who will furnish them, unmounted, for two shillings each, and mounted, for three. And for a foundation of the domestic art-treasure of their establishment, I do not hold this to be an enormous or unjustifiable expense.

---

* Remember, however, that the publication of prime cost, and the absolute knowledge of all circumstances or causes of extra cost, are inviolable laws of established trade under the St. George's Company.

LETTER LX.

I CANNOT finish the letter I meant for my Christmas *Fors;* and must print merely the begun fragment—and such uncrystalline termination must now happen to all my work, more or less, (and more and more, rather than less,) as it expands in range. As I stated in last letter, I have now seven books in the press at once—and any one of them enough to take up all the remainder of my life. *Love's Meinie,* for instance, (Love's Many, or Serving Company,) was meant to become a study of British birds, which would have been occasionally useful in museums, carried out with a care in plume drawing which I learned in many a day's work from Albert Durer; and with which, in such light as the days gave me, I think it still my duty to do all I can towards completion of the six essays prepared for my Oxford schools :— but even the third of these, on the Chough, though already written and in type, is at pause because I can't get the engravings for it finished, and the rest—merely torment me in other work with the thousand things flitting in my mind, like sea-birds for whom there are no sands to settle upon.

Ariadne is nearer its close; but the Appendix is a mass of loose notes which need a very sewing machine to bring together—and any one of these that I take in hand leads me into ashamed censorship of the imperfection of all I have been able to say about engraving; and then, if I take up my Bewick, or return to my old Turner vignettes, I put my Appendix off again—" till next month," and so on.

Proserpina will, I hope, take better and more harmonious form; but it grows under my hands, and needs most careful thought. For it claims nothing less than complete modification of existing botanical nomenclature, for popular use; and in connexion with *Deucalion* and the recast *Elements of Drawing,* is meant to found a system of education in Natural

History, the conception of which I have reached only by thirty years of labour, and the realization of which can only be many a year after I am at rest. And yet none of this work can be done but as a kind of play, irregularly, and as the humour comes upon me. For if I set myself at it gravely, there is too much to be dealt with ; my mind gets fatigued in half an hour, and no good can be done ; the only way in which any advance can be made is by keeping my mornings entirely quiet, and free of care by opening of letters or newspapers ; and then by letting myself follow any thread of thought or point of inquiry that chances to occur first, and writing as thoughts come,—whatever their disorder ; all their connection and co-operation being dependent on the real harmony of my purpose, and the consistency of the ascertainable facts, which are the only ones I teach ; and I can no more, now, polish or neatly arrange my work than I can guide it. So this fragment must stand as it was written, and end,—because I have no time to say more.

Cowley Rectory, 27th October, 1875.

My Christmas letter this year, since we are now definitely begun with our schooling, may most fitly be on the subject, already opened in *Fors* 12th, of the Three Wise Men.

"Three wise men of Gotham," I had nearly written ; the remembrance of the very worst pantomime I ever saw, having from the mere intolerableness of its stupidity, so fastened itself in my memory that I can't now get rid of the ring in my ears, unless I carefully say, "Magi," instead of "wise men."

Such, practically, is the principal effect of the Sacred Art employed by England, in the festivity of her God's birthday, upon the minds of her innocent children, like me, who would fain see something magical and pretty on the occasion—if the good angels would bring it us, and our nurses, and mammas, and governesses would allow us to believe in magic, or in wisdom, any more.

You would not believe, if they wanted you, I suppose, you wise men of the west ? You are sure that no real magicians ever existed ; no real witches—no real prophets ;—that an Egyptian necromancer was only a clever little Mr. Faraday, given to juggling ; and the witch of Endor, only a Jewish Mrs. Somerville amusing herself with a practical joke on Saul; and that when Elisha made the axe swim, he had prepared the handle on the sly—with aluminium ? And you think that in this blessed nineteenth century—though there isn't a merchant, from Dan to Beersheba, too honest to cheat, there is not a priest nor a prophet, from Dan to Beersheba, but he is too dull to juggle ?

You may think, for what I care, what you please in such matters, if indeed you choose to go on through all your lives thinking, instead of ascertaining. But, for my own part, there are a few things concerning Magi and their doings which I have personally discovered, by laborious work among real magi. Some of those things I am going to tell you to-day, positively, and with entire and incontrovertible knowledge of them,—as you and your children will one day find every word of my direct statements in *Fors Clavigera*, to be ; and fastened, each with its nail in its sure place.

A. In the first place, then, concerning stars in the east. You can't see the loveliest which appear there naturally,—the Morning Star, namely, and his fellows,—unless you get up in the morning.

B. If you resolve thus always, so far as may be in your own power, to see the loveliest which are there naturally, you will soon come to see them in a supernatural manner, with a quite—properly so-called—" miraculous " or " wonderful " light which will be a light in your spirit, not in your eyes. And you will hear, with your spirit, the Morning Star and his fellows sing together ; also, you will hear the sons of God shouting together for joy with them ; particularly the little ones,—sparrows, greenfinches, linnets, and the like.

C. You will by persevering in the practice, gradually discover that it is a pleasant thing to see stars in the luminous east ; to watch them fade as they rise ; to hear their Master say, Let there be light—and there is light ; to see the world

made, that day, at the word ; and creation, instant by
instant, of divine forms out of darkness.

D. At six o'clock, or some approximate hour, you will
perceive with precision that the Firm over the way, or
round the corner, of the United Grand Steam Percussion
and Corrosion Company, Limited, (Offices London, Paris,
and New York,) issues its counter-order, Let there be darkness ; and that the Master of Creation not only at once
submits to this order, by fulfilling the constant laws He has
ordained concerning smoke,—but farther, supernaturally or
miraculously, enforces the order by sending a poisonous
black wind, also from the east, of an entirely corrosive,
deadly, and horrible quality, with which, from him that hath
not, He takes away also that light he hath ; and changes
the sky during what remains of the day,—on the average
now three days out of five,*—into a mere dome of ashes,
differing only by their enduring frown and slow pestilence
from the passing darkness and showering death of Pom-
peii.

E. If, nevertheless, you persevere diligently in seeing
what stars you can in the early morning, and use what is
left you of light wisely, you will gradually discover that the
United Grand Steam Percussion and Corrosion Company is
a company of thieves ; and that you yourself are an ass, for
letting them steal your money, and your light, at once. And
that there is standing order from the Maker of Light, and
Filler of pockets, that the company shall not be thieves, but
honest men ; and that you yourself shall not be an ass, but
a Magus.

F. If you remind the company of this law, they will tell
you that people "didn't know everything down in Judee,"
that nobody ever made the world ; and that nobody but the
company knows it.

But if you enforce upon yourself the commandment not
to be an ass, and verily resolve to be so no more, then—hear

---

* It is at this moment, nine o'clock, 27th October, tearing the Virginian creeper round my window into rags rather than leaves.

the word of God, spoken to you by the only merchant city
that ever set herself to live wholly by His law.*

    " I willed, and sense was given to me.
      I prayed, and the Spirit of Wisdom was given to me.
      I set her before Kingdoms and Homes,
      And held riches nothing, in comparison of her."

That is to say,—If you would have her to dwell with you,
you must set her before kingdoms ;—(as, for instance, at
Sheffield, you must not think to be kings of cutlery, and let
nobody else in the round world make a knife but you ;)—
you must set her before homes ; that is to say, you must not
sit comfortably enjoying your own fireside, and think you
provide for everybody if you provide for that :—and as for
riches—you are only to *prefer* wisdom,—think her, of two
good things, the best, when she is matched with kingdoms
and homes ; but you are to esteem riches—*nothing* in comparison of her. Not so much as *mention* shall be made " of
coral, nor of pearls, for the price of wisdom is above rubies."

You have not had the chance, you think, probably, of
making any particular mention of coral, or pearls, or rubies ?
Your betters, the Squires and the Clergy, have kept, if not
the coral, at least the pearls, for their own wives' necks, and
the rubies for their own mitres ; and have generously
accorded to you heavenly things,—wisdom, namely, con-
centrated in your responses to Catechism. I find St. George,
on the contrary, to be minded that you shall at least know
what these earthly goods are, in order to your despising them
in a sensible manner ;—for you can't despise them if you
know nothing about them.

I am going, under His orders, therefore, to give you some
topazes of Ethiopia,—(at least, of the Ural mountains, where
the topazes are just as good,)—and all manner of coral, that
you may know what co-operative societies are working, to
make your babies their rattles and necklaces, without any
steam to help them, under the deep sea, and in its foam ;
also, out of the Tay, the fairest river of the British Isles, we

* See *Fourth Morning in Florence,* "The Vaulted Book."

will fetch some pearls that nobody shall have drawn short breath for : and, indeed, all the things that Solomon in his wisdom sent his ships to Tarshish for,—gold, and silver, ivory, and apes, and peacocks,—you shall see in their perfection, and have as much of as St. George thinks good for you : (only remember, in order to see an ape in perfection, you must not be an ape yourself, whatever Mr. Darwin may say ; but must admire, without imitating their prehensile activities, nor fancy that you can lay hold on to the branches of the tree of life with your tails instead of your hands, as you have been practising lately).

And, in the meantime, I must stop writing, because I've to draw a peacock's breast-feather, and paint as much of it as I can without having heaven to dip my brush in. And when you have seen what it is, you shall despise it—if you can—for heaven itself. But for nothing less !

My fragment does not quite end here ; but in its following statements of plans for the Sheffield Museum, anticipates more than I think Atropos would approve ; besides getting more figurative and metaphysical than you would care to read after your Christmas dinner. But here is a piece of inquiry into the origin of all riches, Solomon's and our own, which I wrote in May, 1873, for the *Contemporary Review,* and which, as it sums much of what I may have too vaguely and figuratively stated in my letters, may advisably close their series for this year.

It was written chiefly in reply to an article by Mr. Greg, defending the luxury of the rich as harmless, or even beneficent to the poor. Mr. Greg had, on his part, been reproving Mr. Goldwin Smith—who had spoken of a rich man as consuming the means of living of the poor. And Mr. Greg pointed out how beneficially for the poor, in a thousand channels, the rich man spent what he had got.

Whereupon I ventured myself to inquire, " How he got it ? " and the paper went on thus,—' Which is indeed the first of all questions to be asked when the economical relations of any man with his neighbour are to be examined.

Dick Turpin is blamed—suppose—by some plain-minded

person, for consuming the means of other people's living.
"Nay," says Dick to the plain-minded person, "observe
how beneficently and pleasantly I spend whatever I get ! "

" Yes, Dick," persists the plain-minded person, " but how
do you get it ? "

" The question," says Dick, "is insidious, and irrelevant."

Do not let it be supposed that I mean to assert any irreg-
ularity or impropriety in Dick's profession—I merely assert
the necessity for Mr. Greg's examination, if he would be
master of his subject, of the manner of *Gain* in every case,
as well as the manner of *Expenditure.* Such accounts must
always be accurately rendered in a well-regulated society.

" Le lieutenant addressa la parole au capitaine, et lui dit
qu'il venait d'enlever ces mannequins, remplis de sucre, de
cannelle, d'amandes, et de raisins secs, à un épicier de Bénavente. Après qu'il eut rendu compte de son expédition au
bureau, les dépouilles de l'épicier furent portées dans l'office.
Alors il ne fut plus question que de se réjour ; je débutai
par le buffet, que je parai de plusieurs bouteilles de ce bon
vin que le Seigneur Rolando m'avoit vanté."

Mr. Greg strictly confines himself to an examination of
the benefits conferred on the public by this so agreeable
festivity ; but he must not be surprised or indignant that
some inquiry should be made as to the resulting condition
of the épicier de Bénavente.

And it is all the more necessary that such inquiry be instituted, when the captain of the expedition is a minion, not
of the moon, but of the sun ; and dazzling, therefore, to all
beholders. " It is heaven which dictates what I ought to do
upon this occasion," * says Henry of Navarre ; " my retreat
out of this city, before I have made myself master of it, will
be the retreat of my soul out of my body. Accordingly, all

---

* I use the current English of Mrs. Lennox's translation, but Henry's
real saying was (see the first – green leaf—edition of Sully), "It is
written above what is to happen to me on *every* occasion." " Toute
occasion" becomes " Cette occasion " in the subsequent editions, and
finally " what is to happen to me " (ce que doit être fait de moi) becomes " what I ought to do " in the English.

the quarter which still held out, we forced," says M. de Rosny; "after which the inhabitants, finding themselves no longer able to resist, laid down their arms, and the city was given up to plunder. My good fortune threw a small iron chest in my way, in which I found about four thousand gold crowns."

I cannot doubt that the Baron's expenditure of this sum would be in the highest degree advantageous to France, and to the Protestant religion. But complete economical science must study the effect of its abstraction on the immediate prosperity of the town of Cahors ; and even beyond this —the mode of its former acquisition by the town itself, which perhaps, in the economies of the nether world, may have delegated some of its citizens to the seventh circle.

And the most curious points, in the modes of study pursued by modern economical science, are, that while it always *waives this question of ways and means* with respect to *rich* persons, it studiously pushes it in the case of *poor* ones ; and while it asserts the consumption of such an article of luxury as wine (to take that which Mr. Greg himself instances) to be economically expedient, when the wine is drunk by persons who are *not* thirsty, it asserts the same consumption to be altogether inexpedient, when the privilege is extended to those who *are*. Thus Mr. Greg dismisses, at page 618, with compassionate disdain, the extremely vulgar notion " that a man who drinks a bottle of champagne worth five shillings, while his neighbour is in want of actual food, is in some way wronging his neighbour ; " and yet Mr. Greg himself, at page 624, evidently remains under the equally vulgar impression that the twenty-four millions of much thirstier persons who spend fifteen per cent. of their incomes in drink and tobacco, *are* wronging their neighbours by *that* expenditure.

It cannot, surely, be the difference in degree of refinement between malt liquor and champagne which causes Mr. Greg's conviction that there is moral delinquency and economical error in the latter case, but none in the former ; if that be all, I can relieve him from his embarrassment by putting the cases in more parallel form. A clergyman writes to me, in distress of mind, because the able-bodied labourers who come begging to him in winter, drink port wine out of buckets in summer.   Of course Mr. Greg's logical mind will at once admit (as a consequence of his own very just argumentum ad hominem in page 617) that the consumption of port wine out of buckets must be as much a benefit to society in general as the consumption of champagne out of bottles ; and yet, curiously enough, I am certain he will feel my question, " Where does the drinker get the means for his drinking ? " more relevant in the case of the imbibers of port than in that of the imbibers of champagne.   And although Mr. Greg proceeds, with that lofty contempt for the dictates of nature and Christianity which radical economists cannot but feel, to observe (p. 618) that "while the natural man and the Christian would have the champagne drinker forego his bottle, and give the value of it to the famishing wretch beside him, the radical economist would condemn such behaviour as distinctly criminal and pernicious," he would scarcely, I think, carry out with the same triumphant confidence the conclusions of the unnatural man and the Anti-Christian with respect to the labourer as well as the idler ; and declare that while the extremely simple persons who still believe in the laws of nature, and the mercy of God, would have the port-drinker forego his bucket, and give the value of it to the famishing wife and child beside him, " the radical economist would condemn such behaviour as distinctly criminal and pernicious."

Mr. Greg has it indeed in his power to reply that it is proper to economise for the sake of one's own wife and children, but not for the sake of anybody else's.   But since, according to another exponent of the principles of Radical Economy, in the *Cornhill Magazine*, a well-conducted agricultural labourer must not marry till he is forty-five, his economies, if any, in early life, must be as offensive to Mr. Greg on the score of their abstract humanity, as those of the richest bachelor about town.

There is another short sentence in this same page 618, of which it is difficult to overrate the accidental significance.

The superficial observer, says Mr. Greg, " recollects a te͞ which he heard in his youth, but of which he never considered the precise applicability—' He that hath two coats, let him impart to him that hath none.' "

The assumptions that no educated Englishman can ever have heard that text *except* in his youth, and that those who are old enough to remember having heard it, " never considered its precise applicability," are surely rash, in the treatment of a scientific subject. I can assure Mr. Greg that a few grey-headed votaries of the creed of Christendom still read—though perhaps under their breath—the words which early associations have made precious to them ; and that in the bygone days, when that Sermon on the Mount was still listened to with respect by many not illiterate persons, its meaning was not only considered, but very deliberately acted upon. Even the readers of the *Contemporary Review* may perhaps have some pleasure in retreating from the sunshine of contemporary science, for a few quiet moments, into the shadows of that of the past ; and hearing in the following extracts from two letters of Scott's (the first describing the manner of life of his mother, whose death it announces to a friend ; the second, anticipating the verdict of the future on the management of his estate by a Scottish nobleman) what relations between rich and poor were possible, when philosophers had not yet even lisped in the sweet numbers of Radical Sociology.

" She was a strict economist, which she said enabled her to be liberal ; out of her little income of about £300 a year she bestowed at least a third in well-chosen charities, and with the rest, lived like a gentlewoman, and even with hospitality more general than seemed to suit her age ; yet I could never prevail on her to accept of any assistance. You cannot conceive how affecting it was to me to see the little preparations of presents which she had assorted for the New Year, for she was a great observer of the old fashions of her period—and to think that the kind heart was cold which delighted in all these arts of kindly affection."

" The Duke is one of those retired and high-spirited men

who will never be known until the world asks what became
of the huge oak that grew on the brow of the hill, and sheltered such an extent of ground.   During the late distress,
though his own immense rents remained in arrears, and
though I know he was pinched for money, as all men were,
but more especially the possessors of entailed estates, he ab-
sented himself from London in order to pay, with ease to
himself, the labourers employed on his various estates.
These amounted (for I have often seen the roll and helped
to check it) to nine hundred and fifty men, working at day
wages, each of whom on a moderate average might maintain
three persons, since the single men have mothers, sisters,
and aged or very young relations to protect and assist.   Indeed it is wonderful how much even a small sum, compara-
tively, will do in supporting the Scottish labourer, who in
his natural state is perhaps one of the best, most intelligent,
and kind-hearted of human beings ; and in truth I have limited my other habits expense very much since I fell into the
habit of employing mine honest people.   I wish you could
have seen about a hundred children, being almost entirely
supported by their fathers' or brothers' labour, come down
yesterday to dance to the pipes, and get a piece of cake and
bannock, and pence apiece (no very deadly largess) in honour of hogmanay.   I declare to you, my dear friend, that
when I thought the poor fellows who kept these children so
neat, and well taught, and well behaved, were slaving the
whole day for eighteen-pence or twenty-pence at most, I
was ashamed of their gratitude, and of their becks and bows.
But after all, one does what one can, and it is better twenty
families should be comfortable according to their wishes and
habits, than that half that number should be raised above
their situation."

I must pray Mr. Greg farther to observe, if he has con-
descended to glance at these remains of almost pre-historic
thought, that although the modern philosopher will never
have reason to blush for any man's gratitude, and has totally
abandoned the romantic idea of making even so much as one
family comfortable according to their wishes and habits, the

alternative suggested by Scott, that *half* " the number should be raised above their situation," may become a very inconvenient one if the doctrines of Modern Equality and competition should render the *other* half desirous of parallel promotion.

It is now just sixteen years since Mr. Greg's present philosophy of Expenditure was expressed with great precision by the Common Councilmen of New York, in their report on the commercial crisis of 1857, in the following terms * :—

" Another erroneous idea is that luxurious living, extravagant dressing, splendid turn-outs, and fine houses, are the cause of distress to a nation. No more erroneous impression could exist. Every extravagance that the man of 100,000 or 1,000,000 dollars indulges in, adds to the means, the support, the wealth of ten or a hundred who had little or nothing else but their labour, their intellect, or their taste. If a man of 1,000,000 dollars spends principal and interest in ten years, and finds himself beggared at the end of that time, he has actually made a hundred who have catered to his extravagance, employers or employed, so much richer by the division of his wealth. He may be ruined, but the nation is better off and richer, for one hundred minds and hands, with 10,000 dollars apiece, are far more productive than one with the whole."

Now that is precisely the view also taken of the matter by a large number of Radical Economists in England as well as America ; only they feel that the time, however short, which the rich gentleman takes to divide his property among them in his own way, is practically wasted ; and even worse, because the methods which the gentleman himself is likely to adopt for the depression of his fortune will not, in all probability, be conducive to the elevation of his character. It appears, therefore, on moral as well as economical grounds, desirable that the division and distribution should at once be summarily effected ; and the only point still open to discussion in the views of the Common Councilmen is to what degree of minuteness they would think it advisable to carry the subsequent *sub*-division.

* See the *Times* of November 23rd of that year.

I do not suppose, however, that this is the conclusion which Mr. Greg is desirous that the general Anti-Christian public should adopt ; and in that case, as I see by his paper in the last number of the *Contemporary*, that he considers the Christian life itself virtually impossible, may I recommend his examination of the manners of the Pre-Christian ? For I can certify him that this important subject, of which he has only himself imperfectly investigated one side, had been thoroughly investigated on all sides, at least seven hundred years before Christ ; and from that day to this, all men of wit, sense, and feeling have held precisely the same views on the subjects of economy and charity, in all nations under the sun. It is of no consequence whether Mr. Greg chooses the experience of Bœotia, Lombardy, or Yorkshire, nor whether he studies the relation of each day to its labour under Hesiod, Virgil, or Sydney Smith. But it is desirable that at least he should acquaint himself with the opinions of some of these persons, as well as with those of the Common Councilmen of New York ; for though a man of superior sagacity may be pardoned for thinking, with the friends of Job, that Wisdom will die with him, it can only be through neglect of the existing opportunities of general culture that he remains distinctly under the impression that she was born with him.

It may perhaps be well that, in conclusion, I should state briefly the causes and terms of the economical crisis of our own day, which has been the subject of the debate between Mr. Goldwin Smith and Mr. Greg.

No man ever became, or can become, largely rich merely by labour and economy. All large fortunes (putting treasure-trove and gambling out of consideration) are founded either on occupation of land, usury, or taxation of labour. Whether openly or occultly, the landlord, money-lender, and capital-holding employer, gather into their possession a certain quantity of the means of existence which other people produce by the labour of their hands. The effect of this impost upon the condition of life of the tenant, borrower, and workman, is the first point to be studied ;—the results, that is to say, of the mode in which Captain Roland *fills* his purse.

Secondly, we have to study the effects of the mode in which Captain Roland *empties* his purse. The landlord, usurer, or labour-master, does not, and cannot, himself consume all the means of life he collects. He gives them to other persons, whom he employs in his own behalf—growers of champagne ; jockeys ; footmen ; jewellers ; builders ; painters ; musicians, and the like. The diversion of the labour of these persons from the production of food to the production of articles of luxury is very frequently, and, at the present day, very grievously, a cause of famine. But when the luxuries are produced, it becomes a quite separate question who is to have them, and whether the landlord and capitalist are entirely to monopolise the music, the painting, the architecture, the hand-service, the horse-service, and the sparkling champagne of the world.

And it is gradually, in these days, becoming manifest to the tenants, borrowers, and labourers, that instead of paying these large sums into the hands of the landlords, lenders, and employers, that *they* may purchase music, painting, etc. ; the tenants, borrowers, and workers, had better buy a little music and painting for themselves ! That, for instance, instead of the capitalist-employer's paying three hundred pounds for a full-length portrait of himself, in the attitude of investing his capital, the united workmen had better themselves pay the three hundred pounds into the hands of the ingenious artist, for a painting, in the antiquated manner of Lionardo or Raphael, of some subject more religiously or historically interesting to *them ;* and placed where they can always see it. And again, instead of paying three hundred pounds to the obliging landlord, that he may buy a box at the opera with it, whence to study the refinements of music and dancing, the tenants are beginning to think that they may as well keep their rents partly to themselves, and therewith pay some Wandering Willie to fiddle at their own doors ; or bid some grey-haired minstrel

> " Tune, to please a peasant's ear,
> The harp a king had loved to hear."

And similarly the dwellers in the hut of the field, and

garret of the city, are beginning to think that, instead of paying half-a-crown for the loan of half a fireplace, they had better keep their half-crown in their pockets till they can buy for themselves a whole one.

These are the views which are gaining ground among the poor ; and it is entirely vain to endeavour to repress them by equivocations. They are founded on eternal laws ; and although their recognition will long be refused, and their promulgation, resisted as it will be, partly by force, partly by falsehood, can only take place through incalculable confusion and misery, recognised they must be eventually ; and with these three ultimate results :—that the usurer's trade will be abolished utterly ;—that the employer will be paid justly for his superintendence of labour, but not for his capital ; and the landlord paid for his superintendence of the cultivation of land, when he is able to direct it wisely :— that both he, and the employer of mechanical labour, will be recognised as beloved masters, if they deserve love, and as noble guides when they are capable of giving discreet guidance ; but neither will be permitted to establish themselves any more as senseless conduits, through which the strength and riches of their native land are to be poured into the cup of the fornication of its Babylonian city of the Plain.'

So ends my article, and enough said for 1875, I think. And I wish you a merry Christmas, my masters ; and honest ways of winning your meat and pudding.

NOTES AND CORRESPONDENCE.

I AM busy, and tired, this month ; so shall keep my making up of accounts till January. The gist of them is simply that we have got £8000 worth of Consols ; and we had a balance of £501 7*s.* at the bank, which balance I have taken, and advanced another hundred of my own, making £600, to buy the Sheffield property with : this advance I shall repay myself as the interest comes in, or farther subscription ; and then use such additional sums for the filling of the museum, and building a small curator's house on the ground. But I shall not touch any of the funded sum ; and hope soon to see it raised to £10,000. I have no word yet from our lawyer about our constitution. The Sheffield property, like the funded, stands in the names of the Trustees.

I have accepted, out of our forty subscribers, some eight or nine for Companions, very gratefully. Others wish well to the cause, but dislike the required expression of creed and purpose. I use no persuasion in the matter, wishing to have complete harmony of feeling among the active members of the Society.

E. L.'s courteous, but firm, reply to Mrs. Green's letter reaches me too late for examination. In justice to both my correspondents, and to my readers, I must defer its insertion, in such abstract as may seem desirable, until next month.

I. The extract in the following letter makes me wonder if it has never occurred to the Rev. Dr. Mullens that there should be immediately formed a Madagascar Missionary Society, for the instruction of the natives of England.

" My dear Sir,—*Apropos* of your strictures on usury which have from time to time appeared in *Fors,* I have thought you would be interested in the following extract from a recent work on Madagascar, by the Rev. Dr. Mullens, of the London Missionary Society.

" After describing a ' Kabáry,'—a public assembly addressed by the Queen,—in the Betsileo * province, he goes on to say : ' Having expressed in a clear and distinct voice her pleasure in meeting her people once more, the Queen uttered several sentences usual to these assemblies, in which she dwelt upon the close and affectionate relations subsisting between them and herself. '' You are a father and mother to me : having you, I have all. . . . And if you confide in me, you have a father and a mother in me. Is it not so, O ye under heaven ? "

* I can't answer for Madagascar nomenclature.

To which, with a deep voice, the people reply, "It is so." Passing at length to the subject specially before her, the Queen said, "My days in the South are now few ; therefore I will say a word about the Schools. And I say to you all, here in Betsileo, . . . cause your children to attend the Schools. My desire is, that whether high or low, whether sons of the nobles, or sons of the judges, or sons of the officers, or sons of the centurious, your sons and your daughters should attend the Schools and become lovers of wisdom." The Prime Minister, then, in the Queen's name, addressed the assembly on the subject of usury,—a great evil among poor nations, and only too common in stages of society like that in Madagascar,—and said, "Thus saith the Queen : *All the usury exacted by the Hovas from the Betsileo is remitted*, and only the original debt shall remain !' "

"I am, dear Sir, faithfully yours,
"JOSEPH HALSEY."

II. (Letter from a clergyman, now an accepted Companion) :—

"You say when I agree in your opinions I may come, but surely you do not exact the unquestioning and entire submission of the individual opinion which the most arrogant of churches exacts.* With your leading principles, so as I am yet able to judge of them, I entirely and unreservedly agree. I see daily such warped morality, such crooked ways in the most urgent and important concerns of life, as to convince me that the axe should be laid to the root of the tree. Mainly I am disgusted—no more tolerant word will do—with the prevalent tone of thought in religious matters, and the resulting tortuous courses in daily work and worship. What a worse than Pagan misconception of Him whom they ignorantly worship—

"'Ille opifex rerum, mundi melioris origo'—

is shown by the mass of so-called religious persons ! How scurrilously the Protestant will rail against Papist *intolerance*—making his private judgment of Scripture the infallible rule, 'blushing not (as Hooker says) in any doubt concerning matters of Scripture to think his own bare Yea as good as the Nay of all the wise, grave, and learned judgments that are in the whole world.'

"'Which insolency must be repressed, or it will be the very bane of Christian Religion.'—(Ecc. Polity, Book II.)

III. (Useful letter from a friend) :—

"I believe the St. George's Company contains the germ of a healthy and vigorous constitution. I see that you are planting that germ, and fostering it with all deliberation and cautious directness of advance ; but what Titanic obstacles ! It seems to me the fittest plant of this age to survive, but in the complexities of the struggle for existence, its rearing must be a Herculean labour. Yet wherein is this age singular ? When was there any time whose sentence we might not write thus : "L'etat agité par les brigues des ambitieux, par les largesses des riches factieux, par la venalité des pauvres oiseux, par l'empirisme des ora-

---

* By no means : but *practical* obedience, yes,—not to *me*, but to the Master of the Company, whoever he may be ; and this not for his pride's sake, but for your comfort's.

teurs, par l'audace des hommes pervers, par la faiblesse des hommes
verteux," was distracted and disintegrate.'

"When I can get better words than my own I like to use them—and
it is seldom I cannot.   In the selfish pleasure of writing to you I forget the tax on your time of reading my vagaries; but I feel a kind of
filial unburdening in writing thus freely.   Will that excuse me?

"Always sincerely and affectionately yours,

"JAMES HOOPER."

WOOD *versus* COAL.—Subject to such correction as may be due to the
different quantity of carbon contained in a load of wood as in a ton of
coal, the product of the coal-field is seven times as much [of fuel] per mile,
as that of the forest.   To produce a yield of fuel equal to that obtainable from the known coal measures of the world, if worked with an
activity equal to that of our own, seven times the area of cultivated
forest is required.   But the actual area, as estimated, is not seven, but
twenty-seven times that of the coal measures.   It is thus four times
as important, regarded as a source of fuel.   But while the life of the
coal-field has been taken at 150 years, that of the forest, if rightly
cared for, will endure as long as that of the human family.   A wealth
such as this is not to be measured in tons of gold.—*Edinburgh Review*, p. 375, Oct., 1875.

"I think Sheffield is more likely 'Schaf-feld' than Sheaf-field.
'Sheep-fold' the sheltered hollow with moors all round it.   I know
a place called 'Theescombe,' meaning 'theaves-combe,' or 'young
lambs-combe.' "—*Note by a Companion.*

LETTER LXI.

November 28th, 1875.

(In the house of a friend who, being ashamed of me and my words, requests that this *Fors* may not be dated from it.)

'LIVE AND LEARN.' I trust it may yet be permitted me to fulfil the adage a few years longer, for I find it takes a great deal of living to get a little deal of learning. (Query, meaning of 'deal'?—substantive of verb deal—as at whist? —no Johnson by me, and shall be sure to forget to look when I have.) But I *have* learned something this morning, —the use of the holes in the bottom of a fireshovel, to wit. I recollect, now, often and often, seeing my mother sift the cinders ; but, alas, she never taught *me* to do it. Did not think, perhaps, that I should ever have occasion, as a Bishop, to occupy myself in that manner ; nor understand,—poor sweet mother,—how advisable it might be to have some sort of holes in my shovel-hat, for sifting cinders of human soul.

Howsoever, I have found out the art, this morning, in the actual ashes ; thinking all the time how it was possible for people to live in this weather, who had·no cinders to sift. My hostess's white cat, Lily, woke me at half-past five by piteous mewing at my window ; and being let in, and having expressed her thanks by getting between my legs over and over again as I was shaving, has at last curled herself up in my bed, and gone to sleep,—looking as fat as a little pillow, only whiter ; but what are the cats to do, to-day, who have no one to let them in at the windows, no beds to curl up into, and nothing but skin and bones to curl ?

' It can't be helped, you know ;—meantime, let Lily enjoy her bed, and be thankful, (if possible, in a more convenient manner). And do you enjoy your fire, and be thankful,' say the pious public : and subscribe, no doubt, at their Rector's request, for an early dole of Christmas coals. Alas, my pious public, all this temporary doling and coaling is worse than useless. It drags out some old women's lives a month or two longer,—makes, here and there, a hearth savoury with smell of dinner, that little knew of such frankincense ; but, for true help to the poor, you might as well light a lucifer match to warm their fingers ; and for the good to your own hearts,—I tell you solemnly, all your comfort in such charity is simply, Christ's dipped sop, given to you for signal to somebody else than Christ, that it is *his* hour to find the windows of your soul open—to the Night, whence very doleful creatures, of other temper and colour than Lily, are mewing to get in.

Indeed, my pious public, you cannot, at present, by any coal or blanket subscription, do more than blind yourselves to the plain order " Give to him that asketh thee ; and from him that would borrow of thee, turn not thou away."

To him that asketh us, say the public,—but then—everybody would ask us.

Yes, you pitiful public,—pretty nearly everybody would : that is indeed the state of national dignity, and independence, and gushing prosperity, you have brought your England into ; a population mostly of beggars, (at heart) ; or, worse, bagmen, not merely bearing the bag—but nothing else *but* bags ;— sloppy star-fishy, seven-suckered stomachs of indiscriminate covetousness, ready to beg, borrow, gamble, swindle, or write anything a publisher will pay for.

Nevertheless your order is precise, and clear ; ' Give to him that asketh thee '—even to the half of your last cloak— says St. Martin ; even to the whole of it, says Christ : ' whosoever of you forsaketh not *all* that he hath, cannot be my disciple.'

' And you yourself, who have a house among the lakes, and rooms at Oxford, and pictures, and books, and a Dives dinner every day, how about all that ? '

Yes, you may well ask,—and I answer very distinctly and frankly, that if once I am convinced (and it is not by any means unlikely I should be so) that to put all these things into the hands of others, and live, myself, in a cell at Assisi, or a shepherd's cottage in Cumberland, would be right, and wise, under the conditions of human life and thought with which I have to deal—very assuredly I will do so.

Nor is it, I repeat, unlikely that such conviction may soon happen to me ; for I begin to question very strictly with myself, how it is that St. George's work does not prosper better in my hands.

Here is the half-decade of years, past, since I began the writing of *Fors*, as a byework, to quiet my conscience, that I might be happy in what I supposed to be my own proper life of Art-teaching, at Oxford and elsewhere ; and, through my own happiness, rightly help others.

But Atropos has ruled it quite otherwise. During these five years, very signal distress has visited me, conclusively removing all possibilities of cheerful action ; separating and sealing a great space of former life into one wide field of Machpelah ; and leaving the rest sunless. Also, everything I have set hand to has been unprosperous ; much of it even calamitous ;—disappointment, coupled with heavy money loss, happening in almost every quarter to me, and casting discredit on all I attempt ; while, in things partly under the influence and fortune of others, and therefore more or less successful,—the schools at Oxford especially, which owe the greater part of their efficiency to the fostering zeal of Dr. Acland, and the steady teaching of Mr. Macdonald,—I have not been able, for my own share, to accomplish the tenth part of what I planned.

Under which conditions, I proceed in my endeavour to re-model the world, with more zeal, by much, than at the beginning of the year 1871.

For these following reasons.

First, that I would give anything to be quit of the whole business ; and therefore that I am certain it is not ambition, nor love of power, nor anything but absolute and mere com-passion, that drags me on. That shoemaker, whom his son left lying dead with his head in the fireplace the other day,*—I wish he and his son had never been born ;—but as the like of them will be born, and must so die, so long as things remain as they are, there's no choice for me but to do all I know to change them, since others won't.

Secondly. I observe that when all things, in early life, appeared to be going well for me, they were by no means going well, in the deep of them, but quite materially and rapidly otherwise. Whence I conclude that though things appear at present adverse to my work and me, they may not at all be adverse in the deep of them, but quite otherwise.

Thirdly. Though in my own fortune, unprosperous, and in my own thoughts and labour, failing, I find more and more every day that I have helped many persons unknown to me ; that others, in spite of my failures, begin to understand me, and are ready to follow ; and that a certain power is indeed already in my hands, woven widely into the threads of many human lives ; which power, if I now laid down, that line (which I have always kept the murmur of in my ears, for warning, since first I read it thirty years ago,)—

      " Che fece per viltate 'l gran rifiuto," †

would be finally and fatally true of me.

Fourthly, not only is that saying of Bacon's of great comfort to me, "therefore extreme lovers of their country, or masters, were never fortunate ; neither can they be, for when a man placeth his thoughts without himself, he goeth not his own way," ‡ for truly I have always loved my masters, Turner, Tintoret, and Carlyle, to the exclusion of my own thoughts ; and my country more than my own garden : but also, I do not find in the reading of history that any victory

* See first article in Notes.

† *Inferno*, III. 60. I fear that few modern readers of Dante understand the dreadful meaning of this hellish outer district, or suburb, full of the refuse or worthless scum of Humanity—such numbers that "non haverei creduto, che morte tanta n' havesse disfatta,"—who are stung to bloody torture by insects, and whose blood and tears together —the best that human souls can give—are sucked up, on the hellground, by worms.

‡ Essay XI.

worth having was ever won without cost ; and I observe that too open and early prosperity is rarely the way to it.

But lastly, and chiefly. If there be any truth in the vital doctrines of Christianity whatsoever,—and assuredly there is more than most of us recognise, or than any of us believe,—the offences committed in this century by all the nations of Christendom against the law of Christ have been so great, and insolent, that they cannot but be punished by the withdrawal of spiritual guidance from them, and the especial paralysis of efforts intelligently made for their good. In times of more ignorant sinning, they were punished by plagues of the body ; but now, by plagues of the soul, and widely infectious insanities, making every true physician of souls helpless, and every false effort triumphant. Nor are we without great and terrible signs of supernatural calamity, no less in grievous changes and deterioration of climate, than in forms of mental disease, * claiming distinctly to be necromantic, and, as far as I have examined the evidence relating to them, actually manifesting themselves as such. For observe you, my friends, countrymen, and brothers—*Either*, at this actual moment of your merry Christmas-time, that has truly come to pass, in falling London, which your greatest Englishman wrote of falling Rome, "the sheeted dead, do squeak and gibber in your English streets,"—*Or*, such a system of loathsome imposture and cretinous blasphemy is current among all classes of England and America, as makes the superstition of all past ages divine truth in comparison !

One of these things *is* so—gay friends ;— have it which way you will : one or other of these, to me, alike appalling ; and in your principal street of London society, you have a picture of highly dressed harlots gambling, of naked ones, called Andromeda and Francesca of Rimini and of

* I leave this passage as it was written : though as it passes through the press, it is ordered by Atropos that I should hear a piece of evidence on this matter no less clear as to the present ministry of such powers as that which led Peter out of prison, than all the former, or nearly all, former evidence examined by me was of the presence of the legion which ruled among the Tombs of Gennesaret.

Christ led to be crucified, exhibited, for your better enter‹
tainment, in the same room ; and at the end of the same
street, an exhibition of jugglery, professedly imitating, *for
money*, what a large number of you believe to be the efforts
of the returned Dead to convince you of your Immortality.

Meantime, at the other end—no, at the very centre of
your great Babylon, a son leaves his father dead, with his
head, instead of a fire, in the fireplace, and goes out himself
to his day's darg.

*   *   *   *   *   *

'We are very sorry ;—What can we do ? How can we
help it ? London is so big, and living is so very expensive,
you know.'

Miserables,—who makes London big, but you, coming
to look at the harlotries in it, painted and other? Who
makes living expensive, but you, who drink, and eat,* and
dress, all you can ; and never in your lives did one stroke of
work to get your living,—never drew a bucket of water,
never sowed a grain of corn, never spun a yard of thread ;—
but you devour, and swill, and waste, to your fill, and think
yourselves good, and fine, and better creatures of God, I
doubt not, than the poor starved wretch of a shoemaker, who
shod whom he could, while you gave him food enough to
keep him in strength to stitch.

We, of the so-called ' educated ' classes, who take it upon
us to be the better and upper part of the world, cannot
possibly understand our relations to the rest better than we
may where actual life may be seen in front of its Shakes-
pearean image, from the stalls of a theatre. I never stand
up to rest myself, and look round the house, without renewal
of wonder how the crowd in the pit, and shilling gallery,
allow us of the boxes and stalls to keep our places ! Think
of it ;—those fellows behind there have housed us and fed us;
their wives have washed our clothes, and kept us tidy ;—they
have bought us the best places,—brought us through the
cold to them ; and there they sit behind us, patiently, seeing

* See second article in Notes.

and hearing what they may. There they pack themselves, squeezed and distant, behind our chairs ;—we, their elect toys and pet puppets, oiled, and varnished, and incensed, lounge in front, placidly, or for the greater part, wearily and sickly contemplative. Here we are again, all of us, this Christmas ! Behold the artist in tumbling, and in painting with white and red,—our object of worship, and applause : here sit we at our ease, the dressed dolls of the place, with little more in our heads, most of us, than may be contained inside of a wig of flax and a nose of wax ; stuck up by these poor little prentices, clerks, and orange-sucking mobility, Kit, and his mother, and the baby—behind us, in the chief places of this our evening synagogue. What for ? 'They did not stick you up,' say you,—you paid for your stalls with your own money. Where did you get your money ? Some of you— if any Reverend gentlemen, as I hope, are among us,—by selling the Gospel ; others by selling Justice ; others by sell- ing their Blood—(and no man has any right to sell aught of these three things, any more than a woman her body,)—the rest, if not by swindling, by simple taxation of the labour of the shilling gallery,—or of the yet poorer or better persons who have not so much, or will not spend so much, as the shilling to get there ? How else should you, or could you, get your money,—simpletons ?

Not that it is essentially your fault, poor feathered moths, —any more than the dead shoemaker's. That blasphemous blockheadism of Mr. Greg's,* and the like of him, that you can swill salvation into other people's bodies out of your own champagne-bottles, is the main root of all your national miseries. Indeed you are willing enough to believe that devil's-gospel, you rich ones ; or most of you would have detected the horror of it before now ; but yet the chief wrong lies with the assertors of it,—and once and again I tell you, the words of Christ are true,—and not theirs ; and that the day has come for fasting, and prayer, not for feasting ; but,

---

* Quoted in last *Fors*, p. 85, lines 18–19, from *Contemporary Review*. Observe that it is blasphemy, definitively and calmly uttered, first against Nature, and secondly against Christ.

above all, for labour—personal and direct labour—on the Earth that bears you, and buries—as best it can. ,

9th December.—I heard yesterday that the son of the best English portrait-painter we have had. since Gainsborough, had learnt farming ; that his father had paid two hundred pounds a year to obtain that instruction for him ; and that the boy is gone, in high spirits, to farm—in Jamaica ! So far, so good. Nature and facts are beginning to assert themselves to the British mind. But very dimly.

For, first, observe, the father should have paid nothing for that boy's farming education. As soon as he could hold a hoe, the little fellow should have been set to do all he could for his living, under a good farmer for master ; and as he became able to do more, taught more, until he knew all that his master knew,—winning, all the while he was receiving that natural education, his bread by the sweat of his brow.

' But there are no farmers who teach—none who take care of their boys, or men.'

Miserables again, whose fault is that ? The landlords choose to make the farmers middlemen between the peasants and themselves—grinders, not of corn, but of flesh,—for their rent. And of course you dare not put your children under them to be taught.

Read Gottheif's *Ulric the Farm Servant* on this matter. It is one of his great novels,—great as Walter Scott's, in the truth and vitality of it, only inferior in power of design. I would translate it all in *Fors*, if I had time ; and indeed hope to make it soon one of my school series, of which, and other promised matters, or delayed ones, I must now take some order, and give some account, in this opening letter of the year, as far as I can, only, before leaving the young farmer among the Blacks, please observe that he goes there because you have all made Artificial Blacks of yourselves, and unmelodious Christys,—nothing but the whites of your eyes showing through the unclean skins of you, here, in Merry England, where there was once green ground to farm instead of ashes.

And first,—here's the woodcut, long promised, of a rose-leaf cut by the leaf-cutting bee, true in size and shape ; a sound contribution to Natural History, so far as it reaches. Much I had to say of it, but am not in humour to-day. Happily, the letter from a valued Companion, Art. III. in Notes, may well take place of any talk of mine.*

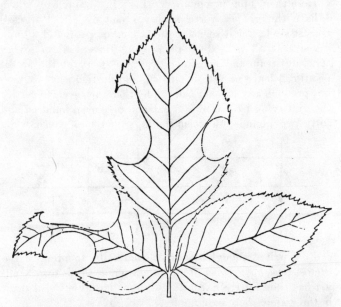

Secondly, I promised a first lesson in writing, of which, therefore, (that we may see what is our present knowledge on the subject, and what farther we may safely ask Theuth † to teach,) I have had engraved two examples, one of writing in the most authoritative manner, used for modern service, and the other of writing by a practised scribe of the fourteenth century. To make the comparison fair, we must take the religious, and therefore most careful, scripture of both dates;

* The most valuable notes of the kind correspondent who sent me this leaf, with many others, and a perfect series of nests, must be reserved till spring-time : my mind is not free for them, now.

† Compare Letter XVI., p. 218, and XVII., p. 227.

so, for example of modern sacred scripture, I take the casting up of a column in my banker's book ; and for the ancient, a letter A, with a few following words, out of a Greek Psalter, which is of admirable and characteristic, but not (by any honest copyist,) inimitable execution.

Here then, first, is modern writing ; in facsimile of which I have thought it worth while to employ Mr. Burgess's utmost skill ; for it seems to me a fact of profound significance that all the expedients we have invented for saving time, by steam and machinery, (not to speak of the art of printing,) leave us yet so hurried, and flurried, that we cannot produce any lovelier caligraphy than this, even to certify the gratifying existence of a balance of eleven hundred and forty-two pounds, thirteen shillings, and two pence, while

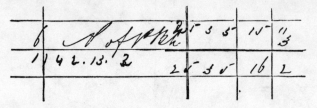

the old writer, though required, eventually, to produce the utmost possible number of entire psalters with his own hand, yet has time for the execution of every initial letter of them in the manner here exhibited.

Respecting which, you are to observe that this is pure *writing ;* not painting or drawing, but the expression of form by lines such as a pen can easily produce, (or a brush used with the point, in the manner of a pen ;) and with a certain habitual currency and fluent habit of finger, yet not dashing or flourishing, but with perfect command of direction in advance, and moment of pause, at any point.

You may at first, and very naturally, suppose, good reader, that it will not advance your power of English writing to copy a Greek sentence. But, with your pardon, the first need, for all beautiful writing, is that your hand should be, in the true and virtuous sense, *free ;* that is to say, able to

move in any direction it is ordered, and not cramped to
a given slope, or to any given form of letter. And also,
whether you can learn Greek or not, it is well, (and perfectly
easy,) to learn the Greek alphabet, that if by chance a questionable word occur in your Testament, or in scientific
books, you may be able to read it, and even look it out in a
dictionary. And this particular manner of Greek writing I
wish you to notice, because it is such as Victor Carpaccio
represents St. Jerome reading in his study; and I shall be
able to illustrate by it some points of Byzantine character of
extreme historical interest.

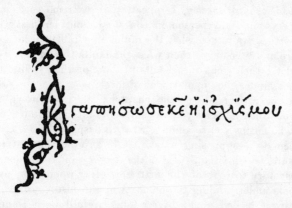

Copy, therefore, this letter A, and the following words, in
as perfect facsimile as you can, again and again, not being
content till a tracing from the original fits your copy to the
thickness of its penstroke. And even by the time next *Fors*
comes out, you will begin to know how to use a pen. Also,
you may at spare times practise copying any clearly-printed
type, only without the difference of thickness in parts of
letters; the best writing for practical purposes is that which
most resembles print, connected only, for speed, by the
current line.

Next, for some elementary practice of the same kind in
the more difficult art of Reading.

A young student, belonging to the working classes, who

has been reading books a little too difficult or too grand for him, asking me what he shall read next, I have told him, *Waverley*—with extreme care.

It is true that, in grandeur and difficulty, I have not a whit really lowered his standard ; for it is an achievement as far beyond him, at present, to understand *Waverley*, as to understand the *Odyssey ;* but the road, though as steep and high-reaching as any he has travelled, is smoother for him. What farther directions I am now going to give him, will be good for all young men of active minds who care to make such activity serviceable.

Read your *Waverley*, I repeat, with extreme care : and of every important person in the story, consider first what the virtues are ; then what the faults inevitable to them by nature and breeding ; then what the faults they might have avoided ; then what the results to them of their faults and virtues, under the appointment of fate.

Do this after reading each chapter ; and write down the lessons which it seems to you that Scott intended in it ; and what he means you to admire, what to despise.

Secondly,—supposing you to be, in any the smallest real measure, a Christian,—begin the history of Abraham, as preparatory to that of the first Law-giver whom you have in some understanding to obey. And the history of Abraham must be led up to, by reading carefully from Genesis ix. 20th, forward, and learning the main traditions which the subsequent chapters contain.

And observe, it does not matter in the least to you, at present, how far these traditions are true. Your business is only to know what is said in Genesis. That does not matter to you, you think? Much less does it matter what Mr. Smith or Mr. Robinson said last night at that public meeting ; or whether Mr. Black, or his brother, shot Mrs. White ; or anything else whatever, small or great, that you will find said or related in the morning papers. But to know what is said in Genesis will enable you to understand, in some sort, the effect of that saying on men's minds, through at least two thousand years of the World's History. Which, if

you mean to be a scholar and gentleman, you *must* make
some effort to do.

And this is the way to set about it. You see the tenth
chapter of Genesis names to you the children, and children's
children, of Noah, from whom the nations of the world (it
says) came, and by whom the lands of the world (it says)
were divided.

You must learn them by rote, in order. You know already,
I suppose, the three names, Shem, Ham, and Japhet; begin
with Shem, and learn the names of his sons, thus :

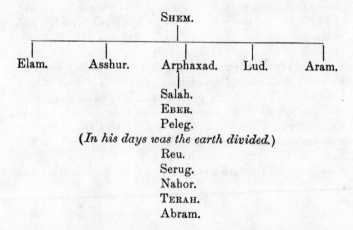

Shem.

| Elam. | Asshur. | Arphaxad. | Lud. | Aram. |

Salah.
Eber.
Peleg.
(*In his days was the earth divided.*)
Reu.
Serug.
Nahor.
Terah.
Abram.

Now, you see that makes a pretty ornamental letter T,
with a little joint in the middle of its stalk.

And this letter T you must always be able to write, out
of your head, without a moment's hesitation. However
stupid you may be at learning by rote, thus much can always be done by dint of sheer patient repetition. Read the
centre column straight down, over and again, for an hour
together, and you will find it at last begin to stick in your
head. Then, as soon as it is fast there, say it over and over
again when it is dark, or when you are out walking, till you
can't make a mistake in it.

Then observe farther that Peleg, in whose days the earth

was divided, had a brother named Joktan, who had thirteen children. Of these, you need not mind the names of ten; but the odd three are important to you. Sheba, Ophir, and Havilah. You have perhaps heard of these before; and assuredly, if you go on reading *Fors*, you will hear of them again.

And these thirteen children of Joktan, you see, had their dwelling "from Mesha, as thou goest unto Sephar, a mount of the East." I don't know anything about Mesha and Sephar, yet; but I may: in the meantime, learn the sentence, and recollect that these people are fixed *somewhere*, at any rate, because they are to be Masters of Gold, which is fixed in Eastern, or Western, mountains; but 'that the children of the other brother, Peleg, can go wherever they like, and often where they shouldn't—for "in his days was the earth divided." Recollect also that the children of both brothers, or, in brief, the great Indian gold-possessing race, and the sacred race of prophets and kings of the higher spiritual world, are in the 21st verse of this chapter called "all the children of EBER." If you learn so much as this well, it's enough for this month: but I may as well at once give you the forms you have to learn for the other two sons.

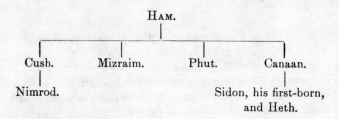

HAM.

Cush.   Mizraim.   Phut.   Canaan.

Nimrod.   Sidon, his first-born,
                                           and Heth.

The seventh verse is to be noted as giving the gold-masters of Africa, under two of the same names as those of Asia, but must not be learned for fear of confusion. The form above given must be amplified and commented on variously, but is best learned first in its simplicity.

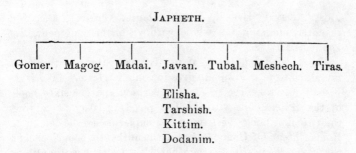

JAPHETH.

Gomer. Magog. Madai. Javan. Tubal. Meshech. Tiras.

Elisha.
Tarshish.
Kittim.
Dodanim.

I leave this blunt-stalked and flat-headed letter T, also, in its simplicity, and we will take up the needful detail in next *Fors.*

Together with which, (all the sheets being now printed, and only my editorial preface wanting), I doubt not will be published the first volume of the classical series of books which I purpose editing for St. George's library ;—Xenophon's *Economist,* namely, done into English for us by two of my Oxford pupils ; this volume, I hope, soon to be followed by Gotthelf's *Ulric the Farm-servant,* either in French or English, as the second Fors, faithfully observant of copyright and other dues, may decide ; meantime, our first historical work, relating the chief decision of Atropos respecting the fate of England after the Conquest, is being written for me by a friend, and Fellow of my college of Corpus Christi, whose help I accept, in St. George's name,—all the more joyfully because he is our head gardener, no less than our master-historian.

And for the standard theological writings which are ultimately to be the foundation of this body of secular literature, I have chosen seven authors, whose lives and works, so far as the one can be traced or the other certified, shall be, with the best help I can obtain from the good scholars of Oxford, prepared one by one in perfect editions for the St. George's schools. These seven books will contain, in as many volumes as may be needful, the lives and writings of the men who have taught the purest theological truth hitherto known to the Jews, Greeks, Latins, Italians, and English ; namely,

Moses, David, Hesiod, Virgil, Dante, Chaucer, and, for seventh, summing the whole with vision of judgment, St John the Divine.

The Hesiod I purpose, if my life is spared, to translate myself (into prose), and to give in complete form. Of Virgil I shall only take the two first *Georgics*, and the sixth book of the *Æneid*, but with the Douglas translation ; * adding the two first books of Livy, for completion of the image of Roman life. Of Chaucer, I take the authentic poems, except the *Canterbury Tales ;* together with, be they authentic or not, the *Dream*, and the fragment of the translation of the *Romance of the Rose*, adding some French chivalrous literature of the same date. I shall so order this work, that, in such measure as it may be possible to me, it shall be in a constantly progressive relation to the granted years of my life. The plan of it I give now, and will explain in full detail, that my scholars may carry it out, if I cannot.

And now let my general readers observe, finally, about all reading,—You must read, for the nourishment of your mind, precisely under the moral laws which regulate your eating for the nourishment of the body. That is to say, you must not eat for the pleasure of eating, nor read, for the pleasure of reading. But, if you manage yourself rightly, you will intensely enjoy your dinner, and your book. If you have any sense, you can easily follow out this analogy : I have not time at present to do it for you ; only be sure it holds, to the minutest particular, with this difference only, that the vices and virtues of reading are more harmful on the one side, and higher on the other, as the soul is more precious than the body. Gluttonous reading is a worse vice than gluttonous

---

* " A Bishop by the altar stood,
A noble Lord of Douglas blood,
With mitre sheen, and rocquet white,
Yet showed his meek and thoughtful eye
But little pride of prelacy ;
More pleased that, in a barbarous age,
He gave rude Scotland Virgil's page,
Than that beneath his rule he held
The bishopric of fair Dunkeld."

eating ; filthy and foul reading, a much more loathsome habit than filthy eating. Epicurism in books is much more difficult of attainment than epicurism in meat, but plain and virtuous feeding the most entirely pleasurable.

And now, one step of farther thought will enable you to settle a great many questions with one answer.

As you may neither eat, nor read, for the pleasure of eating or reading, so you may do *nothing else* for the pleasure of it, but for the use. The moral difference between a man and a beast is, that the one acts primarily for use, the other for pleasure. And all acting for pleasure before use, or instead of use, is, in one word, 'Fornication.' That is the accurate meaning of the words 'harlotry,' or 'fornication,' as used in the Bible, wherever they occur spoken of nations, and especially in all the passages relating to the great or spiritual Babylon.

And the Law of God concerning man is, that if he acts for use—that is to say, as God's servant ;—he shall be rewarded with such pleasure as no heart can conceive nor tongue tell ; only it is revealed by the Spirit, as that Holy Ghost of life and health possesses us ; but if we act for pleasure instead of use, we shall be punished by such misery as no heart can conceive nor tongue tell ; but which can only be revealed by the adverse spirit, whose is the power of death. And that— I assure you—is absolute, inevitable, daily and hourly Fact for us, to the simplicity of which I to-day invite your scholarly and literary attention.

NOTES AND CORRESPONDENCE.

THE St. George's Company is now distinctly in existence; formed of about twenty accepted Companions, to whose number I am daily adding, and to whom the entire property of the Company legally belongs, and who have the right at any moment to depose the Master, and dispose of the property in any manner they may think fit. Unless I believed myself capable of choosing persons for Companions who might be safely entrusted with this' power, I should not have endeavoured to form the society at all. Every one of these Companions has a right to know the names and addresses of the rest, which the Master of the Company must furnish him with; and of course the roll of the names, which will be kept in Corpus Christi College, is their legal certificate. I do not choose to begin this book at the end of the year, but at the beginning of the next term it will be done; and as our lawyer's paper, revised, is now—15th December—in my hands, and approved, the 1st of January will see us securely constituted. I give below the initials of the Companions accepted before the 10th of this month, thinking that my doing so will be pleasing to some of them, and right, for all.

Initials of Companions accepted before 10th December, 1875. I only give two letters, which are I think as much indication as is at present desirable:—

1.	D. L.	14.	A. H.
2.	F. C.	15.	W. S.
3.	L. B.	16.	W. S.
4.	B. B.	17.	J. B.
5.	F. T.	18.	B. G.
6.	R. T.	19.	H. L.
7.	G. S.	20.	J. F.
8.	B. A.	21.	J. M.
9.	A. H.	22.	R. S.
10.	T. D.	23.	H. C.
11.	M. K.	24.	J. T.
12.	S. B.	25.	J. S.
13.	G. A.		

This *Fors* is already so much beyond its usual limits, and it introduces subject-matter so grave, that I do not feel inclined to go into further business details this month; the rather because in the February

Fors, with the accounts of the Company, I must begin what the Master of the Company will be always compelled to furnish—statement of his own personal current expenditure. And this will require some explanation too long for to-day. I defer also the Wakefield correspondence, for I have just got fresh information about the destruction of Wakefield chapel, and have an election petition to examine.

I. Our notes for the year 1876 may, I think, best begin with the two pieces of news which follow ; and which, by order of Atropos, also followed each other in the column of the *Morning Advertiser,* from which I print them.

For, though I am by this time known to object to Advertisement in general, I beg the public to observe that my objection is only to bought or bribed Advertisement (especially if it be Advertisement of one's self). But that I hold myself, and this book of mine, for nothing better than Morning, Noon, and Evening Advertisers, of what things appear verily noteworthy in the midst of us. Whereof I commend the circumstances of the death, beneath related, very particularly to the attention of the Bishops of London and York.

SHOCKING DEATH FROM STARVATION.—Last night Mr. Bedford, the Westminster coroner, held an inquest at the Board-room, Dean Street, Soho, on the body of Thomas Gladstone, aged 58, of 43, King Street, Seven Dials, a shoemaker, who was found dead on Thursday last.

William Gladstone, a lad of 15, identified the body as that of his father, with whom he and three other children lived. Deceased had been ailing for some time past, and was quite unable to do any work. The recent cold weather had such an effect upon him that he was compelled to remain in his room on Wednesday last, and at three the next morning witness found him sitting up in bed complaining of cold, and that he was dying. Witness went to sleep, and on awaking at eight that morning he found deceased with his head in the fireplace. Thinking he was only asleep, witness went to work, and on returning two hours later he was still in the same position, and it was then found that he was dead.

Coroner.—" Why did you not send for a doctor ? "

Witness.—" I didn't know he wanted one until he was dead, and we found out amongst us that he was dead."

Jane Gladstone, the widow, said she had been living apart from her husband for some months, and first heard of his death at 2.30 on Thursday afternoon, and upon going to his room found him dead lying upon a mattress on the floor. He was always ailing, and suffered from consumption, for which he had received advice at St. George's Hospital. They had had seven children, and for some time prior to the separation they had been in the greatest distress ; and on the birth of her last child, on December 7, 1874, they applied at the St. James's workhouse for relief, and received two loaves and 2 lb. of meat per week for a month, and at the end of that time one of the relieving officers stopped the relief, saying that they were both able to work. They told the relieving officer that they had no work, and had seven children to keep, but he still refused to relieve them.

By the Coroner.—They did not ask again for relief, as deceased said " he had made up his mind that, after the way he had been turned away like a dog, he would sooner starve," and she herself would also rather do so.   Deceased was quite unable to earn sufficient to maintain the family, and their support fell mainly upon her, but it was such a hard life that she got situations for two of the boys, got a girl into a school, and leaving the other three boys with deceased, took the baby and separated from him.   He was in great want at that time.

The Coroner.—" Then why did you not go to the workhouse and represent his case to them ? "

Witness.—" What was the good when we had been refused twice ? "

Mr. Green, the coroner's officer, said that he believed the witness had been in receipt of two loaves a week from the St. James's workhouse, but had not called lately for the loaves.

The Coroner said he hardly thought that so poor a woman would refuse or neglect to apply for so valuable a contribution to the needs of a family as two loaves of bread; and some of the jury said that Mr. Green must be mistaken, and that such a statement should be made upon oath if at all.   The officer, however, was not sworn.

John Collins, of 43 King Street, said that about eleven o'clock on Thursday morning he met a gentleman on the stairs, who said that he had been up to the room of deceased to take him some work to do, but that the room door was locked, and a child had called out, " Father is dead, and you can't come in." Witness at once went for the police, who came, and broke open the door.   Upon going into the room witness found a piece of paper (produced) in which was written, " Harry, get a pint of milk for the three of you ; father is dead. Tell your schoolmaster you can't come to school any more. Cut your own bread, but don't use the butter."   He believed that the eldest boy had returned home at ten o'clock in the morning, and finding two of the boys at school had left the note for them.

Police-constable Crabb, 18 C R., deposed to breaking open the door and finding deceased dead on the floor, with a little child crouching by him shivering with cold.

Dr. Howard Clarke, of 19, Lisle Street, Leicester Square, and Gerrard Street, Soho, said that he was called to see the deceased, and found him lying upon the floor of his room dead and cold, with nothing on him but stockings and a shirt, the room being nearly destitute of furniture.   The place was in a most filthy condition, and deceased himself was so shockingly dirty and neglected, and so overrun with vermin, that he (witness) was compelled to wash his hands five times during the post-mortem examination.   By the side of the corpse sat a little child about four years old, who cried piteously, " Oh, don't take me away ; poor father's dead ! "   There was nothing in the shape of food but a morsel of butter, some arrowroot, and a piece of bread, and the room was cold and cheerless in the extreme.   Upon making a post-mortem he found the brain congested, and the whole of the organs of the body more or less diseased.   The unfortunate man must have suffered fearfully.   The body was extremely emaciated, and there was not a particle of food or drop of liquid in the stomach or intestines.   Death had resulted probably from a complication of ailments, but there was no doubt whatever that such death had been much accelerated by want of the common necessaries of life.

The Coroner.—" Starvation, in short ? "

Witness.—" Precisely so. 1 never in all my experience saw a greater case of destitution."

The Coroner.—" Then I must ask the jury to adjourn the case. Here is a very serious charge against workhouse officials, and a man dying clearly from starvation, and it is due alike to the family of the deceased, the parish officials, and the public at large, that the case should be sifted to the very bottom, and the real cause of this death elucidated."

Adjourned accordingly.

SHOCKING DISCOVERY.—A painful sensation was, says the *Sheffield Telegraph*, caused in the neighbourhood of Castleford, near Pontefract, on Friday evening, by the report made to a police-constable stationed at Allerton Bywater that a woman and child had been found dead in bed in Lock Lane, Castleford, under most mysterious circumstances, and that two small children were also found nearly starved to death beside the two dead bodies. The report, however, turned out to be correct. The circumstances surrounding the mystery have now been cleared up. An inquest, held on Saturday at Allerton Bywater, before Dr. Grabham, of Pontefract, reveals the following :—It appears on Sunday, the 28th ult., John Wilson, miner, husband of Emma Wilson, aged thirty-six years (one of the deceased), and father of Fred, aged eighteen months (the other deceased), left home to proceed to his employment at Street House Colliery, and would remain away all the week. Mrs. Wilson was seen going into her house on Monday evening, but was not seen again alive. There were besides the woman three children of very tender years in the house. The neighbours missed the woman and children from Monday night, but finding the blinds were drawn down, concluded that the family had gone to the husband. On Friday evening a neighbour, named Ann Foggett, rapped at the door, and hearing the faint bark of a dog, which was found to be fastened up in a cupboard, continued to knock at the door, and ultimately heard the voice of a child. The door was subsequently burst open, and on proceeding upstairs the sight was horrifying. On the bed lay the mother and infant child dead, beside whom were two other small children in their night dresses. They, too, were nigh death's door, having been without proper food and clothing evidently since their mother's death, which must have occurred on the Monday night. Beside the corpse of the mother lay a knife and portions of a loaf of bread, which had been no doubt taken to her by the children to be supplied with some, but being unable to get an answer from her, they had nibbled the middle of the loaf clean away. A post-mortem examination showed that the mother had died from heart disease, and the child on the following day from starvation. The jury returned a verdict to that effect.—*Morning Advertiser*, December 7th, 1875.

II. The following is sent me by a correspondent. Italics mine throughout. The passage about threshing is highly curious ; compare my account of the threshers at Thun. Poor Gilbert had been doubtless set to thresh, like Milton's fiend, by himself, and had no creambowl afterwards.

24th October, 1800.

GILBERT BURNS TO JAMES CURRIE, M.D.

The evils peculiar to the lower ranks of life derive their power to wound us from the suggestions of false pride, and the contagion of luxury, rather than from the refinement of our taste. There is little labour which custom will not make easy to a man in health, if he is not ashamed of his employment, or does not begin to compare his situation with those who go about at their ease. But the man of enlarged mind feels the respect due to him as a man; he has learnt that no employment is dishonourable in itself; that, while he performs aright the duties of the station in which God has placed him, he is as great as a king in the eyes of Him whom he is principally desirous to please. *For the man of taste, who is constantly obliged to labour, must of necessity be religious.* If you teach him only to reason, you may make him an atheist, a demagogue, or any vile thing; but if you teach him to feel, his feelings can only find their proper and natural relief in devotion and religious resignation. *I can say from my own experience that there is no sort of farm labour inconsistent with the most refined and pleasurable state of the mind, that I am acquainted with,* threshing alone excepted. That, indeed, I have always considered insupportable drudgery, and think the man who invented the threshing-machine ought to have a statue among the benefactors of his country.

Perhaps the thing of most importance in the education of the common people is to prevent the intrusion of artificial wants. I bless the memory of my father for almost everything in the dispositions of my mind and the habits of my life, which I can approve of, and for none more than the pains he took to impress my mind with the sentiment that *nothing was more unworthy the character of a man than that his happiness should in the least depend on what he should eat and drink.*

To this hour I never indulge in the use of any delicacy but I feel a degree of reproach and alarm for the degradation of the human character. If I spent my halfpence in sweetmeats, every mouthful I swallowed was accompanied with shame and remorse. . . . . Whenever vulgar minds begin to shake off the dogmas of the religion in which they have been educated, the progress is quick and immediate to downright infidelity, and nothing but refinement of mind can enable them to distinguish between the pure essence of religion and the gross systems which men have been perpetually connecting it with. Higher salaries for village schoolmasters, high English reading-classes, village libraries, —if once such high education were to become general, the low delights of the public-house, and other scenes of riot, would be neglected; while industry, order, and cleanliness, and every virtue which taste and independence of mind could recommend, would prevail and flourish. Thus possessed of a virtuous and enlightened populace, with delight I should consider my country at the head of all the nations of the earth, ancient or modern.—' *From the Life of Robert Burns.*'

III. The following letter is, as I above said, from a valued, and, at present, my *most* valued,—Companion;—a poor person, suffering much and constant pain, confined to her room, and seeing from her window only a piece of brick wall and a little space of sky. The bit about the spider is the most delightful thing to me that has ever yet come of my teaching :—

I have told the only two children I have seen this summer, about the bees, and both were deeply interested, almost awe-stricken by the wonderful work. How could they do it without scissors? One, an intelligent boy of six years, is the well-cared-for child of well-to-do parents. He came into my room when I was sorting some of the cut leaves, and I gave him a very cleanly-cut specimen, saying, "What do you think cut this, Willie?" "It was *somebody* very clever, wasn't it?" he asked. "Very clever indeed," I said. "Then it was Miss Mildred!"—his governess. "No, not Miss Mildred." I replied. He stood silent by the side of the bed for a minute, looking intently at the leaf in his hand, and evidently puzzling out some idea of his own; and I waited for it—a child's own thoughts are lovely;—then my little visitor turned eagerly to me : "I know,—I know who did it : it was God."

My second pupil is a girl of twelve years. She was a veritable "little ragamuffin" when—ten months back—we took her, motherless, and most miserably destitute, into our home, in the hope of training her for service; and my sister is persistently labouring—with pleasing success, and disheartening failure—to mould her into an honest woman, while I try to supplement her efforts by giving the child—Harriet—lessons according to *Fors*. But I regret to say it is only partially done, for I am but a learner myself, and sorely hindered by illness : still the purpose is always in my mind, and I do what I can.

Taking advantage of every trifle that will help to give Harriet a love for *innocent* out-of-door life, we told her—as soon as we could show her some of the cut leaves—of the work of the cutter bees, much to her delight. "And then she forgot all about them," many persons would assert confidently, if they heard this story.

Not so, for some weeks after she told me with great pride that she had two of "the bees' leaves." Thinking they were probably only eaten by caterpillars, I asked to see them; and then, how she obtained them. She had found them in a glass of withered flowers sent out of the parlour, and carefully dried them—(she had seen me press leaves); and she added, "all the girls" in her class in the Sunday-school "did want them." I wondered why the leaves were taken there, until I discovered that she *keeps them in her Testament*.

So far the possibility; may I now give a proof of the utility of such teaching? When Harriet first came to us, she had an appetite for the horrible that quite frightened me, but it is gradually, I hope, dying out, thanks to the substitution of child-like pleasures. Imagine a child of eleven years coolly asking—as Harriet did a few days after she came—"If you please, has anybody been hanged, or anything, this week?" and she added, before I could reply, and looking quite wistfully at a newspaper lying near, "I should love to hear about it, please." I could have cried, for I believe there are many lovable young ladies in this town who are fretting out weary lives, to whom *work* would be salvation, and who can tell the number of such children all about them, who have not a soul to care *how* they live, or if they die.

Harriet used to catch and kill flies for pleasure, and would have so treated any living insect she saw; but she now holds bees in great re-

spect, and also, I hope, some other insect workers, for one day she
was much pleased to find one of the small spotted spiders, which had
during the night spun its web across the fire-grate. She asked me
many questions about it. (I permit her to do so on principle, at certain
times, as a part of her education); she said it was "a shame" to break
"such beautiful work," and left it as long as she could; and then,
(entirely of her own accord) she carefully slipped her dusting brush
under web and spider, and so put the "pretty little dear" outside the
window, with the gentle remark, "There, now you can make another." Was not this hopeful? This child had lived all her life in one
of the low, crowded courts in the centre of the town, and her ignorance of all green life was inconceivable. For instance, to give her a
country walk I sent her last March with a parcel to a village near
the town, and when she came back—having walked *a mile* through
field paths—she said she did not think there were "such a many trees
and birds in the world." *And on that memorable day she first saw the
lambs in the field—within two miles of the house where she was born.* Yet
she has the purest love for flowers, and goes into very real ecstasies
over the commonest weeds and grasses, and is nursing with great pride
and affection some roots of daisy, buttercup, and clover which she has
brought from the fields, and planted in the little yard at the back of
our house; and every new leaf they put forth is wonderful and lovely
to her, though of course her ideas of "gardening" are as yet most
elementary, and will be for some time, apparently. But it is really
helpful to me to see her happiness over it, and also when my friends
send me a handful of cut flowers—we have no garden; and the eagerness with which she learns even their names, for it makes me feel more
hopeful about the future of our working classes than some of your correspondents.

The despairing letter from Yorkshire in last *Fors*—on their incapacity to enjoy wholesome amusements—has prompted me, as I am
writing to you, to tell you this as an antidote to the pain that letter must
have given you. For if we can do nothing for this generation, cannot
we make sure that the next shall be wiser? Have not young ladies a
mighty power in their own hands here, if they but use it for good, and
especially those who are Sabbath-school teachers? Suppose each one
who has a garden felt it to be her *duty* to make all her scholars as familiar with all the life in it as she is herself, and every one who can take
a country walk her duty to take her girls with her—two or three at
a time—until they know and love every plant within reach; would not
teacher and pupils learn with this much more that would also be invaluable? * And if our Sunday-school children were not left to killing
flies and stoning cats and dogs during the week, would there be so
many brutal murders and violent assaults? The little English heathen
I have named has attended a Sunday-school for about six years, and
the Sunday-school teachers of this town are—most of them—noble men
and women, who devoutly labour year after year "all for love, and
nothing for reward." But even good people too often look on the degradation of the lower classes as a matter of course, and despise them
for ignorance they cannot help. Here the sneer of "those low shoe-
makers" is for ever on the lip, yet few ask *how* they became so much

* Yes, dear lady ; see, therefore, the next article.

lower than ourselves; still I have very pleasing proof of what may be done even for adults by a little wise guidance, but I must not enter into that subject. Pray forgive me for writing so much : I have been too deeply interested, and now feel quite ashamed of the length of this.

Again thanking you most earnestly for all you have taught me to see and to do,

I remain, very faithfully yours.

IV. What the young ladies, old ladies, and middle-aged ladies *are* practically doing with the blessed fields and mountains of their native land, the next letter very accurately shows. For the sake of fine dresses they let their fathers and brothers invest in any Devil's business they can steal the poor's labour by, or destroy the poor's gardens by ; pre-eminently, and of all Devil's businesses, in rushing from place to place, as the Gennesaret swine. And see here what comes of it.

A gentleman told me the other night that trade, chiefly in cotton from India, was going back to Venice. One can't help being sorry—not for our sake, but Venice's—when one sees what commercial prosperity means now.

There was a lovely picture of Cox's of Dollwydellan (I don't think it's spelt right) at the Club. All the artists paint the Slidr valley ; and do you know what is being done to it ? It's far worse than a railway to Ambleside or Grasmere, because those places are overrun already ; but Dollwydellan is such a quiet out-of-the-way corner, and no one in the world will be any the better for a railway there. I went about two months ago, when I was getting better from my first illness ; but all my pleasure in the place was spoiled by the railway they are making from Betwys. It is really melancholy to see the havoc it makes. Of course no one cares, and they crash, and cut, and destroy, like utter barbarians, as they are. Through the sweetest, wildest little glens, the line is cleared—rocks are blasted for it, trees lie cut—anything and everything is sacrificed—and for what ? The tourists will see nothing if they go in the train ; the few people who go down to Betwys or Llanwrst to market, will perhaps go oftener, and so spend more money in the end, and Dollwydellan will get some more people to lodge there in the summer, and prices will go up.* In the little village, a hideous 'traction engine' snorted and puffed out clouds of black smoke, in the mornings, and then set off crunching up and down the roads, to carry coals for the works, I think ; but I never in my life saw anything more incongruous than that great black monster getting its pipes filled at a little spring in the village, while the lads all stood gaping round. The poor little clergyman told us his village had got sadly corrupted since the navvies came into it ; and when he pointed out to us a pretty old stone bridge that was being pulled down for the railway, he said, " Yes,

---

* Yes, my dear, shares down ; and—it is some poor comfort for you and me to know *that.* For as I correct this sheet for press, I hear from the proprietor of the chief slate quarry in the neighbourhood, that the poor idiots of shareholders have been beguiled into tunnelling four miles under Welsh hills—to carry slates ! and even those from the chief quarry in question, they cannot carry, for the proprietors are under contract to send them by an existing line,

I shall miss that, *very* much ; " but he would not allow that things so orthodox as railways could be bad on the whole. I never intended, when I began, to trouble you with all this, but Cox's picture set me off, and it really is a great wrong that any set of men can take possession of one of the few peaceful spots left in England, and hash it up like that. Fancy driving along the road up the Slidr valleys and seeing on boards a notice, to " beware when the horn was blowing," and every now and then hearing a great blasting, smoke, and rocks crashing down. Well, you know just as well as I how horrible it all is. Only I can't think why people sit still, and let the beautiful places be destroyed.

The owners of that property,—I forget their name, but they had monuments in the little old church,—never live there, having another ' place ' in Scotland,—so of course they don't care.*

V. A fragment to illustrate the probable advantage of sulphurous air, and articles, in the country.

I did not think to tell you, when speaking of the fatality of broken limbs in our little dressmaker and her family, that when in St. Thomas's Hospital with a broken thigh, the doctors said in all probability the tenderness of her bones was owing to the manufacture of sulphur by her *mother's grandfather*. Dr. Simon knows her family through operating on the brother of our dressmaker, and often gáve them kindly words at the hospital.

I am, dear Sir,
Yours faithfully.

* Will any charitable Christian tell me who the owners are ?—in the meantime, "confusion on their banners wait."

LETTER LXII.

THERE were more, and more harmful misprints in last *Fors* than usual, owing to my having driven my printers to despair, after they had made all the haste they could, by late dubitation concerning the relative ages of Shem, Ham, and Japheth, which forced me to cut out a sentence about them, and displace corrected type. But I must submit to all and sundry such chances of error, for, to prevent them, would involve a complete final reading of the whole, with one's eye and mind on the look-out for letters and stops all along, for which I rarely allow myself time, and which, had I a month to spare, would yet be a piece of work ill spent, in merely catching three t's instead of two in a " lettter." The name of the Welsh valley is wrong, too ; but I won't venture on correction of that, which I feel to be hopeless ; the reader must, however, be kind enough to transfer the 'and,' now the sixth word in the upper line of the note at page 119, and make it the fourth word, instead ; to put a note of interrogation at the end of clause in the fiftieth line of page 117, and to insert an s, changing ' death ' into ' deaths ' in the seventeenth line of page 113 ;— the death in Sheffield being that commended to the Episcopic attention of York, and that in London to the Episcopic attention of London.

And this commendation, the reader will I hope perceive to be made in sequel to much former talk concerning Bishops, Soldiers, Lawyers, and Squires ;—which, perhaps, he imagined me to have spoken jestingly ; or it may be, in witlessness ; or it may be, in voluble incipient insanity. Admitting myself in no small degree open to such suspicion, I am now about to re-word some matters which madness would gambol from ; and I beg the reader to observe that any former gambolling on my part, awkward or untimely as it may have seemed, has been quite as serious, and intentionally progressive, as Morgiana's dance round the captain of the Forty Thieves.

If, then, the reader will look at the analysis of Episcopacy in *Sesame and Lilies,* the first volume of all my works; next at the chapter on Episcopacy in *Time and Tide ;* and lastly, refer to what he can gather in the past series of *Fors,* he will find the united gist of all to be, that Bishops cannot take, much less give, account of men's souls unless they first take and give account of their bodies : and that, therefore, all existing poverty and crime in their dioceses, discoverable by human observation, must be, when they are Bishops indeed, clearly known to, and describable by them, or their subordinates. Of whom the number, and discipline in St. George's Company, if by God's grace it ever take the form I intend, will be founded on the institution of the same by the first Bishop, or more correctly Archbishop, whom the Christian church professes to obey. For what can possibly be the use of printing the Ten Commandments which he delivered, in gold,—framing them above the cathedral altar,—pronouncing them in a prelatically sonorous voice,—and arranging the responsive supplications of the audience to the tune of an organ of the best manufacture, if the commanding Bishops institute no inquiry whatever into the physical power of—say this starving shoemaker in Seven Dials,—to obey such a command as ' thou shalt not covet' in the article of meat ; or of his son to honour in any available measure either the father or mother, of whom the one has departed to seek her separate living, and the other is lying dead with his head in the fireplace.

Therefore, as I have just said, our Bishops in St. George's Company will be constituted in order founded on that appointed by the first Bishop of Israel, namely, that their Primate, or Supreme Watchman, shall appoint under him " out of all the people, able men, such as fear God, men of truth, hating covetousness, and place such over them to be rulers (or, at the *least,* observers) of thousands, rulers of hundreds, rulers of fifties, and rulers of tens ; " * and that of

* Exodus, xviii. 21,

these episcopic centurions, captains of fifty, and captains of ten, there will be required clear account of the individual persons they are set over ;—even a baby being considered as a decimal quantity not to be left out of their account by the decimal Bishops,—in which episcopacy, however, it is not improbable that a queenly power may be associated, with Norman caps for mitres, and for symbol of authority, instead of the crosier, (or crook, for disentangling lost sheep of souls from among the brambles,) the broom, for sweeping diligently till they find lost silver of souls among the dust.

You think I jest, still, do you ? Anything but that ; only if I took off the Harlequin's mask for a moment, you would say I was simply mad. Be it so, however, for this time.

I simply and most utterly mean, that, so far as my best judgment can reach, the present Bishops of the English Church, (with only one exception, known to me,—the Bishop of Natal,) have forfeited and fallen from their Bishoprics by transgression ; and betrayal of their Lord, first by simony, and secondly, and chiefly, by lying for God with one mouth, and contending for their own personal interests as a professional body, as if these were the cause of Christ. And that in the assembly and Church of future England, there must be, (and shall be so far as this present body of believers in God and His law now called together in the name of St. Michael and St. George are concerned,) set up and consecrated other Bishops ; and under them, lower ministering officers and true "Dogs of the Lord," who, with stricter inquisition than ever Dominican, shall take knowledge—not of creeds, but of every man's way and means of life ; and shall be either able to avouch his conduct as honourable and just, or bound to impeach it as shameful and iniquitous, and this down to minute details ;—above all, or before all, particulars of revenue, every companion, retainer, or associate in the Company's work being bound to keep such accounts that the position of his affairs may be completely known to the Bishops at any moment : and all bankruptcies or treacheries in money matters thus rendered impossible. Not that direct inquisition will be often necessary ; for when the true nature of Theft, with the other particulars of the Moral Law, are rightly taught in our schools, grown-up men will no more think of stealing in business than in burglary. It is merely through the quite bestial ignorance of the Moral Law in which the English Bishops have contentedly allowed their flocks to be brought up, that any of the modern English conditions of trade are possible.

Of course, for such work, I must be able to find what Jethro of Midian assumes could be found at once in Israel, these "men of truth, hating covetousness," and all my friends laugh me to scorn for thinking to find any such.

Naturally, in a Christian country, it will be difficult enough; but I know there are still that kind of people among Midianites, Caffres, Red Indians, and the destitute, afflicted, and tormented, in dens and caves of the earth, where God has kept them safe from missionaries :—and, as I above said, even out of the rotten mob of money-begotten traitors calling itself a ' people' in England, I do believe I shall be able to extricate, by slow degrees, some faithful and true persons, hating covetousness, and fearing God.

And you will please to observe that this hate and fear are flat opposites one to the other ; so that if a man fear or reverence God, he must hate covetousness ; and if he fear or reverence covetousness, he must hate God ; and there is no intermediate way whatsoever. Nor is it possible for any man, wilfully rich, to be a God-fearing person ; but only for those who are involuntarily rich, and are making all the haste they prudently and piously can, to be poor ; for money is a strange kind of seed ; scattered, it is poison ; but set, it is bread : so that a man whom God has appointed to be a sower must bear as lightly as he may the burden of gold and of possessions, till he find the proper places to sow them in. But persons desiring to be rich, and accumulating riches, always hate God, and never fear Him ; the idol they do fear—(for many of them are sincerely religious) is an imaginary, or mind-sculptured God of their own making, to their own liking ; a God who allows usury, delights in strife and contention, and is very particular about everybody's going to his synagogues on Sunday.

Indeed, when Adam Smith formally, in the name of the philosophers of Scotland and England, set up this opposite God, on the hill of cursing against blessing, Ebal against Gerizim ; and declared that all men 'naturally' desired their neighbours' goods ; and that in the name of Covetousness, all the nations of the earth should be blessed,—it is true, that the half-bred and half-witted Scotchman had not gift enough in him to carve so much as his own calf's head on a whinstone with his own hand ; much less to produce a well molten and forged piece of gold, for old Scottish faith to break its tables of ten commandments at sight of. But, in leaving to every artless and ignorant boor among us the power of breeding, in imagination, each his own particular calf, and placidly worshipping that privately fatted animal ; or, perhaps,—made out of the purest fat of it in molten Tallow instead of molten Gold,—images, which may be in any inventive moment, misshapen anew to his mind, Economical Theology has granted its disciples more perfect and fitting privilege.

From all taint or compliance with such idolatry, the Companions of St. George have vowed to withdraw themselves ; writing, and signing their submission to, the First and great Commandment, so called by Christ,—and the Second which is like unto it.

And since on these two hang all the Law and the Prophets, in signing these two promises they virtually vow obedience to all the law of which Christ then spoke ; and belief of all the Prophets of which Christ then spoke. What that law is ; who those prophets are ; whether they *only* prophesied 'until John,' or whether St. Paul's command to all Christians living, " Follow after charity, and desire spiritual gifts, but rather that ye may prophesy,"—is an important *little* commandment following the two great ones, I cannot tell you in a single letter, even if I altogether knew myself. Partly I do know ;—and can teach you, if you will work. No one can teach you anything worth learning but through manual labour ; the very bread of life can only be got out of the chaff of it by "rubbing it in your hands."

You vow, then, that you will at least strive to keep both of these commandments—as far as, what some would call the corruption, but what in honest people is the weakness, of flesh, permits. If you cannot watch an hour, because you don't love Christ enough to care about His agony, that is your weakness ; but if you first sell Him, and then kiss Him, that is your corruption. I don't know if I can keep either you or myself awake ; but at least we may put a stop to our selling and kissing. Be sure that you are serving Christ, till you are tired and can do no more, for that time : and then, even if you have not breath enough left to say "Master, Master " with,—He will not mind.

Begin therefore 'to-day,'—(which you may, in passing, note to be your present leader's signal-word or watch-word), —to do good work for Him—whether you live or die,—(see first promise asked of you, Letter II., page 29, explained in Letter VII., page 98, etc.,)—and see that every stroke of this work—be it weak or strong, shall therefore be done in love of God and your neighbour, and in hatred of covetousness. Which that you may hate accurately, wisely, and well, it is needful that you should thoroughly know, when you see it, or feel it. What covetousness is, therefore, let me beg you at once clearly to understand, by meditating on these following definitions.

AVARICE means the desire to collect money, not goods. A 'miser' or 'miserable person' desires to collect goods only for the sake of turning them into money. If you can read French or German, read Molière's *l'Avare*, and then get Gotthelf's *Bernese Stories*, and read *Schnitzfritz*, with great care.

Avarice is a quite natural passion, and, within due limits, healthy. The addition of coin to coin, and of cipher to cipher, is a quite proper pleasure of human life, under due rule ;' the two stories I ask you to read are examples of its disease ; which arises mainly in strong and stupid minds, when by evil fortune they have never been led to think or feel.

FRUGALITY. The disposition to save or spare what we have got, without any desire to gain more. It is constantly, of course, associated with avarice ; but quite as frequently with generosity, and is often merely an extreme degree of housewifely habit. Study the character of Alison Wilson in *Old Mortality.*

COVETOUSNESS. The desire of possessing more than we have, of any good thing whatsoever of which we have already enough for our uses, (adding house to house, and field to field). It is much connected with pride ; but more with restlessness of mind and desire of novelty ; much seen in children who tire of their toys and want new ones. The pleasure in having things 'for one's very own' is a very subtle element it it. When I gave away my Loire series of Turner drawings to Oxford, I thought I was rational enough to enjoy them as much in the University gallery as in my own study. But not at all ! I find I can't bear to look at them in the gallery, because they are 'mine' no more.

Now, you observe, that your creed of St. George says you believe in the nobleness of human nature—that is to say, that all our natural instincts are honourable. Only it is not always easy to say which of them are natural and which not.

For instance, Adam Smith says that it is 'natural' for every person to covet his neighbour's goods, and want to change his own for them ; wherein is the origin of Trade, and Universal Salvation.

But God says, 'Thou shalt *not* covet thy neighbour's goods ;' and God, who made you, does in that written law express to you *His* knowledge of your inner heart, and instruct you in the medicine for it. Therefore on due consideration, you will find assuredly it is quite *un*natural in you to covet your neighbour's goods.

Consider, first, of the most precious, the wife. It is natural for you to think your own the best and prettiest of women ; not at all to want to change her for somebody else's wife. If you like somebody else's better than yours, and this somebody else likes yours better than his, and you both want to change, you are both in a non-natural condition, and entirely out of the sphere of happy human love.

Again. It is natural for you to think your own nouse and garden the nicest house and garden that ever were. If, as should always be, they were your father's before you, and he and you have both taken proper care of them, they are a treasure to you which no money could buy,—the leaving them is always pain,—the return to them, a new thrill and wakening to life. They are a home and place of root to you, as if you were founded on the ground like its walls, or grew into it like its flowers. You would no more willingly transplant yourself elsewhere than the espalier pear-tree of your own graffing would pull itself out by the roots to climb another trellis. That is the natural mind of a man. "Thou shalt not covet thy neighbour's house." You are in an entirely non-natural state if you do, and, properly speaking, never had a house in your life.

"Nor his man-servant, nor his maid-servant." It is a 'natural' thing for masters to get proud of those who serve them ; and a 'natural' thing for servants to get proud of the masters they serve. (You see above how Bacon connects the love of the master with the love of the country.) Nay, if the service has been true, if the master has indeed asked for what was good for himself, and the servant has done what was good for his master, they cannot choose but like each other ; to have a new servant, or a new master, would be a mere horror to both of them. I have got two Davids, and a Kate, that I wouldn't change for anybody else's servants in the world ; and I believe the only quarrel they have with me is that I don't give them enough to do for me :—this very morning, I must stop writing, presently, to find the stoutest of the Davids some business, or he will be miserable all day.

"Nor his ox, nor his ass." If you have petted both of your own, properly, from calf and foal, neither these, nor anything else of yours, will you desire to change for "anything that is his." Do you really think I would change my pen for yours, or my inkstand, or my arm-chair, or my

Gainsborough little girl, or my Turner pass of St. Gothard ?
I would see you——very uncomfortable—first. And that is
the natural state of a human being who has taken anything
like proper pains to make *himself* comfortable in God's good
world, and get some of the right good, and true wealth of it.

For, you observe farther, the commandment is only that
thou shalt not covet *thy neighbour's* goods. It does not say
that you are not to covet *any* goods. How *could* you covet
your neighbour's, if both your neighbour and you were forbidden to have any ? Very far the contrary ; in the first
piece of genealogic geography I have given you to learn,
the first descriptive sentence of the land of Havilah is,—
"where there is gold ; " and it goes on to say, "And the
gold of that land is of the best : there is bdellium, and the
onyx stone." In the Vulgate, ' dellium ' and ' lapis onichi-
nus.' In the Septuagint, ' anthrax,' and the ' prase-stone.'

Now, my evangelical friends, here is this book which you
call "Word of God," and idolatrously print for your little
children's reading and your own, as if your eternal lives depended on every word of it. And here, of the very beginning of the world—and the beginning of property—it professes to tell you something. But what? Have you the
smallest idea what ' dellium ' is ? Might it not as well be
bellium, or gellium, or pellium, or mellium, for all *you* know
about it ? Or do you know what an onyx is ? or an anthrax ? or a prase ? Is not the whole verse pure and absolute gibberish and gabble to you ; and do you expect God
will thank you for talking gibberish and gabble to your
children, and telling them—*that* is His Word ? Partly,
however, the verse is only senseless to you, because you
have never had the sense to look at the stones which God
has made. But in still greater measure, it is necessarily
senseless, because it is *not* the word of God, but an imperfectly written tradition, which, however, being a most ven-
erable and precious tradition, you do well to make your
children read, provided also you take pains to explain to
them so much sense as there *is* in it, and yourselves do reverently obey so much law as there is in it. **Towards** which

intelligence and obedience, we will now take a step or two farther from the point of pause in last *Fors*.

Remember that the three sons of Noah are, respectively,

SHEM, the father of the Imaginative and Contemplative races.

JAPHETH,   "   "   Practical and Constructive.

HAM,   "   "   Carnal and Destructive.

The sons of Shem are the perceivers of Splendour ;—they see what is best in visible things, and reach forward to the invisible.

The sons of Japheth are the perceivers of Justice and Duty ; and deal securely with all that is under their hand.

The sons of Ham are the perceivers of Evil or Nakedness and are slaves therefore for ever—'servants of servants' when in power, therefore, either helpless or tyrannous.

It is best to remember among the nations descending from the three great sires, the Persians, as the sons of Shem ; Greeks, as the sons of Japheth ; Assyrians, as the sons of Ham. The Jewish captivity to the Assyrian then takes its perfect meaning.

This month, therefore, take the first descendant of Ham— Cush ; and learn the following verses of Gen. x. :—

" And Cush begat Nimrod ; he began to be a mighty one in the earth.

" He was a mighty hunter before the Lord.

" And the beginning of his kingdom was Babel in the land of Shinar.

" Out of that land went forth Asshur, and builded Nineveh."

These verses will become in future a centre of thought to you, whereupon you may gather, as on one root-germ, what you farther learn of the influence of hunting on the minds of men ; and of the sources of Assyrian power, and causes of the Assyrian ruin in Birs Nimroud, out of which you have had those hunting-pieces brought to the narrow passage in the British Museum.

For further subject of thought, this month, read of Carey's
Dante, the 31st canto of the *Inferno*, with extreme care ;
and for your current writing lesson, copy these lines of Italics, which I have printed in as close resemblance as I can to
the Italics of the Aldine edition of 1502.

> *P   ero che come in su la cerchia tonda*
> *Monte reggion di torri si corona,*
> *Cosi la proda che'l pozzo circonda*
> *T   orregiavan di mezza la persona*
> *Gli orribili giganti ; cui minaccia*
> *Giove del ciclo anchora, quando tona.*

The putting of the capital letters that begin the stanza,
outside, is a remaining habit of the scribes who wrote for
the illuminator, and indicated the letter to be enlarged with
ornament at the side of the text.

Of these larger capitals, the A given in last *Fors,* is of a
Byzantine Greek school, in which though there is much
quiet grace, there is no elasticity or force in the lines. They
are always languid, and without spring or evidence of nervous force in the hand. They are not, therefore, perfect models for English writers, though they are useful as exercises
in tranquillity of line : and I chose for that and many more
reasons, that letter and sentence for our first exercise. But
my letter B is to be given from the Northern Schools ; and
will have spring and power in it, which you cannot at once
hope to imitate in a complete letter ; and must be prepared
for by copying a mere incipient fragment or flourish of ornamental line.

This line has been drawn for you, very leisurely indeed,
by one of the gentlest of the animals living on our English
south downs,—and yet, quietly done as it is, being the result of wholly consistent energy, it is a line which a Byzantine Greek would never have produced in writing, nor even
in architecture, except when he was imitating an Ionian one.

You are to draw a horizontal line through the point in

the centre of this figure.　Then measure the breadth of the six coils on each side, counting from the centre backwards and forwards.

Then draw a vertical line through centre, and measure the breadths above and below.　Then draw the complete curve lightly through these fixed points—alter it to your mind—and then paint over it the determined line, with any dark colour and a camel's hair brush.

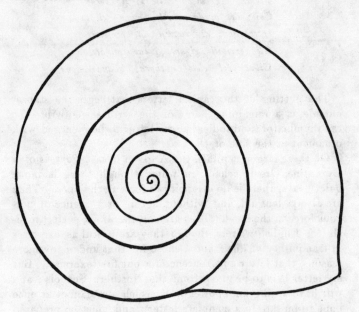

The difficulty is to draw it so that there shall not be the smallest portion of it which is not approaching the inner curve, and narrowing the intermediate space.　And you will find no trick of compasses will draw it.　Choose any number of centres you like, and still I defy you to draw the curve mechanically ; it can be done only as I have done it myself, with the free hand, correcting it and correcting till I got it right.*

* The law of its course will be given in the *Laws of Fésole*, Plate V.

When you have succeeded, to any moderate extent, in doing this, your hand will have begun to receive the power of executing a serene and dignified flourish instead of a vulgar 'dash.' And you may also begin to understand that the word 'flourish' itself, as applied to writing, means the springing of its lines into floral exuberance,—therefore, strong procession and growth, which must be in a spiral line, for the stems of plants are always spirals. (See *Proserpina*, Number IV.) ; and that this bursting out into foliage, in calm swiftness, is a totally different action from the impudent and useless sweeps and loops of vulgar writing.

Further. As your eyes get accustomed to the freely drawn, unmechanical, immeasurable line, you will be able, if you care about architecture, to know a Greek Ionic volute from a vulgar day-labourer's copy of it—done with compasses and calculations. And you will know how the volute of the throne of Lippi's Madonna, (though that is studied from the concave side of the shell) shows him to have been Etruscan-bred ; and you will begin to see what his power was ; and to laugh at the books of our miserable modern builders, filled with elaborate devices for drawing volutes with bits of circles : —the wretches might as well try to draw the lips of Sir Joshua's Circe,—or the smile in her cat's triangular eyes, in that manner. Only in Eleutheria of soul and body, shall any human creature draw so much as one rightly bending line.

Any *human* creature, I say. Little freedom, either of body or soul, had the poor architect who drew this our first model line for us ; and yet and yet, simple as his life and labours may be, it will take our best wits to understand them. I find myself, at present, without any startpoint for attempt to understand them. I found the downs near Arundel, being out on them in a sunny day just after Christmas, sprinkled all over with their pretty white shells, (none larger than a six-pence, my drawing being increased as about seven to one, in line, or fifty to one, square,) and all empty, unless perchance some spectral remnant of their dead masters remain inside ; —and I can't answer a single question I ask myself about them. I see they most of them have six whirls, or whorls.

Had they six when they were young ? have they never more when they are old ? Certainly some shells have periodical passion of progress—and variously decorative stops and rests ; but these little white continuities down to this woful time of their Christmas emptiness, seem to have deduced their spiral caves in peace.

But it's of no use to waste time in ' thinking.' I shall go and ask some pupil of. my dear old friend Dr. Gray at the British Museum, and rejoice myself with a glance at the volutes of the Erectheium—fair home of Athenian thought.

NOTES AND CORRESPONDENCE.

í. I am surprised to find that my Index to Vols. I. and II. of *Fors* does not contain the important article "Pockets"; and that I cannot therefore, without too much trouble, refer to the place where I have said that the Companions of St. George are all to have glass pockets; so that the absolute contents of them may be known of all men. But, indeed, this society of ours is, I believe, to be distinguished from other close brotherhoods that have been, or that are, chiefly in this, that it will have no secrets, and that its position, designs, successes, and failures, may at any moment be known to whomsoever they may concern.

More especially the affairs of the Master and of the Marshals, when we become magnificent enough to have any, must be clearly known, seeing that these are to be the managers of public revenue. For although, as we shall in future see, they will be held more qualified for such high position by contentment in poverty than responsibility of wealth; and, if the society is wise, be chosen always from among men of advanced age, whose previous lives have been recognised as utterly without stain of dishonesty in management of their private business,— the complete publication of their accounts, private as well as public, from the day they enter on the management of the Company's funds, will be a most wholesome check on the glosses with which self-interest, in the minds even of the honestest people, sometimes may colour or confuse their actions over property on a large scale; besides being examples to the accountants of other public institutions.

For instance, I am myself a Fellow of the Horticultural Society; and, glancing the other day at its revenue accounts for 1874, observed that out of an expenditure of eleven thousand odd pounds, one thousand nine hundred and sixty-two went to pay interest on debts, eleven hundred and ninety to its 'salaries'—two hundred to its botanical adviser, a hundred and fifty to its botanical professor, a hundred and twenty-six to its fruit committee, a hundred and twenty to its floral committee, four hundred and twenty to its band, nine hundred and ten to its rates and taxes, a hundred and eighty-five to its lawyers, four hundred and thirty-nine to its printers, and three pounds fifteen shillings to its foreign importations' account, (being interest on Cooper's loan): whereupon I wrote to the secretary expressing some dissatisfaction with the proportion borne by this last item to the others, and asking for some further particulars respecting the 'salaries'; but was informed that none could be had. Whereas, whether wisely or foolishly directed, the expenditure of the St. George's Company will be always open, in all particulars, to the criticism not only of the Companions, but of the outside public. And Fors has so arranged matters that I cannot at all, for my own part, invite such criticism to-day with feelings of gratified vanity; my own immediate position (as I generally stated in last letter) being not in the least creditable to my sagacity, nor likely to induce a large measure of public confidence in me as the Company's Master. Nor are even the affairs of the Company itself, in my estimate, very brilliant, our collected subscriptions for the reform of the world amounting, as will be seen, in five years, only to some seven hundred and odd pounds. However, the Company and its Master may perhaps yet see better days.

First, then, for the account of my proceedings in the Company's affairs. Our eight thousand Consols giving us £240 a year, I have appointed a Curator to the Sheffield Museum, namely, Mr. Henry Swan, an old pupil of mine in the Working Men's College in London; and known to me since as an estimable and trustworthy person, with a salary of forty pounds a year, and residence. He is obliged at present to live in the lower rooms of the little house which is to be the nucleus of the museum:—as soon as we can afford it, a curator's house must be built outside of it.

I have advanced, as aforesaid, a hundred pounds of purchase-money, and fifty for current expenses; and paid, besides, the lawyers' bills for the transfer, amounting to £48 16s. 7d.; these, with some needful comments on them, will be published in next *Fors;* I have not room for them in this.

I have been advised of several mistakes in my subscribers' list, so I reprint it below, with the initials attached to the numbers, and the entire sum, (as far as I can find out,) hitherto subscribed by each; and I beg of my subscribers at once to correct me in all errors.

The names marked with stars are those of Companions. The numbers 10, 17, 36, 43, and 48 I find have been inaccurately initialled, and are left blank for correction.

List of Subscriptions.

	£	s.	d.			£	s.	d.
1. D. L.*	24	0	0	10.		1	1	0
2. R. T.*	80	0	0	11. G. S.*		2	2	0
3. T. K.	5	0	0	12. J. S.		4	0	0
4. C. S.	75	0	0	13. B. A.		9	0	0
5. A. R.	20	0	0	14. A. P.		13	10	0
6. J. M.*	4	4	0	15. W. P.		5	0	0
7. P. S.	45	0	0	16. A. H.*		25	0	0
8. D. A.	20	0	0					
9. A. B.	25	0	0	Carried forward	... £357	17	0	

	£	s.	d.		£	s.	d.
Brought forward.....	357	17	0	37. A. H...............	10	0	0
17.	1	1	0	38. S. S...............	1	0	0
18. F. E...............	10	0	0	39. H. W...............	50	0	0
19. J. S...............	25	0	0	40. J. F...............	8	0	0
20. — D...............	2	0	0	41. J. T...............	5	0	0
21. C. W...............	10	10	0	42. J. O...............	25	0	0
22. S. B.*...............	2	0	0	43.	1	1	0
23. E. G...............	6	1	0	44. A. C...............	1	0	0
24 — L...............	1	1	0	45. J. G...............	5	0	0
25. S. W...............	55	0	0	46. T. M...............	5	5	0
26. B. B.*...............	2	3	4	47. J. B.*...............	2	11	0
27. J. W...............	1	1	0	48.	1	1	0
28. E. F...............	50	0	0	49. J. D...............	0	5	0
29. L. L...............	1	5	0	50. G	15	15	0
30. A. A...............	0	2	6	51. F. B...............	1	1	0
31. T. D...............	5	0	0	52. C. B...............	6	0	0
32. M. G...............	3	3	0	53. H. L...............	10	0	0
33. J. F...............	40	0	0	54. A. G...............	0	10	0
34. W. S...............	10	0	0				
35. H. S...............	9	0	0		£741	14	10
36.	1	1	0				

II. Affairs of the Master.

When I instituted the Company by giving the tenth of my available property to it, I had, roughly, seventy thousand pounds in money or land, and thirty thousand * in pictures and books. The pictures and books I do not consider mine, but merely in my present keeping, for the country, or the persons I may leave them to. Of the seventy thousand in substance, I gave away fourteen thousand in that year of the Company's establishment (see above, Letter XLIX., p. 324,) and have since lost fifteen thousand by a relation whom I tried to support in business. As also, during my battle with the booksellers, I have been hitherto losing considerably by my books, (last year, for instance, paying three hundred and ninety-eight pounds to my assistant, Mr. Burgess, alone, for plates and woodcutting, and making a profit, on the whole year's sales, of fifty pounds), and have been living much beyond my income besides, my seventy thousand is reduced to certainly not more than thirty ; and it is very clear that I am too enthusiastically carrying out my own principles, and making more haste to be poor than is prudent, at my present date of possible life, for, at my current rate of expenditure, the cell at Assisi, above contemplated as advisably a pious mortification of my luxury, would soon become a necessary refuge for my 'holy poverty.' The battle with the booksellers, however, is now nearly won ; and the publishing accounts will soon show better

---

* An under-estimate, at present prices for Turner drawings, and I have hitherto insured for full thirty thousand, but am now going to lower the insurance, for no money would replace the loss of them, and I less and less regard them as exchangeable property.

balance : what changes in my mode of living may, nevertheless, be soon either exemplary or necessary will be better understood after I have given account of it for a year.

Here are my opening expenses, then, from 1st January to 20th, and in each following *Fors* they will be given from 20th to 20th of the month. I content myself, being pressed for space in this number, with giving merely the sums of checques drawn ; somewhat lengthy gossipping explanation of items being also needed, which will come in due place. The four first large sums are, of course, payments of Christmas accounts.

	£	s.	d.	£	s.	d.
Balance in Bank, 1st Jan., 1876				1344	17	9
Paid by cheque :						
Jan. 1. Jackson, (outdoor Steward, Brantwood)	50	0	0			
1. Kate Smith, (indoor Stewardess, Brantwood)	160	0	0			
1. David Downes, (Steward in London)..	115	0	0			
1. David Fudge, (Coachman in London)..	60	0	0			
1. Secretary, 1st quarter, 1876	25	0	0			
4. Frederick Crawley, in charge of schoolrooms at Oxford.	10	0	0			
6. Self, pocket-money	20	0	0			
17. Arthur Burgess, assistant engraver....	27	10	0			
20. New carriage	190	0	0			
20. Gift to Carshalton, for care of spring..	110	0	0			
20. Madame Nozzoli, charities at Florence.	10	0	0			
20. Mrs. Wonnacott, charities at Abingdon.	3	10	0			
20. William Ward, for two copies of Turner.	21	0	0			
20. Charles Murray, for rubbings of brasses and copy of Filippo Lippi	15	0	0			
				817	0	0
Balance Jan. 20				527	17	9

III. I am gradually rising into greater indignation against the baseness and conceit of the modern scientific mob, than even against the mere money-seekers. The following fragment of a letter from a Companion bears notably on this matter :—

" The only earnest folks I know are cold-hearted ' Freethinkers,' and not very earnest either. My church-going friends are not earnest, except about their form of sound words. But I get on best with them. They are warmer, and would be what I wish, were circumstances not so dead set against it. My ' Freethinking ' acquaintances say that with Carlyle the last of the great dreamers *who have impeded the advance of science* will pass away, and that, in fact, he is dead already, for nobody minds him. I don't heed such words now as I used to do. Had I lived when Socrates was condemned, I would have felt hope extinguished ; yet Jesus came long after him, and I will not fear that God

will fail to send His great and good men, any more than that the sun
will forget to rise.

" My Freethinking friends sneer even at the mention of any God ;
and their talk of methods of reformation that infer any wisdom above
their own has long since sickened me. One Sunday evening last year,
I accompanied one of them to what they call the ' Eclectic Hall ' here,
to hear a Mrs. Law speak. There were from two to three hundred
present,—few women—almost all toil-worn looking men. Mrs. Law,
the lecturess—a stout, coarse-looking lady, or woman who might have
been a lady—based her address on another by Mr. Gladstone, M.P.
One thing she said will give you an idea of the spirit of her lecture,
which was full of sadness to me, because highly appreciated by her audience : ' Jesus tells you,' she shouted, ' " Blessed are the poor, for theirs
is the kingdom of Heaven," but *I* tell you, Blessed are the rich, for
theirs is no myth-world, but *this* substantial one with its tangible, sat-
isfying joys.'

" I got one of them to read the October Letter—and then Volumes
I. and IV. of *Fors*. Another young fellow, a Londoner, read them too,
and then at leisure moments there was a talk over them for some days.
But, with the exception of the first referred to, they talked pitifully
enough. Your incidental remark about destroying the new town of
Edinburgh, and other items of dubious sort, blinded them to any good,
and it was a blessing when something else came athwart their vacant
minds, and they ceased to remember you."

IV. I am grateful for the following note on the name ' Sheffield ' :—

"LEEDS, 29*th Dec.*, 1875.

" Sir,—The town, in all probability, took its name from the river
' Sheaf,' which flows into the Don.

"Doncaster is a case in point out of hundreds of others. It may be
that the river has been named in recent times, but it is unlikely ; for
as a rule a river always has some name by which it is known before any
settlements are made on its banks."

V. I must now request my reader's attention somewhat gravely to
the questions in debate between my correspondents at Wakefield ; not
that these are in themselves of any importance, but they are of extreme
importance in their general issue. In the first place, observe the extreme difficulty of writing history. You shall have one impertinent
coxcomb after another in these days, writing constitutional Histories of
England and the like, and telling you all the relationships and all the
motives of Kings and Queens a thousand years dead ; and here is question respecting the immediate ancestor of a living lady, which does not
appear at once or easily determinable ; and which I do not therefore
pursue ;—here again is question respecting the connection of her husband with the cases of bribery reported in the subjoined evidence on
the Wakefield election petition, also indeterminable ;—here are farther
two or three questions respecting the treatment of his workmen, respecting which the evidence is entirely conflicting ; and finally, here is

the chapel on Wakefield bridge pulled down,[*] a model of it built in its place, and the entire front of the historical building carried away to decorate a private boathouse ; and I, quite as knowing in architecture as most people, am cheated into some very careful and quite useless work, and even into many false conclusions, by the sculpture of the sham front, decayed and broken enough in thirty years to look older than sculpture of 500 years B.C. would, or *does*, in pure air.

Observe, in the second place, how petulant and eager people are, the moment a single word touches themselves, while universal abuses may be set before them enough to bring all the stones in heaven but what serve for the thunder, down about their ears,—and they will go on talking about Shakespeare and the musical glasses undisturbed, to the end of their lives ; but let a single word glance at their own windows, or knock at their own doors, and—instantly—' If Mr. Ruskin is what I think him, he will retract,' etc. etc. But, alas ! Mr. Ruskin is not the least what Mrs. Green thinks him,—does not in the smallest degree care for a lady's "Fie's," and, publishing the following letters and newspaper extracts for the general reader's satisfaction and E. L.'s justification, very contentedly, for his part, ends the discussion, though of course *Fors* shall be open to any further communication, if not too long, which either Mrs. Green or her husband may desire to have inserted.

In the following letter I have left all the passages containing due apology, while I have removed some which contained matter of further debate, if not offence, thereby much weakening the whole.

"Dear Mr. Ruskin,—I have been away from home, and have only recently seen Mrs. Green's letter in *Fors* of last month.

"I am sorry to have vexed her ; I did not think that you would print the passages referring to her husband in the form in which they stood. [†]

"When you said that you would assume my permission to print passages from the letter, I supposed that they would be those relating to the general life of Wakefield. All that I have written is essentially true, but I do not wish to hold any controversy on the matter, for if I defended myself publicly I should have to wound still further the feelings of one who is no doubt a devoted wife.

"It is for your satisfaction alone that I write these lines. I have been inaccurate on two points, on which I wrote too hastily, from hearsay, gleaned on brief visits to Wakefield. Mr. Green has not a Scotch estate, only occasional shooting, and he is not concerned in the forges that stand near the bridge, as I was wrongly informed.

"I did not say, though I may have led your readers to infer it, that the so-called ' American devil ' was his. I knew, or rather was told, that it belonged to Whithams, who have the largest foundry. He (Mr. Green) does not forge iron, it seems ; he makes it into machines. He

---

[*] I have not space in this *Fors* to give the letter certifying me of this.
[†] See my reason stated, Letter LIX., p. 72.

can hardly be classed as an engineer ; he is a machine-maker. If he is not an ' iron lord,' on what is his wealth based ?

" Robin the Pedlar is no myth. I often heard him mentioned, when a girl, as being Mrs. Green's father. I dare say that Mrs. Edward Green never heard of him. She came into the family in its genteeler days; but there are old people in Wakefield who remember all about him. I send by this post a Wakefield paper containing some speeches highly illustrative of the town of which Mr. Green is the hero and model." (These I do not think it necessary to publish.) " Party feeling still runs high at Wakefield, and when the next election occurs, Mrs. Green expects to find big yellow bills on the gate-pillars of Heath Common, 'Professor Ruskin on Ned Green,' and she is naturally angry.

" Of course he is not the sole offender. This case occurred to me because he is the most prominent type of the modern successful men who are to inaugurate a new era in the town's history. It is the blind leader of the blind in the downward way that things are going. Everybody wants to get rich like him ; everybody who has greed and competence pushes to the front. The town council promise them that they will make of Wakefield a second Bradford. Meanwhile they squabble about their duties, the streets are filthy, smallpox breeds there, and they set up a hospital in a tent. It catches fire, and nurse and patients are burnt together. I think that was eight or nine years since. Possibly arrangements are better now.

" You say truly that quickly acquired fortunes must be ill acquired, but you must live on my level to realize fully how the prospect and possibility of such gains are disorganizing middle-class life. English people do not lift their families along with them, as we reproach the ' clannish' Scotch with doing.

" Ignorant pride on the one hand, envy on the other, breed hate between those who should be a mutual stay. As classes are estranged, so are families.

" In conclusion, I must again say that I shall always feel regret at having pained Mrs. Green, but what I have said is true in all essentials.

" He is the hero of the men who are changing Wakefield so rapidly. I liked it better thirty years since, when, if it was poor, it was clean and honest.

" I am, dear Mr. Ruskin, yours truly,
" E. L."

I print the following first portion (about the fourth part) of a column and a half of the evidence on the Wakefield election petition, sent me by my correspondent; though I do not suppose it to indicate anything more than compliance on Mr. Green's part with the ordinary customs of English electioneering.

" The trial of the petition against the return of Mr. Green, the Conservative member for Wakefield, was resumed this morning before Mr. Justice Grove. Mr. Hawkins, Q.C., and Mr. Chandos Leigh again appeared for the petitioners, and Mr. C. Russell, Q. C., and Mr. Forbes for the respondent. There was again a crowded attendance.

" John Thompson, a tailor, and a voter in the Northgate Ward, said that about half-past six o'clock, on Sunday, the 1st February—the day before the polling—'Counciller Joe' (Mr. J. Howden) called at his house and solicited his vote for Mr. Green. Witness said he did not think that he could give it, but if he did he must 'have something.' Mr. Howden said, 'If it's worth anything I'll let you know.' About half-past one o'clock on the polling day witness again saw him. Mr. Howden said, 'If you vote for Green, I'll send you 10s. for your day's wage.' Witness said, 'No;' and they parted.

"Cross-examined: Witness did not say to Mr. Howden that he had already been offered a couple of pounds. He was a strong Radical. Mr. Howden was at witness's house several times, but he only saw him once. He (witness) voted about half-past two in the afternoon.

"Elizabeth Thompson, wife of the last witness, said that on the Saturday and Sunday before the polling day Mr. J. Howden called to solicit her husband's vote, and he said, 'If he votes for Green, I'll see that he is paid.' On the Monday, when Mr. Howden called, he said, 'If your husband votes for Green I'll give him 5s. out of my own pocket, and see that he is "tipped" in the committee room.' Later in the day, her husband was at home when Howden called, and they left the house together.

"Henry Blades, a blacksmith's striker, and a voter in the Westgate Ward, said that on the day of the election Mr. Ough gave him £2 in the Finisher Off public-house, on condition that he voted for Mr. Green. Witness voted in the course of the day.

"Cross-examined: Witness, since he received his subpœna, had met Mr. Gill, the respondent's solicitor, and others, at the Bull Hotel, and put his name to a paper, of the nature of which he was ignorant.

"Mr. Russell: 'Was it not a statement, made by yourself, and taken down in writing, to the effect that you had never received any bribe or offer of a bribe?'

"Witness: 'I don't know. They asked me to sign the paper, and I signed it. I was not sober.'

"Re-examined by Mr. Hawkins: Witness was sent for to the Bull. He received there, after making his statement, two glasses of beer, and 5s. in money—the latter from Mr. Ough.

"Henry Lodge said that on the afternoon of the election he was in Farrar's beerhouse, in Westgate. Blade was there 'fresh,' and taking three half-sovereigns from his pocket, he threw them on the table, and said, 'That's the sort to have.'

"James Meeghan, an Irish labourer, said that he was a voter for the borough, and on the polling day was canvassed by Mr. Kay for the Conservatives. He met Mr. Kay in the polling booth, and received from him 10s. Before voting, witness said to Mr. Kay that he was a poor man and could not afford to lose his day's wage. Mr. Kay said, 'I can't give you a bribe—that's against the law; but as you have had to pay your mates for doing your work, you shall have something.' In the polling station Mr. Kay held a half-sovereign in his hand, behind him, and witness took it.

"Cross-examined: Mr. Kay offered witness the 10s. out of his own pocket.

"Mr. Russell (to the Judge): 'What this man says is quite true. Mr. Kay does not deny that he gave him half a sovereign for his loss of time.'

"Patrick M'Hugh, an Irish labourer, and a voter in the Northgate

Ward, said that on the polling day he visited the Conservative Committee-room at the Zetland School, and saw Mr. Tom Howden. Mr.
Howden said, 'Are you going to vote?' Witness replied, 'I suppose
so;' and Mr. Howden said, 'Come this way and I'll show you how.'
Witness was taken into a back room, and there Mr. Howden said,
'Well, how much?' Witness said, 'Three,' and Mr. Howden took
them out of his pocket (three sovereigns), and said, 'See there.' Witness took the money and voted. He had, since receiving his subpœna,
been away from Wakefield.

"Cross-examined: Witness had visited Harrogate—staying a week
there to take the waters—(laughter),—and afterwards Thirsk. He
paid his own expenses and travelled alone, having been recommended
by a doctor to go away for the benefit of his health.

"Mr. Russell: 'Who was the doctor?'

"Witness: 'Mr. Unthank'—(great laughter);—Mr. Unthank being a
chemist, and a prominent Liberal. 'He said that if I could go, and
was strong enough, a bit of an out would do me good.' (Laughter.)
'The £3 that I received at the election supported me while I was
away.'

"James Wright, a police officer of the borough of Wakefield, said
that on the polling day he was acting as door-keeper at the Zetland
Street polling station, and observed Mr. Priestly hand some money to
one who presented himself as a voter. Witness followed the voter into
the booth, and pointed him out to his superior officer. The man voted,
and then left. Mr. Priestly was busily employed during the polling
hours in conducting voters from the Conservative committee-room to
the polling station.

"Cross-examined: At half-past three Priestly was 'fresh' in drink,
and it was found necessary to keep him out of the polling station. He
was in Mr. Green's employment. Witness could not say what amount
of money passed; but some one in the crowd, who also saw the transac-
tion, said to Priestly, 'You are doing it too brown.' (Laughter.)"

The letters next following are from an entirely honest engineer
workman, a Companion of St. George.

"Dear Master,—I read Mrs. Green's letter in the November *Fors*
two or three days ago, and yesterday I adopted the hint in it to inquire amongst the workmen. I asked one working beside me, who I
knew came from Yorkshire, if he ever worked in Wakefield, and, curiously enough, he belongs there, and was apprenticed in a workshop
close to Mr. Green's. He says he knows the place well, and that certainly when he was there, 'At six o'clock or some approximate hour,'
the firm of Green and Son, 'issued its counter-order' with a horrible
noise; and not only at six o'clock, but also after meals.

"He also tells me that the wages of a working engineer in the workshop of Green and Son average 22s. a week, and I know that here, in
London, they average 38s. a week, and Wakefield is close to coal and
iron, while London is not. It may be, as I once heard it, urged that
the workmen in London are superior as workmen to those in the provinces; but my experience, which has been considerable in London
and the provinces as a working engineer, enables me to assert that this
is not the case. Also it may be urged that low wages prevail in the

provinces, but in Glasgow I got 30s. a week two years ago, and this week meant fifty-one hours, while in Wakefield a week's work means fifty-four hours.

"Since Mr. Green derives no pecuniary benefit from Wakefield, it is evident from the above that the London and Glasgow engineers are very ingenious persons indeed, if they contrive to get pecuniary benefit from the cities in which they issue their 'counter-order.'

"Moreover, my fellow-workman tells me that there is a system of piece-work carried on in the workshop of Green and Son, which is extended to the *apprentices*, so that the boys are set to think, not how to learn to work properly, but how to learn to get hold of the greatest number of shillings they can in a week. In the man the desire for more money is tempered with forethought: he knows that if he earns more than a certain amount the price of his job will be cut down ; but the boy does not consider this, and *his* price, to use the language of the workshop, is cut down accordingly.

"Mrs. Green in her letter says Mr. Green never had a forge. This means that he never had a place which exclusively turned out forgings. But connected with Mr. Green's establishment, my fellow-workman tells me, are forges, as indeed there are in every engineering work I have seen. Besides, there is constantly carried on a process of moulding ' pig iron ' at Mr. Green's place, which requires the most intense heat, and to which the workmen are exposed, as they are at the forge Mrs. Green speaks of. (In your lectures to the students at Oxford in 1870, you say that work requiring the use of fire must be reduced to its minimum, and speak of its effects in Greek. I know some of its evil effects on the blacksmiths, but I wonder if it is desirable for me to know the meaning of the Greek language you use on that occasion.) (Yes ; but you need not be in any hurry about it.)

"It would seem, then, that Mr. Green stays at Heath Hall, and cultivates an ideal refinement in art, while he is instrumental in causing two or three hundred men and boys in Wakefield, from whom he derives no pecuniary benefit, to cultivate there the fine art of music in the shriek and roar of machines all day, to cultivate a trader's eagerness for bargaining, instead of a wish to do good work, and to cultivate an acquaintance with the sort of work which, over ten years constant experience in it tells me, is the most effective in this country for qualifying themselves and others for admission to the Ophthalmic, Orthopedic, and other institutions mentioned by your correspondent, E. L.

"Last week I had intelligence of the death of a young engineer friend of mine. A boiler burst while he was standing by, and shot him a distance of 60 yards, killing him instantly.

"Dear Master, if I have made a mistake in troubling you with these notes on Mrs. Green's letter, I am sorry, but I could not resist the impulse to write to you after what I learned from my fellow-workman. I believe the facts are reliable, and at any rate I can give the workman's name who furnished them, if it is wanted."

"Dear Master,—Since I wrote to you last I chanced on another workman, who has worked in Green's shop. He tells me it is known among the workmen as ' The Port in a Storm.'

"My first informant also, unasked, wrote to Wakefield for further information. He showed me the letter in reply, which says that Green's whistle (it is also called a ' buzzard ') was not stopped till force was applied.

" ' The Port in a Storm ' means that only when assailed by the fierce storm of hunger do the workmen think of applying for work at Green's place ; that is, when they can't get work anywhere else in the neighbourhood."

These letters appear to me entirely to justify the impression under which E. L. wrote ; but of course I shall be most happy if Mr. Green will furnish me with more accurate indication of the persons who have made Wakefield the horrible spectacle that it is. For although many of my discreet friends cry out upon me for allowing ' personalities,' it is my firm conviction that only by justly personal direction of blame can any abuse be vigorously dealt with. And, as I will answer for the sincerity and impartiality of attack, so I trust to make it always finally accurate in aim and in limitation.

LETTER LXIII.

I FIND it wholly impossible to crush into one *Fors* what I have been gathering of Bible lesson, natural history lesson, and writing lesson, and to leave room enough for what I have to give of immediate explanation to the Companions, now daily increasing in number. My readers must bear with me—I cannot do more than I am doing, though every day I wonder more at there being so many things apparently my duty to do, while I have only two feeble hands for all of them.

But this much of general statement of the meaning of our Companionship is now absolutely necessary.

Of course, the first natural idea taken up by persons who merely hear talk, or read newspapers, about the Company, is that their domain is intended for a *refuge* for the persons who join it—that within its walls the poor are at once to be made rich, and the sorrowful happy.

Alas, this is not by any means the notion of the St. George's Company. It is to be a band of delivering knights —not of churls needing deliverance ; of eager givers and servants—not of eager beggars, * and persons needing service. It is only the Rich, and the Strong, whom I receive for Companions,—those who come not to be ministered unto, but to minister. Rich, yet some of them in other kind of riches than the world's ; strong, yet some in other than the world's strength. But this much at least of literal wealth and strength they *must* have,—the power, and formed habit, of self-support. I accept no Companion by whom I am not convinced that the Society will be aided rather than burdened ; and although I value intelligence, resolution, and personal strength, more than any other riches, I hope to find, in a little while, that there are people in the world who can hold money without being blinded, by their possession of it, to justice or duty.

* See note at end of this letter.

The Companions whom I accept will be divided, according to their means and circumstances, into three classes.

The first and highest class will be called "Comites Ministrantes," "Companions Servant." It will be composed of the few who devote their main energy to the work of the Company ; and who, as I do myself, and as the Master must always, pursue their private avocations only in subjection to its interests, being at the same time in positions absolutely independent, and openly shown to be so.

The second, or middle class, will be called "Comites Militantes," "Companions Militant."

These will be persons occupied actually in manual labour on the ground, or in any work which the Master may order, for the fulfilment of the Society's functions ; being dependent on such labour for their maintenance, under the conditions fixed by the Company's statutes.

The third and lowest order will be called "Comites Consilii," (Friends of, or in, Council,) "Companions Consular," who will form the general body of the Society, being occupied in their own affairs as earnestly as before they joined it ; but giving it the tenth of their income ; and in all points, involving its principles, obeying the orders of the Master. Thus almost any tradesman may continue his trade, being a Companion ; but, if a jeweller, he must not sell false jewels ; or if a butcher, (I have one accepted already, and I very much want to get a butcher's daughter, if I could ; but she won't come,) must not sell bad meat.

I at first meant them to be called Censors, or Companions Estimant, because when the Society comes into real work, the sentences of fine, or other disgrace, pronounced by the marshals' officers, and the general modes of determining quality and value of goods, must be always ratified by majority of this order of the Companions, in whom also, by virtue of their number, the election, and therefore censorship, of the Master, will necessarily be vested.

To these last, especially, I have now some special matters to write.

Will you please look back to the *Fors* of December 24th,

last year, p. 278, and tell me,—or rather, which is chiefly needful, answer to yourselves, how far you have reflected, since reading it, on the nature of "unfruitful works of darkness; " how many you have abandoned, and how many reproved. It is too probable that you have not, even yet, the slightest idea what works of darkness are. You know,— they can't mean merely murder, or adultery, or theft. You don't, when you go to church, mean to pray that you may have grace to give up committing murder or adultery, or that you may 'rather reprove *them*'? But what then is it that you pray to give up? If you don't know, are you not, yet, in the least, ashamed of yourselves, for going every Sunday, if not every day, to pray to God, without having the dimmest idea what you mean to ask Him for?

Well,—not to be farther teazing about it,—in the first and simple sense, works of darkness are useless, or ill-done, or half-done, things, which pretend to be good, or to be wholly done ; and so mislead or betray.

In the deeper and final sense, a work of darkness is one that seeks concealment, and conceals facts ; or even casts disdain and disgrace on facts.

A work of light is one that seeks light, and that, not for its own sake, but to light all men ; so that all workers of good work delight in witnesses ; only with true desire that the witnesses' pleasure may be greater than theirs ; and that the Eternal witnesses—the Cloud around us, and Powers above—may have chief pleasure of all :—(see on this matter, *Eagle's Nest*, page 43). So that, of these works, what was written of St. Bernard must be always true, "Opera sancti Patris velut Sol in conspectu Dei ; " for indeed they are a true Light of the world, infinitely better in the Creator's sight than its dead sunshine ; and the discovery by modern science that all mortal strength is from the Sun, while it has thrown foolish persons into atheism, is, to wise ones, the most precious testimony to their faith yet given by physical nature ; for it gives us the arithmetical and measurable assurance that men vitally active are living sunshine, having the roots of their souls set in sunlight, as the roots of a tree are in the earth ; not that the dust is therefore the God of the tree, but the Tree is the animation of the dust, and the living Soul, of the sunshine. And now you will understand the meaning of the words on our St. George's wealth,— "Sit splendor."

And you must take care that your works do shine before men, if it may be, as a lamp ; but at least, as a shield ;—nay, if your Captain in Heaven wills it, as a sword.

For the failure of all good people nowadays is that, associating politely with wicked persons, countenancing them in their wickedness, and often joining in it, they think to avert its consequences by collaterally labouring to repair the ruin it has caused ; and while, in the morning, they satisfy their hearts by ministering to the wants of two or three destitute persons, in the evening they dine with, envy, and prepare themselves to follow the example of, the rich speculator who has caused the destitution of two or three thousand. They are thus destroying more in hours than they can amend in years ; or, at the best, vainly feeding the famine-struck populations, in the rear of a devouring army, always on the increase in mass of numbers, and rapidity of march.

Now I call on the St. George's Company, first, to separate themselves clearly, as a body, from persons who practise recognized, visible, unquestionable iniquity. They are to have no fellowship with the unfruitful works of Darkness ; but to walk as Children of Light.

Literally, observe. Those phrases of the Bible are entirely evaded, because we never apply them to immediate practice.

St. George's Companions are to have *no fellowship* with works of darkness ; no companionship whatsoever with recognizable mischief, or mischievous men. Of every person of your acquaintance, you are solemnly to ask yourselves, '*Is* this man a swindler, a liar, a gambler, an adulterer, a selfish oppressor, and taskmaster ?'

Don't suppose you can't tell. You can tell with perfect ease ; or, if you meet any mysterious personage of whom it proves difficult to ascertain whether he be rogue or not, keep clear of him till you know. With those whom you *know* to

be honest, *know* to be innocent, *know* to be striving, with
main purpose, to serve mankind and honour their God, you
are humbly and lovingly to associate yourselves : and with
none others.

"You don't like to set yourself up for being better
than other people? You dare not judge harshly of your
fellow-creatures?"

I do not tell you to judge them. I only tell you not
to dine with them, and not to deal with them. That they
lose the pleasure of your company, or the profit on your
custom, is no crushing punishment. To their own Master
they stand or fall ; but to *your* Master, Christ,* *you* must
stand, with your best might ; and in this manner only, self-
asserting as you may think it, can you confess Him before
men. Why do you suppose that thundrous word of His im-
pends over your denial of Him, "Whosoever shall deny me
before men, him will I also deny before Angels," but because
you are sure to be constantly tempted to such denial?

How, therefore, observe, in modern days, are you so
tempted. Is not the temptation rather, *as it seems*, to confess Him? Is it difficult and shameful to go to church?
—would it not require more courage to stay away? Is it
difficult or shameful to shut your shop on Sunday, in the
East,—or, to abstain from your ride in the Park on Sunday,
in the West? Is it dangerous to hold family worship in
your house, or dishonourable to be seen with a cross on your
Prayer Book? None of these modes or aspects of confession
will bring any outcry against you from the world. You will
have its good word, on the contrary, for each and all of them.
But declare that you mean to speak truth,—and speak it,
for an hour ; that you mean to abstain from luxury,—and
abstain from it, for a day ; that you, obeying God's law, will
resolutely refuse fellowship with the disobedient ;—and be
'not at home' to them, for a week : and hear *then* what the
High Priest's servants will say to you, round the fire.

And observe, it is in charity for them, much more than by

* I have got no Turks yet in the Company : when any join it, I will
give them Koran enough for what I ask of them.

duty to others, that you are required to do this. For half, at least, of these Caiaphas' servants sin through pure ignorance, confirmed by custom. The essential difference in business, for instance, between a man of honour and a rogue, is that the first tries to give as *much* to his customer for his money as he can, and the second to give as *little ;* but how many are at present engaged in business who are trying to sell their goods at as high a price as possible, supposing that effort to be the very soul and vital principle of business! Now by simply asserting to these ignorant persons that they *are* rogues, whether they know it or not ; and that, in the present era of general enlightenment, gentlemen and ladies must not only learn to spell and to dance, but also to know the difference between cheating their neighbours and serving them ; and that, as on the whole it is inexpedient to receive people who don't know how to express themselves grammatically, in the higher circles of society, much more is it inexpedient to receive those who don't know how to behave themselves honestly. And by the mere assertion, practically, of this assured fact to your acquaintance' faces, by the direct intervention of a deal door between theirs and yours, you will startle them out of their Rogues' Paradise in a most healthful manner, and be the most orthodox and eloquent evangelical preacher to them that they have ever heard since they were born.

But all this must, of course, be done with extreme tenderness and modesty, though with absolute decision ; and under much submission to their elders by young people—especially those living in their father's houses. I shall not, of course, receive any companions under age ; but already there are some names on my list of young unmarried women : and, while I have shown in all former writings that I hold the power of such to be the greatest, because the purest, of all social ones, I must as definitely now warn them against any manifestation of feeling or principle tending to break the unity of their home circles. They are bound to receive their father's friends as their own, and to comply in all sweet and subjected ways with the wishes and habits of their parents ;

remaining calmly certain that the Law of God, for them, is that while they remain at home they shall be spirits of Peace and Humility beneath its roof. In all rightly ordered households, the confidence between the parent and child is such that in the event of a parent's wish becoming contrary to a child's feeling of its general duty, there would be no fear or discomfort on the child's part in expressing its thoughts. The moment these are necessarily repressed, there is wrong somewhere ; and in houses ordered according to the ways of modern fashionable life, there *must* be wrong, often, and everywhere. But the main 'curse of modern society is that, beginning by training its youth to be 'independent' and disobedient, this carefully cultivated independence shows itself, of course, by rejecting whatever is noble and honourable in their father's houses, and never by healing or atoning what is faultful.

Of all St. George's young Companions, therefore, he requires first the graces of gentleness and humility ; nor, on the whole, much independent action of any kind ; but only the quiet resolve to find out what is absolutely right, and so far as it may be kindly and inoffensively practised to fulfil it, at home ; and so far as it may be modestly and decorously uttered, to express the same abroad. And a well-bred young lady has always personal power enough of favour and discouragement, among persons of her own age, to satisfy the extremest demands of conscience in this direction.

And now let me see what room I have left for talk of present matters. Here is a piece printed a fortnight since, which I can't be plagued to keep in type till next month.

CORPUS CHRISTI COLLEGE, OXFORD,
8th February, 1876.

I am fifty-seven to-day : and may perhaps be allowed to talk a little of myself.

Among several pretty love-letters from my pets, which only make me sorrier that I'm fifty-seven—but I really don't think some of the letters could be nicer if I were only twenty-seven—there's one with a ghost story in it, more precious to me than all the others, seeing I draw more quickly * near, now, daily, to the Loyal land.

I may as well write it as I read, thus :

" I heard such a pretty story last night of something that happened at a school in Germany, not long since. It was the custom of one of the masters to go round every night to the dormitories to see that the boys were asleep, all right. One night he was astonished to see a lady go up to one of the boys, stoop over him and kiss him, and then vanish. Next morning, news came that the mother of that particular boy had died at the time. Isn't it lovely ? Even A. believes that."

Yes ; and A. does wisely ; and so may B., and C.: but yet I should much like to know *what* particular boy, in what particular school in Germany.

Nevertheless, the story has more value for me because it is written to me by a person who herself saw the shade—or rather light—of her sister, at the time of that sister's death on the other side of the world ; being a member of that branch of my family in which some gift of the Scottish second sight remains, inherited by my maternal grandmother, who ran away with my paternal grandfather when she was not quite sixteen ; and my aunt Jessie, (my father's only sister,) was born a year afterwards ; a few weeks after which event, my grandmother, not yet seventeen, was surprised, (by a friend who came into her room unannounced,) dancing a threesome reel, with two chairs for her partners, she having found at the moment no other way of adequately expressing the pleasure she took in this mortal life, and its gifts, and promises.

The latter failed somewhat afterwards ; and my aunt Jessie, a very precious and perfect creature, beautiful in her dark-eyed, Highland way ; utterly religious, in her quiet Puritan way, and very submissive to Fates mostly unkind, married, or was married to—I never could make out exactly which, or why,—a somewhat rough tanner, with a fairly good business, in the good town of Perth ; and, when I was

* Every day taking more away than the one before it.

old enough to be taken first to visit them, as aforesaid, my aunt and my uncle the tanner lived in a good square-built gray stone house at the 'Bridge-End' of Perth, some fifty yards north of the bridge ; their garden sloping steeply to the Tay, which eddied, three or four feet deep of sombre crystal, round the steps where the servants dipped their pails.

My aggrieved correspondent of Wakefield thought to cure me with her delicate 'Fie,' of what she supposed my coarse habit of sneering at people of no ancestry. I have it not ; yet might have fallen into it in my youth, for I remember now, with more grief and shame than I can speak, being once ashamed of my own father and mother in Mr. Ryman's shop here in Oxford ; nor am I entirely at ease, at this moment, in writing of my uncles the baker and the tanner; yet my readers may trust me when I tell them, that in now remembering my dreams in the house of the entirely honest chief baker of Market Street, Croydon ; and of Peter—not Simon—the tanner, whose house was by the riverside of Perth, I would not change the dreams, far less the tender realities, of those early days, for anything I hear now remembered by lords or dames, of their days of childhood in castle halls, and by sweet lawns and lakes in park-walled forest.

I do not mean this for a republican sentiment ; quite the opposite. I hate republicans, as I do all other manner of fools. I love Lords and Ladies, (especially unmarried ones, with beautiful three-syllabled Christian-names. I know a simple two-syllabled one, also, very charming) ; and Earls, and Countesses, and Marquises, and Marchionesses, and Honourables, and Sirs ; and I bow down before them and worship them, in the way that Mr. Thackeray thought 'snobs' did ; he never perceiving with all the wit of him, (being mostly spent in mean smell-fungus work, which spoiled its scent,) that it is *himself* the snob truly worships, all the time, and not the Lord he looks at. But my way of worship was Walter Scott's, which my father taught me (always excepting such recreance as that in Mr. Ryman's shop). And therefore, when I say I would not change my dreams of Market Street, and Bridge End, and Rose Terrace, (where we used to live after my uncle died, briefly apoplectic, at Bridge End,) for anything that the Palatial and Maxime-Pontifical abodes of Nobles and Bishops give them—I mean simply that I had a home, being a child, and loved it, and did not then, and do not now, covet my neighbour's house ; * but cling to every likeness findable in these ruinous days to the places of peace given me in that lowly time.

Peace, and the knowledge of God it gave me. For, by the way, observe in that sacredest of benedictions, which my Dean gave me in my own cathedral last Sunday, (I being an honorary student of Christ Church ;—and there *are* only eight, if you please to look in the Oxford Calendar,) " The peace of God, which passeth all understanding, keep your hearts and minds in the knowledge and love of God ; "—observe, I say, for we do not always think of this, it is not the knowledge that is to give peace ; but the peace which is to give knowledge ; so that as long as we fast for strife and debate, and to smite with the fist of wickedness, and bite and devour one another, and are consumed one of another—every traveller paying an eight per cent. tax in his fare, for dividend to a consuming railroad company—we can't know anything about God at all. And compare again *Eagle's Nest*, p. 138.

There, then, at Rose Terrace, I lived in peace in the fair Scotch summer days, with my widowed aunt, and my little cousin Jessie, then traversing a bright space between her sixth and ninth year ; dark-eyed deeply, like her mother, and similarly pious ; and she and I used to compete in the Sunday evening Scriptural examinations ; and be as proud as two little peacocks because Jessie's elder brothers, and sister Mary, used to get ' put down,' and either Jessie or I was always ' Dux.' We agreed upon this that we would be married, when we were a little older ; not considering it preparatorily necessary to be in any degree wiser.

* Compare Letter XXI., p. 279.

9th February.

I couldn't go on about my cousin Jessie, for I was interrupted by the second post with more birthday compliments, from young ladies now about Jessie's age—letters which of course required immediate answer,—some also with flowers, which required to be immediately put into water, and greatly worried me by upsetting themselves among my books all day afterwards ; but I let myself be worried, for love ;—and, from a well-meaning and kindly feeling friend, some very respectful and respectable poetry, beautifully written, (and I read part of it, for love, but I had much rather he had sent me sixpence, for I hate poetry, mostly, and love pence, always) ; and to-day, half-past seven before chapel, my mind is otherwise set altogether, for I am reading Leviticus carefully now, for my life of Moses ; and, in working out the law of the feast of harvest, chanced on the notable verse, xxiii. 24 : "In the seventh month, in the first day of the month, shall ye have a Sabbath, a memorial of blowing of trumpets, an holy convocation ; " and then flashed on me, all in a minute, the real meaning of Holbein's introduction to the Dance of Death, (the third woodcut in the first edition,) which till this moment I only took for his own symbol of the Triumph of Death, adopted from Orcagna and others, but which I see now, in an instant, to be the *un*-Holy Convocation ; the gathering together to their temple of the Tribes of Death, and the blowing of trumpets on their solemn feast day, and sabbath of rest to the weary in evil doing.

And, busy friends, in the midst of all your charming preparations for the Spring season, you will do well to take some method of seeing that design, and meditating, with its help, upon the grave question, what kind of weariness *you* will have to rest from. My own thoughts of it are disturbed, as I look, by that drummer-death, in front,* with his rattling

---

* I have desired Mr. Ward to prepare small photographs of this design, in case any reader cares to have it,—but mind, it is not altogether done according to Mr. Stopford Brooke's notion of the object of true art, " to please "—(see page 88 of the *Manual of English Literature,* just published by that omniscient divine—under the auspices of the all-and-

and ringing kettledrums (*he* the chief Musician in the Psalm
for the sons of Korah—Dathan and Abiram, because his
sounding is on Skin, with sticks of Bone,) not only because
of my general interest in drummers, but because, after being
much impressed, when I was a child, by the verses I had to
learn about the last trump, out of the 15th of 1st Corinthians,
—when I became a man, and put away childish things, I used
often to wonder what we should all say of any sacred Saga
among poor Indians whose untutored mind sees God in clouds,
if it told them that they were all to rise from the dead at the
sound of the last drum.

And here I'm interrupted again by a delightful letter about
the resurrection of snails, Atropos really managing matters,
at present, like the daintiest and watchfullest housewife for
me,—everything in its place, and under my hand.

" Dear Mr. Ruskin,—As I have just read the last part of
February *Fors*, I want to say what I know about the little
shells (Helix virgata—I suppose). I think—indeed, am pretty
sure, nearly, if not quite—all those shells had little live snails
in them. I have found them in quantities on the South
Downs near Lewes, on Roundway Hill near Devizes, near
Lyme Regis, in North Wales ; and before any of those places,
on our own Hampton Common in Gloucestershire, where my
sisters and myself used to gather those and other pretty ones
when we were children. If you have any stored by, in a few
months I think you will find them (if not shut up) walk away.

" When I was a girl I once had to choose a birthday present from one of my aunts, and asked for *Turton's British
Shells*, for I always wanted to know the name and history of
everything I found ; then I collected all the land and fresh-
water shells I could find, as I could not get *sea* shells—one of
my longings—for I never saw the sea till after I was twenty,
except for a few hours at Munsley in Norfolk, when I was

---

sundry-scient Mr. T. R. Green, M.A.,— so, if you only want to be pleased,
you had better not order it. But at any rate, order, if you wish to understand the next coming *Fors*, the Etruscan Leucothea, for comparison
with your Lippi Madonna. Mr. Ward will have it ready with my signature about the time next *Fors* comes out ;—or you can get it unmounted,
for a shilling, from Mr. Parker's agent in Rome.

eight years old. I have my little shells still ; and have four
or five varieties of Helix virgata : I think the number of rings
increases as the shell goes on growing.

" In the autumn these shells are often suddenly observed
in such great numbers as to give rise to the popular notion of
their having fallen from the clouds. This shell is very hardy,
and appears nearly insensible to cold, as it does not hiber-
nate even when the ground is covered with snow.

" I always fancied the Lord let them lie about in such
numbers to be food for some little birds, or may be rooks and
starlings, robins, etc., in cold weather when there was so little
to eat.

" I dare say you know how the blackbirds and thrushes eat
the larger snails. I have often seen in the woods a very
pretty coloured shell lying on a white stone,—the birds had
put it there to crack a hole in it and to take out the snail.
The shell looked such a pretty clear colour because it was
alive, and yet empty."

Yes ; the Holy Ghost of Life, not yet finally departed, can
still give fair colours even to an empty shell. Evangelical
friends,—worms, as you have long called yourselves, here is a·
deeper expression of humility suggested possible : may not
some of you be only painted shells of worms,—alive, yet
empty ?

Assuming my shell to be Helix virgata, I take down my
magnificent French—(let me see if I can write its title
without a mistake)—*Manuel de Conchyliologie et de Palé-
ontologie Conchyliologique*, or, in English, "Manual of Shell-
talking and Old-body-talking in a Shell-talking manner."
Eight hundred largest octavo—more like folio—pages of close
print, with four thousand and odd (nearly five thousand) exquisite engravings of shells ; and among them I look for the
creatures elegantly, but inaccurately, called by modern naturalists Gasteropods ; in English, Belly-feet, (meaning, of
course, to say Belly-walkers, for they haven't got any feet) ;
and among these I find, with much pains, one that is rather
like mine, of which I am told that it belongs to the sixteenth
sort in the second tribe of the second family of the first sub-
order of the second order of the Belly-walkers, and that it is

called ' Adeorbis subcarinatus,'—Adeorbis by Mr. Wood, and
subcarinatus by Mr. Montagu ; but I am not told where it is
found, nor what sort of creature lives in it, nor any single
thing whatever about it, except that it is " sufficiently depressed," (" assez déprimée "), and " deeply enough navelled "
(assez profondement ombiliquée,—but how on earth can I tell
when a shell is navelled to a depth, in the author's opinion,
satisfactory ?) and that the turns (taken by the family), are
'little numerous' (peu nombreux). On the whole, I am not
disposed to think my shell is here described, and put my
splendid book in its place again.

I next try my English Cuvier, in sixteen octavo volumes ;
in which I find no notice whatever taken of these minor
snails, except a list of thirty-three species, finishing with an
etc. ; out of which I mark 'Cretacea,' 'Terrestris,' and
' Nivea,' as perhaps likely to fit mine ; and then I come, by
order of Atropos, on this amazing account of the domestic
arrangements of a little French snail, " Helix decollata "
(Guillotined snail ?) with references to " Cm. Chemn. cxxxvi.
1254—1257," a species which " has the singular habit of
successively fracturing the whorls at the top, (origin, that is,
—snails building their houses from heaven towards earth,) of
the spire, so that at a particular epoch, of all the whorls of
the spire originally possessed by this bulimus, not a single
one remains." Bulimus,—what's a bulimus ? Helix is certainly a screw, and bulimus—in my Riddle's dictionary—is
said to be " empty-bellied." Then this French snail, revolu-
tionary in the manner of a screw, appears to be a belly-walker
with an empty belly, and no neck,—who literally " breaks
up " his establishment every year ! Query—breaks ? or
melts ? Confraction or confusion ?

I must put my fine English book back in its place, too ;—
but here, at last, comes a ' work of light' to help us, from my
favourite pupil, who was out with me that day on the Downs,
and nearly killed himself with keeping a fox in sight on foot,
up and down them ; happily surviving, he has pursued the
slower creature for me to its cave of silver earth ; and writes
thus.

" I have sent you two little boxes—one containing common garden snail shells of various ages, and the other black striped Down shells ; and you will see that in box 1 the full-grown ones, with the strong finished lip, have four whorls each, and all the full-grown garden shells I have noticed had the same number, though they varied a little in size.   The next largest in the box have only three and a half turns, but if they had lived longer they would have added on another half turn, bigger than all the rest of the shell put together.   In fact, if one looks at this shell, one sees that any half whorl is half as large again as all the rest of the shell before it.   Then, be-

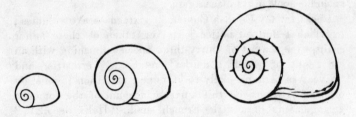

sides these, there are four or five younger shells, the smallest of which has only two and a half whorls, which exactly cor- respond to two and a half whorls taken from any of the larger shells ; so I think we may conclude that a shell grows by adding on *length only* to the large end of a tapering tube, like a dunce's cap, which, however, is curled up like a ram's horn, to look prettier, take up less room, and allow the occu- pant to beat a retreat round the corner when a robin comes. By-the-bye, I wonder some birds don't grow bills like cork- screws, to get at the snails with.

" Then in box No. 2 there are several black striped Down shells, and the full-grown ones have six whorls, and the smallest ones, which died young, some four and some five, according to age ; but the dunce's cap is longer, and so there are more whorls.

" I couldn't get these facts clearly stated in two hand- books which I read. I suppose they took it for granted that one knew ; but I found, what after all would lead one to infer the rest, that the young snail at birth corresponds to the colourless APEX of the shell, and that the colour only comes in that part which grows under the influence of light and air."

" Another fact is, that all the shells I ever remember looking at grow in the direction of the sun.

" Another fact. Since the shells have been in this room, my chimneypiece has been full of sleepy, small, long-bodied spiders, which had gone to sleep for the winter in these black and white caverns, out of the reach of flocks of half-starved larks and starlings."

I drew the three advancing stages of the common snail's houses, thus sent me, forthwith ; and Mr. Burgess swiftly and rightly engraves them. Note that the apparent irregularities in the spirals are conditions of perspective, necessarily affecting the deeply projecting forms ; note also that each whorl is partly hidden by the subsequent one, built with its edge lapping over it ; and finally, that there is really, I believe, a modification, to some extent, and enlargement, of the inner whorls ; until the domestic creature is satisfied with its length of cave, and expresses its rest in accomplished labour and full age, by putting that binding lip round its border, and term to its hope.

Wherein, building for the earth, we may wisely imitate it. Of other building, not with slime for mortar, yet heavenward, we may perhaps conceive in due time.

I beg all my readers, but especially my Companions, to read with their best care the paper by Mr. Girdlestone, which, by the author's kindly gift, I am enabled to send them with this *Fors.* It is the most complete and logical statement of Economic truth, in the points it touches, that I have ever seen in the English language : and to master it will be the best possible preparation for the study of personal duties to which I shall invite my Companions in my next letter.

NOTES AND CORRESPONDENCE.

I. Affairs of the Company.

I give below our banker's account to the end of last year, drawn up by my friend Mr. W. Walker, whom I asked to take salary as the Company's accountant, but who, as will be seen by the part of his letter I take leave here to print, gives us his work in true sympathy.

18, YONGE PARK, HOLLOWAY, N., *Nov.* 11*th*, 1875.

Dear Sir,—I am of the same opinion as your printseller, and agree with him that "it is delightful to do business with you,"—so you must please let me volunteer to be of any practical service so far as keeping accounts, etc., can be useful to you or the St. George's Company.

I readily accept the duties as *honorary* but not *titled* accountant, and as the labour is light, entailing very little trouble, my reward shall be the self-satisfaction in thinking I have done very little in the cause wherein you have done and are doing so very much.

Nevertheless, your kindly worded offer was gratefully received, and I was really pleased.

The enclosed accounts are a mere copy of the ledger items. I would have put all the names of the donors, (I found a few,) but you have a record, if I may judge from the notices in the December number of *Fors.*

With sincere respect, yours faithfully,

John Ruskin, Esq., LL. D.   WM. WALKER.

Dr. THE UNION BANK OF LONDON (CHANCERY LANE BRANCH) IN ACCOUNT WITH ST. GEORGE'S FUND. *Cr.*

		£	s.	d.			£	s.	d.
1872.					**1872.**				
Nov. 27.	To Cash..................	100	0	0	Dec. 4. By Cheque Book..........		0	4	2
Dec. 11.	" Draft at Peckham......	25	0	0	Dec. 27. Power of Attorney to receive Dividend on Consols....		0	5	0
					Dec. 31. By Balance..........		124	10	10
		£125	0	0			£125	0	0
1873					**1873.**				
Jan. 1.	To Balance.............	124	10	10	March 13. By Postage..........		0	0	3
Jan. 2.	" John Ruskin, Esq.....	30	0	0					
Feb 10.	" Ditto	20	0	0					
"	" Dividend on Consols, Jan., 1872	29	5	0					
"	" Ditto July, 1872	103	5	0					
"	" Ditto Jan., 1873	103	5	0					
April 15.	" Draft at Blackheath.....	7	0	0					
June 10.	" Draft at Bury St. Edmund's...	13	10	0					
July 8.	" R. J. Tyrwhitt..........	20	0	0					
July 9	" Dividend on £7000 Consols...	103	13	9					
July 29	" John Ruskin, Esq.......	20	0	0					
July 30.	" No. 18...............	5	0	0	By Balance..........		579	9	4
		£579	9	7			£579	9	7

THE UNION BANK OF LONDON (Chancery Lane Branch) IN ACCOUNT WITH ST. GEORGE'S FUND.

Dr.		£	s.	d.	Cr.		£	s.	d.
1874.					**1874.**				
Jan. 1.	To Balance....................	579	9	4	Dec. 10. By Postage..................		0	0	3
	" Interest on Current Account Balance......	2	13	4	" Purchase of £1000 Consols......		918	15	0
	" Draft at Durham by A. Hunt	25	0	0					
Jan. 7.	" Dividend on £7000 Consols......	103	13	9					
Jan. 17.	" John Ruskin, Esq.......	31	10	0					
Feb. 13.	" Cash....................	10	0	0					
July 1.	" Interest on Current Account Balance......	7	4	8					
July 8.	" Dividend on £7000 Consols......	104	*2	6					
Dec. 3.	" John Ruskin, Esq........	20	0	0					
Dec. 6.	" Ditto	*40	0	0					
Dec. 5.	" Draft at Bilston (Wilkins)........	5	0	0					
Dec. 11.	" H. F. Smith.............	9	0	0					
	" E. R. Gill.............	5	0	0					
	" Mrs. Barnard............	1	13	4					
	" J. Temple.............	5	0	0					
Dec. 28.	" Draft at Sheffield (Fowler)........	20	0	0	By Balance.............		50	11	8
		£969	6	11			£969	6	11

* The £40 here acknowledged was an additional subscription from No. 8 subscriber, whose total subscription is therefore £60, not £20, as in above subscriber's account; in which also the initials of No. 38 should be S. G., and the sum £2 2s. These errors will be corrected in next *Fors*, in which also I will separate the interest from the subscriptions.

THE UNION BANK OF LONDON (CHANCERY LANE BRANCH) IN ACCOUNT WITH ST. GEORGE'S FUND.

Dr.		£	s.	d.		Cr.	£	s.	d.
1875.						**1875.**			
Jan. 1.	To Balance..........	50	11	8		Nov. 13. By Cheque to John Ruskin, Esq	500	0	0
Jan. 7.	" Dividend on £7000 Consols.....	104	2	6					
Feb. 4.	" John Ruskin, Esq..........	105	10	0					
Feb. 8.	" Draft at Manchester (Walker)...	1	1	0					
March 1.	" John Ruskin, Esq..........	17	2	0					
March 5.	" Ditto	8	17	0					
"	" Draft at Bilston (Wilkins).......	8	3	4					
April 23.	" Irvine................	1	0	0					
May 1.	" John Ruskin, Esq.............	20	0	0					
July 7.	" Dividend on £8000 Consols.....	119	0	0					
July 15.	" John Ruskin, Esq.............	50	0	0					
Sept. 11.	" G. Gilbert.............	5	0	0					
Sept. 28.	" Draft at Bridgewater (Talbot)...	11	0	4					
Nov. 23.	" By G. Allen..............	12	14	0		Dec. 31. By Balance......	14	1	10
		£514	1	10			£514	1	10
1876.		£	s.	d.					
Jan. 1.	To Balance......	14	1	10					

II. Affairs of the Master.*

		£	s.	d.
Balance in Bank, 20th Jan., 1876		527	17	9
Received: Mr. Allen, on Publishing Account		50	0	0
Mr. Ellis, on ditto		7	0	0
Lecture, London Institution		10	10	0
		595	7	9

Jan.	24.	Royal Insurance Company (*a*)	37 10 0			
	27.	F. Crawley (*b*)	25 0 0			
	31.	Taxes on Armorial Bearings, etc.	7 19 0			
Feb.	4.	Warren and Jones—Tea for Shop	36 1 0			
	6.	Buying a lad off who had enlisted and repented	20 0 0			
	7.	Christmas Gifts in Oxford	14 10 0			
	7.	Klein (*c*)	5 0 0			
	7.	Pocket Money	10 10 0			
	7.	Crawley	5 0 0			
	8.	Miss Rudkin, Clifford Street (*d*)	14 14 0			
	11.	Dr. Parsons (*e*)	21 0 0			
	11.	The Bursar of Corpus (*f*)	27 7 3			
	13.	Professor Westwood (*g*)	50 0 0			
	14.	Mr. Sly (*h*), Coniston, Waterhead Inn	33 0 0			
	19.	Downs (*i*)	25 0 0			
	20.	Subscriptions to Societies, learned and other (*k*)	37 11 0			
				360	2	0

Balance Feb. 20 ....£225 5 9

(*a*) Insurance on £15,000 worth of drawings and books in my rooms at Oxford.

(*b*) Particulars of this account to be afterwards given ; my Oxford assistant having just lost his wife, and been subjected to unusual expenses.

(*c*) My present valet, a delightful old German, on temporary service.

(*d*) Present, on my birthday, of a silk frock to one of my pets. It became her very nicely; but I think there was a little too much silk in the flounces.

(*e*) My good doctor at Coniston. Had to drive over from Hawkshead every other winter day, because I wouldn't stop drinking too much tea—also my servants were ill.

(*f*) About four times this sum will keep me comfortably—all the year round—here among my Oxford friends—when I have reduced myself to the utmost allowable limit of a St. George's Master's income—366 pounds a year, (the odd pound for luck).

* My friends (see a really kind article in the *Monetary Gazette*,) much doubt, and very naturally, the wisdom of this exposition. I indeed expected to appear to some better advantage ; but that the confession is not wholly pleasant, and appears imprudent, only makes it the better example. Fors would have it so.

(*g*) For copies of the Book of Kells, bought of a poor artist Very beautiful, and good for gifts to St. George.

(*h*) My honest host (happily falsifying his name), for friends when I haven't houseroom, etc. This bill chiefly for hire of carriages.

(*i*) Downs shall give account of himself in next *Fors*.

(*k*)	£	s.		£	s.
Athenæum	7	7	Historical	1	1
Alpine Club	1	1	Anthropological	2	2
Early English Text Society	10	10	Consumption Hospital	3	3
Horticultural	4	4	Lifeboat	5	0
Geological	2	2			
Architectural	1	1		£37	11

LETTER LXIV.

I WILL begin my letter to-day with our Bible lesson, out of which other necessary lessons will spring. We must take the remaining three sons of Ham together, in relation to each other and to Israel.

Mizraim, the Egyptian ; Phut, the Ethiopian ; Sidon, the Sidonian : or, in breadth of meaning the three African powers,—A, of the watered plain, B, of the desert, and C, of the sea ; the latter throning itself on the opposite rocks of Tyre, and returning to culminate in Carthage.

A. Egypt is essentially the Hamite slavish *strength* of body and intellect.

B. Ethiopia, the Hamite slavish *affliction* of body and intellect ; condemnation of the darkened race that can no more change its skin than the leopard its spots ; yet capable, in its desolation of nobleness. Read the "What doth hinder me to be baptized?—If thou believest with all thine heart thou mayest" of the Acts ; and after that the description in the *Daily Telegraph* (first Monday of March), of the Nubian king, with his sword and his Bible at his right hand, and the tame lioness with her cubs, for his playmates, at his left.

C. Tyre is the Hamite slavish *pleasure* of sensual and idolatrous art, clothing her nakedness with sea purple. She is lady of all beautiful carnal pride, and of the commerce that feeds it,—her power over the Israelite being to beguile, or help for pay, as Hiram.

But Ethiopia and Tyre are always connected with each other : Tyre, the queen of commerce ; Ethiopia, her gold-bringing slave ; the redemption of these being Christ's utmost victory. "They of Tyre, with the Morians—*there*, even *there*, was He born." "Then shall princes come out of Egypt, and Ethiopia stretch forth her hands unto God."

" He shall let go my captives, not for price ; and the *labour* of Egypt, and *merchandise* of Ethiopia, shall come over unto thee, and shall be thine." *

Learn now after the fifteenth, also the sixteenth verse of Genesis x., and read the fifteenth chapter with extreme care. If you have a good memory, learn it by heart from beginning to end ; it is one of the most sublime and pregnant passages in the entire compass of ancient literature.

Then understand generally that the spiritual meaning of Egyptian slavery is *labour without hope*, but having all the reward, and all the safety, of labour absolute. Its beginning is to discipline and adorn the body,—its end is to embalm the body ; its religion is first to restrain, then to judge, " whatsoever things are done in the body, whether they be good or evil." Therefore, whatever may be well done by measure and weight,—what force may be in geometry, mechanism, and agriculture, bodily exercise, and dress ; reverent esteem of earthly birds, and beasts, and vegetables ; reverent preparation of pottage, good with flesh ;—these shall Egypt teach and practise, to her much comfort and power. " And when Jacob heard that there was corn in Egypt, he called his sons."

And now remember the scene at the threshing floor of Atad (Gen. 50th, 10 and 11).

" A grievous mourning." They embalmed Jacob. They put him in a coffin. They dutifully bore him home, for his son's sake. Whatsoever may well be done of earthly deed, they do by him and his race. And the end of it all, for *them*, is a grievous mourning.

Then, for corollary, remember,—all fear of death, and embalming of death, and contemplating of death, and mourning for death, is the pure bondage of Egypt.

And whatsoever is formal, literal, miserable, material,

---

* Psalm lxviii. 31 ; lxxxiii. 7 and 8 ; lxxxvii. 4 ; Isaiah xlv. 14. I am not sure of my interpretation of the 87th Psalm ; but, as far as any significance exists in it to our present knowledge, it can only be of the power of the Nativity of Christ to save Rahab the harlot, Philistia the giant, Tyre the trader, and Ethiopia the slave.

in the deeds of human life, is the preparatory bondage of Egypt; of which, nevertheless, some formalism, some literalism, some misery, and some flesh-pot comfort, will always be needful for the education of such beasts as we are. So that, though, when Israel was a child, God loved him, and called his son out of Egypt, He preparatorily sent him *into* Egypt. And the first deliverer of Israel had to know the wisdom of Egypt before the wisdom of Arabia; and for the last deliverer of Israel, the dawn of infant thought, and the first vision of the earth He came to save, was under the palms of Nile.

Now, therefore, also for all of us, Christians in our nascent state of muddy childhood, when Professor Huxley is asking ironically, 'Has a frog a soul?' and scientifically directing young ladies to cut out frogs' stomachs to see if they can find it,—whatsoever, I say, in our necessary education among that scientific slime of Nile, is formal, literal, miserable, and material, is necessarily Egyptian.

As, for instance, brickmaking, scripture, flogging, and cooking,—upon which four heads of necessary art I take leave to descant a little.

And first of brickmaking. Every following day the beautiful arrangements of modern political economists, obeying the law of covetousness instead of the law of God, send me more letters from gentlemen and ladies asking me 'how they are to live'?

Well, my refined friends, you will find it needful to live, if it be with success, according to God's Law; and to love that law, and make it your meditation all the day. And the first uttered article in it is, "In the sweat of thy face thou shalt eat bread."

"But you don't really expect us to work with our hands, and make ourselves hot?"

Why, who, in the name of Him who made you, are you then, that you shouldn't? Have you got past the flaming sword, back into Eden; and is your celestial opinion there that we miserable Egyptians are to work outside, here, for *your* dinners, and hand them through the wall to you at a

tourniquet ? or, as being yet true servants of the devil, while
you are blessed, dish it up to you, spiritually hot, through a
trap-door ?

Fine anti-slavery people you are, forsooth ! who think it
is right not only to make slaves, but *accursed* slaves, of
other people, that you may slip your dainty necks out of the
collar !

" Ah, but we thought Christ's yoke had *no* collar ! "

It is time to know better. There may come a day, indeed,
when there shall be no more curse ;—in the meantime, you
must be humble and honest enough to take your share of it.

So what *can* you do, that's useful ? Not to ask too much
at first ; and, since we are now coming to particulars,
addressing myself first to gentlemen,—Do you think you
can make a brick, or a tile ?

You rather think not ? Well, if you are healthy, and fit
for work, and can do nothing better,—go and learn.

You would rather not ? Very possibly : but you can't
have your dinner unless you do. And why would you so
much rather not ?

" So ungentlemanly ! "

No ; to beg your dinner, or steal it, is ungentlemanly.
But there is nothing ungentlemanly, that I know of, in beating clay, and putting it in a mould.

" But my wife wouldn't like it ! "

Well, that's a strong reason : you shouldn't vex your
wife, if you can help it ; but why will she be vexed ? If she
is a nice English girl, she has pretty surely been repeating
to herself, with great unction, for some years back, that
highly popular verse,—

> " The trivial round, the common task,
>   Will give us all we ought to ask,—
>   Room to deny ourselves ; a road
>   To bring us daily nearer God."

And this, which I recommend, is not a trivial round, but an
important square, of human business ; and will certainly
supply any quantity of room to deny yourselves in ; and will

bring you quite as near God as, for instance, writing lawyers' letters to make appointments, and charging five shillings each for them.   The only difference will be that, instead of getting five shillings for writing a letter, you will
only get it for a day and a half's sweat of the brow.

"Oh, but my wife didn't mean *that* sort of 'common task'
at all !"

No ; but your wife didn't know what she meant ; neither
did Mr. Keble.   Women and clergymen have so long been
in the habit of using pretty words without ever troubling
themselves to understand them, that they now revolt from
the effort, as if it were an impiety.   So far as your wife had
any meaning at all, it was that until she was made an angel
of, and had nothing to do but be happy, and sing her flatter-
ing opinions of God for evermore,—dressing herself and her
children becomingly, and leaving cards on her acquaintances,
were sufficiently acceptable services to Him, for which trivial
though they were, He would reward her with immediate
dinner, and everlasting glory.   That was your wife's real
notion of the matter, and modern Christian women's generally,
so far as they have got any notions at all under their bonnets,
and the skins of the dead robins they have stuck in them,—
the disgusting little savages.   But that is by no means the
way in which either your hands are to be delivered from
making the pots, or her head from carrying them.

Oh, but you will do it by deputy, and by help of capital,
will you ?   Here is the Grand Junction Canal Brick, Tile,
and Sanitary Pipe Company, Limited ; Capital, £50,000, in
10,000 shares of £5 each; "formed for the purpose of pur-
chasing and working an estate comprising fifty-eight acres
of land known as the 'Millpost Field,' and 'The Duddles,'
situate at Southall, in the county of Middlesex."   You will
sit at home, serene proprietor, not able, still less willing, to
lift so much as a spadeful of Duddles yourself ; but you will
feed a certain number of brickmaking Ethiopian slaves
thereon, as cheap as you can ; and teach them to make bricks,
as basely as they can ; and you will put the meat out of
their mouths into your own, and provide for their eternal

salvation by gracious ministries from Uxbridge. A clerical friend of mine in that neighbourhood has, I hear, been greatly afflicted concerning the degenerate natures of brickmakers. Let him go and make, and burn, a pile or two with his own hands ; he will thereby receive apocalyptic visions of a nature novel to his soul. And if he ever succeeds in making one good brick, (the clay must lie fallow in wind and sun two years before you touch it, my master Carlyle tells me,) he will have done a good deed for his generation which will be acknowledged in its day by the Stone of Israel, when the words of many a sermon will be counted against their utterers, every syllable as mere insolent breaking of the third commandment.

In the meantime, it seems that no gracious ministries from Uxbridge, or elsewhere, can redeem this untoward generation of brickmakers. Like the navvies of Furness, (Letter XI., p. 143,) they are a fallen race, fit for nothing but to have dividends got out of them, and then be damned. My fine-lady friends resign themselves pacifically to that necessity, though greatly excited, I perceive, at present, concerning vivisection. In which warmth of feeling they are perfectly right, if they would only also remember that England is spending some thirty millions of pounds a year in making machines for the vivisection, not of dogs, but men ; nor is this expenditure at all for anatomical purposes ; but, in the real root of it, merely to maintain the gentlemanly profession of the Army, and the ingenious profession of Engineers.

Oh, but we don't want to live by soldiering, any more than by brickmaking ; behold, we are intellectual persons, and wish to live by literature.

Well, it is a slavish trade,—true. Hamite ; nevertheless, if we will learn our elements in true Egyptian bondage, some good may come of it.

For observe, my literary friends, the essential function of the slavish Egyptian, in the arts of the world, is to lose the picture in the letter ; as the essential function of the Eleutherian Goth is to illuminate the letter into the picture.

The Egyptian is therefore the scribe of scribes,—the supremely literary person of earth. The banks of Nile give him his rock volume : the reeds of Nile his paper roll. With cleaving chisel, and cloven reed, he writes thereon, exemplarily : the ark which his princess found among the paper reeds, is the true beginning of libraries,—Alexandrian, and all other. What you call Scripture, in special, coming out of it ; the first portion written in Egyptian manner, (it is said,) with the finger of God. Scribe and lawyer alike have too long forgotten the lesson,—come now and learn it again, of Theuth, with the ibis beak.*

When next you are in London on a sunny morning, take leisure to walk into the old Egyptian gallery of the British Museum, after traversing which for a third of its length, you will find yourself in the midst of a group of four massy sarcophagi,—two on your left, two on your right. Assume

B   ↑   **C**

that they are represented by the letters on the cut, and that you are walking in the direction of the arrow, so that you have the sarcophagi A and B on your left, and the sarcophagi C and D on your right.

In my new *Elements of Drawing,* I al-

A | **D**

ways letter the corners of a square all round thus, so that A C is always the diagonal, A B the upright side on the left, and A D the base.

The sarcophagus A is a king's ; B, a scribe's ; C, a queen's; and D, a priest's.

A is of a grand basaltic rock with veins full of agates, and white onyx,—the most wonderful piece of crag I know ; B and C are of grey porphyry ; D of red granite.

The official information concerning sarcophagus A, (Nectabenes,) is to the effect that it dates from the 30th dynasty, or about 380 B.C.

B, (Hapimen,) of the 26th dynasty, or about 525.

C, (the Queen's,) of the same dynasty and period.

D, (Naskatu,) of the 27th dynasty, or about 500 B.C.

The three sarcophagi, then, B, C, and D, were, (we are

---

* Letter XVII., p. 227.

told,) cut exactly at the time when, beyond the North Sea, Greek art, just before Marathon, was at its grandest.

And if you look under the opened lid of the queen's, you will see at the bottom of it the outline portrait, or rather symbol, of her, engraved, with the hawk for her crest, signifying what hope of immortality or power after death remained to her.

But the manner of the engraving you must observe. This is all that the Egyptian Holbein could do on stone, after a thousand years at least of practised art; while the Greeks, who had little more than begun only two hundred years before, were already near to the strength of carving their Theseus, perfect for all time.

This is the Hamite bondage in Art: of which the causes will teach themselves to us as we work, ourselves. Slavery is good for us in the beginning, and for writing-masters we can find no better than these Mizraimites: see what rich lines of Scripture they are, along the black edges of those tombs. To understand at all how well they are done, we must at once begin to do the like, in some sort ourselves.

By the exercise given in *Fors* of January, if you have practised it, you have learned something of what is meant by merit and demerit in a pure line, however produced. We must now consider of our tools a little.

You can make a mark upon things in three ways—namely, by scratching them, painting on them with a brush, or letting liquid run on them out of a pen. Pencil or chalk marks are merely a kind of coarse painting with dry material.

The primitive and simplest mark is the scratch or cut, which shall be our first mode of experiment. Take a somewhat blunt penknife, and a composition candle; and scratch or cut a fine line on it with the point of the knife, drawing the sharp edge of the knife towards you.

Examine the trace produced through a magnifying glass, and you will find it is an angular ditch with a little ridge raised at its side, or sides, pressed out of it.

Next, scratch the candle with the point of the knife, turn-

ing the side of the blade forwards : you will now cut a
broader furrow, but the wax or composition will rise out of
it before the knife in a beautiful spiral shaving, formed like
the most lovely little crimped or gathered frill ; which I've
been trying to draw, but can't ; and if *you* can, you will be
far on the way to drawing spiral staircases, and many other
pretty things.

Nobody, so far as I have myself read, has yet clearly explained why a wood shaving, or continuously driven portion
of detached substance, should thus take a spiral course ; nor
why a substance like wax or water, capable of yielding to
pressure, should rise or fall under a steady force in successive undulations. Leaving these questions for another time,
observe that the first furrow, with the ridge at its side, represents the entire group of incised lines ploughed in soft
grounds, the head of them all being the plough furrow itself. And the line produced by the flat side of the knife is
the type of those produced by complete *excision*, the true
engraver's.

Next, instead of wax, take a surface of wood, and, drawing first as deep and steady a furrow in it as you can with
the edge of the knife, proceed to deepen it by successive
cuts.

You will, of course, find that you must cut from the two
sides, sloping to the middle, forming always a deeper angular
ditch ; but you will have difficulty in clearing all out neatly
at the two ends.

And if you think of it, you will perceive that the sim
plest conceivable excision of a clear and neat kind must be
that produced by three cuts given triangularly.* For
though you can't clear out the hollow with two touches, you
need not involve yourself in the complexity of four.

And unless you take great pains in keeping the three
sides of this triangle equal, two will be longer than the

---

* You may indeed dip softly into the ground and rise gradually out
of it ; but this will give you not a clear, but an infinitely graduated excision, exquisite in drawing, but not good for writing.

third. So the type of the primitive incised mark is what grand persons call ' cuneiform '—wedge-shaped.

If you cut five such cuneiform incisions in a star group, thus, with a little circle connecting them in the middle, you will have the element of the decorative upper border both on the scribe's coffin and the queen's. You will also have an elementary picture of a starfish—or the portrait of the pentagonal and absorbent Adam and Eve who were your ancestors, according to Mr. Darwin.

You will see, however, on the sarcophagi that the rays are not equidistant, but arranged so as to express vertical position,—of that afterwards ; to-day observe only the manner of their cutting ; and then on a flat surface of porphyry,— do the like yourself.

You don't know what porphyry is—nor where to get it ? Write to Mr. Tennant, 149, Strand, and he will send you a little bit as cheap as he can. Then you must get a little vice to fix it, and a sharp-pointed little chisel, and a well-poised little hammer ; and, when you have cut your asterisk, you will know more about Egypt than nine hundred and ninety-nine people out of a thousand,—Oxford scholars and all. Awaiting the result of your experiment, I proceed to the other instrument of writing, the reed, or pen.

Of which the essential power is that it can make a narrow stroke sideways, and a broad one when you press it open.

Now our own current writing, I told you, is to be equal in thickness of line. You will find that method the quickest and servicablest. But in quite beautiful writing, the power of the pen is to be exhibited with decision ; and of its purest and delicatest exertion, you will see the result on the opposite page ; facsimile by Mr. Burgess, coloured afterwards by hand, from a piece of Lombardic writing, of about the eleventh century,—(I shall not say where the original is, because I don't want it to be fingered)—which the scribe has entirely delighted in doing, and of which every line and touch is perfect in its kind. Copy it, with what precision you can, (and mind how you put in the little blue dash to thicken the s of Fides,) for in its perfect uprightness, exquisite use of the diamond-shaped touches obtained by mere pressure on the point, and reserved administration of colour, it is a model not to be surpassed ; standing precisely halfway between old Latin letters and mediæval Gothic. The legend of it is—

"Fides catholica edita ab Athana-
sio Alexandrie sedis episcopo."

Towards the better understanding of which Catholic faith, another step may be made, if you will, by sending to Mr. Ward for the Etruscan Leucothea,* with Dionysus on her knees, which also stands just half-way in imagination, though only a quarter of the way in time, between the Egyptian Madonna, (Isis with Horus,) of fifteen hundred years before Christ, and the Florentine Madonna by Lippi, fifteen hundred years after Christ. Lippi, being true-bred Etruscan, simply raises the old sculpture into pure and sacred life, retaining all its forms, even to the spiral of the throne ornament, and the transgression of the figures on the bordering frame, acknowledging, in this subjection to the thoughts and laws of his ancestors, a nobler Catholic Faith than Athanasius wrote : faith, namely, in that one Lord by whose breath, from the beginning of creation, the children of men are born ; and into whose hands, dying, they give up their spirit.

This photograph of Etruscan art is therefore to be the second of our possessions, and means of study ; affording us at once elements of art-practice in many directions, according to our strength ; and as we began with drawing the beads of cap, and spiral of chair, in the Lippi, rather than the Madonna, so here it will be well to be sure we can draw the throne, before we try the Leucothea. Outline it first by

---

* I take the title of this relief from Mr. Parker's catalogue, not being certain of the subject myself, and rather conceiving it to be Latona with Apollo.

the eye, then trace the original, to correct your drawing ; and by the time next *Fors* comes out, I hope your power of drawing a fine curve, like that of the back of this throne, will be materially increased ; by that time also I shall have got spirals to compare with these Etruscan ones, drawn from shells only an hour or two old, sent me by my good friend Mr. Sillar, (who taught me the wrongness of the infinite spiral of money interest,) by which I am at present utterly puzzled, finding our conclusions in last *Fors* on this point of zoology quite wrong ; and that the little snails have no less twisted houses than the large. But neither for drawing nor architecture is there to-day more time, but only to correct and clarify my accounts, which I have counted a little too far on my power of keeping perspicuous without trouble ; and have thereby caused my subscribers and myself a good deal more than was needful.

Henceforward I must ask their permission, unless I receive definite instruction to the contrary, to give names in full, as the subscriptions come in, and give up our occult notation.

I am not quite so well pleased with my good friend Mr. Girdlestone's pamphlet on luxury as I was with that on classification of society, though I am heartily glad to be enabled by him to distribute it to my readers, for its gentle statements may be more convincing than my impatient ones. But I must protest somewhat against their mildness. It is not now merely dangerous, but criminal, to teach the lie that the poor live by the luxury of the rich. Able men—even Pope himself—have been betrayed into thinking so in old times, (blaming the luxury, however, no less,) but the assertion is now made by no intelligent person, unless with the deliberate purpose of disguising abuses on which all the selfish interests of society depend.

I have to acknowledge a quite magnificent gift of Japanese inlaid work to our Sheffield Museum, from my kind friend Mr. Willett, of Arnold House, Brighton. A series of some fifty pieces was offered by him for our selection : but I have only accepted a tithe of them, thinking that the fewer examples of each school we possess, the better we shall learn from them. Three out of the five pieces I have accepted are of quite unsurpassable beauty, and the two others of extreme interest. They are sent to the Curator at Sheffield.

NOTES AND CORRESPONDENCE.

I. Affairs of the Company.

I give on next two pages our banker's account to 14th March of this year. Calling this "Account B," and that given to the end of last year, in last *Fors*, "Account A," the following abstract of both is, I hope, accurate.

```
By Account A:                            £   s.  d.
    Cash paid into bank  ................653  1   0
    Interest accumulated ................780  5   6
By Account B :
    Cash paid into bank ..................324 11   1
    Interest ...............................119  0   0
                                                     _____
        Giving total to our credit...................1876 17   7

Per contra, we have—
    Petty expenses........................  0 10   9
    Purchase of £1000 Consols ............918 15   0
    Cheques to myself.....................800  0   0
    Balance ......................  .......157 11  10
                                                     _____
                                              1876 17   7
```

Of the cheques for £800 I will give account presently ; but first, we must compare the cash paid in with the subscription list.

```
    The total cash paid in is—Account A.......653  1   0
                              Account B.......324 11   1
                                                     _____
                                                977 12   1
```

Now see subscription list, after banker's account, page 183.

THE UNION BANK OF LONDON (Chancery Lane Branch) IN ACCOUNT WITH
ST. GEORGE'S FUND.

Dr.			£	s.	d.	Cr.			£	s.	d.
1876.						1876.					
Jan.	1.	To Balance	14	1	10	Feb.	22.	By Charges on two local notes	0	0	10
Jan.	6.	" Dividend on £8000 Consols	119	0	0	Feb.	25.	" Postage of Pass Book	0	0	3
Jan.	13.	" Geo. Allen	24	11	1	March	3.	" John Ruskin, Esq.	300	0	0
Feb.	15.	" John Ruskin, Esq.	25	0	0						
Feb.	15.	" Draft at Sheffield	8	0	0						
Feb.	15.	" " Ambleside	6	0	0						
Feb.	15.	" " Bridgewater	100	0	0						
Feb.	15.	" " Birmingham	5	0	0						
Feb.	22.	" Cash	35	0	0						
March	4.	" Draft at Windsor	20	0	0						
March	7.	" Cash	25	0	0						
March	7.	" Draft at Oxford	50	0	0						
March	14.	" Cash	6	0	0						
March	14.	" Draft at Sheffield	20	0	0	March	15.	By Balance	157	11	10
			£457	12	11				£457	12	11

			£	s.	d.
1876.					
March	15.	To Balance	157	11	10

Subscription List.

To March 14th of this Year.

	£	s.	d.
Total in *Fors* of February	741	14	10
(Corrections received note of.)			
No. 8. Additional	40	0	0
" 26. "	1	5	0
" 38. Subscriptions 1875, 1876	2	2	0
	785	1	10

Now continuing the list.

	£	s.	d.
No. 55. J. W..............................	50	0	0
" 56. The mother of the first donor of land			
to St. George	100	0	0
" 57. The Curator of our Museum.........	8	0	0
" 58. B. A., Subscription, 1876...........	3	0	0
" 59. J. T. S............................	50	0	0
" 60. E. L...............................	20	0	0
" 61. S. I..............................	2	0	0
" 62. R. R..............................	5	0	0
" 63. L. L..............................	0	10	0
	1023	11	10
Cash paid in	977	12	1
Balance in my hands......................	45	19	9

The sum in my hands, thus amounting to £845 19s. 9d., has been distributed as follows:—

	£	s.	d.
Purchase of land and house at Sheffield	600	0	0
Henry Swan—Two quarters' salary to 31st			
March, 1876............................	20	0	0
Expenses of repair, Sheffield................	41	0	0
Prints (Colnaghi). See November *Fors*	29	10	0
Messrs. Tarrant and Mackrell, 29th December,			
1876 ....£20 17 5			
26 15 11—47	13	4
Balance in my hands.......:..............	106	16	5
	£845	19	9

Messrs. Tarrant and Mackrell's accounts follow. I had an offer from Sheffield to do this legal work for nothing; but I wanted to be sure that everything was in due form, and I can trust this London firm. My very good friend Mr. Tarrant must, however, pardon my pointing out to him how much more pleasantly, for all parties, he might be employed, as suggested in *Fors* XVI., page 218, than in taxing this transfer of property to the amount of nearly fifty pounds—(seven pounds odd worth of letters merely). For, were the members of the legal profession employed generally in illuminating initials, and so got out of our way, and the lands of the country properly surveyed and fenced, all that would be really needful for the sale of any portion of them by anybody to anybody else, would be the entry in a roll recording the tenure of so many square miles round each principal town. " The piece of land hitherto belonging to A B, is this day sold to and henceforward belongs to C D, whereof we (city magistrate and a head of any county family) are witnesses."

THE ST. GEORGE'S COMPANY,

To TARRANT & MACKRELL,

Costs of Purchase of Freehold Land and Messuage in Bell Hagg Road, Sheffield.

1875.

	£	s.	d.
Sept. 20.			
On receipt of letters from Messrs. Webster, and from Mr. Ruskin, as to purchase of land and a house at Sheffield, writing Messrs. Webster, the vendor's solicitors, to send us contract......................	0	5	0
Writing Mr. Ruskin as to amount of purchase money, he having stated it to be £600, and Messrs. Webster £630	0	3	6
Oct. 4.			
On receipt of draft contract for approval from Messrs. Webster, with abstract of title for inspection, looking through abstract, when we found it would be necessary to have a copy of plan on deed of 1st May, 1857, and an abstract of the Rivelin View Society's Deed of Covenants, before investigating the title, or approving contract..	0	13	4
Writing Messrs. Webster accordingly	0	5	0
Copy contract to keep, fo. 15.......................	0	5	0
Oct. 11.			
Perusing abstract of title, nine sheets................	1	0	0
Perusing the Rivelin View Company's Deed of Covenants, four sheets	0	10	0
Perusing and approving draft contract....	0	6	8
Writing vendor's solicitors with contract approved and thereon, and for plan which they had omitted to send	0	5	0
Oct. 13.			
Writing Messrs. Webster. acknowledging letter approving of our alterations in contract, and asking for plan which they had omitted to send, although in their letter they stated it was enclosed	0	5	0
Engrossing one part of the contract for signature of Mr. Ruskin, and paid stamp thereon....................	0	10	6
Drawing plan thereon...............................	0	7	6

	£	s.	d.
Writing Mr. Ruskin, with contract for his signature, and fully thereon, and as to the contents of the Rivelin View Society's Deed of Covenants, and as to Trustees of the Company to whom the property might be conveyed, and for cheque for £60 for deposit...........	0	5	0

Oct. 18.

On receipt of letter from Mr. Ruskin with contract signed and cheque for deposit, writing him acknowledging receipt....................................	0	3	6
Writing with appointment to exchange contracts and pay deposit......................................	0	3	6
Attending exchanging contracts, and paying deposit...	0	6	8

Oct. 19.

Writing our agents at Sheffield (Messrs. Broomhead and Co) with abstract of title to examine, with deeds, and instructing them..................................	0	5	0

Oct. 20.

Writing vendor's solicitors that contract exchanged and deposit paid to their London agent, and as to examination of title deeds.............................	0	5	0

Oct. 21.

On receipt of abstract from Messrs. Broomhead and Co., with remarks on title, writing them to examine probate of H. Norton's will in hands of Messrs. Tattershall, and on subject of duties, etc., under that will, and returning abstract to them....................	0	3	6

Oct. 23.

Attending perusing conditions of sale under which Mr. Bagshawe bought the property before drawing requisitions on title..................................	0	6	8

Oct. 29.

Drawing requisitions and copy........................	0	10	0
Writing vendor's solicitors therewith	0	3	6

Nov. 5.

Instructions for deed of conveyance..................	0	6	8
Drawing same, fo. 16	0	16	0
Fair copy for perusal	0	5	4
Writing Messrs. Webster therewith and fully thereon ..	0	5	0

Nov. 10.

Engrossing conveyance.............................	0	13	4
Paid parchment....................................	0	5	0
Writing Mr. Ruskin on subject of completion, and for cheque for £540 balance of purchase money, and with consent to be signed by him to conveyance being taken to the Right Hon. W. C. Temple and Sir T. D. Acland as Trustees for the Company, Mr. Ruskin having entered into the contract.............................	0	5	0
Writing vendor's solicitors, with engrossment for examination, and fully thereon	0	5	0

	£	s.	d.
Writing Messrs. Broomhead, our agents, instructing them to make proper searches in the Land Registry at Wakefield, and as to completion of purchase	0	3	6

Nov. 12.

	£	s.	d.
Writing our agents at Sheffield, with cheque for £540 purchase money, and very fully as to registering deed of conveyance, searches, and settling..............	0	5	0
Writing Mr. Ruskin acknowledging receipt of his two letters, with two cheques for, together, £540........	0	3	6

Nov. 15.

	£	s.	d.
Attending examining certificates of searches, with abstract, when we found same satisfactory............	0	6	8

Nov. 16.

	£	s.	d.
On receipt of conveyance executed by the vendor and his mortgagee, attending stamping, and afterwards, for same...	0	6	8
Paid stamp	3	0	0
Writing our agents, with stamped deed conveyance for registration, and fully thereon.....................	0	3	6

Nov. 22.

	£	s.	d.
Making schedule of documents received from agents (Messrs. Broomhead), and writing them acknowledging receipt of deeds, and for account of their charges	0	3	6

Nov. 29.

	£	s.	d.
On receipt of account of agents' charges, amounting to £10 14s. 11d., writing them with cheque............	0	3	6
Writing Mr. Ruskin on subject of insurance..........	0	5	0
Incidentals...	0	10	0
	16	1	0
Paid Messrs. Broomhead's charges..............	10	14	11
	£26	15	11

THE ST. GEORGE'S COMPANY,

To WM. B. TARRANT.

General Bill of Costs to 10th December, 1875.

1875.

Feb. 13.

	£	s.	d.
On receipt of letter from Mr. Ruskin, attending him at Herne Hill, and conferring on course to be taken on subject of letter from Messrs. Griffith and Son, of Dolgelly, as to conveyance of cottage property at Barmouth, and on the necessity of trust deed for the purpose of such conveyance, so as to carry out the wishes of Mr. Ruskin and others for improving the condition of agriculturists, and paid rail.....................	1	2	0

Feb. 15.

	£	s.	d.
Writing Messrs. Griffith and Son, as arranged.........	0	5	0

Feb. 18.

		£	*s.*	*d.*
Attending Sir Sydney Waterlow, Mr. W. J. Thompson, and others, as to the Industrial Dwellings Company, of which they had been promoters, with a view to obtaining information to guide me in the formation of the St. George's Company		0	6	8

Feb. 22.

	£	*s.*	*d.*
Instructions to counsel to advise in conference on course to be adopted to carry out the scheme	0	6	8
Making copy of Mr. Ruskin's letter to accompany instructions	0	5	0
Attending counsel therewith, when it was arranged that conference should be postponed until Mr. Ruskin could attend	0	6	8
Writing Mr. Ruskin to let me know on what day he could attend conference	0	5	0

Feb. 23.

	£	*s.*	*d.*
On receipt of letter from Messrs. Griffith and Son, writing them fully in reply	0	5	0

March 10.

	£	*s.*	*d.*
Attending counsel, Mr. Barber appointing conference for 3.30 on Monday	0	6	8
Writing Mr. Ruskin, with appointment	0	3	6

March 15.

	£	*s.*	*d.*
Attending conference with Mr. Ruskin, at Mr. Barber's, when it was decided that he should draw a deed for the purpose of carrying out Mr. Ruskin's wishes, and paid cab	1	3	0
Paid counsel's fee and clerk	1	6	0
Drawing proposal circular	0	12	0

March 21.

	£	*s.*	*d.*
Attending counsel therewith to settle	0	6	8
Paid his fee and clerk	1	3	6

March 26.

	£	*s.*	*d.*
Attending counsel, appointing conference on draft	0	6	8

April 26.

	£	*s.*	*d.*
Attending conference	0	13	4
Paid counsel's fee and clerk	1	6	0

April 29.

	£	*s.*	*d.*
Fair copy of proposed circular as settled	0	4	0
Letter to Mr. Ruskin therewith and thereon	0	5	0

To TARRANT & MACKRELL.

June 9.

	£	*s.*	*d.*
On receipt of letter from Mr. Ruskin on draft circular, making copy of Mr. Ruskin's suggestions to place before counsel three brief sheets	0	10	0
Perusing and considering same	0	10	0
Drawing memoranda of constitution of the Company, to take place of the circular	0	10	0

	£	s.	d.

June 10.

    Instructions to counsel to settle same, and with Mr.

        Ruskin's suggestions, etc. 0 6 8

    Attending counsel therewith. 0 6 8

    Paid his fee and clerk. 2 4 6

June 11.

    Long letter to Mr. Ruskin in reply to his of the 27th

        and 28th ult., and 8th inst. 0 5 0

June 15

    Fair copy memoranda of Constitution of the Company,

        as settled by counsel, fo. 30.... ....   0 10 0

    Writing Mr. Ruskin therewith and thereon. 0 5 0

June 23.

    Attending Mr. Ruskin on his calling and handing us

        print of the proposed memoranda in a number of

        his *Fors Clavigera*, and with Mr. Ruskin's sugges-

        tions for some alterations ; and we were to submit

        same to counsel, and obtain a conference with him in

        about a month's time, which Mr. Ruskin would attend   0 6 8

Oct. 7.

    On receipt of the July and October *Fors* from Mr. Rus-

        kin, attending, perusing, and considering remarks

        and suggestions contained therein, and bearing on the

        formation of the St. George's Company, and also your

        letter to us of the 2nd inst., returning us the draft

        memoranda sent you on the 15th June, with your re-

        marks thereon, and letter you had received from a

        correspondent on the subject, attending, perusing,

        and considering the several letters and documents to

        enable us to revise the memoranda as desired. 1 1 0

Oct. 15.

    Writing Mr. Ruskin very fully on subject of revision of

        memoranda and statutes, and for further information

        as to marshals, etc. 0 5 0

Oct. 24.

    On receipt of letter from Mr. Ruskin withdrawing all

        reference to marshals from the proposed memoranda,

        making fresh copy of the memoranda as drawn, and

        adding in the margin thereof all suggestions and com-

        ments thereon contained in the *Fors*, and the several

        letters we had received in connection with the matter   0 10 0

Oct. 30.

    Instructions to counsel to revise memoranda. 0 6 8

    Attending him therewith and thereon. 0 6 8

    Paid his fee and clerk. 1 3 6

Dec. 10.

    Writing Mr. Ruskin, with draft memoranda and coun-

        sel's amendments, and with counsel's opinion at foot

        thereof, and also as to insurance of the Sheffield prem-

        ises. 0 5 0

    Petty disbursements and incidentals. 0 10 0

                                            £22 0 8

II. Affairs of the Master.

	£	s.	d.
Balance, Feb. 20th......................................	225	5	9
Cash (Portsdown mortgage, paid March 2nd)............	1522	12	4
	1747	18	1

		£	s.	d.			
Feb. 28.	Klein (*a*).........................	40	0	0			
March 1.	Raffaelle Carloforti (*b*).............	15	0	0			
2.	Thomas Wade, Esq. (*c*)............	31	10	0			
6.	Self (*d*).....................	35	0	0			
6.	Arthur Burgess....................	30	0	0			
9.	F. Crawley (*e*)....................	40	0	0			
10.	Charles F. Murray, Esq. (*f*)	10	0	0			
11.	Antonio Valmarana (*g*)............	50	0	0			
16.	Antonio Coletti (*h*)...............	25	0	0			
					276	10	0

	£	s.	d.
Balance..	£1471	8	1

(*a*) Travelling and personal expenses since January 1st, of which I have no space for the detail in this *Fors;* it will be given in its place. Klein has ten pounds a month, himself, besides his expenses in Oxford when I've no rooms for him.

(*b*) A youth, whom I am maintaining in art-study at Venice. He has £7 10s. monthly. This payment is to end of April.

(*c*) Water-colour drawing of a cottage at Coniston, likely to be soon destroyed by ' improvements.'

(*d*) £10 pocket-money, £25 to St. George, money of his in my hands included in my banker's January balance, acknowledged in St. George accounts, March 7th.

(*e*) £21 of this my own upholsterer's and other bills at Oxford; the rest, Crawley will account for.

(*f*) Drawings made for me at Siena.

(*g*) Fifty drawings made for me by Signor Caldara of Venice, being part of a complete Venetian Herbal in process of execution. I count none of my money better spent than this.

(*h*) Annual gift to monastery of Assisi, for 1875: not sent last year because I meant to go there. Due always on the Corpus Domini.

III.

" 6, MOIRA PLACE, SOUTHAMPTON, 15*th Feb.*, 1876.

"Dear Sir,—On referring to *Helix ericetorum* (the species I take your outline to be enlarged from) in Dr. Turton's *British Land and Freshwater Shells*, with additions by Dr. Gray, I find it stated, on the authority of M. Bouchard, that the eggs of *H. ericetorum* are laid from July to November, and are from forty to sixty in number, the time of hatching being twenty days after laying, and the length of the snail's life is eighteen months. It is not, however, stated whether these particulars refer to *H. ericetorum* in England or France.

"The only extra information I can get from my other book is that heavy rains kill great numbers of them.

"Your drawing refers to the shell of a full-grown snail, shown by its having six whorls, and by the slight reflex curve at the outer end of the spiral.*

"With regard to the formation of the shell, I can state that it was formed by successive additions during the life of the snail, the small dark transparent portion in the centre of the spiral being the nucleus, and the lines and ridges crossing the spiral indicate the different rings or layers of shell added to suit the convenience of the snail.

"I enclose specimens of *H. ericetorum* from Deal,† to enable you to compare them with those from Arundel, to make sure that they are the same species.

"I am, dear Sir, your obedient servant,

"H. L."

IV. "A Swedish newspaper contains a lengthy account of the gallant rescue of a Swedish steamer by the people of the village of Creswell, Northumberland. Thirteen out of the fifteen male inhabitants manned the boat, to launch which the women waded to their waists. A fisher-girl named Bella Brown ran ten miles to the next lifeboat station for assistance, and had to wade through several bays on an icy January night. The brave girl was seized with cramp on returning, and nearly lost her life."

V. Part of a letter from one of my best friends, Fellow and Tutor of Corpus, communicating some recent notes on English scenery :—

"I next went to the Isle of Wight, which is very pretty, but all over-builded. It threatens soon to become a mere suburb of London. Portsmouth detained me a day,—all too brief a time for its beauties and horrors, its relics of past naval glories and picturesque bits on land and sea, its nightmare sea-going caldrons, misnamed men-of-war, at the present. I went on board the Thunderer, twin ship of the Devastation. I had expected something ugly and horrible, both inside and out; but my expectations were surpassed tenfold, especially with regard to the inside of the ship. The crew are confined altogether in utterly dark dungeons at each end of the ship, wholly under water, and hardly high enough for a man to walk in upright. An iron-shielded and very high deck in the middle of the ship is the only place where a man can see the light of day, and live when this witch's kettle is at sea, as the ends of the vessel cut under the waves. The bull of Phalaris would have been an eligible prison to me in comparison of this ; victims, at any rate, were not sent to sea in it."

VI.

"LAXEY, ISLE OF MAN, *March 4th*, 1876.

"Dear Sir,—In this month's *Fors*, page 107—'Affairs of the Master,'—if you add up the amounts paid out, I think you will find, instead

---

* Exaggerated a little, I'm afraid.—J. R.
† The shells sent, for which I heartily thank my correspondent, are, I think, the same as mine, only not so white.

of £360 2*s.* 0*d.*, the amount should be £370 2*s.* 3*d.*, and leaves a proper balance of £225 5*s.* 6*d.*

"I hope you will not be offended at me for troubling you with these trifling errors, of no moment ; but I have got a singular habit—that I can never pass over a column of added figures, no matter what length,' without testing their correctness.

"Yours truly,
"E. RYDINGS."

(If only my good correspondent—now a Companion—will indulge himself constantly in this good habit as respects the *Fors* accounts I shall be much more at ease about them. But his postscript is more important.)

"P. S. You say that the girls of St. George's Company shall learn to *spin* and *weave*, etc. There is a good deal of hand-spinning done on this little island, but I am sorry to say that there are no young girls learning now to spin ; and in a few years more, the common spinning wheel here will be as great a curiosity as it is in Lancashire, where one is never seen—only at the theatre. I have gone to some little trouble to ascertain why the young girls are not learning now to spin ; and the principal reason I can gather is that home-spun 'Manks-made dresses,' as they are called, last *too long*, and therefore do not give the young women a chance of having four or five new dresses in the year. I could give you some interesting information about hand-spinning and weaving here, but must reserve it for another time, and will send you patterns of cloth, etc. All our blankets, sheets, flannels, skirts, jacket cloth, stockings, and yarns, have been spun by my wife and her mother before her. We have now linen sheets in wear, not a hole or a tear in them, that were spun by my wife's mother.—and she, poor body, has been dead twenty-eight or twenty-nine years.—the flax grown on their own farm. Fine and white they are, and would compare favourably in *fineness* with machine-made Irish linen. The daughters of Lord Auckland, when he was bishop here, used to go every Saturday afternoon to my wife's mother's, (who lived just behind Bishop Court,) to learn to spin.

"But I must write you a special letter on the subject when I have got my patterns ready."

LETTER LXV.

I TOLD you in last *Fors* to learn the 15th chapter of Genesis by heart. Too probably, you have done nothing of the sort ; but at any rate, let us now read it together, that I may tell you, of each verse, what I wanted, (and still beg,) you to learn it for.

1. "The word of God came to Abram " Of course you can't imagine such a thing as that the word of God should ever come to *you?* Is that because you are worse, or better, than Abram ?—because you are a more, or less, civilized person than he ? I leave you to answer that question for yourself ;—only, as I have told you often before, but cannot repeat too often, find out first what the Word *is ;* and don't suppose that the printed thing in your hand, which you call a Bible, is the Word of God, and that the said Word may therefore always be bought at a pious stationer's for eighteenpence.

Farther, in the *Explanatory and Critical Commentary and Revision of the Translation* (of the Holy Bible) by Bishops and other Clergy of the Established Church, published in 1871, by Mr. John Murray, you will find the interesting statement, respecting this verse, that "This is the first time that the expression—so frequent afterwards—'the Word of the Lord' occurs in the Bible." The expression *is* certainly rather frequent afterwards ; and one might have perhaps expected from the Episcopal and clerical commentators, on this, its first occurrence, some slight notice of the probable meaning of it. They proceed, however, without farther observation, to discuss certain problems, suggested to them by the account of Abram's vision, respecting somnambulism ; on which, though one would have thought few persons more qualified than themselves to give an account of that condition, they arrive at no particular conclusion.

But even their so carefully limited statement is only one-third true. It is true of the Hebrew Law ; not of the New Testament :—of the entire Bible, it is true of the English version only ; not of the Latin, nor the Greek. Nay, it is very importantly and notably *un*true of these earlier versions.

There are three words in Latin, expressive of utterance in three very different manners ; namely, 'verbum,' a word, ' vox,' a voice, and 'sermo,' a sermon.

Now, in the Latin Bible, when St. John says "the Word was in the beginning," he says, the 'Verbum' was in the beginning. But here, when somebody (nobody knows who, and that is a bye question of some importance,) is represented as saying, "The word of the Lord came to Abram," what somebody really says, is that "There was made to Abram a 'Sermon' of the Lord."

Does it not seem possible that one of the almost unconscious reasons of your clergy for not pointing out this difference in expression, may be a doubt whether you ought not rather to desire to hear God preach, than them ?

But the Latin word 'verbum,' from which you get 'verbal' and 'verbosity,' is a very obscure and imperfect rendering of the great Greek word 'Logos,' from which you get 'logic,' and 'theology,' and all the other logies.

And the phrase "word of the Lord," which the Bishops, with unusual episcopic clairvoyance, have really observed to 'occur frequently afterwards' in the English Bible, is, in the Greek Bible always "the Logos of the Lord." But this Sermon to Abraham is only 'rhema,' an actual or mere *word ;* in his interpretation of which, I see, my good Dean of Christ Church quotes the Greek original of Sancho's proverb, "Fair words butter no parsneps." Which we shall presently see to have been precisely Abram's—(of course cautiously expressed)—feeling, on this occasion. But to understand his feeling, we must look what this sermon of the Lord's was.

The sermon (as reported), was kind, and clear. "Fear not, Abram, I am thy Shield, and thy exceeding great Reward," ('reward' being the poetical English of our translators—the real phrase being 'thy exceeding great pay, or gain'). Meaning, "You needn't make an iron tent, with a revolving gun in the middle of it, for I am your tent and artillery in one ; and you needn't care to get a quantity of property, for *I* am your property ; and you needn't be stiff about your rights of property, because nobody will dispute your right to *Me*."

To which Abram answers, "Lord God, what wilt Thou give me, seeing I go childless."

Meaning,—"Yes, I know that ;—but what is the good of *You* to me, if I haven't a child? I am a poor mortal : I don't care about the Heavens or You ; I want a child."

Meaning this, at least, if the Latin and English Bibles are right in their translation—"*I* am thy great gain." But the Greek Bible differs from them ; and puts the promise in a much more tempting form to the modern English mind. It does not represent God as offering Himself ; but something far better than Himself, actually exchangeable property ! Wealth, according to Mr. John Stuart Mill. Here is indeed a prospect for Abram !—and something to refuse, worth thinking twice about. For the Septuagint reads, "Fear not, Abram. I am thy Protector, and *thou shalt have* an exceeding great pay." Practically, just as if, supposing Sir Stafford Northcote to represent the English nation of the glorious future, a Sermon of the Lord should come just now to him, saying, "Fear not, Sir Stafford, I am thy Devastation ; and thou shalt have an exceeding great surplus."

On which supposition, Abram's answer is less rude, but more astonishing. "Oh God, what wilt thou give me? What good is money to me, who am childless?"

Again, as if Sir Stafford Northcote should answer, in the name of the British people, saying, "Lord God, what wilt thou give me? What is the good to me of a surplus? What can I make of surplus? It is children that I want, not surplus ! "

A truly notable parliamentary utterance on the Budget, if it might be ! Not for a little while yet, thinks Sir Stafford ; perhaps, think wiser and more sorrowful people than he, not

until England has had to stone, according to the law of
Deuteronomy xxi. 18, some of the children she has got : or
at least to grapeshot them. I couldn't get anything like
comfortable rooms in the Pea Hen at St. Alban's, the day
before yesterday, because the Pea Hen was cherishing, for
chickens under her wings, ever so many officers of the Royal
Artillery ; and some beautiful sixteen-pounders,—exquisite
fulfilments of all that science could devise, in those machines ;
which were unlimbered in the market-place, on their way to
Sheffield—where I am going myself, as it happens. I wonder much, in the name of my mistress, whose finger is certainly in this pie, what business we have there, (both of us,)
the black machines, and I. As Atropos would have it, too, I
had only been making out, with good Mr. Douglas's help, in
Woolwich Repository on Wednesday last, a German Pea
Hen's inscription on a sixteen-pounder of the fourteenth
century :—

> Ich bin furwahr, ein Grober Baur
> Ver frist mein apr, es wurd ihm Saur.

Verse 5th. "And he brought him forth abroad, and said,
Tell now the stars, if thou be able to number them. So
shall thy seed be."

Of course *you* would have answered God instantly, and
told Him the exact number of the stars, and all their magnitudes. Simple Abram, conceiving that, even if he did
count all he could see, there might yet be a few more out of
sight, does not try.

Verse 6th. "And he believed in the Lord, and He counted
it to him for righteousness."

That, on the whole, is the primary verse of the entire
Bible. If that is true, the rest is worth whatever Heaven is
worth ; if that is untrue, the rest is worth nothing. You
had better, therefore, if you can, learn it also in Greek and
Latin.

"Καὶ ἐπίστευσεν Ἄβραμ τῷ Θεῷ, καὶ ἐλογίσθη αὐτῷ εἰς
δικαιοσύνην."

"Credidit Abram Deo, et reputatum est illo in justitiam."

If, then, that text be true, it will follow that you also, if you would have righteousness counted to you, must believe God. And you can't believe Him if He never says anything to you. Whereupon it will be desirable again to consider if He ever *has* said anything to you ; and if not, why not.

After this verse, I don't understand much of the chapter myself—but I never expect to understand everything in the Bible, or even more than a little ; and will make what I can of it.

Verses 7th, 8th. "And He said, I the Lord brought thee, to give thee this land, to inherit it.

"But he said, Lord, whereby shall I know that I shall inherit it ? "

Now, I don't see how he could know it better than by being told so ; nor how he knew it any better, after seeing a lamp moving between half-carcases. But we will at least learn, as well as we can, what happened ; and think it over.

The star-lesson was of course given in the night ; and, in the morning, Abram slays the five creatures, and watches their bodies all day.

'Such an absurd thing to do—to cut rams and cows in two, to please God !'

Indeed it seems so ; yet perhaps is better than cutting men in two to please ourselves ; and we spend thirty millions a year in preparations for doing that. How many more swiftly divided carcases of horses and men, think you, my Christian friends, have the fowls fed on, *not* driven away,— finding them already carved for their feast, or blown into small and convenient morsels, by the military gentlemen of Europe, in sacrifice to—their own epaulettes, (poor gilded and eyeless idols !) during the past seventy and six years of this *one* out of the forty centuries since Abram ?

"The birds divided he not." A turtle dove, or in Greek "cooing dove" ; and a pigeon, or in Greek "dark dove" ; or black dove, such as came to Dodona ;—these were not to be cut through breast and backbone ! Why ? Why, indeed, any of this butchery and wringing of necks ? Not wholly, perhaps, for Abram's amusement, or God's ; like our coursing and pigeon-shooting ;—but then, all the more earnestly one asks, why ?

The Episcopal commentary tells you, (usefully this time,) that the *beasts* were divided, because among all nations it was then the most solemn attestation of covenant to pass between halves of beasts. But the birds ?

We are not sure, by the way, how far the cleaving might reach, without absolute division. Read Leviticus i., 15 to 17, and v., 6 to 10. 'You have nothing to do with those matters,' you think ? I don't say you have ; but in my schools you must know your Bible, and the meaning of it, or want of meaning, at least a little more definitely than you do now, before I let you throw the book away for ever. So have patience with it a little while ; for indeed until you know something of this Bible, I can't go on to teach you any Koran, much less any Dante or Shakespeare. Have patience, therefore,—and you will need, probably, more than you think ; for I am sadly afraid that you don't at present know so much as the difference between a burnt-offering and a sin-offering ; nor between a sin-offering and a trespass-offering, —do you ? (Lev. v. 15) ; so how can you possibly know anything about Abram's doves, or afterwards about Ion's,— not to speak of the Madonna's ? The whole story of the Ionic migration, and the carving of those Ionic capitals, which our architects don't know how to draw to this day, is complicated with the tradition of the saving of Ion's life by his recognition of a very small 'trespass '—a servant's momentary 'blasphemy.' Hearing it, he poured the wine he was about to drink out upon the ground. A dove, flying down from the temple cornice, dipped her beak in it, and died, for the wine had been poisoned by—his mother. But the meaning of all that myth is involved in this earlier and wilder mystery of the Mount of the Amorite.

On the slope of it, down to the vale of Eshcol, sat Abram, as the sun ripened its grapes through the glowing day ; the shadows lengthening at last under the crags of Machpelah ;

—the golden light warm on Ephron's field, still Ephron's, wild with wood. "And as the sun went down an horror of great darkness fell upon Abram."

Indigestion, most likely, thinks modern philosophy. Accelerated cerebration, with automatic conservation of psychic force, lucidly suggests Dr. Carpenter. Derangement of the sensori-motor processes, having certain relations of nextness, and behaviour uniformly depending on that nextness, condescendingly explains Professor Clifford.

Well, my scientific friends, if ever God does you the grace to give you experience of the sensations, either of horror, or darkness, even to the extent your books and you inflict them on my own tired soul, you will come out on the other side of that shadow with newer views on many subjects than have occurred yet to you,—novelty-hunters though you be.

"Behold, thy seed shall be strangers, in a land not theirs." Again, the importunate question returns, 'When was this written?' But the really practical value of the passage for ourselves, is the definite statement, alike by the Greeks and Hebrews, of dream, as one of the states in which knowledge of the future may be distinctly given. The truth of this statement we must again determine for ourselves. Our dreams are partly in our power, by management of daily thought and food ; partly, involuntary and accidental—very apt to run in contrary lines from those naturally to be expected of them ; and partly, (at least, so say all the Hebrew prophets, and all great Greek, Latin, and English thinkers,) prophetic. Whether what Moses, Homer, David, Daniel, the Evangelists and St. Paul, Dante, Chaucer, Shakespeare, and Bacon, think on this matter, or what the last-whelped little curly-tailed puppy of the Newington University thinks, is most likely to be true—judge as you will.

"In the fourth generation they shall come hither again, for the iniquity of the Amorites is not yet full."

What *was* the iniquity of the Amorites, think you, and what kind of people were they ? Anything like ourselves ? or wide-mouthed and goggle-eyed,—terrifically stalking above the vineyard stakes of Eshcol ? If like us, in any wise, is it possible that we also may be committing iniquity, capable of less and more fulness, through such a space as four hundred years? Questions worth pausing at ; and we will at least try to be a little clear-headed as to Amorite personality.

We habitually speak of the Holy Land as the Land of 'Canaan.' The 'promised' land was indeed that of Canaan, with others. But Israel never got it. They got only the Mount of the Amorites ; for the promise was only to be perfected on condition of their perfect obedience. Therefore, I asked you to learn Genesis x. 15, and Genesis x. 16, separately. For *all* the Canaanites were left, to prove Israel, (Judges iii. 3,) and a good many of the Amorites and Jebusites too, (Judges iii. 5—7,) but in the main Israel subdued the last two races, and held the hill country from Lebanon to Hebron, and the capital, Jerusalem, for their own. And if instead of 'Amorites,' you will read generally 'Highlanders,' (which the word means,) and think of them, for a beginning of notion, simply as Campbells and Macgregors of the East, getting themselves into relations with the pious Israelites closely resembling those of the Highland race and mind of Scotland with its evangelical and economical Lowlanders, you will read these parts of your Bible in at least an incipiently intelligent manner. And above all, you will, or may, understand that the Amorites had a great deal of good in them : that they and the Jebusites were on the whole a generous and courteous people,—so that, when Abram dwells with the Amorite princes, Mamre and Eshcol, they are faithful allies to him ; and when he buys his grave from Ephron the Hittite, and David the threshing floor from Arannah the Jebusite, both of the mountaineers behave just as the proudest and truest Highland chief would. 'What is that between me and thee?' "All these things did Arannah, as a King, give unto the King—and Arannah said unto the King, The Lord thy God accept thee." Not *our* God, you see ;—but giving sadly, as the Sidonian widow begging,—with claim of no part in Israel.

'Mere oriental formulæ,' says the Cockney modern expositor—'offers made in fore-knowledge that they would not be accepted.'

No, curly-tailed bow-wow; it is only you and other such automatic poodles who are 'formulæ.' Automatic, by the way, you are not; we all know how to wind you up to run with a whirr, like toy-mice.

Well, now read consecutively, but quietly, Numbers xiii. 22—29, xxi. 13—26, Deuteronomy iii. 8—13, and Joshua x. 6—14, and you will get a notion or two, which with those already obtained you may best arrange as follows.

Put the Philistines, and giants, or bulls, of Bashan, out of the way at present; they are merely elements of physical malignant force, sent against Samson, Saul, and David, as a half-human shape of lion or bear,—carrying off the ark of God in their mouths, and not knowing in the least what to do with it. You already know Tyre as the trading power, Ethiopia as the ignorant—Egypt as the wise—slave; then the Amorites, among the children of Ham, correspond to the great mountain and pastoral powers of the Shemites; and are far the noblest and purest of the race: abiding in their own fastnesses, desiring no conquest, but as Sihon, admitting no invader;—holding their crags so that nothing can be taken out of the hand of the Amorite but with the sword and bow, (Gen. xlviii. 22;) yet living chiefly by pasture and agriculture; worshipping, in their early dynasties, the one eternal God; and, in the person of their great high priest, Melchizedec, but a few years before this vision, blessing the father of the faithful, and feeding him with the everlasting sacraments of earth,—bread and wine,—in the level valley of the Kings, under Salem, the city of peace.

Truly, 'the iniquity of the Amorites was not yet full.'

I have given you enough to think of, for this time; but you can't work it out rightly without a clearly intelligible map of Palestine, and raised models of the districts of Hebron and Jerusalem, which I will provide as soon as possible, according to St. George's notions of what such things should be, for the Sheffield museum: to the end that at least, in that district of the Yorkshire Amorites, singularly

like the Holy Land in its level summits and cleft defiles, it
may be understood what England also had once to bring
forth of blessing in her own vales of peace ; and how her
gathering iniquity may bring upon her,—(and at this instant,
as I write, early on Good Friday, the malignant hail of
spring time, slaying blossom and leaf, smites rattling on the
ground that should be soft with flowers,) such day of ruin
as the great hail darkened in the going down to Beth-horon,
and the sun, that had bronzed their corn and flushed their
grape, prolonged on Ajalon, implacable.

"And it came to pass, when the sun went down, and it
was dark, behold, a smoking furnace, and a burning lamp
which passed between those pieces."

What a lovely vision, half of it, at any rate, to the eye of
modern progress ! Foretelling, doubtless, smoking furnaces,
and general civilization, in this Amorite land of barbarous
vines and fig-trees ! Yes—my progressive friends. That
was precisely what the vision *did* foretell,—in the first half
of it ; and not very many summer mornings afterwards,
Abram going out for his walk in the dew round his farm,*
saw its fulfilment in quite literal terms, on the horizon. (Gen.
xix. 28.) The smoke of the country went up as the smoke
of a furnace. But what do you make of the other part of
the night-vision ? Striking of oil ? and sale of numerous
patent lamps ? But Abram never did strike any oil—except
olive, which could only be had on the usual terms of laborious

---

* Abram's mountain home seems to have been much like Horace's, as
far as I can make out : but see accounts of modern travellers. Our
translation "in the plain of Mamre" (Genesis xiii. 28 ; xiv. 13) is
clearly absurd ; the gist of the separation between Lot and Abram
being Lot's choice of the plain, as 'the Paradise of God,' and Abram's
taking the rock ground. The Vulgate says ' in the ravine ' of Mamre ;
the Septuagint, ' by the oak.' I doubt not the Hebrew is meant to
carry both senses, as of a rocky Vallombrosa; the Amorites at that
time knew how to keep their rain, and guide their springs. Compare
the petition of Caleb's daughter when she is married, after being
brought up on this very farm, Joshua xv. 17, 18; comparing also
xiv. 14, 15, and of the hill country generally, xvi. 15, and Deut. xi.
10—12, 17.

beating and grinding, and in moderate quantities. What do you make of the second half of the vision ?

Only a minute part of its infinite prophecy was fulfilled in those flames of the Paradise of Lot. For the two fires were the sign of the presence of the Person who accepted the covenant, in passing between the pieces of the victim. And they shone, therefore, for the signature of His Name ; that name which we pray may be hallowed ; and for what that name entirely means ;—'the Lord, merciful and gracious,— and that will by no means clear the guilty.'

For as on the one side He is like a refiner's fire, so that none may abide the day of His coming,—so on the other He is the Light that lighteth every man that cometh into the world. And all the pain of grief and punishment, temporal or eternal, following on the broken covenant ; and all the sweet guidance of the lamp to the feet and the light to the path, granted to those who keep it, are meant by the passing of the darkened and undarkened flames.

Finish now the learning this whole chapter accurately, and when you come to the eighteenth verse, note how much larger the *promised* land was, than we usually imagine it ; and what different manner of possession the Israelites got of its borders, by the waters of Babylon, and rivers of Egypt, (compare Jeremiah xxxix. 9, with xliii. 6 and 7) than they might have had, if they had pleased.

And now, when you have got well into your heads that the Holy Land is, broadly, the mountain or highland of the Amorites, (compare Deut. i. 7, 20, 44, Numbers xiii. 29,) look to the verse which you have probably quoted often, "Behold upon the mountains the feet of Him that bringeth good tidings,"—without ever asking *what* mountains, or what tidings. The mountains are these Amorite crags, and the tidings are of the last destruction of the Hamite power, in the other three great brethren, Cush, Mizraim, and Phut. Read your Nahum through slowly ; and learn the eighth and ninth verses of the third chapter, to be always remembered as the completion of the fifteenth, which you know the first half of so well already—though I suppose you rarely go on to its practical close, "Oh Judah, keep thy solemn feasts, perform thy vows ; for the wicked shall no more pass through thee "—this 'passing,' observe, being the ruinous war of the bitter and hasty nation, (compare Habakkuk i. 6—8, with the last verse of Nahum,) which spiritually is the type of all ruinous and violent passion, such as now passes continually to and fro in this English land of ours.

I am not much in a humour to examine further to-day the passing of its slower molluscous Assyrians; but may at least affirm what I believe at last to be the sure conclusion of my young hunter of Arundel ; that the spiral of the shell uniformly increases its coil, from birth to maturity. Here are examples of the minute species, sent me by Mr. Sillar, in three stages of growth ; the little black spots giving them in their natural size (with much economic skill of Mr. Burgess' touch). The three magnified spirals you may as well copy, and find out how many these little creatures may have. I had taken them for the young of the common snail when I wrote last ; but we will have all our facts clear some day, both concerning bees, and slugs, and the larger creatures, industrious or lazy, whom they are meant to teach.

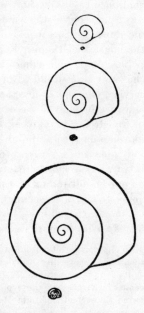

But I want to finish my letter for this time with a word or two more of my Scottish Amorite aunt, after she was brought down into Lowland life by her practical tanner. She, a pure dark-eyed dove-priestess, if ever there was one, of Highland Dodona.* Strangely, the kitchen servant-of-all-work in the

* I need scarcely desire the reader to correct the misprint of ' maternal' for ' paternal ' in line 22 of p. 153 in *Fors* of March. In last *Fors*, please put a comma before and after ' there' in p. 170, line 36.

house at Rose Terrace was a very old "Mause" who might well have been the prototype of the Mause of *Old Mortality,* * but had even a more solemn, fearless, and patient faith, fastened in her by extreme suffering ; for she had been nearly starved to death when she was a girl, and had literally picked the bones out of cast-out dust-heaps to gnaw ; and ever afterwards, to see the waste of an atom of food was as shocking to her as blasphemy. "Oh, Miss Margaret !" she said once to my mother, who had shaken some crumbs off a dirty plate out of the window, "I had rather you had knocked me down." She would make her dinner upon anything in the house that the other servants wouldn't eat ;—often upon potato skins, giving her own dinner away to any poor person she saw ; and would always stand during the whole church service, (though at least seventy years old when I knew her, and very feeble,) if she could persuade any wild Amorite out of the streets to take her seat. Her wrinkled and worn face, moveless in resolution, and patience ; incapable of smile, and knit sometimes perhaps too severely against Jessie and me, if we wanted more creamy milk to our porridge, or jumped off our favourite box on Sunday,—('Never mind, John,' said Jessie to me, once, seeing me in an unchristian state of provocation on the subject, 'when we're married, we'll jump off boxes all day long, if we like !') may have been partly instru-

---

* Vulgar modern Puritanism has shown its degeneracy in nothing more than in its incapability of understanding Scott's exquisitely finished portraits of the Covenanter. In *Old Mortality* alone, there are four which cannot be surpassed ; the typical one, Elspeth, faultlessly sublime and pure ; the second, Ephraim Macbriar, giving the too common phase of the character, which is touched with ascetic insanity ; the third, Mause, coloured and made sometimes ludicrous by Scottish conceit, but utterly strong and pure at heart ; the last, Balfour, a study of supreme interest, showing the effect of the Puritan faith, sincerely held, on a naturally and incurably cruel and base spirit. His last battle-cry—" Down with the Amorites," the chief Amorite being Lord Evandale, is intensely illustrative of all I have asked you to learn to-day. Add to these four studies, from this single novel, those in the *Heart of Midlothian,* and Nicol Jarvie and Andrew Fairservice from *Rob Roy,* and you have a series of theological analyses far beyond those of any other philosophical work that I know, of any period.

mental in giving me that slight bias against the Evangelical
religion which I confess to be sometimes traceable in my later
works : but I never can be thankful enough for having seen,
in her, the Scottish Puritan spirit in its perfect faith and
force ; and been enabled therefore afterwards to trace its
agency in the reforming policy of Scotland with the reverence
and honour it deserves.

My aunt was of a far gentler temper, but still, to me, remained at a wistful distance. She had been much saddened
by the loss of three of her children, before her husband's
death. Little Peter, especially, had been the corner-stone of
her love's building ; and it was thrown down swiftly :—
white-swelling came in the knee ; he suffered much ; and
grew weaker gradually, dutiful always, and loving, and
wholly patient. She wanted him one day to take half a glass
of port wine,—and took him on her knee, and put it to his
lips. 'Not now, mamma ;—in a minute,' said he ; and put
his head on her shoulder, and gave one long, low sigh, and
died. Then there was Catherine ; and—I forget the other
little daughter's name. I did not see them ; my mother told
me of them ;—eagerly always about Catherine, who had been
her own favourite. My aunt had been talking earnestly one
day with her husband about these two children ; planning
this and that for their schooling and what not ; at night, for
a little while she could not sleep ; and as she lay thinking,
she saw the door of the room open ; and two spades come
into it, and stand at the foot of her bed. Both the children
were dead within brief time afterwards. I was about to write
' within a fortnight'—but I cannot be sure of remembering
my mother's words accurately.

But when I was in Perth, there were still—Mary, her eldest
daughter, who looked after us children when Mause was too
busy,—James and John, William and Andrew ; (I can't think
whom the unapostolic William was named after ; he became
afterwards a good physician in London, and Tunbridge Wells ;
his death, last year, is counted among the others that I have
spoken of as recently leaving me very lonely). But the boys
were then all at school or college,—the scholars, William and

Andrew, only came home to tease Jessie and me, and eat
the biggest jargonel pears; the collegians were wholly abstract; and the two girls and I played in our quiet ways on
the North-inch, and by the 'Lead,' a stream, 'led' from the
Tay past Rose Terrace, into the town for molinary purposes;
and long ago, I suppose, bricked over, or choked with rubbish; but then lovely, and a perpetual treasure of flowing
diamond to us children. Mary, by the way, was nearly fourteen—fair, blue-eyed, and moderately pretty; and as pious
as Jessie, without being quite so zealous. And I scarcely
know if those far years of summer sunshine were dreams, or if
this horror of darkness is one, to-day, at St. Albans, where,
driven out of the abbey, unable to bear the sight of its resto-
rations, and out of the churchyard, where I would fain have
stayed to draw, by the black plague-wind, I take refuge from
all in an old apple-woman's shop, because she reminds me of
my Croydon Amorite aunt,—and her little window of the one
in the parlour beside the shop in Market Street. She sells
comic songs as well as apples. I invest a penny in 'The Union
Jack,' and find, in the course of conversation, that the result
of our unlimited national prosperity upon *her*, is, that where
she used to take twopence from one customer, she now takes
five farthings from five,—that her rates are twelve shillings
instead of six,—that she is very tired of it all, and hopes
God will soon take her to heaven.

I have been a little obscure in direction about the Egyptian
asterisk in last *Fors*. The circle in the middle is to be left
solid; the rays round are to be cut quite shallow; not in
deep furrows, as in wood, but like rising, sharp, cliff-edged
harbours with flat bottoms of sand; as little of the hard rock
being cut away as may be.

The Etrurian Leucothea has come at last; but please let
my readers observe that my signature to it means only that
it will answer our purpose, not that it is a good print, for
Mr. Parker's agent is a 'Grober Baur,' and will keep neither
time nor troth in impressions. Farther, I have now put into
Mr. Ward's hands a photograph from a practice-sketch of my

own at Oxford, in pure lead pencil, on grey paper secured with ink on the outlines, and touched with white on the lights. It is of a stuffed Kingfisher,—(one can't see a live one in England nowadays,) and done at full speed of hand; and it is to be copied for a balance practice to the slow spiral lines.

NOTES AND CORRESPONDENCE.

I. Affairs of the Company.

I have given leave to two of our Companions to begin work on the twenty acres of ground in Worcestershire, given us by Mr. George Baker, our second donor of land ; (it was all my fault that he wasn't the first). The ground is in copsewood ; but good for fruit trees ; and shall be cleared and brought into bearing as soon as the two Companions can manage it. We shall now see what we are good for, working as backwoodsmen, but in our own England.

I am in treaty for more land round our Sheffield museum ; and have sent down to it, for a beginning of the mineralogical collection, the agates on which I lectured in February at the London Institution. This lecture I am printing, as fast as I can, for the third number of *Deucalion ;* but I find no scientific persons who care to answer me any single question I ask them about agates ; and I have to work all out myself ; and little hitches and twitches come, in what one wants to say in print. And the days go.

Subscriptions since March 14th to April 16th. I must give names, now ; having finally resolved to have no secrets in our Company,—except those which must be eternally secret to certain kinds of persons, who can't understand either our thoughts or ways :—

		£	s.	d.
March.	F. D. Drewitt (tithe of a first earning)	1	4	1
	Miss M. Guest	2	2	0
April.	James Burdon (tithe of wages)	2	10	0
	Wm. B. Graham (gift)	1	0	0
	Anonymous (post stamp, Birkenhead)	1	10	0
		£8	6	1

II. Affairs of the Master.

		£	s.	d.
March 16.	Balance	1471	8	1
21.	Miss O. Hill, 1½ year's rent on Marylebone Freehold	90	15	0
28.	R. Forsyth (tea-shop)	54	0	0
April 7.	Dividend on £7000 Bank Stock	315	0	0
8.	Petty cash (Dividends on small shares in Building Societies and the like)	25	3	3
		1956	6	4

			£	s.	d.
Brought forward.......................			1956	6	4
March 21. Jackson........................	£50	0	0		
22. Self*........................	100	0	0		
23. Warren and Jones.................	56	16	3		
25, and *April* 7. Crawley.............	40	0	0		
April 1. Secretary......................	25	0	0		
1. Downs........................	25	0	0		
2. Kate, (and 11th April).............	45	0	0		
6. Burgess........................	50	0	0		
6. David........................	53	0	0		
			444	16	3

Balance, April 16.................. ....£1511 10 1

III. I have promised an answer this month to the following pretty little letter; and will try to answer fully, though I must go over ground crossed often enough before. But it is often well to repeat things in other times and words :—

> "16*th March*, 1876.
> "Sir,—Being very much interested in the St. George's Society, we venture to write and ask if you will be so kind as to send us the rules, as, even if we could not join it, we should so like to try and keep them. We hope you will excuse our troubling you, but we do not know how else to obtain the rules.   We remain, yours truly."

My dear children, the rules of St. George's Company are none other than those which at your baptism your godfather and godmother promised to see that you should obey—namely, the rules of conduct given to all His disciples by Christ, so far as, according to your ages, you can understand or practise them. But the Christian religion being now mostly obsolete, (and worse, falsely professed) throughout Europe, your godfather, and godmother, too probably, had no very clear notion of the Devil or his works, when they promised you should renounce them ; and St. George hereby sends you a splinter of his lance, in token that you will find extreme difficulty in putting any of Christ's wishes into practice, under the present basilisk power of society.

Nevertheless, St. George's first order to you, supposing you were put under his charge, would be that you should always, in whatever you do, endeavour to please Christ; (and *He* is quite easily pleased if you try;) but in attempting this, you will instantly find yourself likely to displease many of your friends or relations; and St. George's second order to you is that in whatever you do, you consider what is kind and dutiful to them also, and that you hold it for a sure rule that no manner of disobedience to your parents, or of disrespect and presumption

---

* For accounts in London, to save drawing small cheques. I have not room for detail this month, the general correspondence being lengthy.

towards your friends, can be pleasing to God. You must therefore be doubly submissive ; first in your own will and purpose to the law of Christ ; then in the carrying out of your purpose, to the pleasure and orders of the persons whom He has given you for superiors. And you are not to submit to them sullenly, but joyfully and heartily, keeping nevertheless your own purpose clear, so soon as it becomes proper for you to carry it out.

Under these conditions, here are a few of St. George's orders for you to begin with : —

1st. Keep absolute calm of temper, under all chances ; receiving everything that is provoking and disagreeable to you as coming directly from Christ's hand : and the more it is like to provoke you, thank Him for it the more ; as a young soldier would his general for trusting him with a hard place to hold on the rampart. And remember, it does not in the least matter what happens to you,—whether a clumsy school-fellow tears your dress, or a shrewd one laughs at you, or the governess doesn't understand you. The *one* thing needful is that none of these things should vex you. For your mind is at this time of your youth crystallizing like sugar-candy ; and the least jar to it flaws the crystal, and that permanently.

2nd. Say to yourselves every morning, just after your prayers : " Whoso forsaketh not all that he hath, cannot be my disciple." That is exactly and completely true : meaning that you are to give all you have to Christ to take care of for you. Then if He doesn't take care of it, of course you know it wasn't worth anything. And if He takes anything from you, you know you are better without it. You will not indeed, at your age, have to give up houses, or lands, or boats, or nets ; but you may perhaps break your favourite teacup, or lose your favourite thimble, and might be vexed about it, but for this second St. George's precept.

3rd. What, after this surrender, you find entrusted to you, take extreme care of, and make as useful as possible. The greater part of all they have is usually given to grown-up people by Christ, merely that they may give it away again ; but schoolgirls, for the most part, are likely to have little more than what is needed for themselves : of which, whether books, dresses, or pretty room furniture, you are to take extreme care, looking on yourself, indeed, practically, as a little housemaid set to keep Christ's books and room in order, and not as yourself the mistress of anything.

4th. Dress as plainly as your parents will allow you : but in bright colours, (if they become you,) and in the best materials,—that is to say, in those which will wear longest. When you are really in want of a new dress, buy it, (or make it,) in fashion : but never quit an old one merely because it has become unfashionable. And if the fashion be costly, you must not follow it. You may wear broad stripes or narrow, bright colours or dark, short petticoats or long, (in moderation) as the public wish you : but you must not buy yards of useless stuff to make a knot or a flounce of, nor drag them behind you over the ground. And your walking dress must never touch the ground at all. I have lost much of the faith I once had in the common sense and even in the personal delicacy of the present race of average English women, by seeing how they will allow their dresses to sweep the streets, if it is the fashion to be scavengers.

5th. If you can afford it, get your dresses made by a good dress-maker, with utmost attainable precision and perfection : but let this good dressmaker be a poor person, living in the country ; not a rich person living in a large house in London. ' There are no good dress-makers in the country.' No : but there soon will be if you obey St. George's orders, which are very strict indeed, about never buying dresses in London. ' You bought one there, the other day, for your own pet !' Yes ; but that was because she was a wild Amorite, who had wild Amorites to please ; not a Companion of St. George.

6th. Learn dressmaking yourself, with pains and time ; and use a part of every day in needlework, making as pretty dresses as you can for poor people who have not time nor taste to make them nicely for themselves. You are to show them in your own wearing what is most right, and graceful ; and to help them to choose what will be prettiest and most becoming in their own station. If they see that you never try to dress above yours, they will not try to dress above theirs. Read the little scene between Miss Somers and Simple Susan, in the draper's shop, in Miss Edgeworth's *Parent's Assistant ;* and by the way, if you have not that book, let it be the next birthday present you ask papa or uncle for.

7th. Never seek for amusement, but be always ready to be amused. The least thing has play in it—the slightest word, wit, when your hands are busy and your heart is free. But if you make the aim of your life amusement, the day will come when all the agonies of a pantomime will not bring you an honest laugh. Play actively and gaily ; and cher-ish, without straining, the natural powers of jest in others and your-selves ;—remembering all the while that your hand is every instant on the helm of the ship of your life, and that the Master, on the far shore of Araby the blest, looks for its sail on the horizon,—to its hour.

I can't tell you more till next letter.

IV. Extract from a letter of one of my own girl-pupils and changes :—

"What *is* to be done with town children ? Do you remember going with me to see Mrs. G——, our old servant ? She has died since, and left two children for us to love and care for, for her. The elder, Louie, is thirteen ; unusually intelligent and refined ; I was helping her last

night in her work for an examination. She had Tennys⟨ ⟩ *Dora* to
learn by heart, and said it beautifully, with so much spirit ⟨ ⟩nd then,
asked me what the harvest was. She said she had such a ⟨v⟩ague idea
about it, she shouldn't know how to explain it, if the Insp⟨ ⟩⟨e⟩or asked
her.

"I am just going to take her down to the picture gallery, to give her
a geography lesson on moors and lakes, etc., which is the b⟨e⟩st I can do
for her here; but isn't that dreadful?

"Much love, dear Godfather.

"Ever your loving God⟨c⟩hild."

V. I accept the offer of subjoined letter thankfully. Our Companion,
Mr. Rydings, is henceforward to be answerable for our arithmetic ; and
all sums below fifty pounds are to be sent to him, not to me.

"LAXEY, *April* 1⟨4⟩, 1876.

"My dear Master,—At page 183, April *Fors* Subscription ⟨L⟩ist, bottom of page 183, balance in hand £106 16*s.* 5*d.*, should be £10⟨7⟩ 16*s.* 5*d.*

"Yours, ever truly,

"EGBERT RYDINGS.

"P.S.—Would it be possible to have these items checked befo⟨r⟩e b⟨e⟩-
ing printed? I should feel it a pleasure if I could be of use."

[All Signed Petitions against Rydal Railway to be sent immediately to me at Brantwood, Coniston, Lancashire.]

LETTER LXVI.

BRANTWOOD, 14*th May*, 1876.

THOSE of my readers who have followed me as far as I have hitherto gone in our careful reading of the Pentateuch, must, I think, have felt with me, in natural consequence of this careful reading, more than hitherto, the life and reality of the record ; but, in the degree of this new life, new wonderfulness, and difficult credibility ! For it is always easy to imagine that we believe what we do not understand ; and often graceful and convenient to consent in the belief of others, as to what we do not care about. But when we begin to know clearly what is told, the question if it be fable or fact becomes inevitable in our minds ; and if the fact, once admitted, would bear upon our conduct, its admission can no longer be made a matter of mere social courtesy.

Accordingly, I find one of my more earnest readers already asking me, privately, if I really believed that the hail on Good Friday last had been sent as a punishment for national sin ?—and I should think, and even hope, that other of my readers would like to ask me, respecting the same passage, whether I believed that the sun ever stood still ?

To whom I could only answer, what I answered some time since in my paper on Miracle for the Metaphysical Society, (*Contemporary Review*) that the true miracle, to my mind, would not be in the sun's standing still, but IS in its going on ! We are all of us being swept down to death in a sea of miracle ; we are drowned in wonder, as gnats in a Rhine whirlpool : unless we are worse,—drowned in pleasure, or sloth, or insolence.

Nevertheless, I do not feel myself in the least called upon to believe that the sun stood still, or the earth either, during that pursuit at Ajalon. Nay, it would not anywise amaze me to find that there never had been any such pursuit— never any Joshua, never any Moses ; and that the Jews, "taken generally," as an amiable clerical friend told me from his pulpit a Sunday or two ago, " were a Christian people."

But it does amaze me—almost to helplessness of hand and thought—to find the men and women of these days careless of such issue ; and content, so that they can feed and breathe their fill, to eat like cattle, and breathe like plants, questionless of the Spirit that makes the grass to grow for them on the mountains, or the breeze they breathe on them, its messengers, or the fire that dresses their food, its minister. Desolate souls, for whom the sun—beneath, not above, the horizon—stands still for ever.

'Amazed,' I say, ' almost to helplessness of hand and thought '—quite literally of both. I was reading yesterday, by Fors' order, Mr. Edward B. Taylor's idea of the Greek faith in Apollo : " If the sun travels along its course like a glittering chariot, forthwith the wheels, and the driver, and the horses are there ; " * and Mr. Frederick Harrison's gushing article on Humanity, in the *Contemporary Review ;* and a letter about our Cotton Industry, (hereafter to be quoted, †) and this presently following bit of Sir Philip Sidney's 68th Psalm ;—and my hands are cold this morning, after the horror, and wonder, and puzzlement of my total Sun-less-day, and my head is now standing still, or at least turning round, giddy, instead of doing its work by Shrewsbury clock ; and I don't know where to begin with the quantity I want to say,—all the less that I've said a great deal of it before, if I only knew where to tell you to find it. All up and down

---

* *Early History of Mankind,* (a book of rare value and research, however,) p. 379.

† In the meantime, if any of my readers will look at the leading articles of the *Monetary Gazette,* whose editor I thank with all my heart and soul, for the first honest commercial statements I ever saw in English journals, they will get sufficient light on such matters.

my later books, from *Unto This Last* to *Eagle's Nest,* and
again and again throughout *Fors,* you will find references to
the practical connection between physical and spiritual light
—of which now I would fain state, in the most unmistakable
terms, this sum : that you cannot love the real sun, that is
to say physical light and colour, rightly, unless you love the
spiritual sun, that is to say justice and truth, rightly. That
for unjust and untrue persons, there is no real joy in physical light, so that they don't even know what the word means.
That the entire system of modern life is so corrupted with
the ghastliest forms of injustice and untruth, carried to the
point of not recognising themselves as either—for as long as
Bill Sykes knows that he is a robber, and Jeremy Diddler
that he is a rascal, there is still some of Heaven's light left
for both—but when everybody steals, cheats, and goes to
church, complacently, and the light of their whole body is
darkness, how great is that darkness ! And that the physical result of that mental vileness is a total carelessness of the
beauty of sky, or the cleanness of streams, or the life of
animals and flowers : and I believe that the powers of Nature
are depressed or perverted, together with the Spirit of Man ;
and therefore that conditions of storm and of physical darkness, such as never were before in Christian times, are developing themselves, in connection also with forms of loathsome insanity, multiplying through the whole genesis of
modern brains.

As I correct this sheet for press, I chance, by Fors' order,
in a prayer of St. John Damascene's to the Virgin, on this,
to me, very curious and interesting clause : "Redeem me
from the dark metamorphosis of the angels, rescuing me
from the bitter law-giving of the farmers of the air, and the
rulers of the darkness."

"*τῆς σκοτεινῆς με τῶν δαιμόνων λυτρου μέτημορφῆς,* (I am not
answerable either for Damascene Greek, or for my MS. of it,
in 1396,) *τοῦ πικροτάτου λογοθεσίου τῶν τελωνῶν τοῦ ἀέρος καὶ τῶν
ἀρχόντων τοῦ σκότους ἐξαίρουσα.*"

And now—of this entangling in the shrine of half born
and half-sighted things, see this piece of Sir Philip Sidney's

psalm. I want it also for the bit of conchology at the end. The italics are mine.

"And, call ye this to utter what is just,
You that of justice hold the sov'raign throne?
And call yee this to yield, O sonnes of dust,
To wronged brethren ev'ry one his own?
O no: it is your long malicious will
Now to the world to make by practice known,
With whose oppression you the ballance fill,
Just to your selves, indiff'rent else to none.

But what could they, who ev'n in birth declin'd,
From truth and right to lies and injuries?
To shew the *venom of their cancred mynd*
The adder's image scarcely can suffice.
Nay, scarce the aspick may with them contend,
On whom the charmer all in vaine applies
His skillful'st spells: aye, missing of his end,
While shee *self-deaf, and unaffected* lies.

Lord, crack their teeth, Lord, crush Thou these lions' jawes,
Soe lett them sinck as water in the sand:
When deadly bow their aiming fury drawes,
Shiver the shaft, ere past the shooter's hand.
So make them melt as the dishowsed snaile,
Or as the embrio, whose vitall band
Breakes ere it holdes, and formlesse eyes doe faile
To see the sun, though brought to lightfull land."

'*Dis*housed' snail! That's a bit, observe, of Sir Philip's own natural history, perfecting the image of the psalm, " as a snail which melteth." The 'housed' snail can shelter himself from evil weather, but the poor houseless slug, a mere slimy mass of helpless blackness,—shower-begotten, as it seems,—what is to become of *it* when the sun is up!

Not that even houseless snails melt,—nor that there's anything about snails at all in David's psalm, I believe, both Vulgate and LXX. saying 'wax' instead, as in Psalms lxviii. 2, xcvii. 5, etc.; but I suppose there's some reptilian sense in the Hebrew, justifying our translation here—all the more interesting to me because of a puzzle I got into in Isaiah, the other day; respecting which, lest you should fancy I'm too ready to give up Joshua and the sun without taking trouble about them, please observe this very certain condition of your Scriptural studies : that if you read the Bible with predetermination to pick out every text you approve of—that is to say, generally, any that confirm you in the conceit of your own religious sect,—that console you for the consequences of your own faults,—or assure you of a pleasant future though you attend to none of your present duties—on these terms you will find the Bible entirely intelligible, and wholly delightful : but if you read it with a real purpose of trying to understand it, and obey ; and so read it all through, steadily, you will find it, out and out, the crabbedest and most difficult book you ever tried ; horribly ill written in many parts, according to all human canons ; totally unintelligible in others ; and with the gold of it only to be got at by a process of crushing in which nothing but the iron teeth of the fiercest and honestest resolution will prevail against its adamant.

For instance, take the 16th of Isaiah. Who is to send the Lamb ? why is the Lamb to be sent ? what does the Lamb mean ? There is nothing in the Greek Bible about a Lamb at all, nor is anybody told to send anything. But God says *He* will send something, apostolically, as reptiles !

Then, are the daughters of Moab the outcasts, as in the second verse, or other people, as in the fourth? How is Moab's throne to be established in righteousness, in the tabernacle of David, in the fifth ? What are his lies not to be, in the sixth? And why is he to howl for himself, in the seventh ?' Ask any of the young jackanapes you put up to chatter out of your pulpits, to tell you even so much as this, of the first half-dozen verses ! But above all, ask them who the persons are who are to be sent apostolically as reptiles ?

Meanwhile, on the way to answer, I've got a letter,* not from a jackanapes, but a thoroughly learned and modest clergyman, and old friend, advising me of my mistake in April *Fors,* in supposing that Rahab, in the 89th Psalm, means the harlot. It is, he tells me, a Hebrew word for the

* Corr., Art. VI.

Dragon adversary, as in the verse " He hath cut Rahab, and wounded the Dragon." That will come all the clearer and prettier for us, when we have worked it out, with Rahab herself and all ; meantime, please observe what a busy creature she must have been—the stalks of her flax in heaps enough to hide the messengers ! doubtless also, she was able to dye her thread of the brightest scarlet, a becoming colour. *

Well, I can't get that paper of Mr. Frederick Harrison's out of my head ; chiefly because I know and like its writer ; and I *don't* like his wasting his time in writing that sort of stuff. What I have got to say to him, anent it, may better be said publicly, because I must write it carefully, and with some fulness ; and if he won't attend to me, perhaps some of his readers may. So I consider him, for the time, as one of my acquaintances among working men, and dedicate the close of this letter to him specially.

My dear Harrison,—I am very glad you have been enjoying yourself at Oxford ; and that you still think it a pretty place. But why, in the name of all that's developing, did you walk in those wretched old Magdalen walks ? They're as dull as they were thirty years ago. Why didn't you promenade in our new street, opposite Mr. Ryman's ? or under the rapturous sanctities of Keble ? or beneath the lively new zigzag parapet of Tom Quad ?—or, finally, in the name of all that's human and progressive, why not up and down the elongating suburb of the married Fellows, on the cock-horse road to Banbury ?

However, I'm glad you've been at the old place ; even though you wasted the bloom of your holiday-spirits in casting your eyes, in that too childish and pastoral manner, " round this sweet landscape, with its myriad blossoms and foliage, its meadows in their golden glory," etc. ; and declaring that all you want other people to do is to " follow out in its concrete results this sense of collective evolution." Will you only be patient enough, for the help of this old head of mine on stooping shoulders, to tell me one or two of the inconcrete results of separate evolution ?

* See, on that subject, the third number of *Deucalion*.

Had you done me the honour to walk through my beautifully developing schools, you would have found, just outside
of them, (turned out because I'm tired of seeing it, and
want something progressive) the cast of the Elgin Theseus.
I am tired thereof, it is true ; but I don't yet see my way,
as a Professor of Modern Art, to the superseding it. On
the whole, it appears to me a very satisfactory type of the
human form ; arrived at, as you know, two thousand and
two hundred years ago. And you tell me, nevertheless, to
" see how this transcendent power of collective evolution
holds *me* in the hollow of its hand ! " Well, I hope I *am*
handsomer than the Theseus ; it's very pleasant to think so,
but it did not strike me before. May I flatter myself it is
really your candid opinion ? Will you just look at the
" Realization of the (your ?) Ideal," in the number of *Vanity Fair* for February 17th, 1872, and confirm me on this
point ?

Granting whatever advance in the ideal of humanity you
thus conclude, I still am doubtful of your next reflection.
" But these flowers and plants which we can see between
the cloisters, and trellised round the grey traceries—" (My
dear boy, what have *you* to do with cloisters or traceries ?
Leave that business to the jackdaws ; their loquacious and
undeveloped praise is enough for such relics of the barbarous past. You don't want to shut yourself up, do you ?
and you couldn't design a tracery, for your life ; and you
don't know a good one from a bad one : what in the name
of common sense or common modesty do you mean by chat-
tering about these ?) " What races of men in China, Japan,
India, Mexico, South America, Australasia, first developed
their glory out of some wild bloom ? " Frankly, I don't
know—being in this no wiser than you ; but also I don't
care : and in this carelessness *am* wiser than you, because I
do know this—that if you will look into the Etruscan room
of the British Museum, you will find there an Etruscan
Demeter of—any time you please—B.C., riding on a car
whose wheels are of wild roses : that the wild rose of *her*
time is thus proved to be precisely the wild rose of *my* time,

growing behind my study on the hillside ; and for my own part, I would not give a spray of it for all Australasia, South America, and Japan together. Perhaps, indeed, apples have improved since the Hesperides' time ; but I know they haven't improved since I was a boy, and I can't get a Ribston Pippin, now, for love or money.

Of Pippins in Devonshire, of cheese in Cheshire, believe me, my good friend,—though I trust much more than you in the glorified future of both,—you will find no development in the present scientific day ;—of Asphodel none ; of Apples none demonstrable ; but of Eves ? From the ductile and silent gold of ancient womanhood to the resonant bronze, and tinkling—not cymbal, but shall we say—saucepan, of Miss Frances Power Cobbe, there *is* an interval, with a vengeance ; widening to the future. You yourself, I perceive, have no clear insight into this solidified dispersion of the lingering pillar of Salt, which *had* been good for hospitality in its day ; and which yet would have some honour in its descendant, the poor gleaning Moabitess, into your modern windily progressive pillar of Sand, with "career open to it" indeed other than that of wife and mother—good for nothing, at last, but burial heaps. But are you indeed so proud of what has been already achieved ? I will take you on your own terms, and study only the evolution of the Amazonian Virgin. Take first the ancient type of her, leading the lucent Cobbes of her day, ' florentes aere catervas.'

> " Bellatrix.   Non illa colo, calathisve Minervae
> Foemineas assueta manus.
> Illam omnis tectis agrisqu' effusa juventus
> Turbaque miratur matrum ; et prospectat euntem.
> Attonitis inhians animis : ut regius ostro
> Velet honos leves humeros ; ut fibula crinem
> Auro internectat ; Lyciam ut gerat ipsa pharetram
> Et pastoralem praefixa cuspide myrtum."

With this picture, will you compare that so opportunely furnished me by the author of the *Angel in the House*,[*] of the modern Camilla, in "white bodice, purple knee-

* Article III. of Correspondence.

breeches, which she had borrowed from an Ethiopian serenader, red stockings, and shoes." From this sphere of Ethiopian aspiration, may not even the divinely emancipated
spirit of Cobbe cast one glance—" Backward, Ho " ?

But suppose I grant your Evolution of the Japanese Rose,
and the Virginian Virago, how of other creatures? of other
things? I don't find the advocates of Evolution much given
to studying either men, women, or roses ; I perceive them to
be mostly occupied with frogs and lice. Is there a Worship-
ful Batrachianity—a Divine Pedicularity ?—Stay, I see at
page 874 that Pantheism is "muddled sentiment"; but it
was you, my dear boy, who began the muddling with your
Japanese horticulture. *Your* Humanity has no more to do
with roses than with Rose-chafers or other vermin ; but I
must really beg you not to muddle your terms as well as
your head. " *We*, who *have* thought and studied," do not
admit that " humanity is an aggregate of men." An aggregate of men is a mob, and not ' Humanity '; and an aggregate
of sheep is a flock, and not Ovility ; and an aggregate of
geese is——perhaps you had better consult Mr. Herbert
Spencer and the late Mr. John Stuart Mill for the best
modern expression,—but if you want to know the proper
names for aggregates, in good old English, go and read Lady
Juliana's list in the book of St. Albans.

I do not care, however, to pursue questions with you of
the ' concrete developments.' For, frankly, I conceive myself
to know considerably more than you do, of organic Nature
and her processes, and of organic English and its processes ;
but there is one development of which, since it is your special
business to know it, and I suppose your pleasure, I hope you
know much more than I do, (whose business I find by no
means forwarded by it, still less my pleasure)—the Development of Law. For the concrete development of beautifully
bewigged humanity, called a lawyer, I beg you to observe
that I always express, and feel, extreme respect. But for
Law itself, in the existent form of it, invented, as it appears
to me, only for the torment and taxation of Humanity, I
entertain none whatsoever. I may be wrong, and I don't want

to be wrong ; and you, who know the law, can show me if I am wrong or not. Here, then, are four questions of quite vital importance to Humanity, which if you will answer to me positively, you will do more good than I have yet known done by Positivism.

1. What is 'Usury' as defined by existing Law?

2. Is Usury, as defined by existing law, an absolute term, such as Theft, or Adultery? and is a man therefore a Usurer who only commits Usury a little, as a man is an Adulterer who only commits Adultery a little?

3. Or is it a sin incapable of strict definition, or strictly retributive punishment; like 'Cruelty'? and is a man criminal in proportion to the quantity of it he commits?

4. If criminal in proportion to the quantity he commits, is the proper legal punishment in the direct ratio of the quantity, or inverse ratio of the quantity, as it is in the case of theft?

If you will answer these questions clearly, you will do more service to Humanity than by writing any quantity of papers either on its Collective Development or its Abstract being. I have not touched upon any of the more grave questions glanced at in your paper, because in your present Mercutial temper I cannot expect you to take cognizance of anything grave. With respect to such matters, I will "ask for you to-morrow," not to-day. But here—to end my *Fors* with a piece of pure English,—are two little verses of Sir Philip's, merry enough, in measure, to be set to a Fandango if you like. I may, perhaps, some time or other, ask you if you can apply them personally, in address to Mr. Comte. For the nonce I only ask you the above four plain questions of English law ; and I adjure you, by the soul of every Comes reckoned up in unique Comte—by all that's positive, all that's progressive, all that's spiral, all that's conchoidal, and all that's evolute—great Human Son of Holothurian Harries, answer me.

> " Since imprisoned in my mother
> Thou me feed'st, whom have I other
> Held my stay, or made my song?
> Yea, when all me so misdeemed,
> I to most a monster seemed
> Yet in thee my hope was strong.

> Yet of thee the thankful story
> Filled my mouth : thy gratious glory
> Was my ditty all the day.
> Do not then, now age assaileth,
> Courage, verdure, vertue faileth,
> Do not leave me cast away."

I have little space, as now too often, for any definite school work. My writing-lesson, this month, is a facsimile of the last words written by Nelson ; in his cabin, with the allied fleets in sight, off Trafalgar. It is entirely fine in general structure and character.

Mr. Ward has now three, and will I hope soon have the fourth, of our series of lesson photographs, namely,—

1. Madonna by Filippo Lippi.
2. The Etruscan Leucothea.
3. Madonna by Titian.
4. Infanta Margaret, by Velasquez.

On these I shall lecture, as I have time, here and in the *Laws of Fésole ;* but, in preparation for all farther study, when you have got the four, put them beside each other, putting the Leucothea first, the Lippi second, and the others as numbered.

Then, the first, the Leucothea, is entirely noble religious art, of the fifth or sixth century B.C., full of various meaning and mystery, of knowledges that are lost, feelings that have ceased, myths and symbols of the laws of life, only to be traced by those who know much both of life and death.

Technically, it is still in Egyptian bondage, but in course of swiftly progressive redemption.

The second is nobly religious work of the fifteenth century of Christ,—an example of the most perfect unison of religious myth with faithful realism of human nature yet produced in this world. The Etruscan traditions are preserved in it even to the tassels of the throne cushion : the pattern of these, and of the folds at the edge of the angel's drapery, may be seen in the Etruscan tomb now central in the first compartment of the Egyptian gallery of the British Museum ; and the double cushion of that tomb is used, with absolute obedience to his tradition, by Jacopo della Quercia, in the tomb of Ilaria di Caretto.

The third represents the last phase of the noble religious art of the world, in which realization has become consummate ; but all supernatural aspect is refused, and mythic teaching is given only in obedience to former tradition, but with no anxiety for its acceptance. Here is, for certain, a sweet Venetian peasant, with her child, and fruit from the market-boats of Mestre. The Ecce Agnus, topsy-turvy on the finely perspectived scroll, may be deciphered by whoso list.

But the work itself is still sternly conscientious, severe, reverent, and faultless.

The fourth is an example of the highest reach of technical perfection yet reached in art ; all effort and labour seeming to cease in the radiant peace and simplicity of consummated human power. But all belief in supernatural things, all hope of a future state, all effort to teach, and all desire to be taught, have passed away from the artist's mind. The Child and her Dog are to him equally real, equally royal, equally mortal. And the History of Art since it reached this phase—cannot be given in the present number of *Fors Clavigera.*

NOTES AND CORRESPONDENCE.

I. Affairs of the Company.

No. 50. G. £10 10*s.*

This is a subscription of five guineas for each year : this amount completes that sum (with the £15 15*s.* which appeared at p. 137, February *Fors*) for each of the five years.

The publication of the following letter, with its answer, will, I hope, not cause Mr. Tarrant any further displeasure. I have only in the outset to correct his statement that the payment of £10 14*s.* 11*d.* was on *my* behalf. It is simply payment to another lawyer. And my first statement was absolutely accurate ; I never said Mr. Tarrant had himself taxed, but that he had been " employed in taxing " ; I do not concern myself with more careful analysis, when the accounts are all in print. My accusation is against the 'legal profession generally,' not against a firm which I have chosen as an entirely trustworthy one, to be employed both in St. George's business and my own.

2, BOND COURT, WALBROOK, 25*th April*, 1876.

Dear Mr. Ruskin,—I have the April *Fors*, in which I see you have published our account of costs against you, amounting to £47 13*s.* 4*d.* The document was yours, and you had a perfect right to lay it before your readers, but you are the first client who has ever thought it necessary to put such a document of mine to such a use. I don't know, however, that it will do me any injury, although the statement preceding it is somewhat inaccurate, because our costs of the transfer of the Sheffield property were £26 15*s.* 11*d.*, which included a payment of £10 14*s.* 11*d.* made on your behalf, leaving our costs at £16 1*s.*, the other portion of the £47 13*s.* 4*d.* being costs relating to the constitution of the St. George's Company, leaving altogether £29 14*s.* 11*d.* only payable to us beyond money paid on your account. It is hardly fair, therefore, to say that I *employed myself* in taxing the transfer of the property to nearly £50.

As to the charge for letters (the writing which is really not brickmakers' work), you must bear in mind that the entire of your matters had to be done by correspondence, for which you are fairly chargeable ; and I cannot accuse myself of having written a single letter that was unnecessary.

As to the position of the St. George's Company, it is not a legal company, if by that you mean a company recognised by law : it has neither the advantages nor disadvantages of companies incorporated in accordance with the provisions of the several Acts of Parliament relating to such matters. It is not a legal trust of a charitable nature, if by that term be meant a trust which is liable to the supervision or interference of the Charity Commissioners. It is a number of persons unincorporated, but associated for other purposes than that of gain. It is on a similar footing to such a society as that for the Promotion of Christian Knowledge. The Master will be personally responsible for the debts of the Company contracted by his order. If you desire to have a legal-Company, or the supervision of the Charity Commissioners, you must give way in many points which you have hitherto considered indispensable to your scheme. On the 29th February last we sent you a specimen of the form in which we proposed to draw up the memorandum for each Companion to subscribe. If you will return us this with any remarks upon it which may occur to you, we will at once have it engrossed, and send it you to be signed by all the Companions.

We were expecting a call from you when you were in town some time since, and should have then have discussed this subject with you, and also the subject of the trust deed which will have to be executed by the Master of the Company.

We will act upon your suggestion, and forward the deed of the Sheffield property to Mr. Bagshawe. Shall I also send all the title deeds to him relating to the property? Tell me this.

Faithfully yours,

Professor Ruskin,　　　　　　　　　　　W. P. TARRANT.
　　Arthur Severn, Esq., Herne Hill, S.E.

(Answer.)

PATTERDALE, 6th May, 1876.

Dear Mr. Tarrant,—I was surprised and vexed by the opening of your letter of 25th April, showing that you had not in the least hitherto understood the scope or meaning of my present work. There is not the smallest unfriendliness in my publication of your account. No client ever had occasion to do it before, of course;—you never had a client before engaged in steady and lifelong contest with the existing principles of the Law, the Church, and the Army,—had you? The publication of your accounts of course can do you no harm, if they are fair; nor have, or had I, the slightest idea of their being otherwise. All accounts for St. George are to be printed: the senders-in must look to the consequences.

The delay in my returning your draft of the rules of Company is because every lawyer I speak to tells me of a new difficulty. The whole piece of business, you remember, arose from my request to you simply to secure a piece of ground to our trustees, which had been given us by Mr. Baker. Now I find at the last moment that neither Mr. Baker nor anybody else can *give* us a piece of land at all, but must sell it us.

Next, I want to know if this form, as you have drawn it up, is approved by me, what are you going to do with it? What is the good of it? Will the writing of it in black letter make us a legal compar , like a railway company, capable of holding land? Do the Charity Commissioners interfere with *their* business? or must we blow some people to bits or smash them into jelly, to prove our want of charity,—and get leave, therefore, to do what we like with our own?

Fix your minds, and Mr. Barber's, on this one point—the grip of the land. If you can't give us that, send us in your accounts, and let us be done with the matter. If you can, on the document as it stands, write it out on the rubbish your modern stationers call parchment, and do what you will with it, so.

I am really ashamed to give any farther account, just now, of the delays in our land work, or of little crosses and worries blocking my first attempt at practice. One of the men whom I thought I had ready for this Worcestershire land, being ordered, for trial, to do a little bit of rough work in Yorkshire that I might not torment Mr. Baker with his freshmanship, threw up the task at once, writing me a long letter of which one sentence was enough for me,—that "he would do *his share*, but no more." These infernal notions of Equality and Independence are so rooted, now, even in the best men's minds, that they don't so much as know even what Obedience or Fellowship mean! Fancy one of Nelson's or Lord Cochrane's men retreating from his gun, with the avowed resolution to 'do no more than his share'! However, I know there's good in this man, and I doubt not he will repent, and break down no more; but I shall not try him again for a year. And I must be forgiven my St. George's accounts this month. I really can't let the orchises and hyacinths go out of flower while I'm trying to cast sums; and I've been two whole days at work on the purple marsh orchis alone, which my botanical readers will please observe is in St. George's schools to be called 'Porphyria veris,' 'Spring Purplet.' It is, I believe, Ophelia's "long purple." There are a quantity of new names to be invented for the whole tribe, their present one's being not by St. George endurable.

The subjoined letter gives me great pleasure : it is from a son of my earliest Oxford friend : who, as his father helped me in educating myself, is now helping me in the education of others. I print it entire ; it may give some of my readers an idea of the minor hindrances which meet one at every step, and take as much time to conquer as large ones. The work to be done is to place a series of the simple chemical elements as 'Imps' in a pretty row of poetical Bottles at Sheffield.

"BROAD STREET, OXFORD, *March* 30, 1876.

"My dear Mr. Ruskin,—I knocked in vain at your 'oak' last night when I came to Corpus to report progress, and also to ask you two questions, which must be put to you by letter, as there is not much time to lose if you wish to have the alkaline earths ready by the time you go to Sheffield. Firstly, do you wish me to see about getting the *metals* of the alkalies, and if so which of them do you want? Some of them are extremely expensive,—calcium, for instance, being 2*d* a grain;

but then, as it is very light a very small quantity would be required as
a specimen. The other questions were about the amount of the
oxides, and about the shape of the bottles to hold them. I have in
your absence chosen some long sample bottles which are very beautiful
of their kind, and even if they do not meet your approval they can easily
be changed when you return to Oxford. I am progressing fairly well
with the earths—Magnesia is ready ; Alumina and Baryta partly made,
but not yet pure, for it is not more easy in chemistry to get a perfect
thing than in any other matter with which man has anything to do,
and to-day I have been extremely unfortunate with the Baryta, having
tried two methods of making it, broken four crucibles, and, worst of
all, failed to make it in a state of purity: however I shall have one
more try to-morrow, and no doubt shall succeed. If there is any chance
of your being in Oxford before Easter, I will not make the Silica, since
the process is very beautiful, and one which no doubt you would like
to see. Please excuse the length of my letter, and believe me,

                         " Affectionately yours,
                                   "THEODORE D. ACLAND."

II. Affairs of the Master.

I am aghast at the columnar aspect of any account given in satisfactory detail ; and will only gradually, as I have space, illustrate my own
expenditure and its course. That unexplained hundred of last month,
diminished itself, I find, thus :

	£	s.	d.
Pocket	10	0	0
Klein, (final account on dismissal to Rotterdam, pay- ing his passage, and a shilling or two over).....	30	0	0
Downs, for my London quarterly pensioners........	25	0	0
Morley, (Oxford bookbinding)....................	3	1	6
Easter presents.............................	5	0	0
	73	1	6
Leaving a balance of.................	26	18	6

to be added to the £200 of personal expenses in this month's accounts.
About a hundred and twenty of this has gone in a fortnight's posting,
with Mr. and Mrs. Severn, from London to Coniston, stopping to see
St. Albans, Peterborough, Croyland, Stamford and Burleigh, Grantham,
Newark, Lincoln, our new ground at Sheffield, Pomfret, Knaresborough,
Ripon, Fountain's, Richmond, Mortham Tower, and Brougham Castle.
A pleasant life, you think ? Yes,—if I led an unpleasant one, however
dutiful, I could not write any of my books, least of all, *Fors.* But I am
glad, if you honestly think it a pleasant life ; why, if so, my richer
readers, do you drive only round the parks, every day, instead of from
place to place through England, learning a thing or two on the road ?
Of the rest of the 'self' money, I leave further account till next month :
it is not all gone yet. I give, however, for a typical example, one of
Downs's weekly bills, reaching the symmetrical total of £7 7*s.* 7*d.*, or a

guinea and a penny a day, which I think is about the average. Of the persons named therein as receiving weekly wage, Hersey is our old under-gardener, now rheumatic, and as little able to earn his dinner as I am myself; Rusch, my old lapidary, who cuts in the course of the week what pebbles he can for me; Best, an old coachman, who used to come to us from livery-stable on occasion, and now can't drive any more; Christy, an old woman who used to work for my mother.

1876.		£	s.	d.
April 22.	Cash in hand......................	30	12	8
29.	Men's Wages......................	4	1	0
	Coachman's Book.................	1	16	10
	Charities.......................	0	16	0
	Sundries	0	13	9
		£7	7	7
April 29.	Balance in hand..................	23	5	1

Men's Wages.		£	s.	d.
April 29.	David Downs.....................	1	15	0
	Thomas Hersey..................	1	5	0
	John Rusch.....................	1	1	0
		£4	1	0

Coachman's Book.		£	s.	d.
April 29.	Plate Powder, 1s.; Oil, 10d........	0	1	10
	Soap and Sand..................	0	1	0
	Wages..........................	1	14	0
		£1	16	10

Charities.		£	s.	d.
	William Best.....................	0	10	0
	Mrs. Christy	0	6	0
		£0	16	0

Sundries.		£	s.	d.
April 22.	Postage	0	0	5
24.	Rail and 'Bus, British Museum.....	0	1	0
	Cord for Boxes, 1s. 6d.; Postage, 1s. 6½d....................	0	3	0½
25.	Horse and Cart, Boxes to Station..	0	7	6
	Carman, 1s ; Booking ditto, 6d.....	0	1	6
	Postage..	0	0	1
26 and 28.	Postage..................	0	0	2½
		£0	13	9

After thus much of miniature illustration, I have only to explain of the broad effects in the account below, that my Oxford secretary, who has £200 a year, does such work for me connected with my Professorship as only a trained scholar could do, leaving me free here to study hyacinths. I wish I could give him the Professorship itself, but must do as I am bid by Oxford. My younger secretary, who has £100 a year, is this year put into office, for St. George's correspondence; and I must beg my good friends—now. I am thankful to say, gathering a little to St. George's work,—not to think themselves slighted in being answered by his hand, for mine is weary.

1876.	£	s.	d.
April 16. Balance	1511	10	1
May 1. Half-year's Stipend of Slade Professorship....................	179	0	0
	1690	10	1
	464	11	0
Balance, May 16th............	£1225	19	1

	£	s.	d.
April 20 and 30. Self......................	200	0	0
20. Downs........................	50	0	0
22. Photographs (Leucothea and Lippi)	16	5	0
25. Tailor's Account.................	33	6	0
May 1. Oxford Secretary.................	100	0	0
1. Raffaelle for May and June........	15	0	0
15. Burgess........................	50	0	0
	£464	11	0

III.

"HASTINGS, *May* 15.

"My dear Ruskin,—I enclose two extracts, cut from the same day's paper, which contain so grimly humorous a parallel between the ways in which the 'Protestant Church' and 'the world' are engaged in 'obliterating all traces of the Virgin Mary,' that I thought you might possibly use them in *Fors* or elsewhere.

"Yours affectionately,
"C. PATMORE."

(The following are the two extracts. Before giving them, I must reply to my greatly honoured and loved friend, that both the Bristol destroyers of images and New York destroyers of humanity, are simply—Lost Sheep of the great Catholic Church; account of whom will be required at *her* hand.)

"ICONOCLASM AT BRISTOL.—Our Bristol correspondent writes: The removal of the 'imagery' from the north porch of Bristol Cathedral has created considerable excitement in the city and in Clifton. As a member of the capitular body who is known to strongly object to the figures was seen near the Cathedral late on Wednesday night, the clerk of the works employed 'watchers,' his intention being to refuse admission to other than his own workmen. On Thursday morning he had occasion to leave the works to go to the quarries at Corsham, and while he was absent a gang of men, under the orders of the chapter clerk, entered the gates, and before the clerk of the works, who was telegraphed for, could return, hauled down the four statues and *obliterated all traces of the Virgin Mary*, doing much damage to other carving in the process of removal. The last has by no means been heard of this affair. The statues cost over £100 each, but the money value of the 'imagery' is not considered by the Restoration Committee. Their contention is that, until the work was completed and handed over to the Cathedral body, it belonged to the Restoration Committee; and it is believed that the right of the Chapter to act as they have done will be tested in a court of law. Feeling is so strong against the action of the Dean and Chapter that plenty of money would be forthcoming to prosecute such an inquiry."—*Pall Mall Gazette, April* 7, 1876.

"One of the latest 'sensations' in New York has been a 'female boxing match,' aptly described by the *New York Times* as a 'novel and nonsensical exhibition.' The combatants—or 'lady contestants,' as they are called in the report of the proceedings—were two ballet-girls, of the kind known as 'variety dancers.' One, Miss Saunders, wore a white bodice, purple knee-breeches, which she had borrowed from an Ethiopian serenader, red stockings, and shoes. The other, Miss Harland, was attired in blue trunks and white tights. Both appeared nervous, were very pale, tried to blush, and 'partially succeeded.' When the fighting began, Miss Harland 'did not know what to do with her hands.' Miss Saunders, however, had her fists more at command, and, after some preliminary sparring, succeeded in striking her opponent 'square in the face.' Miss Harland, on her side, 'by a vicious blow from the shoulder,' managed to disarrange Miss Saunders's back hair. Both ladies then smiled. In the end Miss Harland lost the match, 'owing to her confirmed habit of swinging her hands around in the air.' Miss Saunders was declared the winner, and carried off a prize of 200 dols. and a piece of silver plate; Miss Harland received a ten-dollar bill from an amateur who thought she deserved consolation; and the two 'lady contestants' left the stage arm-in-arm."—*Pall Mall Gazette, April* 7, 1876.

IV. In last *Fors*, though I thought I knew my *Old Mortality* well enough, I carelessly wrote 'Elspeth,' for ' Elizabeth,' (meaning Bessie Maclure); and the misprint ' Araunah' for 'Arauah' escaped my eyes three times over. The more grotesque one of 'changes' for ' charges,' in p. 211, line 40, was I suppose appointed by Fors to chastise me for incurable flirtation. I wish I knew who these two schoolgirls are, whom I've got to finish my letter to if I can, this time.

My dears, will you please, for I can't rewrite what I've said so often, read, when you have opportunity, the letter to a young lady in *Fors* 34, pp. 96, 97.* Respecting the third article in that letter, I have now

* I should like my lady readers in general to have, of back *Fors* numbers, at least, 30, 34, 36, 45, 46, and 48: those who have the complete book should scratch out the eleventh line in ρ. 18 of the last Index, and put the 10th line of it thus: "Ladies, and girls, advice to, 30, 2; 34, 29; 45, 212; 48, 271."

a few words to add ; (read also, if you can, what is said of the Word
of God, in Letters XLV. and XLVI). I told you in last *Fors* that you
would have great difficulty in getting leave from English society to obey
Christ. Fors has since sent me, in support of this statement, a paper
called *The Christian,*—the number for Thursday, May 11,—in the
fifteenth page of which is an article on young ladies headed " What
can they do ? " from which I take the following passage :—

" There have been times of special prayer for young men and women.
Could there not be also for the very large class of young ladies who do
not go out into society ? They have no home duties to detain them, as
many in a humbler condition; they have hours and hours of leisure,
and know not how to spend them—partly from need of being directed,
but more so from the prejudices and hindrances in their way. Their
hearts are burning to do something for Christ, but they are not allowed,
partly because it is considered ' improper,' and for a variety of reasons.
" There is a cry on every side for laborers. There are numbers longing to respond ; if not wholly to dedicate their lives, at least a portion
of their days, to active Christian service, and only a wave of united
prayer can throw these objections aside, and free the large band who
are so willing.
" A bright young Christian came to me this week. She is tired of
meetings to which she is constantly taken, but never allowed to work in
the inquiry-room at them,—hindered from taking up the least bit of
work, till at last she cannot even *ask* for it. Almost to ' kill time,' she
has taken up a secular corresponding agency."

Now that it is ' considered improper ' by the world that you should do
anything for Christ, is entirely true, and always true ; and therefore it
was that your Godfathers and Godmothers, in your name, renounced
the " vain pomp and glory of the world," with all covetous desires of
the same—see baptismal service—(I wonder if you had pretty names—
won't you tell me ?) but I much doubt if you, either privately or from
the pulpit of your doubtless charming church, have ever been taught
what the " vain pomp and glory of the world " was.
Well, do you want to be better dressed than your schoolfellows ?
Some of them are probably poor, and cannot afford to dress like you ;
or, on the other hand, you may be poor yourselves, and may be morti-
fied at their being dressed better than you. Put an end to all that at
once, by resolving to go down into the deep of your girl's heart, where
you will find, inlaid by Christ's own hand, a better thing than vanity ;
pity. And be sure of this, that, although in a truly Christian land,
every young girl would be dressed beautifully and delightfully,—in this
entirely heathen and Baal-worshipping land of ours, not one girl in ten
has either decent or healthy clothing, and that you have no business
now to wear anything fine yourself, but are bound to use your full
strength and resources to dress as many of your poor neighbors as you
can. What of fine dress your people insist upon your wearing, take—

and wear proudly and prettily, for their sakes; but, so far as in you
lies, be sure that every day you are labouring to clothe some poorer
creatures. And if you cannot clothe, at least help, with your hands.
You can make your own bed; wash your own plate; brighten your own
furniture,—if nothing else.

'But that's servant's work'? Of course it is. What business have
you to hope to be better than a servant of servants? 'God made you a
lady'? Yes, He has put you, that is to say, in a position in which you
may learn to speak your own language beautifully; to be accurately
acquainted with the elements of other languages; to behave with
grace, tact, and sympathy to all around you; to know the history of
your country, the commands of its religion, and the duties of its race.
If you obey His will in learning these things, you will obtain the power
of becoming a true 'lady;' and you will become one, if while you
learn these things you set yourself, with all the strength of your youth
and womanhood, to serve His servants, until the day come when He
calls you to say, "Well done, good and faithful servant: enter thou
into the joy of thy Lord."

You may thus become a Christ's lady, or you may, if you will,
become a Belial's lady, taking Belial's gift of miserable idleness, living
on the labor and shame of others, and deceiving them and yourself by
lies about Providence, until you perish in hell with the rest of such,
shrieking the bitter cry, " When saw we *Thee?* "

V.

" 3, ATHOLE CRESCENT, PERTH, 10*th May*, 1876.

"Sir,—Thinking that it may interest you, I take the liberty of
writing to let you know that the 'Lead' is not at all in the state you
suppose it to be; but still runs down, very clear, by the side of the
North Inch and past Rose Terrace, and, judging from the numbers of
them at this moment playing by it, affords no small delight to the
children.

" I am, yours most respectfully,

"A READER OF ' FORS.' "

VI.

"EASTHAMPSTEAD RECTORY, BRACKNELL,

" *April* 20, 1876.

" My dear Ruskin,—I have just received this month's *Fors*, but not
read it, (of course not; my friends never do, except to find the mistakes,) as I am off to Dublin, but as regards Psalm lxxxvii., (note, p.
169,) I expounded it in a sermon some time since, and was talking of
it to a very learned Hebraist last Monday. Rahab, there, is generally
understood to mean 'the monster,' and has nothing to do, beyond
resemblance of sound, with Rahab the harlot. And the monster is the
crocodile, as typical of Egypt. In Psalm lxxxix. 10, (the Bible version,
not the Prayer Book,) you will see Rahab explained in the margin, by
' *or Egypt.*'

" Perhaps Rahab the harlot was called by the same name from the rapacity of her class, just as in Latin *lupa.*

" The whole Psalm is badly translated, and, as we have it, unintelligible. But it is really charged with deep prophetical meaning. I cannot write more, so believe me,

"Ever yours affectionately,

"O. GORDON.

" I hope you will have had a pleasant journey when you receive this. The Greek Septuagint is much better than the English, but not good. As regards the general meaning, you have divined it very correctly."

LETTER LXVII.

As I am now often asked, in private letters, the constitution of St. George's Company, and cannot, hitherto, refer,
in answer, to any clear summary of it, I will try to write
such a summary in this number of *Fors;* that it may henceforward be sent to inquirers as alone sufficiently explanatory.

The St. George's Company is a society established to
carry out certain charitable objects, towards which it invites,
and thankfully will receive, help from any persons caring to
give it, either in money, labour, or any kind of gift. But the
Company itself consists of persons who agree in certain general principles of action, and objects of pursuit, and who
can, therefore, act together in effective and constant unison.

These objects of pursuit are, in brief terms, the health,
wealth, and long life of the British nation : the Company
having thus devoted itself, in the conviction that the British
nation is at present unhealthy, poor, and likely to perish, as
a power, from the face of the earth. They accordingly propose to themselves the general medicining, enriching, and
preserving in political strength, of the population of these
islands ; they themselves numbering at present, in their
ranks, about thirty persons,—none of them rich, several of
them sick, and the leader of them, at all events, not likely to
live long.

Whether the nation be healthy, or in unwholesome degradation of body and mind ; wealthy, or in continual and shameful distress ; strong, or in rapid decline of political power
and authority,—the reader will find debated throughout the
various contents of the preceding volumes of *Fors.* But
there is one public fact, which cannot be debated—that the
nation is in debt. And the St. George's Company do practically make it their *first*, though not their principal, object,
to bring *that* state of things to an end ; and to establish, in-

stead of a National Debt, a National Store. (See the last
line of the fifth page of the first letter of the series, published
1st January, 1871, and the eleventh, and twenty-seventh,
letters, throughout.)

That very few readers of *this* page have any notion, at this
moment, what a National Debt is, or can conceive what a
National Store should be, is one of many evil consequences
of the lies which, under the title of "Political Economy,"
have been taught by the ill-educated, and mostly dishonest,
commercial men, who at present govern the press of the
country.

I have again and again stated the truth in both these
matters, but must try once more to do it, emphatically,
and intelligibly.

A 'civilized nation' in modern Europe consists, in broad
terms, of (A) a mass of half-taught, discontented, and mostly
penniless populace, calling itself the people ; of (B) a thing
which it calls a government—meaning an apparatus for collecting and spending money ; and (C) a small number of capitalists,
many of them rogues, and most of them stupid persons, who
have no idea of any object of human existence other than
money-making, gambling, or champagne-bibbing. A certain
quantity of literary men, saying anything they can get paid
to say,—of clergymen, saying anything they have been
taught to say,—of natural philosophers, saying anything
that comes into their heads,—and of nobility, saying nothing
at all, combine in disguising the action, and perfecting the
disorganization, of the mass ; but with respect to practical
business, the civilized nation consists broadly of mob, money-
collecting machine, and capitalist.

Now when this civilized mob wants to spend money for
any profitless or mischievous purposes,—fireworks, illuminations, battles, driving about from place to place, or what
not,—being itself penniless, it sets its money-collecting machine to borrow the sum needful for these amusements from
the civilized capitalist.

The civilized capitalist lends the money, on condition that,
through the money-collecting machine, he may tax the

civilized mob thenceforward for ever. The civilized mob
spends the money forthwith, in gunpowder, infernal machines,
masquerade dresses, new boulevards, or anything else it has
set its idiotic mind on for the moment ; and appoints its
money-collecting machine to collect a daily tax from its children, and children's children, to be paid to the capitalists
from whom it had received the accommodation, thenceforward for ever.

That is the nature of a National Debt.

In order to understand that of a National Store, my
readers must first consider what any store whatever, serviceable to human beings, consists of. A store properly means
a collection of useful things. Literally, it signifies only a
quantity, or much of *any*thing. But the heap of broken
bottles which, I hear, is accumulating under the principal
cliff of Snowdon, through the contributions of tourists from
the summit, is not properly to be called a store ; though a
binfull of old wine is. Neither is a heap of cannon-balls a
store ; * though a heap of potatoes is. Neither is a cellar
ful of gunpowder a store ; though a cellar full of coals is.
A store is, for squirrels, of nuts ; for bees, of honey ; for
men, of food, clothes, fuel, or pretty things, such as toys or
jewels,—and, for educated persons, of books and pictures.

And the possession of such a store by the nation would
signify, that there were no taxes to pay ; that everybody had
clothes enough, and some stuff laid by for next year ; that
everybody had food enough, and plenty of salted pork, pickled
walnuts, potted shrimps, or other conserves, in the cupboard ;
that everybody had jewels enough, and some of the biggest
laid by, in treasuries and museums ; and, of persons caring
for such things, that everybody had as many books and
pictures as they could read or look at ; with quantities of
the highest quality besides, in easily accessible public libraries
and galleries.

Now the wretches who have, at present, the teaching of

---

* They may serve for the *defence* of the store, of course ;—so may the
broken bottles, stuck on the top of a wall. But the lock of your cupboard is not the contents of it.

the people in their hands, through the public press, tell them
that it is not "practical" to attempt to bring about this state
of things ;—and that their government, or money-collecting
machine, must not buy wine, potatoes, jewels, or pictures for
them ; but *must* buy iron plates two feet thick, gunpowder,
and red tape. And this popular instruction is given, you
will find, in the end, by persons who know that they could
not get a percentage themselves, (without the public's coming to know it,) on buying potatoes or pictures ; but *can* get
it, and a large one, on manufacturing iron, on committing
wholesale murder, or on tying up papers with red tape.

Now the St. George's Company propose to themselves,—
and, if the God they believe in, lives, will assuredly succeed
in their proposition,—to put an end to this rascally and inhuman state of things, and bring about an honest and human
state of them, instead. And they have already actually
begun the accumulation of a National Store of good and
useful things ; by the collection and administration of which,
they are not themselves to derive any gain whatsoever, but
the Nation only.

We are, therefore, at present, as I said at first, a company
established for a charitable purpose ; the object of charity
being the entire body of the British nation, now paying
taxes to cheating capitalists. But we hope to include,
finally, in our ranks a large number of the people themselves,
and to make quite a different sort of people of them, carrying out our company's laws, to the abolition of many existing interests and in abrogation of many existing arrangements.

And the laws which we hope thus to see accepted are none
of them new ; but have been already recommended by all
wise men, and practised by all truly prosperous states ; nor
is there anything whatever new in the modes of administration proposed ;—and especially be it noted, there is nothing
of the present leader's fancies, in any part or character of
the scheme—which is merely the application, to our nation-
ally diseased thoughts and practices, of the direct precepts
of the true sages of past time, who are every one of them in

harmony concerning all that is necessary for men to do, feel, and know.

And we hope to establish these laws, not by violence, but by obeying them ourselves, to the extent of which existing circumstances admit ; and so gradually showing the advantage of them, and making them acceptable to others. Not that, for the enforcement of some of them, (the abolition of all manufactures that make the air unwholesome, for instance,) we shall hesitate to use the strong hand, when once our hands are strong. But we shall not begin by street riots to throw down our neighbour's chimneys, or break his machinery ;—though what we shall *end* in doing — God knows, not I,—but I have my own thoughts concerning it ; not at present needing exposition.

The Companions, for the most part, will remain exactly in the condition of life they held before entering the Society ; but they will direct all their powers, and some part of their revenues, in that condition, to the advance of its interests. We hold it shortsighted and ruinous policy to form separate institutions, or attempt the sudden establishment of new systems of labour. Every one of us must use the advantages he now possesses, whatever they may be, and contend with the difficulties arising out of his present position, gradually modifying it, as he can, into conformity with the laws which the Society desires may be ultimately observed by all its members.

The first of our conditions of Companionship is Honesty. We are a company of honest persons, vowing to have no fellowship with dishonest ones. Persons who do not know the meaning of the word ' Honesty,' or who would in anywise, for selfish convenience, tolerate any manner of cheating or lying, either in others or themselves, we class indiscriminately with the self-conscious rogues, for whom we have more respect ; and our separation from all such is to be quite manifest and unmistakable. We do not go into monasteries,—we seek no freedom of conscience in foreign lands,—we profess no severities of asceticism at home. We simply refuse to have any dealings with rogues, whether at home or abroad.

I repeat, for this must be strictly understood ; we are a company of honest persons ; and will add to ourselves none but persons of that quality. We, for our own part, entirely decline to live by passing bad half-crowns, by selling bad goods, or by lying as to their relative quality. And we hold only such communication with persons guilty of such practices, as we should with any other manner of thieves or liars.

It will follow that anything gravely said by a Companion of St. George may be, without investigation, believed ; and anything sold by one, without scrutiny, bought for what it is said to be,—of which recovery of old principles of human speech and commerce, no words can set forth the infinitude of beneficial consequences, when it is once brought about among a discernible and every day increasing body of persons.

The second condition of Companionship is the resolution, so far as we have ability, to earn our own living with our own hands, and not to allow, much less compel, other people to work for us : this duty being of double force,—first, as necessary to our own health and honour ; but much more, as striking home at the ghastly universal crime of modern society,—stealing the labourer's bread from him, (making him work, that is to say, for ours, as well as his own,) and then abusing and despising him for the degradation of character which his perpetual toil involves ; * deliberately, in many cases, refusing to encourage him in economy, that we may have him at our mercy to grind in the mill ; always selling as much gin and beer to him as we can persuade him to swill, at the rate of twenty-pence for twopence' worth, (see Letter XXVII.,) to fill our own pockets ; and teaching him pious catechisms, that we may keep him our quiet slave.

We cannot, at present, all obey this great law concerning labour, however willing we may be ; for we may not, in the condition of life in which we have been brought up, have

* See Letter XI. (November '71,) pages 142 to 145, the most pregnant four pages in the entire series of these letters ; and compare that for January of this year, pp. 100—101, and for April, p. 170.

been taught any manual labour by which we now could make a living. I myself, the present Master of the Society, cannot obey this, its second main law ; but then I am only a make-shift Master, taking the place till somebody more fit for it be found. Sir Walter Scott's life, in the full strength of it at Ashestiel, and early at Abbotsford, with his literary work done by ten, or at latest twelve, in the morning ; and the rest of the day spent in useful work with Tom Purdie in his woods, is a model of wise moral management of mind and body, for men of true literary power ; but I had neither the country training of body, nor have the natural strength of brain, which can reach this ideal in anywise. Sir Walter wrote as a stream flows ; but I do all my brain-work like a wrung sponge, and am tired out, and good for nothing, after it. Sir Walter was in the open air, farm-bred, and playing with lambs, while I was a poor little Cockney wretch, play-ing, in a dark London nursery, with a bunch of keys. I do the best I can, and know what ought to be ; and that is all the Company really need of me. I would fain, at this mo-ment, both for pleasure and duty's sake, be cutting the dead stems out of my wood, or learning to build a dry stone wall under my good mason, Mr. Usher, than writing these insti-tutes of St. George ; but the institutes are needed, and must be written by me, since there is nobody else to write them.

Any one, therefore, may be a Companion of St. George who sincerely does what they can, to make themselves useful, and earn their daily bread by their own labour : and some forms of intellectual or artistic labour, inconsistent (as a musician's) with other manual labour, are accepted by the Society as useful ; provided they be truly undertaken for the good and help of all ; and that the intellectual labourer ask no more pay than any other workman. A scholar can gen-erally live on less food than a ploughman, and there is no conceivable reason why he should have more.* And if he be

---

* Again, I have more myself—but that is because I have been ill-bred ; and I shall be most thankful to take less, as soon as other people cease to be paid for doing nothing. People cry out upon me for asking ten shillings for a year's *Fors ;* but never object to Mr. Barber's paying

a false-hearted scholar, or a bad painter or fiddler, there is infinite reason why he should have less. My readers may have been surprised at the instant and eager assertion, as of a leading principle, in the first of these letters, (January '71,) that people cannot live by art. But I spoke swiftly, because the attempt so to live is among the worst possible ways they can take of injurious begging. There are a few, a very few persons born in each generation, whose words are worth hearing ; whose art is worth seeing. These born few will preach, or sing, or paint, in spite of you ; they will starve like grasshoppers, rather than stop singing ; and even if you don't choose to listen, it is charitable to throw them some crumbs to keep them alive. But the people who take to writing or painting as a means of livelihood, because they think it genteel, are just by so much more contemptible than common beggars, in that they are noisy and offensive beggars. I am quite willing to pay for keeping our poor vagabonds in the workhouse ; but not to pay them for grinding organs outside my door, defacing the streets with bills and caricatures, tempting young girls to read rubbishy novels, or deceiving the whole nation to its ruin, in a thousand leagues square of dirtily printed falsehood, every morning at breakfast. Whatever in literature, art, or religion, is done for money, is poisonous itself ; and doubly deadly, in preventing the hearing or seeing of the noble literature and art which have been done for love and truth. If people cannot make their bread by honest labour, let them at least make no noise about the streets ; but hold their tongues, and hold out their idle hands humbly ; and they shall be fed kindly.

Then the third condition of Companionship is, that, after we have done as much manual work as will earn our food, we all of us discipline ourselves, our children, and any one else willing to be taught, in all the branches of honourable knowledge and graceful art attainable by us. Having honestly obtained our meat and drink, and having sufficiently eaten and drunken, we proceed, during the rest of the day, to seek

his clerk a guinea for opening his study door to me five times, charging the same to St. George's account. (See *Fors* of April, pp. 186, 187, 188.)

after things better than meat and drink ; and to provide for the nobler necessities of what, in ancient days, Englishmen used to call their souls.

To this end, we shall, as we increase in numbers, establish such churches and schools as may best guide religious feeling, and diffuse the love of sound learning and prudent art. And when I set myself first to the work of forming the Society, I was induced to do so chiefly by the consciousness that the balanced unison of artistic sensibility with scientific faculty, which enabled me at once to love Giotto, and learn from Galileo, gave me singular advantages for a work of this kind. More particularly, the course of study through which, after being trained in the severest schools of Protestant divinity, I became acquainted with the mythology of Greece, and legends of Rome, in their most vivid power over the believing minds of both nations, permits me now to accept with freedom and respect the concurrence of a wider range of persons holding different views on religious subjects, than any other scholar I know, at the present day, in England, would feel himself secure in the hope of reconciling to a common duty, and in uncontested elements of faith.

The scheme, and elementary means, of this common education, I am now occupied in arranging and choosing as I best may.* In especial, I have set myself to write three grammars—of geology, botany, and zoology, which will contain nothing but indisputable facts in those three branches of proper human learning ; and which, if I live a little longer, will embrace as many facts as any ordinary schoolboy or schoolgirl need be taught. In these three grammars, (*Deucalion, Proserpina,* and *Love's Meinie,*†) I shall accept every aid that sensible and earnest men of science can spare me, towards the task of popular education : and I hope to keep thankful records of the names of the persons who are making true discoveries in any of these sciences, and of the dates of such discovery, which shall be unassailably trustworthy

---

* See *Fors* for January of this year, pp. 109, 110.

† This book I shall extend, if time be given me, from its first proposed form into a parallel one with the two others.

as far as they extend. I hope also to be able to choose, and in some degree provide, a body of popular literature of entirely serviceable quality. Of some of the most precious books needed, I am preparing, with the help of my friends, new editions, for a common possession in all our school libraries.

If I have powers fitted for this task, (and I should not have attempted it but in conviction that I have,) they are owing mainly to this one condition of my life, that, from my youth up, I have been seeking the fame, and honouring the work, of others ;—never my own. I first was driven into literature that I might defend the fame of Turner ; since that day I have been explaining the power, or proclaiming the praise, of Tintoret,—of Luini,—of Carpaccio,—of Botticelli,—of Carlyle ;—never thinking for an instant of myself : and sacrificing what little faculty, and large pleasure, I had in painting, either from nature or noble art, that, if possible, I might bring others to see what I rejoiced in, and understand what I had deciphered. There has been no heroism in this, nor virtue ;—but only, as far as I am myself concerned, quaint ordering of Fate ; but the result is, that I *have* at last obtained an instinct of impartial and reverent judgment, which sternly fits me for this final work, to which, if to anything, I was appointed.

And for the right doing of it, and for all future work of the same kind, requiring to be done for the Society by other persons, it is absolutely needful that the person charged with it should be implicitly trusted, and accurately obeyed by the Companions, in all matters necessary to the working of the Society. He cannot lose his time in contention or persuasion ; he must act undisturbedly, or his mind will not suffice for its toil ; and with concurrence of all the Society's power, or half their power will be wasted, and the whole perverted, by hesitation and opposition. His authority over them must correspond precisely, in the war against the poverty and vice of the State, to that of a Roman Dictator, in his war against its external enemies.

Of a Roman '*Dictator*,' I say, observe : not a Roman '*Em*-

peror.' It is not the command of private will, but the dictation of necessary law, which the Society obeys :—only, the obedience must be absolute, and without question ; faithful to the uttermost,—that is to say, trusting to the uttermost. The practice of faith and obedience to some of our fellow-creatures is the alphabet by which we learn the higher obedience to heaven ; and it is not only needful to the prosperity of all noble united action, but essential to the happiness of all noble living spirits.

I have not, in my past letters, much noticed this condition of the Society's work ; because its explanation will involve that of our religious creed to the full ; and its enforcement must be in the very teeth of the mad-dog's creed of modernism, " I will not be dictated to," which contains the essence of all diabolical error. For, in sum, the moral scale is raised exactly according to the degree and motive of obedience. To be disobedient through temptation, is human sin ; but to be disobedient for the sake of disobedience, fiendish sin. To be obedient for the sake of success in conduct, is human virtue ; but to be obedient for the sake of obedience, angelic virtue.

The constitution of the Society is to be, therefore, that of an aristocracy electing an absolute chief, (as the Senate of Rome their Dictator, or the Senate of Venice their Doge,) who is to be entirely responsible for the conduct of the Society's affairs ; to appoint its principal officers, and to grant or refuse admission to candidates for Companionship. But he is liable to deposition at any moment, by a vote of the majority of the Companions ; and is to have no control over the property of the Society, but through the Trustees in whom that property is vested.

And now, for farther explanation of the details of our constitution and design, I must refer the reader to the *Fors* for March of this year ; and, if he desires to pursue his inquiry, to the 8th, 9th, 11th, 17th, and 19th Letters of the previous series. These state clearly what we propose to do, and how : but, for defence of our principles, the entire series of Letters must be studied ; and that with quiet attention, for not a word of them has been written but with purpose. Some parts of the plan are confessedly unexplained, and others obscurely hinted at ; nor do I choose to say how much of this indistinctness has been intentional. But I am well assured that if any patient and candid person cares to understand the book, and master its contents, he may do so with less pains than would be required for the reading of any ordinary philosophical treatise on equally important subjects.

Only readers should be clearly aware of one peculiarity in the manner of my writing in *Fors*, which might otherwise much mislead them :—namely, that if they will enclose in brackets with their pen, passages of evident irony, all the rest of the book is written with absolute seriousness and literalness of meaning. The violence, or grotesque aspect, of a statement may seem as if I were mocking ; but this comes mainly of my endeavour to bring the absolute truth out into pure crystalline structure, unmodified by disguise of custom, or obscurity of language ; for the result of that process is continually to reduce the facts into a form so contrary, if theoretical, to our ordinary impressions, and so contrary, if moral, to our ordinary practice, that the straightforward statement of them looks like a jest. But every such apparent jest will be found, if you think of it, a pure, very dreadful, and utterly imperious, veracity.

With this understanding, the following series of aphorisms contain the gist of the book, and may serve to facilitate the arrangement of its incidental matter.

1. Any form of government will work, provided the governors are real, and the people obey them ; and none will work, if the governors are unreal, or the people disobedient. If you mean to have logs for kings, no quantity of liberty in choice of the wood will be of any profit to you :—nor will the wisest or best governor be able to serve you, if you mean to discuss his orders instead of obeying them. Read carefully on this matter Letter XIII., pp. 176 and 177.

2. The first duty of government is to see that the people have food, fuel, and clothes. The second, that they have means of moral and intellectual education.

3. Food, fuel, and clothes can only be got out of the ground, or sea, by muscular labour ; and no man has any business to have any, unless he has done, if able, the muscular work necessary to produce his portion, or to render, (as the labour of a surgeon or physician renders,) equivalent benefit to life. It indeed saves both toil and time that one man should dig, another bake, and another tan ; but the digger, baker, and tanner are alike bound to do their equal day's duty ; and the business of the government is to see that they have done it, before it gives any one of them their dinner.

4. While the daily teaching of God's truth, doing of His justice, and heroic bearing of His sword, are to be required of every human soul according to its ability, the mercenary professions of preaching, law-giving, and fighting must be entirely abolished.

5. Scholars, painters, and musicians, may be advisedly kept, on due pittance, to instruct or amuse the labourer after, or at, his work ; provided the duty be severely restricted to those who have high special gifts of voice, touch, and imagination ; * and that the possessors of these melodious lips, light-fingered hands, and lively brains, do resolutely undergo the normal discipline necessary to ensure their skill ; the people whom they are to please, understanding, always, that they cannot employ these tricksy artists without working double-tides themselves, to provide them with beef and ale.

6. The duty of the government, as regards the distribution of its work, is to attend first to the wants of the most necessitous ; therefore, to take particular charge of the back streets of every town ; leaving the fine ones, more or less, according to their finery, to take care of themselves. And it is the duty of magistrates, and other persons in authority, but especially of all bishops, to know thoroughly the numbers, means of subsistence, and modes of life of the poorest persons in the community, and to be sure that *they* at least

* Such limitation being secured by the severity of the required education in the public schools of art, and thought ; and by the high standard of examination fixed, before granting license of exhibition, in the public theatres, or picture galleries.

are virtuous and comfortable ; for if poor persons be not virtuous, after all the wholesome discipline of povery, what must be the state of the rich, under their perilous trials and temptations ? *—but, on the other hand, if the poor are made comfortable and good, the rich have a fair chance of entering the kingdom of heaven also, if they choose to live honourably and decently.

7. Since all are to be made to labour for their living, and it is not possible to labour without materials and tools, these must be provided by the government, for all persons, in the necessary quantities. If bricks are to be made, clay and straw must be provided ; if sheep are to be kept, grass ; if coats are to be made, cloth ; if oakum to be picked, oakum. All these raw materials, with the tools for working them, must be provided by the government, at first, free of cost to the labourer, the value of them being returned to them as the first-fruits of his toil ; and no pawnbrokers or usurers may be allowed to live by lending sea to fishermen, air to fowlers, land to farmers, crooks to shepherds, or bellows to smiths.

8. When the lands and seas belonging to any nation are all properly divided, cultivated, and fished, its population cannot be increased, except by importing food in exchange for useless articles,—that is to say, by living as the toy-manufacturers of some independent nation, which can both feed itself, and afford to buy toys besides. But no nation can long exist in this servile state. It must either emigrate, and form colonies to assist in cultivating the land which

* Here is just an instance of what might at first seem to be a jest ; but is a serious and straightforward corollary from the eternally true fact stated by St. Timothy : " They that will be rich fall into temptation and a snare, and into many foolish lusts, which drown men in destruction and perdition ; " and by Horace :

" Quanto quisque sibi plura negaverit
Ab Dis plura feret."

The passage might at first be thought inconsistent with what is said above of the 'degradation' which perpetual toil involves. But toil and poverty are two different things. Poverty ennobles, and secures ; toil degrades, and endangers. We are all bound to fulfil our task : but happy only if we can also enter into our rest.

feeds it, or become entirely slavish and debased. The moment any nation begins to import food,* its political power and moral worth are ended.

9. All the food, clothing, and fuel required by men can be produced by the labour of their own arms on the earth and sea ; all food is appointed to be so produced, and *must* be so produced at their peril. If instead of taking the quantity of exercise made necessary to their bodies by God, in the work appointed by God, they take it in hunting or shooting, they become ignorant, irreligious, and finally insane, and seek to live by fighting as well as by hunting ; whence the type of Nimrod in the circle of the Hell-towers, which I desired you to study in Dante. If they do not take exercise at all, they become sensual, and insane in worse ways. *And it is physically impossible that true religious knowledge, or pure morality, should exist among any classes of a nation who do not work with their hands for their bread.* Read Letter XI. carefully.

10. The use of machinery † in agriculture throws a certain number of persons out of wholesome employment, who must thenceforward either do nothing or mischief. The use of machinery in art destroys the national intellect ; and, finally, renders all luxury impossible. All machinery needful in ordinary life to supplement human or animal labour may be moved by wind or water ; while steam, or any mode of *heat-power*, may only be employed justifiably under extreme

---

* It may always import such food as its climate cannot produce, in exchange for such food as it can ; it may buy oranges with corn, or pepper with cheese. But not with articles that do not support life. Separate *cities* may honourably produce saleable art ; Limoges its enamel, Sheffield its whittle ; but a *nation* must not live on enamel or whittles.

† Foolish people are continually quibbling and stupefying themselves about the word ' machine.' Briefly, any instrument is a machine so far as its action is, in any particular, or moment, beyond the control of the human hand. A violin, a pencil, and plough, are tools, not machines. A grinding organ, or a windmill, is a machine, not a tool ; often the two are combined ; thus a lathe is a machine, and the workman's chisel, used at it, a tool.

or special conditions of need ; as for speed on main lines of communication, and for raising water from great depths, or other such work beyond human strength.

11. No true luxury, wealth, or religion is possible to dirty persons ; nor is it decent or human to attempt to compass any temporal prosperity whatever by the sacrifice of cleanliness. The speedy abolition of all abolishable filth is the first process of education ; * the principles of which I state in the second group of aphorisms following.

12. All education must be moral first ; intellectual secondarily. Intellectual, before—(much more without)—moral education, is, in completeness, impossible ; and in incompleteness, a calamity.

13. Moral education begins in making the creature to be educated, clean, and obedient. This must be done thoroughly, and at any cost, and with any kind of compulsion rendered necessary by the nature of the animal, be it dog, child, or man.

14. Moral education consists next in making the creature practically serviceable to other creatures, according to the nature and extent of its own capacities ; taking care that these be healthily developed in such service. It may be a question how long, and to what extent, boys and girls of fine race may be allowed to run in the paddock before they are broken ; but assuredly the sooner they are put to such work as they are able for, the better.† Moral education is summed when the creature has been made to do its work with delight, and thoroughly ; but this cannot be until some degree of intellectual education has been given also.

15. Intellectual education consists in giving the creature the faculties of admiration, hope, and love.

* The ghastly squalor of the once lovely fields of Dulwich, trampled into mud, and strewn with rags and paper by the filthy London population, bred in cigar smoke, which is attracted by the Crystal Palace, would alone neutralize all possible gentlemanly education in the district.

† See an entirely admirable paper on school-sports, in *The World* for February of this year.

These are to be taught by the study of beautiful Nature ; the sight and history of noble persons ; and the setting forth of noble objects of action.

16. Since all noble persons hitherto existent in the world have trusted in the government of it by a supreme Spirit, and in that trust, or faith, have performed all their great actions, the history of these persons will finally mean the history of their faith ; and the sum of intellectual education will be the separation of what is inhuman, in such faiths, and therefore perishing, from what is human, and, for human creatures, eternally true.

These sixteen aphorisms contain, as plainly as I can speak it, the substance of what I have hitherto taught, and am now purposed to enforce practice of, as far as I am able. It is no business of mine to think about possibilities ;—any day, any moment, may raise up some one to take the carrying forward of the plan out of my hands, or to furnish me with larger means of prosecuting it ; meantime, neither hastening nor slackening, I shall go on doing what I can, with the people, few or many, who are ready to help me.

Such help, (to conclude with what simplest practical direction I can,) may be given me by any persons interested in my plans, mainly by sending me money ; secondly, by acting out as much as they agree with of the directions for private life given in *Fors ;* and thirdly, by promulgating and recommending such principles. If they wish to do more than this, and to become actual members of the Company, they must write to me, giving a short and clear account of their past lives, and present circumstances. I then examine them on such points as seem to me necessary ; and if I accept them, I inscribe their names in the roll, at Corpus Christi College, with two of our masters for witnesses. This roll of the Company is written, hitherto, on the blank leaves of an eleventh-century MS. of the Gospels, always kept in my rooms ; and would enable the Trustees, in case of my death, at once to consult the Companions respecting the disposition of the Society's property. As to the legal tenure of that property, I have taken counsel with my lawyer-friends till I am tired ; and, as will be seen by the statement in the first page of the Correspondence, I purpose henceforward to leave all such legal arrangements to the discretion of the Companions themselves.

NOTES AND CORRESPONDENCE.

I. Affairs of the Company.

The new purchases of land round our little museum at Sheffield have been made at rather under than over the market price of land in the district ; and they will enable me, as I get more funds, to extend the rooms of the museum under skylight as far as I wish. I did not want to buy so soon ; but Fors giving me the opportunity, I must take it at her hand. Our cash accounts will in future be drawn up as on p. 254, by our companion, Mr. Rydings, to whom all questions, corrections, etc., are to be sent, and all subscriptions under fifty pounds.

[For Cash Account, see next page (254).]

The following letter from Messrs. Tarrant will be seen to be in reply to mine of the 6th June, printed in last *Fors*. From the tone of it, as well as from careful examination of my legal friends, I perceive that it is out of my power to give the Company a legal status, according to the present law of England, unless it be permitted to gather dividends for itself, instead of store for the nation, and to put its affairs in the hands of a number of persons who know nothing about them, instead of in the hands of one person who is acquainted with them.

Under these circumstances, I consider it to be best that the Companions should settle their own legal status with the lawyers ; and this the more, as I do not choose to run the Society into farther expense by the continuance of correspondence between these legal gentlemen and me without the slightest chance of either party ever understanding the other. Accordingly, I hereby authorize Mr. Robert Somervell, of Hazelthwaite, Windermere, to collect the opinions of the other Companions, (a list of whom I have put in his hands,) and to act in their name, as they shall direct him, respecting the tenure of the Company's lands and property, now and in future. And I hereby hold myself quit of all responsibility touching such tenure, maintaining simply the right of the Master of the Company to direct their current expenditures.

> "*Re* ST. GEORGE'S COMPANY.
> "2, BOND COURT, WALBROOK, LONDON,
> "31*st May*, 1876.

"Dear Sir,—We have carefully considered the points raised in your letter to us of the 6th inst., and have also consulted Mr. Barber upon them, and with reference thereto we advise you that the law stands shortly thus :—by the 13th Eliz., c. 5, a voluntary settlement of real or

Dr.   CASH ACCOUNT OF ST. GEORGE'S COMPANY (*From March 15th to June 15th, 1876*).   **Cr.**

		£	s.	d.			£	s.	d.
1876.					1876.				
March 15.	To Balance at Union Bank, London (see April *Fors*, p. 182) ..	157	11	10	April 17.	By Benjamin Bradshawe (advance on new purchase of land at Sheffield)............	30	0	0
	" Balance in Mr. Ruskin's hand (see May *Fors*, p. 212)......	107	16	5	23.	" Theodore D. Acland (expenses of chemicals for Sheffield Museum)..................	5	0	0
March	" F. D. Drewitt (tithe of first earning)	1	4	1	May 7.	" Henry Swan (Salary and Expenses at Museum).............	55	15	3
	" Miss M. Guest..............	2	2	0					
April	" James Burdon (tithe of wage).	2	10	0					
	" Wm. B. Graham (gift)........	1	0	0	23.	" Mrs. Talbot (repairing expenses on our cottages at Barmouth, with other expenses for educational purposes, afterwards to be explained)............	27	0	0
	" Anon., post stamp, Birkenhead	1	10	0					
April 16	" Egbert Rydings............	25	0	0					
	" Miss S. Beever............	7	0	6					
	" Anon. (tithe gift for half-year 1876)...................	50	0	0	26.	" Benjamin Bagshawe (on completion of purchase at Sheffield)	300	0	0
	" Rev. R. St. J. Tyrwhitt......	20	0	0					
	" No. 50, G................	10	10	0					
June 16	" Balancee du to Mr. Ruskin....	31	10	5					
		£417	15	3			£417	15	3

personal estate will be void and may be set aside by a creditor of the settlor, upon his showing an intent on the part of the settlor to defraud his creditors; and such an intent may be inferred from the circumstances. The Bankruptcy Act 1869 (32 and 33 Vict., c. 71) contains a still more stringent provision where the voluntary settlor is a trader. These are liabilities and risks which your association cannot avoid; but they are more imaginary than real, as the donors of land to the Company are not likely to make a voluntary gift for the purpose of defeating their creditors. By the 27th Eliz., c. 4, a voluntary gift or settlement of real estate, unless it be in favour of a charity, will be avoided by a subsequent *bonâ fide* sale for value, even though the purchaser have notice of the voluntary settlement. This, too, is an ordinary risk from which you cannot escape, unless you are willing to submit to the jurisdiction of the Charity Commissioners. It does not often happen that a person who has made a voluntary settlement of real estate seeks to stultify his own act by a subsequent sale of the same estate, but the payment of a small consideration, or even matter *ex post facto*, would prevent the deed being voluntary, and the risk is not a very serious one.

"We do not recollect Mr. Baker's name, and we find no mention of it in any of your letters to us : we think you must have meant Mr. Talbot, with whose solicitors we were in communication as to some cottages and land, and it was arranged that that matter should stand over until the St. George's Company was constituted.

"As to the writing out of the memorandum and rules for signature of the Companions—the case is this you receive donations from people who give them to you on the faith of a certain scheme of yours being duly carried out; it is therefore necessary that the leading features of that scheme should be reduced to writing, in order that there may be no misunderstanding between the givers and receivers of these donations as to the objects to which they are devoted. The signatures of the Companions are a feature of your published scheme, and in addition will be useful to show who are the acknowledged Companions having a direct interest in it—the right to elect and control the action of the Master, elect Trustees, etc., etc.; and the signatures will be the evidence of the deliberate submission of the Companions to be bound by the rules to which they subscribe their names.

"But all this will not make the St. George's Company other than a voluntary association of persons which the law will not recognize as a corporation.

"The Companions of St. George will be capable of holding land, but not as the St. George's Company,—that is, not as a corporation. Land must be held by or for them as individuals. You may have a piece of land conveyed to, say two hundred Companions; naming each of them; but for the sake of convenience you would have it conveyed to two or three who should hold it upon trust for the Companions generally.

"You can only obtain the countenance and supervision of the law for your Company on certain conditions, and when you came to us we were careful to explain this to you. You at once told us the conditions would not do for your Company, therefore we have had to do the best we could for you, treating your Company as an association without the countenance and supervision of the law.

"Forgive us for quoting from a letter of yours to us of the 27th May, 1875, 'Mr. Barber's notion is the popular one of a Mob of Directors.

But St. George's Company must have only one Master. They may dismiss him at their pleasure, but they must not bother him. I am going
to draw up a form myself, and submit it to Mr. Barber for criticism
and completion.' We think you may rest satisfied with matters as
they are.　　　　　　　　　We remain, dear Sir,
　　　　　　　　　　　　　　" Yours very truly,
　　　　　　　　　　　　　　　　" TARRANT & MACKRELL.
　" John Ruskin, Esq.
　　　" Brantwood, Coniston, Lancashire."

II. Affairs of the Master.

		£	s.	d.
Balance, May 16th		1225	19	1
		460	0	0
		£765	19	1

Spent.			£	s.	d.
May 17.	a.	Messrs. Weldon and Inglis	23	0	0
	b.	Mr. Stowe, Camberwell Green	11	0	0
		Warren and Jones	21	19	3
June 1.	c.	Annie Brickland	10	0	0
8.	d.	Furniture of new Lodge	300	0	0
		Downs	44	0	9
3.		Kate	50	0	0
			£460	0	0

　a and *b.* The first of these bills is for a sealskin jacket; the second
for a gold and pearl frame to a miniature. Respecting my need for
these articles, I have more to say when my lecture on Jewels can be
got published; it is fine weather just now, and I can't see to it.

　c. In 1871, in one of my walks at Abingdon, see *Fors*, Letters IV.
and VI.,) I saw some ragged children playing by the roadside on the
bank of a ditch, and gathering what buttercups they could find.
Watching them a little while, I at last asked what they were doing.
'This is my garden,' answered a little girl about nine years old. 'Well,
but gardens ought to be of use; this is only full of buttercups. Why
don't you plant some strawberries in it?' 'I have none to plant.' 'If
you had a little garden of your own, and some to plant, would you take
care of them?' 'That I would.' Thereupon I told her to come and
ask for me at the Crown and Thistle, and with my good landlady, Mrs.
Wonnacott's help, rented a tiny piece of ground for her. Her father
and mother have since died; and her brothers and sisters (four, in all,)
are in the Union, at Abingdon. I did not like to let this child go there
too; so I've sent her to learn shepherding at a kindly shepherd's; close
to Arundel, on the farm of the friend whose son (with perhaps a little
help from his sister) took me out foxhunting; and examined the snail-

shells for me. This ten pounds is for her board, etc., till she can be made useful.

d. I had settled my servant Crawley, with his wife and his three children, in a good house here at my gate. He spent his savings in furnishing it, in a much more costly manner than I thought quite proper; but that, (as I then supposed,) was his affair, more than mine. His wife died last year : and now both he and I think he will be more useful to me at Oxford than Coniston. So I send him to Oxford,—but have to pay him for his house-furniture, which is very provoking and tiresome, and the kind of expense one does not calculate on. The curious troublesomeness of Fors to me in all business matters has always been one of the most grotesque conditions of my life. The names of Warren and Jones appear for the last time in my accounts, for I have had to give up my tea-shop, owing to the (too surely mortal) illness of my active old servant, Harriet Tovey,—a great grief to me, no less than an utter stop to my plans in London.

III. I somewhat regret, for my friend's sake, that he desires me to print the subjoined letter in its entirety, if at all. I *must* print his answer to my question about Usury, for which I am heartily grateful to him, for reference in next *Fors ;* and can only therefore do as he bids me with the rest, which he has written more hastily than is his habit. What answer it seems to me to need will be found in the attached notes.

"Dear Mr. Ruskin,—It did not need your kind letters by the post to assure me that the rebuke pronounced on me by *Fors* in June was meant in the most friendly spirit—for my good and that of all men. *Fors* set me thinking, and, as you urged me to say what I thought, I began to write you a letter, partly to show that I am not so repulsive a person as you paint, (*a*) or at least that it is not the fault of Comte if I am; partly to show that, whilst agreeing with you very much about modern life, I find other reasons for trusting that the world as a whole improves. I owe you, and the age owes you, profound gratitude for much noble teaching ; and it is very sad to me to find you reviling (*b*) other teachers to whom we owe much, and who know a thousand things about which you have told us nothing. And indiscriminate abuse of all that the human race has now become, wounds my ear as if I heard one cursing our own fathers and mothers, brothers and sisters. If you believe that 'the entire system of modern life is corrupted with the ghastliest forms of injustice and untruth,' I wonder that you believe in God, or any future, in effort at all, or in anything but despair. (*c*)

"But my letter to you grew at last to such a length that I must find for it another place, and you or any reader of *Fors* who may take the trouble to look, may see what I wish to put to you in the *Fortnightly Review*. I wanted especially to point out that the impression you have conveyed about Comte and his teaching is almost exactly the contrary of the truth. You speak as if Comte were a physiologist, (*d*) mostly occupied with frogs and lice, whereas he is mostly occupied with history, morality, and religion; as if he insisted on the origin of man from the protozoa, whereas no one has more earnestly repudiated such speculations; as if he claimed political and public careers for women, whereas no one has said more against everything of the kind; as if he looked on modern industrial and social life with admiration, whereas he preaches a regeneration of our lives far more searching than any which you even contemplate; lastly, you speak of him and his students as if they were forbidden all sympathy with the spirit of ages past, whereas the reverence which Comte has expressed for the Middle Age at its best, its religion, its chivalry, its poetry, and its art, far exceeds in depth and completeness of spiritual insight even all the fine things which you yourself have taught us.

"Now I ask you, who love the very soul of truth, to repair an injustice which you have done in representing Comte (*e*) to teach quite the contrary of what you will find, if you turn to his books, that he does teach. I give a trifling instance. You write as if it were sheer impertinence in me a student of positivism, (*f*) to allude to a mediæval building or speak of a tracery. Now the truth is that some of Comte's profoundest thoughts relate to the moral and spiritual meaning of these sacred relics; and for my own part, though I *know* nothing of the matter, some of the best seasons of my life have been given to companionship with these most sublime monuments, and study of the 'writing on the wall,'—or all that men have spared.

"I say nothing about others whose views you may wish to class under the general title 'Evolution,' or of a lady whom I am sorry to see you speak of as 'Cobbe.' I have never shared all the opinions of those to whom you allude, and they are not followers of Comte. I shall say nothing about them; though I should like to know on what grounds you think yourself entitled to call Mr. Herbert Spencer and Mr. John Stuart Mill—geese. (*g*) The letter addressed to me in *Fors* has reference to Positivism, or it should have been addressed to some one else; and I assure you that every one of the doctrines which you ascribe to Positivists are not held by them at all, but quite the contrary are held.

"Whether the world is wholly worse than it was of old, is a very big matter on which I cannot now enter. I do not think it can be settled by statutes, old MSS., or bits from the poets. Thought and life are very wide; and I will listen to the judgment only of those who have patiently weighed the *whole* of both. (*h*) The grandest times of art are often those of especial vileness in life and society; and the grandest times of one art are sometimes those of utter decadence in another art, even in the same people and place. When the Theseus was carved, Aristophanes gives us the domestic and public life of the Athenians, and it has its dark side. Titian was the contemporary of Palladio, and also of Philip II.; Milton of Sir Peter Lely and Louis XIV.; so too were Bach and Mozart contemporaries of Greuze and Louis XV. I don't quite see what is to be made of these violent contrasts. And by the way, I wish you would work out for us the bearing of musical art on the social and moral life of various ages. It always seemed to me you omitted music.

"Now I will try to answer your questions of law about Usury. There is no such thing as usury in law at all,—that is to say, there is no rate of interest above which the lending of money is criminal or unlawful. BY THE 17 ND 18 VICT., C. 90, (PASSED IN 1854,) "ALL EXISTING

LAWS AGAINST USURY SHALL BE REPEALED." (Caps. mine.) There are a great many cases where courts of law interfere in bargains which seem to them unfair or unreasonable. But they all arise out of the *special relations* of the parties, and it would take a volume to tell you what these may be. For more than twenty years, as I suppose every one knows who reads a newspaper, there has been known to the law no lawful rate of interest which it is punishable to exceed. I cannot imagine for what end you ask me the question. Lawyers do not make the law, be it good or bad; they follow it like policemen or soldiers who obey orders.

"I reserve what else I have to say. I am sure all that you write to me comes from you in the most friendly feeling, as believe me does from me all that I write to you. Your *Fors* fills me with melancholy each time I read it. For it reminds me how many of those to whom we might look to bring more order, pa ience, and faith into the world, are occupied in setting us against one another, in making us rebels against our fathers, and all that they have done for us and taught us.

"Ever gratefully and most sincerely yours,
"FREDERIC HARRISON."

a. I believe there is no other friend, with whom I have had so brief opportunity of intercourse, whom I like so much as I do Mr. Harrison. What reproach this sentence is to me as an artist, I must submit to silently.

b. To 'revile' means, in accurate English, to vilify under the influence of passion. It is not an expression which my friend could have used, except thoughtlessly, of any words of mine, uttered of any person living.

c. I do not 'believe,'—I know, that the entire system of modern life is thus corrupted. But I have long learned to believe in God, without expecting Him to manage everything as I think proper ; and I have no occasion for belief in effort, so long as I know the duty of it.

d. Where, and when ?

e. The only word I have applied to Comte, in my whole letter, is "unique." For the justice of which epithet I trusted my friend's report of him. I have never read a word he has written,—never heard anything about him that interested me,—and never represented, or misrepresented, him, in any manner whatsoever. When I said 'physiologists,' I meant physiologists ; and no more thought of Comte than of Adam.

f. I did not write to my friend as a 'student of Positivism,' for I have no idea what positivism means. I wrote to him as an assertor, in the paper I was reading, of the splendour of Evolution ; and therefore ventured to imply, not that it was an impertinence, but an absurdity, in him to linger under the scholastic architecture dimly evolved from the superstition of Magdalen, when he might have disported himself under the commercial architecture more brightly evolved from the moral consciousness of Oriel.

g. Simply because I know a goose when I see one,—and when my friend has himself learned to know geese from swans, he will not think himself ' entitled ' to call either anything else.

h. Mr. Harrison underlines the word ' whole.' I am bound, therefore, to italicize it. Whether my friend will, hereafter, thank me for so faithfully echoing his emphasis on this sentence, my respect for his general common sense makes very doubtful to me. I do not see anything requiring notice in the rest of the letter so far as it regards myself. I seldom flaunt my poor little ragged feathers in my friends' faces; but must in simplicity confess to my feeling that it is not necessary for the author of *Modern Painters* to defend himself against the charge of uttering '' indiscriminate abuse of all that the human race has now become ; '' nor for the author of *Sesame and Lilies*, to receive lessons in courtesy to women, from modern Anglo-French chivalry, because he chooses to call a Cobbe, a Cobbe, no less plainly than a Plantagenet, a Plantagenet.

IV. '' PIOUS SENTIMENT.—' *I wish to God we could get a good bloody war somewhere*.' It is not without reluctance that we reproduce these awful words, but they were literally spoken in our hearing in that most sober place of business, Mincing Lane, only a few hours ago. They were spoken by a merchant or broker of gentlemanly appearance and apparent respectability, in a public room, and the most melancholy incident in connection with the utterance is that the atrocious sentiment *apparently* created no surprise, and was met with no outburst of indignation. We say *apparently*, for we ourselves were greatly surprised.'' (There is nothing whatever to be surprised at, except the frankness of the expression. Modern Liberal Protestantism has always held that you must not kill a man for his creed ; but you may, for his money,) ''and we felt burning indignation, but we controlled our feelings, and we hope others may have felt as we did, and had equally good reasons for silence. We are accused of taking a pessimist view of mercantile morality and mercantile activity. We commend the expressed wish of an English merchant, publicly expressed, in a public place, where merchants most do congregate, to consideration of those who differ from us in opinion, and we merely place the fact on record without further comment.''—*Monetary Gazette, June* 14th.

I reprint the paragraph for final illustration to Mr. Harrison of the ' evolution ' of British character. I wish I had space for some others which the courage of the editor of this excellent journal has exposed ; or for the leading article in the same number, which is an admirably temperate and clear estimate of the real value of the work of Adam Smith.

V. Lastly, here is some most valuable evidence from the faithful old friend to whom I wrote, in *Time and Tide*, of the increasing ' wealth ' of England, which with the example given in the last extract of her increasing morality, may symmetrically close the summary of St George's designs, and their cause.

"15, SUNDERLAND STREET, SUNDERLAND,
20th June, 1876.

"Dear Sir,—I have read with deep and earnest attention the last small tract of Girdlestone. I feel its tremendous truth, and have long done so too; but there is now a very pressing matter I would like to see gone into, and if possible some remedy proposed for it. It is one I have written many times to you about: I mean the rent question for the poor, the working people. At the present there is a sad depressing trade all over our country, and even in Europe. Yet, despite this awful depression, I note what is termed real estate is now going up gradually in value. I mean property and land. And that in the midst of this very depression and want of all kinds of labour by our workpeople and manufacturers, and in the midst of a tremendous opposition from our foreign competitors; yet nowhere do I see it named in any of our papers in the way I expected to see it treated of: they all seem quite elated with the great advance that has taken place, and the continued activity of all our building trades. Now, it seems to me, here is a question of vital importance that needs some sound information given on it, and some reasons assigned for this strange change in the value of all such property, in a time of such widespread depression of all trade. How are our people and our manufacturers to pay increased rents when there is a depressed trade, and no work for our workmen to do? Our town is now in a sad depressed state—work of all kinds very scarce; yet on all sides I learn the rents are being increased to workmen, manufacturers, and shopkeepers; and I note it also the case in other towns. I would like to see some good report as to the real extent of such advance of property in England. I find the advance in price of hotel, publichouse, and such-like property has been something tremendous within these few years, since I wrote you my letters in *Time and Tide.* To me it is something very sad to reflect upon this great change in the value or cost of a house to our workpeople. I find their food, such as butcher's meat, potatoes, and vegetables, milk, and some other kinds of necessaries, are also increased in price, owing to this advance in rent. So that the outlook for our workpeople, despite all our wealth, is indeed not a very pleasant one, for how are they to tide over this storm with all these necessaries at such prices? I note in the papers the miners of the Forest of Dean in some places are starving. I send you a book:* you can make any use of it you like. I have here and there marked its pages that I thought might serve in some measure to awaken an interest in this question of the workpeople, versus the rise in the value of their necessaries in dull times. "Yours respectfully,
"THOMAS DIXON."

* *Threading My Way*—an excellent one.

LETTER LXVIII.

I FIND that the letter which I wrote in the *Fors* of May
to those two children, generally pleases the parents and
guardians of children. Several nice ones ask me to print it
separately : I have done so ; and commend it, to-day, to the
attention of the parents and guardians also. For the gist
of it is, that the children are told to give up all they have,
and never to be vexed. That is the first Rule of St. George,
as applied to children,—to hold their childish things for
God, and never to mind losing anything.

But the parents and guardians are not yet, it seems to
me, well aware that St. George's law is the same for grown-
up people as for little ones. To hold all they have,—all
their grown-up things,—for God, and never to mind losing
anything,—silver or gold, house or lands, son or daughter ;
—law seldom so much as even attempted to be observed !
And, indeed, circumstances have chanced, since I wrote that
Fors, which have caused me to consider much how curious it
is that when good people lose their own son or daughter,
even though they have reason to think, God has found what
they have lost, they are greatly vexed about it : but if they
only hear of other people's losing *their* sons or daughters,—
though they have reason to think God has *not* found them,
but that the wild beasts of the wilderness have torn them,
—for such loss they are usually not vexed in anywise.
To-day, nevertheless, I am not concerned with the stewardship of these spirit-treasures, but only with the stewardship
of money or lands, and proper manner of holding such by
Christians. For it is important that the accepted Companions should now understand that although, in *creed*, I ask
only so much consent as may include Christian, Jew, Turk,
and Greek,—in *conduct*, the Society is to be regulated at
least by the Law of Christ. It may be, that as we fix our

laws in further detail, we may add some of the heavier
yokes of Lycurgus, or Numa, or John the Baptist : and,
though the Son of Man came eating and drinking, and turning water into wine, we may think it needful to try how
some of us like living on locusts, or, wild honey, or Spartan
broth. But at least, I repeat, we are here, in England, to
obey the law of Christ, if nothing more.

Now the law of Christ about money and other forms of
personal wealth, is taught, first in parables, in which He
likens himself to the masters of this world, and explains the
conduct which Christians should hold to Him, their heavenly Master, by that which they hold on earth, to earthly ones.

He likens himself, in these stories, several times, to unkind or unjust masters, and especially to hard and usurious
ones. And the gist of the parables in each case is, " If ye
do so, and are thus faithful to hard and cruel masters, in
earthly things, how much more should ye be faithful to a
merciful Master, in heavenly things ? "

Which argument, evil-minded men wrest, as they do also
the other scriptures, to their own destruction. And instead
of reading, for instance, in the parable of the Usurer, the intended lesson of industry in the employment of God's gifts,
they read in it a justification of the crime which, in other
parts of the same scripture, is directly forbidden. And there
is indeed no doubt that, if the other prophetic parts of the
Bible be true, these stories are so worded that they *may* be
touchstones of the heart. They are nets, which sift the
kindly reader from the selfish. The parable of the Usurer
is like a mill sieve :—the fine flour falls through it, bolted
finer ; the chaff sticks in it.

Therefore, the only way to understand these difficult parts
of the Bible, or even to approach them with safety, is first
to read and obey the easy ones. Then the difficult ones all
become beautiful and clear :—otherwise they remain ven-
omous enigmas, with a Sphinx of destruction provoking false
souls to read them, and ruining them in their own replies.

Now the orders, " not to lay up treasure for ourselves on
earth," and to " sell that we have, and give alms," and to

" provide ourselves bags which wax not old," are perfectly
direct, unmistakable,—universal ; and while we are not at
all likely to be blamed by God for not imitating Him as a
Judge, we shall assuredly be condemned by Him for not,
under Judgment, doing as we were bid. But even if we do
not feel able to obey these orders, if we must and will lay
up treasures on earth, and provide ourselves bags with holes
in them,—God may perhaps still, with scorn, permit us in
our weakness, provided we are content with our earthly
treasures, when we have got them, and don't oppress our
brethren, and grind down their souls with them. We may
have our old bag about our neck, if we will, and go to heav-
en like beggars ;—but if we sell our brother also, and put
the price of his life in the bag, we need not think to enter
the kingdom of God so loaded. A rich man may, though
hardly, enter the kingdom of heaven without repenting him
of his riches ; but not the thief, without repenting his theft ;
nor the adulterer, without repenting his adultery ; nor the
usurer, without repenting his usury.

The nature of which last sin, let us now clearly understand, once for all.

Mr. Harrison's letter, published in the *Fors* for June, is
perhaps no less valuable as an evidence of the subtlety with
which this sin has seized upon and paralyzed the public
mind, (so that even a man of Mr. Harrison's general intelligence has no idea why I ask a question about it,) than as a
clear statement of the present condition of the law, produced
by the usurers who *are* ' law-makers' for England, though
lawyers are not.

Usury is properly the taking of money for the loan or use
of anything, (over and above what pays for wear and tear,)
such use involving no care or labour on the part of the
lender. It includes all investments of capital whatsoever,
returning ' dividends,' as distinguished from labour wages, or
profits. Thus anybody who works on a railroad as plate-
layer, or stoker, has a right to wages for his work ; and any
inspector of wheels or rails has a right to payment for such
inspection ; but idle persons who have only paid a hundred

pounds towards the road-making, have a right to the return of the hundred pounds,—and no more. If they take a farthing more, they are usurers. They may take fifty pounds for two years, twenty-five for four, five for twenty, or one for a hundred. But the first farthing they take more than their hundred, be it sooner or later, is usury.

Again, when we build a house, and let it, we have a right to as much rent as will return us the wages of our labour, and the sum of our outlay. If, as in ordinary cases, not labouring with our hands or head, we have simply paid say—£1000—to get the house built, we have a right to the £1000 back again at once, if we sell it ; or, if we let it, to £500 rent during two years, or £100 rent during ten years, or £10 rent during a hundred years. But if, sooner or later, we take a pound more than the thousand, we are usurers.

And thus in all other possible or conceivable cases, the moment our capital is 'increased' by having lent it, be it but in the estimation of a hair, that hair's-breadth of increase is usury, just as much as stealing a farthing is theft, no less than stealing a million.

But usury is worse than theft, in so far as it is obtained either by deceiving people, or distressing them ; generally by both : and finally by deceiving the usurer himself, who comes to think that usury is a real increase, and that money can grow of money ; whereas all usury is increase to one person only by decrease to another ; and every grain of calculated Increment to the Rich, is balanced by its mathematical equivalent of Decrement to the Poor. The Rich have hitherto only counted their gain ; but the day is coming, when the Poor will also count their loss,—with political results hitherto unparalleled.

For instance, my good old hairdresser at Camberwell came to me the other day, very uncomfortable about his rent. He wanted a pound or two to make it up ; and none of his customers wanted their hair cut. I gave him the pound or two,—with the result, I hope my readers have sagacity enough to observe, of distinct decrement to *me*, as increment to the landlord ; and then inquired of him, how much he had paid for rent, during his life. On rough calculation, the total sum proved to be between 1500 and 1700 pounds. And after paying this sum,—earned, shilling by shilling, with careful snippings, and studiously skilful manipulation of tongs,—here is my poor old friend, now past sixty, practically without a roof over his head ;—just as roofless in his old age as he was in the first days of life,—and nervously wandering about Peckham Rye and East Norwood, in the east winter winds, to see if, perchance, any old customers will buy some balm for their thinning locks—and give him the blessed balm of an odd half-crown or two, to rent shelter for his own, for three months more.

Now, supposing that £1500 of his had been properly laid out, on the edification of lodgings for him, £500 should have built him a serviceable tenement and shop ; another £500 have met the necessary repairing expenses for forty years ; and at this moment he ought to have had his efficient free-hold cottage, with tile and wall right weatherproof, and a nice little nest-egg of five hundred pounds in the Bank, besides. But instead of this, the thousand pounds has gone in payment to slovenly builders, each getting their own percentage, and doing as bad work as possible, under the direction of landlords paying for as little as possible of any sort of work. And the odd five hundred has gone into the landlord's pocket. Pure increment to him ; pure decrement to my decoratively laborious friend. No gain 'begotten' of money ; but simple subtraction from the pocket of the labouring person, and simple addition to the pocket of the idle one.

I have no mind to waste the space of *Fors* in giving variety of instances. Any honest and sensible reader, if he chooses, can think out the truth in such matters for himself. If he be dishonest, or foolish, no one can teach him. If he is resolved to find reason or excuse for things as they are, he may find refuge in one lie after another ; and, dislodged from each in turn, fly from the last back to the one he began with. But there will not long be need for debate—nor time for it. Not all the lying lips of commercial Europe can much longer deceive the people in their rapidly increasing distress, nor

arrest their straight battle with the cause of it. Through
what confused noise and garments rolled in blood,—through
what burning and fuel of fire, they will work out their victory,—God only knows, nor what they will do to Barabbas,
when they have found out that he *is* a Robber, and not a
King. But that discovery of his character and capacity
draws very near : and no less change in the world's ways
than the former fall of Feudalism itself.

In the meantime, for those of us who are Christians, our
own way is plain. We can with perfect ease ascertain what
usury is ; and in what express terms forbidden. I had
partly prepared, for this *Fors,* and am able to give, as
soon as needful, an analysis of the terms 'Increase' and
'Usury' throughout the Old and New Testaments. But the
perpetual confusion of the English terms when the Greek
and Latin are clear, (especially by using the word 'increase'
in one place, and 'generation' in another, at the English
translator's pleasure,) renders the matter too intricate for the
general reader, though intensely interesting to any honest
scholar. I content myself, therefore, with giving the plain
Greek and plain English of Leviticus xxv. 35 to 37.*

Ἐὰν δὲ πένηται ὁ ἀδελφός σου, καὶ ἀδυνατήσῃ ταῖς χερσὶν αὐτοῦ
παρὰ σοί, ἀντιλήψῃ αὐτοῦ ὡς προσηλύτου καὶ παροίκου, καὶ ζήσεται ὁ
ἀδελφός σου μετὰ σοῦ.

Οὐ λήψῃ παρ' αὐτοῦ τόκον, οὐδὲ ἐπὶ πλήθει, καὶ φοβηθήσῃ τὸν
θεόν σου · ἐγὼ κύριος · καὶ ζήσεται ὁ ἀδελφός σου μετὰ σοῦ.

Τὸ ἀργύριόν σου οὐ δώσεις αὐτῷ ἐπὶ τόκῳ, καὶ ἐπὶ πλεονασμῷ οὐ
δώσεις αὐτῷ τὰ βρώματά σου ·

"And if thy brother be poor, and powerless with his
hands, at thy side, thou shalt take his part upon thee, to
help him,† as thy proselyte and thy neighbour ; and thy

* The twenty-third verse of the same chapter is to be the shield-
legend of the St. George's Company.

† Meaning, to do his work instead of him. Compare Acts xx. 35. "I
have showed you all things, how that, so labouring, ye ought to *support*
the weak."

brother shall live with thee. Thou shalt take no usury of
him, nor anything over and above, and thou shalt fear thy
God. I am the Lord, and thy brother shall live with thee.
Thou shalt not give him thy money, for usury ; and thou
shalt not give him thy food, for increase."

There is the simple law for all of us ;—one of those which
Christ assuredly came not to destroy, but to fulfil : and
there is no national prosperity to be had but in obedience
to it.

How we usurers are to live, with the hope of our gains
gone, is precisely the old temple of Diana question. How
Robin Hood or Cœur de Lion were to live without arrow or
'axe, would have been as strange a question to *them*, in their
day. And there are many amiable persons who will not
directly see their way, any more than I do myself, to an
honest life ; only, let us be sure that this we are leading
now is a dishonest one ; and worse, (if Dante and Shakspeare's mind on the matter are worth any heed, of which
more in due time,) being neither more nor less than a spiritual manner of cannibalism, which, so long as we persist in,
every word spoken in Scripture of those who "eat my
people as they eat bread," is spoken directly of us.* It may
be an encouragement to some of us—especially those evan-
gelically bred—in weaning ourselves slowly from such habits,

---

* Dear Mr. Ruskin,　　　　　　　　　　　*8th July*, 1876.

　　　I see that you intend to speak on the question of usury in next
Fors. Would it not be well, since the Bishops of the Established
Church have not a word to offer in defence of their conduct, to appeal
to some of the other sects that profess to take the teaching of the
Bible and of Christ for their guidance ? The Wesleyans, for instance,
teach that the Bible was given almost verbally by the Spirit of God ;
and John Wesley says his followers are " *to die sooner than put anything in pawn, or borrow and lend on usury.*" Perhaps if you were to
challenge the President and Conference, and call on them either to
state that they do not accept the teaching of Moses, David, and Christ
on this matter, or to bring the sin clearly before the minds of the
members of their body, you might force the question on the attention
of the professedly religious persons in the country.

　　　　　　　　　　　　　　　　　A READER OF FORS.

to think of our dear old converted friend, Friday. We need not fear our power of becoming good Christians yet, if we will : so only that we understand, finally and utterly, that all gain, increase, interest, or whatever else you call it or think it, to the lender of capital, is loss, decrease, and disinterest, to the borrower of capital. Every farthing we, who lend the tool, make, the borrower of the tool loses. And all the idiotical calculations of what money comes to, in so many years, simply ignore the debit side of the book, on which the Labourer's Deficit is precisely equal to the Capitalist's Efficit. I saw an estimate made by some blockhead in an American paper, the other day, of the weight of gold which a hundred years' 'interest' on such and such funds would load the earth with ! Not even of wealth in that solid form, could the poor wretch perceive so much of the truth as that the gold he put on the earth above, he must dig out of the earth below ! But the mischief in real life is far deeper on the negative side, than the good on the positive. The debt of the borrower loads his heart, cramps his hands, and dulls his labour. The gain of the lender hardens his heart, fouls his brain, and puts every means of mischief into his otherwise clumsy and artless hands.

But here, in good time, is one example of honest living sent me, worth taking grave note of.

In my first inaugural lecture on Art at Oxford, given in the theatre, (full crowded to hear what first words might be uttered in the University on so unheard-of a subject,) I closed by telling my audience—to the amusement of some, the offence of others, and the disapproval of all,—that the entire system of their art-studies must be regulated with a view to the primal art, which many of them would soon have to learn, that of getting their food out of the Ground, or out of the Sea.

Time has worn on ; and, last year, a Christ-Church man, an excellent scholar, came to talk with me over his brother's prospects in life, and his own. For himself, he proposed, and very earnestly, considering his youth and gifts, (lying, as far as I could judge, more towards the rifle-ground than

in other directions,) to go into the Church : but for his
brother, he was anxious, as were all his relatives ;—said
brother having broken away from such modes of living as
the relatives held orthodox, and taken to catching and pot-
ting of salmon on the Columbia River; having farther
transgressed all the proprieties of civilized society by providing himself violently with the 'capital' necessary for setting up in that line of business, and 'stealing a boat.' How
many boats, with nine boilers each in them, the gentlemen
of Her Majesty's navy construct annually with money violently abstracted out of my poor pockets, and those of other
peaceful labourers,—boats not to catch salmon with, or any
other good thing, but simply to amuse themselves, and blow
up stokers with,—civilized society may perhaps in time
learn to consider. In the meantime, I consoled my young
St. Peter as well as I could for his brother's carnal falling
away ; represented to him that, without occasional fishing
for salmon, there would soon be no men left to fish for ;
and that even this tremendous violation of the eighth commandment, to the extent of the abstraction of a boat, might
not perchance, with due penitence, keep the young vaga-
bond wholly hopeless of Paradise ; my own private opinion
being that the British public would, on the whole, benefit
more by the proceedings of the young pirate, if he provided
them annually with a sufficient quantity of potted salmon,
than by the conscientious, but more costly, ministry of his
brother, who, provided with the larger boat-apparatus of a
nave, and the mast of a steeple, proposed to employ this
naval capital only in the provision of potted talk.

And finding that, in spite of the opinion of society, there
were still bowels of mercies in this good youth, yearning
after his brother, I got him to copy for me some of the
brother's letters from the Columbia River, confessing his
piratical proceedings, (as to which I, for one, give him a
Christian man's absolution without more ado ;) and account
of his farther life in those parts—a life which appears to me,
on the whole, so brave, exemplary, and wise, that I print
the letters as chief article of this month's correspondence ;

and I am going to ask the boy to become a Companion of St. George forthwith, and send him a collar of the Order, (as soon as we have got gold to make collars of,) with a little special pictorial chasing upon it, representing the Miraculous Draught of Fishes.

NOTES AND CORRESPONDENCE.

I. Affairs of the Master.

		£	s.	d.
Balance, June 16		765	19	1
By cash, (rents, etc.,) May and June		180	11	8
		946	10	9
		328	19	6
Balance, July 16		£617	11	3

		£	s.	d.
June 25.	Downs	16	0	0
July 1.	St. George Secretary	25	0	0
"	Raffaelle, July and August	15	0	0
"	Gift to poor relation, annual	50	0	0
6.	Johns, Camberwell, Bookseller	17	19	6
7.	Jackson	40	0	0
7.	Joseph Sly (*a*)	40	0	0
8.	Crawley	30	0	0
11.	To Assisi (*b*)	45	0	0
11.	Self (*c*)	50	0	0
		£328	19	6

a. Carriage expenses, of which the out-of-the-wayness of Brantwood incurs many, from April 6th to June 19th.

b. Twenty pounds more than usual, the monks being in distress there.

c. I shall take a fit of selfish account-giving, one of these days, but have neither time nor space this month.

II. Affairs of the Company.

I have no subscriptions to announce. My friends send me occasional letters inquiring how I do, and what I am doing. Like Mr. Toots, I am very well, I thank them ; and they can easily find out what I am doing, and help me, if they like ; and if not, I don't care to be asked questions. The subjoined account gives the detail of Sheffield Museum expenses to end of June. I am working hard at the catalogue of its mineral collection ; and the forthcoming number of *Deucalion* will give account of its proposed arrangement. But things go slowly when one has so many in hand, not only because of the actual brevity of time allowable for each, but because, of that short time, much is wasted in recovering the threads of the work.

SHEFFIELD MUSEUM ACCOUNT.

Dr.   £ *s.* *d.*
April 1. To Balance in hand............................ 21   3   3
May 9. " J. Ruskin, by cheque....................... 55 15   3
                                                                      ————————
                                                                       £76 18   6

Cr.   CURRENT EXPENSES.   £ *s.* *d.*
April 26. By H. Swan, (salary)................ 10   0   0
May 2. " Watch Rate   0   5   0
  " " Poor Rate 0 10   0
  17. " Water Rate.....................` 0   5   8
  " " Gas 0 13   3
June 29. " Rate on New Land Allotment.......   0   2   3
                                                                     ———————— 11 16   2

REPAIRS AND FITTINGS.

April 15. By J. Smith, for making paths........   1 19   3
  26. " J. Ashton, brass taps...............   0   3   9
  " " S. Bower, card mounts............   0   3 10
  " " Walter Nield, cases................   5 10   0
  " " J. Smith, paths 1 14 10
May 12. " Sheffield Water Works—repairs......   0   5   8
  13. " Silicate Paint Co..................   2   0   9
  " " J. Smith   1   3   8
  19. " Mr. Bell, for applying silicate......   0 15   0
June 4. " Mr. Aitken, fixtures, etc., pertaining
                   to the two cottages...........   1   0   0
  26. " C. Collingwood, materials for paths..   5   4   0
  29. " G. H. Hovey, floor-cloth............   4 11   0
        Petty expenses 1 13   5
                                                                      ———————— 26   5   2
        Balance in hand.................... 38 17   2

July 20, 1876. Examined and found correct,   £76 18   6
                         E. RYDINGS.

III. I give the following letters without changing a syllable; never
were any written with less view to literary fame, and their extreme
value consists precisely in their expression of the spirit and force of
character which still happily exists in English youth :—

" ASTORIA, COLUMBIA RIVER, OREGON, NORTH AMERICA.

" I hope you flourish still on this terrestrial sphere. I have been
watching my chance to hook it for a long time: however, I may get a
chance to-morrow. If I do, I will write and let you know immediately.
This is a nice country, only there are a great deal too many trees. We
have been up to Portland, and are now down at Astoria again, waiting
for 250 tons more cargo, and the ship will proceed to Queenstown for
orders, so that if I do go home in her, I shall not get home till about
the month of August. There was a bark wrecked here the other night,

and the crew spent a night in the rigging; hard frost on, too. We have had snow, ice, frost, and rain in great abundance. The salmon are just beginning here, and are so cheap and fresh. I am steward now, as the other steward has run away."

. . . .

"BROOKFIELD, COLUMBIA RIVER, OREGON.

" I have just started another business, and knocked off going to sea: yours truly is now going in for salmon fishing. I had quite enough of it, and the ship would have been very unpleasant, because she was very deep, and I think short-handed.

" One night five figures without shoes on (time 1 A.M.) might be seen gliding along the decks, carrying a dingy. We launched her over the side, and put our clothes, provisions, etc., in her, and effected as neat a clear as one could wish to see. We had been watching our chances for the last week or so, but were always baffled by the vigilance of the third mate: however, I happened to hear that he and the boatswain had also arranged to clear, so we all joined together. We were to call the boatswain at twelve o'clock : the third mate and all of us had our clothes up on deck, and the boatswain backed out of it, and the third mate said he wouldn't go; but it would have been impossible for him to go in the ship, for all must have come out " [gentle persuasion, employed on boatswain, given no account of]. " We started: favoured by the tide, we pulled fifteen miles to the opposite shore; concealed the boat, had breakfast, and slept. At twelve that night we started again, and went on a sandbank ; got off again, and found a snug place in the bush. We hauled the boat up, and built a house, and lay there over a fortnight, happy and comfortable. At last the ship sailed, and we got to work. . . . We live like princes, on salmon, pastry, game, etc. These fishermen take as many as 250 (highest catch) in one boat in a night. I suppose there are about five hundred boats out every night ; and the fish weigh " [up to sixty pounds—by corrections from next letter], 'and for each fish they get 10d.—twenty cents. They sell them to canneries, where they are tinned, or salt them themselves. They pay two men a boat from £8 10s. a month. If I can raise coin for a boat and net (£100), I shall make money hand over fist. Land is 10s. an acre : up-country it is cheaper."

. . . .

" *Care of Captain Hodge, Hog'em, Brookfield.*

" *May 9th*, 1875.

" I am now in pretty steady work, and very snug. All the past week I have been helping Hodge build a house, all of wood ; and every morning I sail a boatful of fish up to the cannery, so altogether it is not bad fun. I am getting four pounds a month, and if the fishing season is prosperous, I am to get more. A sixty pound salmon is considered a very big one. There is a small stream runs at the back of the house, wherein small trout do abound. . . . I shall catch some. The houses here generally are about a mile apart, but the one Tom works at is alongside. It is pretty cold of a night-time, but we have a roaring fire. You are not allowed to shoot game during the next three months, but after that you can ; there are plenty of grouse, pheasants, ducks, geese, elk, deer, bears, and all sorts, so perhaps I shall do a little of that. There are some splendid trees about, some of which are 10 feet thick, from 100 to 200 feet high, and as straight as an arrow. Some Indians live at the back of us, —civilized, of course : the men work in the boats : some of the squaws have got splendid bracelets ; whether they are made of gold or brass I don't know. It rains here all the winter, and the moss grows on the people's backs : up around Portland they are called web-feet. There is a train runs from Portland to San Francisco every day. Tom is with a very nice old fellow, who is very fond of him, and gave him a new pair of india-rubber thigh boots the other day, which I con-sider to be very respectable of him.

" The boats go out of a night-time mostly ; they have a little store on board, and we have coffee, cake, and bread and butter, whenever we feel so disposed."

.   .   .   .

" In the first place, I will describe all hands belonging to this shanty. Captain Hodge is a man characteristically lovely, resembling Fagin the Jew whilst he is looking for Oliver Twist. Still he is honest—and honest men are scarce : if he is a rum'un to look at, he is a d—l to go. He has a cat whom he addresses in the following strain : ' It was a bully little dog, you bet it was : it had a handle to it, you bet it had : it was fond of fresh meat, you bet it was.' The next one is Jem the cook : he is a Chinaman, and holds very long and interesting conversa-tions with me, but as I have not the slightest idea of what they are about, I cannot tell you the details. Then comes Swiggler, who is an old married wretch, and says he is a grandson of a German Count. One or two more of less note, the dog Pompey, and myself.

" I can keep myself in clothes and food, but I can't start to make money, under £100.

" So F—— will come for £10 a month, will he ? He could make that anywhere while the fishing season lasts, but that is only three months ; and this is rather a cold, wet climate. I have had my first shot at a bear, and missed him, as it was pretty dark : they are common here, and we see one every day—great big black fellows—about a hundred yards from the house : they come down to eat salmon heads.

" I met an old ' Worcester ' friend, who had run away from his ship, the other day in Astoria : he was going home overland.

" Hodge offers to board me free all the winter, but as friend Hodge says he can t afford wages I ll see friend Hodge a long way off.

" I am very well and contented and shall be about a hundred dollars in pocket at the end of the season."

.   .   .   .

" *July* 19*th.*

" We expect the fishing season to last about a fortnight or three weeks more. Tom and I got some old net from Hodge, and went out fishing : we caught about six salmon the first night, for which we got 4*s.* We went out again on Saturday, and caught eighteen, for which we got 9*s.* 3*d.*, and as that is extra money we profit a little. There are plenty of bears knocking around here, and Tom and I got a boat and went out one night. We don t have to go more than two hundred yards from the house. About dusk, out comes old Bruin. I was very much excited, and Tom fired first, and did not hit him ; then I had a running shot, and did not hit him either. He has taken a sack of salmon heads, which I put out for a bait, right away to his den, and I have not seen him since. However—the time will come, and when it does, let him look well to himself.

" Did you ever taste sturgeon ? I don't remember ever having any in the ' old country,' but it's very nice.

" Hodge has a fisherman who has caught over eight hundred fish in the last seven nights ; he gets 10*d.* per fish, so he is making money hand over fist.

" I have not decided on any particular plans for the winter, but shall get along somehow.

" Send me any old papers you can, and write lots of times."

.   .   .   .

" The last fortnight we have been very busy salting and taking sal-mon to the cannery. I have been out four times with Hodge, whom I call Bill, and the first drift we got twenty-eight ; second, twenty-eight ; third and fourth, thirty-one.

" I like this sort of business very well, and am quite contented.

" I wish you would send me out some English newspapers now and then—*Illustrated London News, Graphics,* etc. It does not much matter if they are not quite new.

" The people out here are a rough lot, but a very goodnatured sort. Hodge has got a nice piece of ground which he intends to cultivate ; he put some potatoes in early last year, and has not looked at them since. However, I am to be put on to work there for a bit, and I'll bet my crop will beat yours.

" There are wild cherries and strawberries growing in the woods, but of course they are not ripe yet.

" My idea was, or is, to stop till I raise money enough to come home and get a farm, which I am able to do in two, three, or four years."

.   .   .   .

" ALDER POINT (so called because we're ' all dere '),

" *Sept. 4th.*

" I have been paid off now about a month. I received fifty-one dollars (a dollar equals 4*s.* 2*d.*). and a present of a pair of gum boots, which every one said was low wages. Tom had fifty, and Jackson a hundred and fourteen dollars. We combined these, and bought a fish-ing boat for ninety dollars, and sail for five more. We then set about to find a land agent ; but they are scarce, so we didn't find one. Then we went down to the sawmills, and bought 2094 feet of assorted lum-ber. I can't tell how they measure this lumber ; but our house is 24 feet by 16½, with walls 9 feet high, and a roof about 8 feet slope. The lumber cost twenty-eight dollars ; hammer, nails, etc., about fifteen dollars. We then chose a spot close to a stream, and built our house. It's built very well, considering none of us ever built a house before.

It is roofed with shingles—*i. e.*, pieces of wood 3 feet by ½ foot, and very thin; they cost seven dollars per 1000. Our house is divided into two rooms—a bedroom, containing a big fireplace and three bunks; and in the other room we grub, etc. At the back of the house we have the sword of Damocles, a tree which has fallen, and rests on its stump, and we know not at what hour he may fall. In the front we have the Siamese twins, a tree about 200 feet high, with another tree, about 100 feet, growing out of him. Nothing but trees all around us, and the nearest house is two miles away."

. . . .

"The Alder Point Mansion.

"I have now shifted my quarters, and am living in my own house, built of rough wood, in the woods on the bank of the river, and free from ornament save 'Sweet Seventeen' and 'The Last Days in Old England,' which I have framed and hung up.

"I am now, to use the words of the poet, 'head cook and bottle-washer, chief of all the waiters,' in my own house. It stands in its own grounds—for a simple reason, it couldn't stand in anybody else's. It has an elevated appearance,—that is, it looks slightly drunk, for we built it ourselves, and my architectural bump is not very largely developed. Our floor is all of a cant, but Tom settled that difficulty by saying we were to imagine ourselves at sea, and the ship lying over slightly.

"I am very poor,—have not had a red cent for some time; spent it all on the house, boat, etc. We have got grub to last us a month and a half, and 'what will poor Hally do then, poor thing?' Probably bust up and retire. I can't help envying you occasionally. I am a rare cad in appearance; an old blue shirt is my uniform. We live principally on bread and butter and coffee, sometimes varied by coffee and butter and bread. I have made a dresser, and we have six knives, forks, tea-spoons, plates, cups and saucers, three big spoons, a kettle, frying-pan, and camp oven, also a condensed sewing machine, which some people call 'needles.'"

. . . .

"Sept. 17th.

"Our house was invaded by wasps the other day for our sugar. I accordingly rigged myself up in shirts, etc., to look something like a man in a diving suit, and went and seized the sugar and put it in the chimney, and then fled for dear life. Whilst I was gone the sugar caught fire, and about forty pounds were burnt, and the chimney also was nearly burned down. Tom and I and hot water then slaughtered about four hundred wasps, but that don't sweeten the coffee.

"I have just been building a slip to haul our boat up on, as it blows very stiff here in the winter, and there is a good sea in consequence. Tom and I have been bathing this week or so, but the water is cold. We see one mountain from here on whose summit there is snow all the year round. It's rather monotonous living here; we see no one for days together. I heard there were two bears below here, so at about nine o'clock one night I started in the canoe. The river was smooth as glass, and it was a glorious night; and I guess Bruin thought so too, for he didn't give me a sight of him. Ducks are beginning to show round here, but my gun, which is a United States musket. don't do much execution. It is dark here about half-past five or six in the evening, so I don't know what our allowance of daylight will be in the winter.

" I remain yours, etc."

. . . .

" *Oct. 27th.*

" Thus far yours truly is progressing favourably. My latest achievement is in the lifeboat line. which you will hear of, no doubt, from other sources. The bears have all retired for the winter. which shows Bruin's sense. To-morrow I'm going to work up at Brookfield, clearing land. I shall probably work there three weeks, and then—well, I mean to go to Portland, and work till Christmas.

" Supper is now ready :—

Poisson.   *Légumés.*
Salmon heads and potatoes.

Entrée.
Potatoes and heads of salmon.

Pièce de resistance.
Salmon heads and spuds.

Dessert.
Bread surmounted with butter.

(Note.—You can't manage the bread without ¾ inch of grease, called for decency's sake ' butter.')

Wines.
Café avec beaucoup de chicorée.

Finish off.
A smoke.

" Having digested supper, and trimmed the yeast powder tin with lard in it for a lamp, I resume. The sport going on here at this time of the year is sturgeon fishing. with lines a fathom or so, and any number of hooks. The sturgeon run very big : I have seen one that measured eight feet from stem to stern. In the spring there are swarms of smelts ; you take them with a net the size of a landing-net, with small meshes. There is good elk shooting, and deer away back in the woods ; but you must go after them for about a week, and that is poor fun in this sort of weather. We got one of our big trees down the other day with a big auger : you bore two holes in the tree, stick a live piece of charcoal in it, and blow like mad, and the tree will catch, and in a few days he'll burn and fall. Very interesting, but it fills up.

. . . .

" *Oct. 28th.*

" It's some time since you last had a letter, and I guess you deserve this. Tom and I are both all right, and the other man, Jackson, is, I think, going home. Since I wrote last the rainy season has commenced, and at times it blows like my namesake ' Old Harry.'

"During a heavy squall some days ago, when Tom and I were returning from Brookfield, a boat about three-quarters of a mile behind us capsized, and a man and boy who were in her managed to climb on to her bottom. Tom and I bore away and picked them up, and they were truly grateful—not without cause, for, but for our assistance, they must have lost their lives.

" The man was * * *, who has lots of money, but he hasn't given us any. Perhaps he saw the necessity of our saving him,—made a virtue of a necessity, and virtue is its own reward. So much for my new ten shilling hat, lost in the rescue.

"I am in with all that s going on in London and England, for I get lots of papers, and as soon as I have done with them they are in great request all along the river. A boat has just called here, and John Eliot, a New Brunswick man, was grateful for a *Graphic*.

"The *London News* has just come to hand,—the 'Prince's visit to India' edition,—and is certainly quite a furore amongst the boys. On Tuesday night there was a hurricane here : it blew a great deal of the cannery down, and the place presents the appearance of a wreck. The house was swaying to and fro, and all hands had to leave for their lives. It nearly blew a man 6 ft. 3 in. off the wharf, and everybody was crawling on their hands and knees. Great trees were rooted up by hundreds : and at the next cannery above this, the owner had just left' his house and gone to play a game of cards, when a tree came down on his house and smashed it into many pieces.

"I am working here clearing land : I don't work when it rains, so I get about four days a week to myself. However, this week has been an exception, for we have had three fine days. Snowed thick last week : weather cold and bracing. Am getting one dollar fifteen cents a day's work, but am living up to it."

.   .   .   .

" *Nov. 23d.*

"You doubtless think I am quite uncivilized : however, whilst I am writing a cat is purring on my knees, if that is any evidence of civilization.

" To-morrow I am going out to work for about three weeks, clearing away bush for a Swede. I shall ask a dollar a day, but I don't expect it. I may add, necessity alone compels me to take this step, as I am beginning to forget what a dollar is like, it is so long since I had one. I am heavy on the axe : I cut down five trees to-day, and the trees out here are by no means small. A troop of five wild-ducks came round here on Saturday, so I loaded my old musket and let rip into the middle of them : singular to relate, they all swam away. Then occurred one of the most vigorous pursuits the human eye has ever witnessed. Hungry H. H. H. *v.* the ducks. I broke three paddles and my own nose, and then they escaped. However, one white one was sighted, and in the evening the old mud-stick (*i. e.* musket) was again prepared, and next day we ate wild-duck for dinner.

" On the whole, I like this much better than being on the ship, and I don't think I shall come home for two or three years.

" I am rigging a model of a ship, and I am not unhandy at it, and I calculate it will fetch me twenty dollars.

.   .   .   .

"*Dec.* 26th.

" I will begin by wishing the house a Merry Christmas and a Happy New Year, if so be it is not too late. We had a quiet Christmas Day with our select few. We were going to have a deer hunt, but the weather, which made a regular old-fashioned Christmas, stopped us. We had a good dinner, but no turkey or sausages. There is a strange old character stopping here, an ex-prizefighter, and in the evening he gave us a short sermon on the Star in the East, and asked us if we remembered Christmas Eve 1800 years ago. He then gave us a stepdance, so as not to dwell too long on one subject. Italian Sam gives a dance on New Year's night, and I may go.

" I got my discharge from Megler on Tuesday week, after putting in 25½ days' work since November 1, in consequence of bad weather, for which I had the large sum of 0 to take, being one dollar in debt. However, I struck a job right away, which is pretty stiff work—cutting cord-wood, making one dollar a day and board. Cord-wood is a pile of wood eight feet long, four high, and four broad, about one foot thick, and it is pretty hard work swinging a heavy oaken maul all day long, splitting the wood with wedges. But it's good for the muscle. Goodbye."

. . . .

"ALDER POINT. *Date uncertain.*

" It's about a month since I last wrote to you ; I had no writing-paper, and no coin to buy any ; however, Oleson paying up enabled me to lay in a stock. The rainy, blowy, galy season has set in, and it is pretty miserable down here. We had a heavy gale the other day, but did not suffer any damage, though many people predicted we should lose our boat ; but the gale is over, and the boat is still there, so that it shows public opinion may sometimes err. We were scared lest some of the big trees should come down, but they did not. If you could spare Gladstone for a bit, I would board him free, and he could wire in all round here free gratis for nothing. After the gale, the next day looked fine, so Tom and I (a puff of wind just came, and I thought the house would succumb, but no ! it holds its own) went up to Brookfield. Coming back, there were lots of squalls ; I was steering, and we saw one coming, so shortened sail : the boat was nearly capsized, and we had to take out the mast and let it rig, and so saved ourselves. There was a boat behind us, and we were watching her as the squall passed up : they shortened sail and tried to run before the wind to Brookfield, but—over she went. So Tom and I made all haste to save the crew. She was about three-quarters of a mile off, so we up sail and ran down for her. The crew, * * * and a boy, were sitting on the bottom of the boat white as ghosts. We took them aboard, picked up his oars and rudder, and then took them ashore to a house where we all got dry clothes and something to eat. They certainly owed their lives to us, and it was very lucky we saw them, for they must otherwise have perished. I lost a new 10*s.* hat in the rescue. * * * has lots of money ; but he has offered us none, yet. Perhaps, as he saw that we must of necessity save him, he made a virtue of a necessity, and virtue they say is its own reward. So much for my new hat.'

IV. I beg all my readers who can afford it, to buy *Threading my Way*, by Robert Dale Owen, (Trübner, 1874). It is full of interest throughout; but I wish my Companions to read with extreme care pages 6 to 14, in which they will find account of the first establishment of cotton industry in these islands ; 101 to 104, where they will find the effect of that and other manufacturing industries on the humanities of life ; and 215 to 221, where they will find the real statistics of that increased wealth of which we hear so constant and confident boasting.

V. Part of letter from an honest correspondent expressing difficulties which will occur to many :—

" I thank you for what you say about the wickedness of ' taking interest' consisting in the cruelty of making a profit out of the distresses of others. And much of the modern spirit of looking for bargains, and buying in the cheapest market, is precisely the same. But is there not a radical moral difference between such deliberate heartlessness, and simply receiving interest from an ordinary investment? Surely it is very important that this matter should be made clear."

The difference between deliberate and undeliberate heartlessness ;— between being intelligently cruel, with sight of the victim, and stupidly cruel, with the interval of several walls, some months, and aid and abetting from many other equally cruel persons, between him and us, is for God to judge; not for me. But it *is* very important that this matter should be made clear, and my correspondent's question, entirely clarified, will stand thus : " If I persist in extracting money from the poor by torture, but keep myself carefully out of hearing of their unpleasant cries, and carefully ignorant of the arrangements of mechanism which enable me, by turning an easy handle, to effect the compression of their bones at that luxurious distance, am I not innocent?" Question which I believe my correspondent quite capable of answering for himself.

VI. Part of a letter from my nice goddaughter :—

" I want to tell you about an old woman we sometimes go to see here" (Brighton), " who was ninety-one yesterday. She lived in service till her health failed, and since then she has had her own little room, which is always exquisitely clean and neat. The bed-hangings and chair-covers are all of white dimity, embroidered by her in patterns of her own designing, with the ravellings of old carpets. She has made herself two sets. Her carpet is made in the same way, on coarse holland covered close with embroidery, which, as she says proudly, never wears out. She is still able to work, though her arrangement of colours isn't quite as good as it used to be. The contrast came into my mind between work like that, and something I was told the other day,*—that it takes a workwoman a week to make one

* Please, some one, tell me if this something be true, or how far true.

inch of the finest Valenciennes lace, and that she has to do it, sitting in a dark cellar, with the light only admitted through a narrow slit, to concentrate it on the work. It's enough to make one give up wearing Valenciennes at all ! "

This last piece of impassioned young lady's English, translated into unimpassioned old gentleman's English, means, I suppose, that " it is very shocking, but not at all enough to make one give up wearing Valenciennes." Nor should it be. But it should be quite enough to make one inquire into the matter; ascertain with what degree of fineness lace *can* be made in the open daylight and fresh air of France; request some benevolent lady friend, who has nothing else to do, to undertake the sale of such lace, with due Episcopal superintendence of the relieved workers; and buy one's lace only from this benevolent lady-Bishop.

LETTER LXIX.

I HAVE just been down to Barmouth to see the tenants on the first bit of ground,—noble crystalline rock, I am thankful to say,—possessed by St. George in the island.

I find the rain coming through roofs, and the wind through walls, more than I think proper, and have ordered repairs ; and for some time to come, the little rents of these cottages will be spent entirely in the bettering of them, or in extending some garden ground, fenced with furze hedge against the west wind by the most ingenious of our tenants.

And in connection with this first—however small—beginning under my own eyes of St. George's work,—(already some repairs had been made by my direction, under the superintendence of the donor of the land, Mrs. Talbot, before I could go to see the place)—I must state again clearly our St. George's principle of rent. It is taken first as the acknowledgment of the authority of the Society over the land, and in the amount judged by the Master to be just, according to the circumstances of the person and place, for the tenant to pay as a contribution to the funds of the Society. The tenant has no claim to the return of the rent in improvements on his ground or his house ; and I order the repairs at Barmouth as part of the Company's general action, not as return of the rent to the tenant. The reader will thus see that our so-called 'rents' are in fact taxes laid on the tenants for the advancement of the work of the Company. And all so-called rents are, in like manner, taxes laid on the labourer for the advancement of the work of his landlord. If that work be beneficial, on the whole, to the estate, and of all who live on it, the rents are on a right footing ; but if they are abstracted by the landlord to his own private uses, he is merely another form of the old mediæval Knight of Evilstone, living as hawk in eyrie.

It chanced, while I set this work on foot at Barmouth, that a paragraph was sent me out of a Carlisle paper, giving the information that all Lord Lonsdale's tenants have received notice to quit, that the farms might be re-valued. I requested my correspondent to ascertain for me the manner of the holdings on Lord Lonsdale's estates ;—his reply is the third article in our correspondence this month, and I beg to recommend it to the reader's most earnest attention. What it says of rents, with the exception indicated in my note, is right ; and cannot be more tersely or clearly expressed. What it says of ground-produce is only partially right. To discover another America at our own doors would not be any advantage to us ;—nor even to make England bigger. We have no business to want England to be bigger, any more than the world to be bigger. The question is not, for *us*, how much land God ought to have given us ; but to fill the land He *has* given us, with the wisest and best inhabitants we can. I could give a plan, if I chose, with great ease, for the maintenance of a greatly increased quantity of inhabitants, on iron scaffolding, by pulverizing our mountains, and strewing the duly pulverized and, by wise medical geology, drugged materials, over the upper stages ; carrying on our present ingenious manufactures in the dark lower stories. But the arrangement, even if it could be at once achieved, would be of no advantage to England.

Whereas St. George's arrangements, which are to take the hills, streams, and fields that God has made for us ; to keep them as lovely, pure, and orderly as we can ; * to gather their carefully cultivated fruit in due season ; and if our children then multiply so that we cannot feed them, to seek other lands to cultivate in like manner,—these arrangements, I repeat, will be found very advantageous indeed, as they always have been ; wheresoever even in any minor degree enforced. In some happy countries they have been so, many a

---

* What *can* be done, ultimately, it is not yet in human imagination to conceive. What *has* been done, by one sensible man, for the land he had under control, may be read in the fourth article of our correspondence.

long year already ; and the following letter from a recent
traveller in one of them, may further illustrate the description given in a *Fors* of early date, of the felicity verily and
visibly to be secured by their practice.

" SALZBURG, *July* 30, 1876.

" Dear Professor Ruskin,—I have long intended to write
to you, but the mountain of matters I had to tell you has increased till Pelion is piled upon Ossa within my mind, and so
I must confine myself to one or two points. In the Black
Forest, and more especially in remote mountain valleys of
Tyrol, I have found the people living more or less according
to principles laid down for the Company of St. George. I have
seen the rules so much descried, and even ridiculed, in England, wrought into the whole life of the people. One may
still find villages and communes where lawsuits are impossible—a head-man of their own deciding all disputes ; where
the simplest honesty and friendliness are all but universal,
and the stranger is taken in only in the better sense of the
phrase ; where the nearest approach to steam power is the
avalanche of early summer ; where there are no wheeled
vehicles, and all burthens are carried on the backs of men and
mules," (my dear friend, I really don't want people to do
without donkey-carts, or pony-chaises ; nay, I was entirely
delighted at Dolgelly, the other day, to meet a four-in-hand
coach—driven by the coachman's daughter ;) " where rich
and poor must fare alike on the simple food and cheap but
sound wine of the country ; where the men still carve wood,
and the women spin and weave, during the long hours of
winter ; and where the folk still take genuine delight in
picturesque dress, and daily church-going, and have not re
duced both to the dreary felon's uniform of English respectability. With these unconscious followers of Ruskin, and
Companions of St. George, I formed deep friendships ; and
for me, if I ever revisit the wild recesses of the Œtzthal,
it will almost be like going amongst my own people and to
my own home. Indeed, wherever I left the beaten track of
tourists, and the further I left it, so did the friendliness
of my entertainers increase. It was evident they regarded
me not as a mere purse-bearing animal, but as an argosy of
quite a different sort—a human spirit coming from afar, from
a land 'belonging,' as one of them conjectured, ' to Spain,'
and laden with all kinds of new knowledge and strange ideas,

of which they would gladly have some share. And so towards the close of a dinner, or supper, the meek-eyed hostess would come and sit beside me, hoping I had enjoyed a 'happy meal;' and after a complimentary sip from my glass, ask me all sorts of delightful and simple questions about myself, and my family, and my country. Or the landlord would come sometimes,—alas, at the very beginning of a meal,—and from huge pipe bowl, wonderfully painted with Crucifixion or Madonna, blow clouds of anything but incense smoke. But the intention of honouring and amusing me were none the less apparent."

With my friend's pleasant days among this wise and happy people, I will forthwith compare the very unpleasant day I spent myself on my journey to Barmouth, among unwise and wretched ones ; one incident occurring in it being of extreme significance. I had driven from Brantwood in early morning down the valley of the Crake, and took train first at the Ulverston station, settling myself in the corner of a carriage next the sea, for better prospect thereof. In the other corner was a respectable, stolid, middle-aged man reading his paper.

I had left my Coniston lake in dashing ripples under a south wind, thick with rain ; but the tide lay smooth and silent along the sands ; melancholy in absolute pause of motion, nor ebb nor flow distinguishable ;—here and there, among the shelves of grey shore, a little ruffling of their apparent pools marked stray threadings of river-current.

At Grange, talking loud, got in two young coxcombs ; who reclined themselves on the opposite cushions. One had a thin stick, with which, in a kind of St. Vitus's dance, partly affectation of nonchalance, partly real fever produced by the intolerable idleness of his mind and body, he rapped on the elbow of his seat, poked at the button-holes of the window strap, and switched his boots, or the air, all the way from Grange to the last station before Carnforth,—he and his friend talking yacht and regatta, listlessly ;—the St. Vitus's, meantime, dancing one expressing his opinion that "the most dangerous thing to do on these lakes was going before the wind." The respectable man went on reading his paper, without notice of them. None of the three ever looked out of the windows at sea or shore. There was not much to look at, indeed, through the driving, and gradually closer-driven, rain,—except the drifting about of the seagulls, and their quiet dropping into the pools, their wings kept open for an instant till their breasts felt the water well ; then closing their petals of white light, like suddenly shut water flowers.

The two regatta men got out, in drenching rain, on the coverless platform at the station before Carnforth, and all the rest of us at Carnforth itself, to wait for the up train. The shed on the up-line side, even there, is small, in which a crowd of third-class passengers were packed close by the outside drip. I did not see one, out of some twenty-five or thirty persons, tidily dressed, nor one with a contented and serenely patient look. Lines of care, of mean hardship, of comfortless submission, of gnawing anxiety, or ill-temper, characterized every face.

The train came up, and my poor companions were shuffled into it speedily, in heaps. I found an empty first-class carriage for myself : wondering how long universal suffrage would allow itself to be packed away in heaps, for my convenience.

At Lancaster, a father and daugher got in ; presumably commercial. Father stoutly built and firm-featured, sagacious and cool. The girl hard and common ; well dressed, except that her hat was cocked too high on her hair. They both read papers all the way to Warrington. I was not myself employed much better ; the incessant rain making the windows a mere wilderness of dirty dribblings ; and neither Preston nor Wigan presenting anything lively to behold, I had settled myself to Mrs. Brown on Spelling Bees, (an unusually forced and poor number of Mrs. Brown, by the way).

I had to change at Warrington for Chester. The weather bettered a little, while I got a cup of tea and slice of bread in the small refreshment room ; contemplating, the while, in front of me, the panels of painted glass on its swinging doors, which represented two troubadours, in broadly striped blue and yellow breeches, purple jackets, and plumed caps ; with golden-hilted swords, and enormous lyres. Both had soft curled moustaches, languishing eyes, open mouths, and faultless legs. Meanwhile, lounged at the counter behind me, much bemused in beer, a perfect example of the special type of youthful blackguard now developing generally in England ; more or less blackly pulpous and swollen in all the features, and with mingled expression of intense grossness and intense impudence,—half pig, half jackdaw.

There got in with me, when the train was ready, a middle-class person of commercial-traveller aspect, who had possessed himself of a *Graphic* from the newsboy ; and whom I presently forgot, in examining the country on a line new to me, which became quickly, under the gleams of broken sunlight, of extreme interest. Azure-green fields of deep corn ; undulations of sandstone hill, with here and there a broken crag at the edge of a cutting ; presently the far-glittering of the Solway-like sands of Dee, and rounded waves of the Welsh hills on the southern horizon, formed a landscape more fresh and fair than I have seen for many a day, from any great line of English rail. When I looked back to my fellow-traveller, he was sprawling all his length on the cushion of the back seat, with his boots on his *Graphic*,— not to save the cushions assuredly, but in the foul modern carelessness of everything which we have ' done with ' for the moment ;— his face clouded with sullen thought, as of a person helplessly in difficulty, and not able to give up thinking how to avoid the unavoidable.

In a minute or two more I found myself plunged into the general dissolution and whirlpool of porters, passengers, and crook-boned trucks, running round corners against one's legs, of the great Chester station. A simply-dressed upper-class girl of sixteen or seventeen, strictly and swiftly piloting her little sister through the populace, was the first human creature I had yet seen, on whom sight could rest without pain. The rest of the crowd was a mere dismal fermentation of the Ignominious.

The train to Ruabon was crowded, and I was obliged to

get into a carriage with two cadaverous sexagenarian spin-
sters, who had been keeping the windows up, all but a chink,
for fear a drop of rain or breath of south wind should come
in, and were breathing the richest compound of products of
their own indigestion. Pretending to be anxious about the
construction of the train, I got the farther window down,
and my body well out of it ; then put it only half-way up
when the train left, and kept putting my head out without
my hat ; so as, if possible, to impress my fellow-passengers
with the imminence of a collision, which could only be avert-
ed by extreme watchfulness on my part. Then requesting,
with all the politeness I could muster, to be allowed to move
a box with which they had occupied the corner-seat—" that I
might sit face to the air "—I got them ashamed to ask that
the window might be shut up again ; but they huddled away
into the opposite corner to make me understand how they suf-
ered from the draught. Presently they got out two bags of
blue grapes, and ate away unanimously, availing themselves
of my open window to throw out rolled-up pips and skins.

General change, to my extreme relief, as to theirs, was
again required at Ruabon, effected by a screwing backwards
and forwards, for three-quarters of an hour, of carriages
which one was expecting every five minutes to get into ; and
which were puffed and pushed away again the moment one
opened a door, with loud calls of 'Stand back there.' A
group of half a dozen children, from eight to fourteen—the
girls all in straw hats, with long hanging scarlet ribands—
were more or less pleasant to see meanwhile ; and sunshine
through the puffs of petulant and cross-purposed steam,
promised a pleasant run to Llangollen.

I had only the conventional 'business man with a paper'
for this run ; and on his leaving the carriage at Llangollen,
was just closing the door, thinking to have both windows at
command, when my hand was stayed by the father of a
family of four children, who, with their mother and aunt,
presently filled the carriage, the children fitting or scram-
bling in anywhere, with expansive kicks and lively struggles.
They belonged to the lower middle-class ; the mother an

ideal of the worthy commonplace, evidently hard put to it
to make both ends meet, and wholly occupied in family concerns ; her face fixed in the ignoble gravity of virtuous persons to whom their own troublesome households have become
monasteries. The father, slightly more conscious of external
things, submitting benevolently to his domestic happiness
out on its annual holiday. The children ugly, fidgety, and
ill-bred, but not unintelligent,—full of questionings, 'when'
they were to get here, or there ? how many rails there were
on the line ; which side the station was on, and who was to
meet them. In such debate, varied by bodily contortions in
every direction, they contrived to pass the half-hour which
took us through the vale of Llangollen, past some of the
loveliest brook and glen scenery in the world. But neither
the man, the woman, nor any one of the children, looked out
of the window once, the whole way.

They got out at Corwen, leaving me to myself for the run
past Bala lake and down the Dolgelly valley ; but more
sorrowful than of late has been my wont, in the sense of my
total isolation from the thoughts and ways of the present
English people. For I was perfectly certain that among all
the crowd of living creatures whom I had that day seen,—
scarlet ribands and all,—there was not one to whom I could
have spoken a word on any subject interesting to me, which
would have been intelligible to them.

But the first broad sum of fact, for the sake of which I
have given this diary, is that among certainly not less than
some seven or eight hundred people, seen by me in the course
of this day, I saw not one happy face, and several hundreds
of entirely miserable ones. The second broad sum of fact is,
that out of the few,—not happy,—but more or less spirited
and complacent faces I saw, among the lower and the mercantile classes, what life or spirit they had depended on a
peculiar cock-on-a-dunghill character of impudence, which
meant a total inability to conceive any good or lovely thing
in this world or any other : and the third sum of fact is, that
in this rich England I saw only eight out of eight hundred
persons gracefully dressed, and decently mannered. But the

particular sign, and prophetic vision of the day, to me, was the man lying with his boots on his *Graphic*. There is a long article in the *Monetary Gazette*, sent me this morning, on the folly of the modern theory that the nation is suffering from 'over-production.' The writer is quite correct in his condemnation of the fallacy in question ; but it has not occurred to him, nor to any other writer that I know of on such matters, to consider whether we may not possibly be suffering from over-*destruction*. If you use a given quantity of steam power and human ingenuity to produce your *Graphic* in the morning, and travel from Warrington to Chester with your boots upon it in the afternoon,—Is the net result, production, my dear editor? The net result is labour with weariness A.M.,—idleness with disgust P.M.,— and nothing to eat next day. And do not think our Warrington friend other than a true type of your modern British employer of industry. The universal British public has no idea of any other use of art, or industry, than he ! It reclines everlastingly with its boots on its *Graphic*. 'To-morrow there will be another,—what use is there in the old?' Think of the quantity of energy used in the 'production' of the daily works of the British press ? The first necessity of our lives in the morning,—old rags in the evening ! Or the annual works of the British naval architect? The arrow of the Lord's deliverance in January, and old iron in June ! The annual industry of the European soldier,—of the European swindler,—of the European orator,—will you tell me, good Mr. Editor, what it is that they produce? Will you calculate for me, how much of all that *is*, they destroy?

But even of what we do produce, under some colour or fancy, of service to humanity,—How much of it *is* of any service to humanity, good Mr. Editor ? Here is a little bit of a note bearing on the matter, written last Christmas in a fit of incontrollable provocation at a Christian correspondent's drawl of the popular sentiment, "living is so very expensive, you know ! "

Why, of course it is, living as you do, in a saucepan full of steam, with no potatoes in it !

Here is the first economical fact I have been trying to teach, these fifteen years; and can't get it, yet, into the desperate, leathern-skinned, death-helmeted skull of this wretched England—till Jael-Atropos drive it down, through skull and all, into the ground;—that you can't have bread without corn, nor milk without kine; and that being dragged about the country behind kettles won't grow corn on it; and speculating in stocks won't feed mutton on it; and manufacturing steel pens, and scrawling lies with them, won't clothe your backs or fill your bellies, though you scrawl England as black with ink as you have strewed her black with cinders.

Now look here: I am writing in a friend's house in a lovely bit of pasture country, surrounding what was once a bright bit of purple and golden heath—inlaid as gorse and heather chose to divide their possession of it; and is now a dusty wilderness of unlet fashionable villas, bricks, thistles, and crockery. My friend has a good estate, and lets a large farm; but he can't have cream to his tea, and has 'Dorset' butter.* If he ever gets any of these articles off his own farm, they are brought to him from London, having been carried there that they may pay toll to the railroad company once as they go up, and again as they come down; and have two chances of helping to smash an excursion train.

Meantime, at the apothecary's shop in the village, I can buy, besides drugs,—cigars, and stationery; and among other stationery, the 'College card,' of "eighteen *useful* articles," —namely, Bohemian glass ruler, Bohemian glass penholder, pen-box with gilt and diapered lid, pen-wiper with a gilt tin fern leaf for ornament, pencil, india-rubber, and twelve steel pens,—all stitched separately and neatly on the card; and the whole array of them to be bought for sixpence.

What times!—what civilization!—what ingenuity!— what cheapness!

Yes; but what does it mean? First, that I, who buy the

* Most London theatre-goers will recollect the Butterman's pity for his son, in "Our Boys," as he examines the remains of the breakfast in their lodgings.

card, can't get cream to my tea ? And secondly, that the unhappy wretches,—Bohemian and other,—glass blowers, iron diggers, pen manufacturers, and the like,—who have made the eighteen useful articles, have sixpence to divide among them for their trouble ! What sort of cream have *they* to their tea ?

But the question of questions about it all, is—Are these eighteen articles 'useful articles' ? For what ? Here's a— nominal—'pencil' on our ' college card.' But not a colle- gian, that I know of, wants to draw,—and if he did, he couldn't draw with *this* thing, which is *not* a pencil, but some sand and coal-dust jammed in a stick. The 'india- rubber' also, I perceive, is not india-rubber ; but a compo- sition for tearing up the surface of paper,—useful only to filthy blunderers ; the nasty glass-handled things, which will break if I drop them, and cut the housemaid's fingers, I shall instantly turn out of the house ; the pens, for which I bought the card, will perhaps be useful to me, because I have, to my much misery, writing to do : but *you*, happier animals, who may exist without scratching either paper or your heads,—what is the use of them to *you ?* (N.B. I couldn't write a word with one of them, after all.)

I must go back to my Warrington friend ; for there are more lessons to be received from him. I looked at him, in one sense, not undeferentially. He was, to the extent of his experience, as good a judge of art as I. He knew what his *Graphic* was worth. Pronounced an entirely divine ver- dict upon it. Put it, beneficently, out of its pictorial pain, —for ever.

Do not think that it is so difficult to know good art from bad. The poorest-minded public cannot rest in its bad pos- sessions,—wants them new, and ever new. I have given my readers, who have trusted me, four art-possessions, which I do not fear their wishing to destroy ; and it will be a long while before I wish them to get another. I have too long delayed beginning to tell them *why* they are good ; and one of my Sheffield men asked Mr. Swan the other day what I had commended the Leucothea for,—" he couldn't see anything in it." To whom the first answer must be—Did you expect to, then? My good manufacturing friend, be assured there was no more thought of pleasing *you* when Leucothea was carved, than of pleasing—Ganymede, when Rosalind was christened. Some day you will come to "like her name."

But, whether you ever come to 'see anything in it' or not, be assured that this and the Lippi, and the Titian, and the Velasquez, are, all four, alike in one quality, which you can respect, even if you do not envy. They are work of men doing their best. And whose *pride* is in doing their best and most. You modern British workmen's pride, I find more and more, is in doing ingeniously the worst, and least, you can.

Again : they all four agree in being the work of men trained under true masters, and themselves able to be true masters to others. They belong, therefore, to what are properly called 'schools' of art. Whereas your modern British workman recognizes no master ; but is, (as the result of his increasing intelligence, according to Mr. Mill,) less and less disposed "to be guided in the way which he should go by any prestige or authority." The result of which is that every British artist has to find out how to paint as he best can ; and usually begins to see his way to it, by the time he is sixty.

Thirdly. They belong to schools which, orderly and obedient themselves, understood the law of order in all things. Which is the chief distinction between Art and Rudeness. And the first aim of every great painter, is to express clearly his obedience to the law of Kosmos, Order, or Symmetry.* The only *perfect* work of the four I have given, the Titian, binds itself by this symmetry most severely.

* The law of symmetry, however, rests on deeper foundations than than that of mere order. It is here, in Greek terms, too subtle to be translated except bit by bit, as we want them.

Τίς οὖν δὴ πρᾶξις φίλη καὶ ἀκόλουθος θεῷ ; μία, καὶ, ἕνα λόγον ἔχουσα ἀρχαῖον, ὅτι τῷ μὲν ὁμοίῳ τὸ ὅμοιον ὄντι μετρίῳ φίλον ἂν εἴη, τὰ δ' ἄμετρα οὔτ' ἀλλυήλοις οὔτε τοῖς ἐμμέτροις.—(Plato, Laws, Book IV.)

Absolutely straight lines of screen behind the Madonna's head,—a dark head on one side, a dark head on the other ; a child on one side, a child on the other ; a veil falling one way on one side, a scroll curling the other way on the other ; a group of leaves in the child's right hand balanced by another in the Madonna's left ; two opposed sprays of leaves on the table, and the whole clasped by a single cherry. In the Lippi, the symmetry is lateral ; the Madonna fronting the group of the child central, with supporting angel on each side. In the Leucothea, the diminishing magnitudes of the attendant goddesses on the right are answered by the diminishing magnitudes from the seated goddess and the child, to the smallest figure at her knee, which clasps both the sides of the chain.

Lastly, in the Velasquez, the little pyramid of a child, with her three tassels and central brooch, and a chair on each side of her, would have been *too* symmetrical, but for the interferent light in the dog.

I said just now, the Titian was the only *perfect* one of the four. Everything there is done with absolute rightness : and you don't see how. The hair in the Lippi is too stiff, —in the Velasquez, too slight ; and one sees that it is drawn in the one, dashed in the other ; but by Titian only, 'painted'—you don't know how.

I say the Titian is the most perfect. It does not follow that it is the best. There are gifts shown in the others, and feelings, which are not in it ; and of which the relative worth may be matter of question. For instance, the Lippi, as I told you before, is a painting wrought in real Religion ; —that is to say, in the binding of the heart in obedience to the conceived nature and laws of God.

The Titian is wrought in what Mr. Harrison calls the Religion of Humanity : but ought more accurately to call, the Religion of Manity, (for the English use of the word 'humane' is continually making him confuse benevolence with religion,)—that is to say, in the binding of the heart in obedience to the nature and laws of Man.

And, finally, the Velasquez is wrought in the still more

developed Modern Religion of Dogity, or obedience of the heart to the nature and laws of Dog ; (the lovely little idol, you observe, dominant on velvet throne, as formerly the Madonna). Of which religion, as faithfully held by the brave British Squire, in its widest Catholic form of horse-and-dog-ity, and passionately and tenderly indulged by the devoted British matron in the sectarian limitation of Lap-dogity,—there is more to be told than Velasquez taught, or than we can learn, to-day.

NOTES AND CORRESPONDENCE.

I. Affairs of the Company.

I leave our accounts now wholly in the hands of Mr. Walker and Mr. Rydings, reserving to myself only the usual—as I understand—and proper functions of Director,—that of spending the Company's money. I have ordered, as above stated, repairs at Barmouth, which will somewhat exceed our rents, I fancy ; and a mineral cabinet for the Museum at Sheffield, in which the minerals are to rest, each in its own little cell, on purple, or otherwise fittingly coloured, velvet of the best.   Permission to handle and examine them at ease will be eventually given, as a moral and mineralogical prize to the men who attain a certain proficiency in the two sciences of Mineralogy and Behaviour.

Our capital, it will be observed, is increased, by honest gift, this month, to the encouraging amount of £16 16*s.* ;—the iniquitous interest, of which our shareholders get none, I have pretty nearly spent in our new land purchase.

CASH ACCOUNT OF ST. GEORGE'S COMPANY.

(*From June 15th to Aug. 15th,* 1876.)

1876.	Dr.	£	s.	d.
June 29.	To Mrs. Jane Lisle	1	1	0
30.	" Chas. Firth...........................	1	1	0
Aug. 7.	" G. No. 50...........................	10	10	0
12.	" Miss Sargood........................	2	2	0
"	" Miss Christina Allen	2	2	0
15.	" Balance due Mr. Ruskin	14	14	5
		£31	10	5

1876.	Cr.	£	s.	d.
June 16.	By Balance due, Mr. Ruskin..............	31	10	5
		£31	10	5

THE UNION BANK OF LONDON (CHANCERY LANE BRANCH) IN ACCOUNT WITH THE ST. GEORGE'S FUND.

1876.		*Dr.*	£	s.	d.
March	15.	To Balance	157	11	10
May	3.	" Cash Paid Mr. John Ruskin	17	11	0
	6.	" Ditto, draft at Bridgwater (J. Talbot)	9	19	3
	9.	" Ditto, draft at Douglas (E, Rydings) ..	24	18	9
June	9.	" Ditto, Cash	5	0	0
	13.	" Ditto, draft at Bridgwater (F. Talbot)	20	12	6
"		" Ditto, draft at Bilston (Wilkins)	50	0	0
	17.	" Ditto, Cash	20	0	0
July	6.	" Dividend on £8000 Consols...........	118	10	0
			£424	3	4

1876.		*Cr.*	£	s.	d.
July	28.	By Cheque to Mr. John Ruskin..........	330	0	0
Aug.	15.	To Balance	94	3	4
			£424	3	4

II. Affairs of the Master.

It was not my fault, but my printers' (who deserve raps for it), that mine came before the Company's in last *Fors*.* It is, I think, now time to state, in general comment on my monotonous account, that the current expenses recorded in the bills of Jackson, Kate, Downs, and David, represent for the most part sums spent for the maintenance or comfort of others; and that I could if need were, for my own part, be utterly at ease in the sunny parlour of a village inn, with no more carriage or coachman than my own limbs,—no more service than a civil traveller's proper share,—and the blessedness of freedom from responsibility from everything. To which condition, if I ever reduce myself by my extravagance, and, (indeed, just after paying my good Mr. Ellis for thirteenth-century MSS.,† etc., a hundred and forty pounds, I am in treaty to-day with Mr. Quaritch for another, which he says is charged at the very lowest penny at three hundred and twenty)—it will be simply to me only occasion for the loadless traveller's song; but as it would be greatly inconvenient to other people, I don't at present intend it. Some day, indeed, perhaps I shall begin to turn a penny by my books. The bills drawn by Mr. Burgess represent now the only loss I incur on them.

---

* Note by printer :—" We did this to avoid an unseemly division of balance-sheet, and of two evils thought this the least."

† One of these is a perfect English Bible, folio, and in beautiful state, sent to Sheffield for the first volume of our Museum library. Of course I must make St. George a present of it.

	£	s.	d.
Stated Balance, July 15th.....................	617	11	3
Repayment and other receipts, July and August...	406	6	5
	1023	17	8
Expenses.......................................	427	5	0
Balance, August 15th...........	£596	12	8

		£	s.	d.
July	16. Geoghegan (blue neckties)..............	4	0	0
"	Naval School.........................	5	5	0
	17. David...............................	65	0	0
"	Downs.............	25	0	0
	30. Jackson............................	50	0	0
"	Kate................................	50	0	0
Aug.	1. Herne Hill ground-rent................	23	0	0
	14. Burgess.............................	40	0	0
	15. Ellis and White......................	140	0	0
"	Lucy Tovey (gift).....................	10	0	0
"	Self (chiefly gone in black quartz from St. Gothard Tunnel)....................	15	0	0
		£427	5	0

III.

"My dear Sir,—I duly received your very kind note referring to the 'notice to quit' to Lord Lonsdale's farmers in West Cumberland, and have delayed to reply till I had made special inquiries, and find that, as a rule, these tenants have no leases, but have held their farms from year to year only.

"Formerly, I am told, some had leases; but as these expired they were not renewed, and the supposition now is that all such have run out, and that all now as yearly tenants have had the notice given them simultaneously.

"The notice is clearly given to allow a re-valuation to be made ; and when the new rents are arranged, it is expected that leases will then be granted, though it is plain to be seen that all the increased prosperity that the prosperity of recent years of the coal and iron industries have caused to farming, *may thus be secured to the landholder;* and the farmers, with or without leases, but with higher rents, may be left to bear alone the ebb of the tide that is evidently on the turn ; and in any or every case, the general public—the consumers of these farmers' produce—will have to pay the extra rent, whatever it may be, that Lord Lonsdale may see fit to lay upon the land.*

* As I correct this sheet, Fors places another Carlyle paper in my hand ; from which I gather that Lord Lonsdale's conceptions of what is fit, and not, are probably now changed. But my correspondent is wrong in *assuming* that the public will have to pay the extra rent. Very probably they will if the farming improvements are fallacious ; but if indeed produce can be raised at less expense, the increased rent *may* represent only the difference between past and present cost of production. In this sense, however, the

" I have been studying this matter—the increase of land-rents—for
many years, and consider it is very much to blame for the present high
prices of all land produce, and the distress amongst the poorest of our
population, as well as being the great hindrance to the carrying out of
any schemes that have for their object the application of more of our
own labour to our own soil. In a letter to my son a few weeks ago, I
ventured to say that the man who was the first to demonstrate by
actual experiment that English soil could be made to double or quad-
ruple its produce, would earn the name of a new Columbus, in that he
had discovered another America at our own doors. This son, my oldest,
having shown a turn for mathematics, I was induced to send to Cambridge, my hope being that a good education might fit him to solve some
of the problems that are so pressing us for solution (and which I had
been essaying myself in the pamphlet on ' Labour and Capital') ; and as
he now, on the completion of his second term, holds the second place in
his year at St. John's, there is a hope that he may take a good place in
the mathematical tripos for 1878 ; and yet, since we got introduced to
your books—two years ago—both he and I think he had best. so soon as
he completes his course, go into farming ; and hence the reference to
growing crops that appeared in his letter last week, and which I am
most happy to find has met with your approbation." (Yes ;—and I trust
with higher approbation than mine.)

IV. The following paragraphs from a county paper gladden me exceedingly, by taking from me all merit of originality in any part of the
design of the operations of St. George's Company, while they prove
to the most incredulous not only the practicability, but the assured
good of such operations, already, as will be seen, carried to triumphant results on a private gentleman's estate.

The *Agricultural Gazette* gives, as one of a series of papers on
" Noteworthy Agriculturists," a sketch of Mr. William Mackenzie,
Achandunie, who, acting for Mr. Matheson, has carried out so many
improvements on the Ardross estates. The sketch is in the form of an
autobiography, which, as the *Gazette* remarks, carries with it a most
pleasant impression of directness and simplicity of character no less
than of industry, energy, and success. It is accompanied by a portrait
of Mr. Mackenzie, which his friends will recognize as a fair likeness.
Mr. Mackenzie states that he was born in 1806, in the parish of Urquhart, Ross-shire, where his ancestors had resided for many generations.
His father, who occupied a small farm, died about five years ago at
the advanced age of ninety. In 1824, he (Mr. William Mackenzie) entered as an apprentice at Belmaduthy (*a*) Gardens, and after serving
there three years, removed to the nurseries of Dickson and Co., Edinburgh, where he remained only a few months. He then went to the
Duke of Buccleuch's gardens at Dalkeith, serving under Mr. Macdonald,
who was in advance of his time as a practical gardener. There he

public *do* pay Lord Lonsdale's extra rent, that their market prices, but for his Lordship,
would have been lowered. As matters stand, they may be thankful if they are not
raised.

(*a*) I can't be responsible for these Scotch names. I sent the slip of paper to my printers,
and ' on their eyes be it.'

assisted in carrying out the improvements which were made in the gardens and pleasure-grounds. New ranges of hothouses and a fine conservatory were erected, into which the hot-water system of heating was, it is believed, first introduced in Scotland. Next Mr. Mackenzie assisted in laying out gardens and grounds at Barcaldine, the seat of Sir Duncan Campbell, in Argyllshire; and coming in 1835 to Rosehaugh, as head-gardener, forester, and superintendent of estate works, he carried out the construction of new gardens, both at Rosehaugh and Kinlochluichart, and the remodelling of private grounds and approaches. These large gardens at Barcaldine and Rosehaugh were made with great care, *especially in selecting and preparing the soil* for the wall and *vinery* borders, *so that after the lapse, in the one case of thirty years, and in the other of forty years, no decay or canker has appeared among the fruit trees.* (*b*)

"In 1847 Mr. Mackenzie commenced the improvements at Ardross, the property of Alexander Matheson, Esq., M.P. for the county of Ross.

"Ardross proper is surrounded by high hills, and with trifling exceptions was in a state of nature, the whole surface of the district being covered with coarse grass and heather, stunted birches, morass or quagmire, and studded with granite boulders drifted from the hills. The place was under sheep and a few black cattle, and, owing to the coarseness of the herbage the cattle were subject to red water. *The tenants' houses were mere hovels, without chimneys, and with little or no glass in the windows. The population of the district of Ardross proper was, in 1847, only 109 souls; and now, in 1875, the population on the same area is 600, and the number of children attending school is about* 140.

"In giving a summary of the improvements, we will begin with the pleasure-grounds. (*c*) They extend to about 800 acres. In forming them, wagons on rails were used for two years in removing knolls, forming terraces, and filling up gullies. The banks of the river and of the burns flowing through the grounds have been planted with upwards of a hundred different varieties of the finest and hardiest ornamental trees that could be procured, from the tulip-tree to the evergreen oak, and from the native pine to the Wellingtonia. Evergreen shrubs cover about 25 acres in detached portions on the banks of the river which flows immediately beneath the castle, as well as on the banks of two romantic burns, with beautiful cascades, and in ravines. The garden is enclosed with a brick-lined wall, and so boggy was the site that the foundation of the wall is more than 6 feet below the sills of some of the doors. The south side is enclosed by a terrace wall 12 feet high, and the north wall is covered with glass, which includes vineries, conservatory, and orchard houses, besides a range of pits, all heated with water. *The soil of the garden was prepared and carted a considerable distance,* (*d*) as there was none to be got on the site.

(*b*) Italics mine (throughout the article, the rest of which is in Mr. Mackenzie's own words). Have the vine-proprietors of Europe yet begun to look to the Earth—not the air, as the power that fails them? (See note *d*.)

(*c*) It will, I hope, not be thought an absurdity in the St. George's Company to retain on their estates 'pleasure-grounds' for their *tenants*, instead of themselves. In this one respect, and in this only, their public work will differ from this admirable piece of 'private enterprise.'

(*d*) Supposing the labour of all navvies, gold-diggers, and bad architects, throughout the world during the last fifty years, had been spent entirely in carting soil to where it was wanted for vegetables,—my dinnerless friends, you would have found the difference, by this time!

"Upwards of 5,000 acres of moor ground have been planted, chiefly with Scotch fir and larch, the thinnings of which are now being shipped for pit props, the plants of the oldest woods only having been taken out of the nursery in 1847.

"The extent of arable land may be best explained by stating that there are twenty-seven farms with threshing mills, paying rents from £50 to £800 each ; and upwards of a hundred ploughs are used in culti-vating the lands improved. The steam plough is also to be seen at work on some of the farms." (St. George does not, however, propose entertaining the curious spectator in this manner.) "Cattle reared on the reclaimed land have taken prizes at the Highland Society's Shows, and at all local shows ; and for cereals and green crops, they will bear a favourable comparison with any part of Scotland.

"At one of the detached properties, great care had to be taken, and engineering skill used, in the drainage. Recently a low-lying part of the lands, a mile and a half long by three-quarters broad, was a mixture of the lower stratum of peaty bog, marsh, and spouty sand, charged with ochrey-coloured water, impregnated with sulphur and saltpetre. Attempts made by former occupants to drain this place were fruitless, from want of depth and proper outfall. We found all the pipes in their drains completely choked by deposited ochrey matter. The whole subsoil was running sand. In order to make the drainage perfect, a main leading drain made, 800 yards long, and in some places 8 feet deep, in which were laid ' spigot and faucet,' vitrified pipes 10 to 15 inches in diameter, jointed with cement to prevent sand from getting in, with junctions to receive pipes of smaller sizes, from 10 inches down to 6 inches. Minor drains are from $3\frac{1}{2}$ to 4 feet deep, with tiles of 2 to 4 inch bore, the smaller sizes having collars on the joints. Large stone cisterns are formed to receive the silt, and ventilating shafts with iron gratings are built to give circulation of air. By these means the whole flat is drained effectually, *and where bog rushes were the prevailing produce, crops of the richest wheat now grow.* THE STUNTED HERBAGE AND WATER WERE SO POISONOUS THAT BLACK CATTLE WERE KNOWN TO HAVE TURNED GRAY IN A SEASON (?). (*e*)

"More than fifty miles of private roads have been made, and twelve miles of walks through the pleasure-grounds. One walk is six miles continuous, along the windings of fine scenery of the Alness. Upwards of forty miles of stone dykes and eighty of wire fences have been erected, enclosing the arable land and plantations.

"For twenty years from three to four hundred men were employed; two hundred of them lived in a square of barracks for nearly eleven years, *and so orderly were they that the services of a policeman were never required.* There are still a number of men employed, but the improve-ments are now coming to a close.

" *All the assistance I had in the engineering and planning was that of a young man only seventeen years old when the works were begun, and we never had occasion to employ a man for a single day re-doing work.*

"I may further add that I have now the great pleasure of seeing my liberal employer reletting all his farms on the Ardross estate to the

(*e*) This passage, in capitals, being wholly astounding to me, I venture to put a note of interrogation to it. I have long myself been questioning the farmers in Westmoreland about the quantity of rank bog grass they let grow. But *their* only idea of improvement is to burn the heather; this being a cheap operation, and dangerous only to their neigh-bours' woods. Brantwood was within an ace of becoming Brantashes last summer.

same tenants, on a second nineteen years' lease," (at increased rents, of course, my friend?) "the second leases having been renewed between two and three years before the expiry of the previous leases, and none of the farms were ever advertised.

"I cannot leave this part of the present brief sketch without noticing a feature in the important work so successfully carried out by my enlightened employer, and one which cannot fail to be a source of great satisfaction to himself. Among the first things he did was to establish a school in the district, with a most efficient teacher, and the result is that sons of the small farmers and labourers are now in respectable positions in various walks of life. They are to be found in the capacities of gardeners, artizans, and merchants, students of law, medicine, and divinity. One of them, Donald Ross, carried the Queen's prize of £100 in the University, and is now one of Her Majesty's Inspectors of Schools. Another is the chief constable of the county. Others are in the colonies of Australia, New Zealand, and America, all doing well; *and out of hundreds working for themselves, to my knowledge, not one has gone astray.* (*f*)

"I will now advert to the improvements on the west coast estates. A mansion-house was built in the parish of Kintail, with pleasure-grounds and gardens, *the former being chiefly reclaimed from the sea. Two islands, which were surrounded by water 11 feet deep on the shore side, are now part of the lawn,* the intervening spaces having been filled up by the removal of a hill of rotten rock. This house is let to a suooting tenant. The garden is excellent for fruit, including peaches, nectarines, and apricots, which come to perfection. At Duncraig, recently, a new mansion-house has been built, with all the modern appliances. New gardens have also been made at Duncraig, the site of which was originally a narrow gully running between high ridges of rock. The gardens are upwards of two acres within the walls. The soil is composed of virgin soil and turfy loam, the whole having been carted a considerable distance. The gardens were completed in 1871, and the different kinds of fruit trees, including pears, peaches, and apricots, are now bearing.

"Duncraig is rarely to be surpassed in scenery and beauty. The view is extensive, embracing the Cuchullin hills in Skye," (etc., etc.) "There are two fresh-water lakes within the grounds, one covering thirty-seven acres, and the other about sixty acres. abounding with excellent trout and char. One of them supplies Duncraig House with water, having a fall about 300 feet. The pipe in its course supplies the gardens; the livery stables and laundry have also connections for applying hose in cases of fire.

"The conformation of the ground is a mingling of winding valleys with high rock hills, on which grow natural wood, such as birch, oak, ash, and mountain ash. Several of the valleys have been improved and laid out under permanent pasture, making the landscape, as seen from the front of the house, with wood, rock, and winding grassy bay, very picturesque.

"There are twelve miles of private drives and walks—miles of them cut out of the solid rock, and in some places in the face of precipices 100

(*f*) The name of the—certainly *very* efficient—teacher of these young people, and the general principles of their tuition, would have been a desirable addition, St. George thinks, to the information furnished by Mr. Mackenzie.

feet sheer up above the sea. A home-farm is in course of being improved at Achandarroch, a mile south of Duncraig House."

The *Gazette* adds: Mr. Mackenzie himself farms some of the land
which he has reclaimed, and nowhere probably is there a better example of what is possible in the way of agricultural improvement under a
northern climate. Excellent crops of barley, clover, wheat, and roots
are grown where nothing but a marshy wilderness once existed. Here
obviously are the circumstances and the experience which should guide
and stimulate the efforts of estate owners and improvers in the way of
the reclamation of land which is now waste and worthless."

> " Holme Head, Carlisle,
> " *Juiy 6th*, 1875.

"Dear Sir,—When I read the number of *Fors* for last April, and
came to your account of the rose-leaf cutting bees, I recollected that I
had seen one of these bees making its fragmentary cell in a hole in a
brick wall, and that I had often seen the remnants of the cut leaves ;
but I never had a chance of watching them when at work till last week ;
and thinking the result may be interesting to you, and may correct the
omission you refer to at the foot of page 387 in the April *Fors*, I
take the liberty to send them to you.

"I had the opportunity of seeing a great many bees—often half a
dozen together at work upon a solitary dog-rose in front of a house at a
small watering-place (Silloth), and I observed that they cut various shapes
at different times. I picked off a great many of the leaves that they had
been at, and send you herewith one or two specimens. I find that these
have occasionally cut through the midrib of the leaf ; but this is a rare
exception. I found they carried the cuttings to some adjoining sand-
hills, where they had bored small holes in the sand ; and in these they
built their leaf-cells. The pollen in these cells was not purple, but
yellow, and may have been gathered from the hawkweed which covers
the banks where their nests are made.

" Since we came home, I have found some more leaves in my own
garden similarly cut. The leaves I find to be cut in this way are the
rose, French bean, and young laburnum.

> " Yours truly,
> " W. Lattimer."

V. Part of a letter from a lady who sent me Helix virgata :—

"We live in a poor neighbourhood, and I have come to know the
history of many poor working people lately ; and I want to understand
so much about it, even more than I used to long to understand the
mysterious life of shells and flowers. Why aren't there public baths, etc.,
for children as much as public schools ? They want washing more than
teaching. 'Hearts sprinkled from an evil conscience, and bodies
washed in pure water," is continually sounding in my ears." (Well—
why don't you go and wash some, then ?)

"A poor woman, whose father was a West Country carrier," (very
good, but what is *she?*—the gist of the story depends on that : at present it's like one of those French twisty Bulimi, with no beginning to
it,) "was so delighted the other day to find we knew the 'West
Country ; and when I was saying something about our intending to take
the children down in May to pick cowslips, her face gleamed with delight

as she said, 'Oh, the years since I have seen a cowslip!' We used to make 'tisties'' (twisties?) "of them, and it sent a thrill of remembrance through me of my own birthday treats, and cowslip-ball days.

"But I'm so glad you like the shells. No, there *is* nothing about vegetables in the word Bulimus; but 'empty-bellied' generally is hungry, and hungry generally eats a great deal when opportunity offers. Now these 'Bulimi' eat a great deal, (of *vegetables*, it happens), so I suppose some one who named them thought they must be very hungry or 'empty-bellied.' That's the way I read the story." Well, its very accommodating and ingenious of you to read it that way; but many snails, thrushes, blackbirds, or old gentlemen of my acquaintance who 'eat a great deal,' appear to me more suggestive of the epithet 'full-' than 'empty-—waistcoated, shall we say?

VI. Week's Diary of a Companion of St. George:—

"*First day.*—Received from Sheffield a dainty 'well-poised little hammer' and three sharp-pointed little chisels : felt quite cheerful about porphyry-cutting.

"*Second day.*—Sent to the village in the morning for a slab of freestone; employed man in the afternoon to chisel a hole in it, and to fix the porphyry therein with plaster-of-Paris; drew a straight line, thinking it wiser not to begin with an asterisk; turned the points of two chisels without making the least impression on my line ; the process turned out to be skating, not engraving. Tried the third chisel, and, after diligent efforts, made a cut equal in depth to about two grains of sand. This is the Hamite bondage of art. Felt an increasing desire that the Master should try it, and a respect for the ancient Egyptians. Bore patiently the scoffs of the Amorites.

"*Third day.*—Sent chisel to the village to be hardened. Was recommended a lead hammer. Finally, a friend went to the village and brought back with him an iron hammer and two shorter chisels. Was asked by an Amorite gardener how I was 'getting on'—unconcealed pleasure on his part to hear that I was not getting on at all. Later, accomplished a beautifully irregular star-fish, which looks *mashed out* rather than *cut*, not the least like 'sharp cliff-edged harbours,' as the Master kindly supposes. I begin to feel for the ancient Egyptians : they must have got a great deal of porphyry-dust into their eyes. I shall rise in the morning to dulled points and splintered chisels ; but '*when* you have cut your asterisk, you will know,' etc., and this is not the voice of a syren, (see *Eagle's Nest*,) but of my honoured Master. . . . A terrible suspicion occurs to me that he thought no one would or could cut it! Obedience is a fine thing! How it works in the midst of difficulties, dust, and worst of all—doubt!

"*Fourth day.*—I think porphyry-cutting is delightful work: it is true that I have not done any to-day, but I have had my chisels sharpened, and two new ones have arrived from the blacksmith this evening, made out of old files. Also, I have covered my chisels with pretty blue paper, and my hammer with blue-and-white ribbon. I feel the importance of the step gained. Surely I may rest righteously after such labour. If they sing 'From Egypt lately come,' in church, I shall think it very personal.

"*Fifth day.*—My piece of porphyry is now enriched by a second star-fish, with a little more backbone in it, and two dividing lines. I worked on the lawn this morning, under the chestnut tree ;—the derision of the Amorite gardener (who was mowing the grass *with a scythe*) was manifested by the remark 'Is *that-t* all!' I told him about the Egyptian tombs, but he probably thinks me mildly insane ; he however suggested a flat edge instead of a point to a chisel, and I will try it.

"*Sixth day.*—Had lead hammer cast, and waited for chisel.

"*Seventh day.*—With third hammer and seventh chisel will surely charm the porphyry.

"But, no ! my latest asterisk is jagged in outline instead of sharp. I wonder what attempts others have made. Any one living in or near a blacksmith's shop would have an advantage, for the chisels are always wanting hardening, or rectifying in some way ; and my blue papers soon disappeared. If obedience for the sake of obedience is angelic, I must be an exalted creature. One Amorite's suggestion was, 'You would do a deal better with a softer material.' This was the voice of the tempter.

"What is gained ?—(besides lifelong affection for porphyry)—a knowledge of one more thing that I can*not* do ; an admiration (to a certain extent) of those who could do it ; and a wonder as to what the Master will require next of (amongst others) his faithful and obedient disciple."

VII. Portion of valuable letter from Mr. Sillar :—

"KINGSWOOD LODGE, LEE GREEN, S.E.,
"*August 7th*, 1876.

"My dear Mr. Ruskin,—It may interest your correspondent, 'A Reader of *Fors*,' and possibly yourself also, to know that interested persons have altered old John Wesley's rules to suit modern ideas.

"Rules of the Methodist Societies (*Tyerman's Life and Times of Wesley*, p. 431.)

"Rule.—Leader to receive once a week what members are willing to give towards *relief of the poor.*

"Altered to ' support of the Gospel.'

"*Going to law* forbidden, is altered to ' *brother* going to law with *brother*.'

"Original Rule.—The giving or taking things on usury, the words have been added, ' that is, unlawful interest.'

"Mr. Tyerman remarks, ' the curious reader will forgive these trifles.'

"I for one do not feel disposed to do so."

(Nor does St. George ; nor has he either leave, or hope, to say, "God forgive them.")

LETTER LXX.

I HAVE been not a little pestered this month by the quantities of letters, which I can't wholly cure myself of the weakness of reading, from people who fancy that, like other political writers of the day, I print, on the most important subjects, the first thing that comes into my head ; and may be made immediately to repent of what I have said, and generally to see the error of my ways, by the suggestions of their better judgment.

Letters of this sort do not surprise me if they have a Scottish postmark, the air of Edinburgh having always had a curiously exciting quality, and amazing power over weak heads ; but one or two communications from modest and thoughtful English friends have seriously troubled me by the extreme simplicity of their objections to statements which, if not acceptable, I had at least hoped would have been intelligible to them.

I had, indeed, expected difficulty in proving to my readers the mischievousness of Usury ; but I never thought to find confusion in their minds between Property itself and its Interest. Yet I find this singular confusion at the root of the objections made by most of my cavilling correspondents : "How *are* we to live" (they say) "if, when we have saved a hundred pounds, we can't make a hundred and five of them, without any more trouble ? "

Gentlemen and ladies all,—you are to live on your hundred pounds, saved ; and if you want five pounds more, you must go and work for five pounds more ; just as a man who hasn't a hundred pounds must work for the first five he gets.

The following sentence, written by a man of real economical knowledge, expresses, with more than usual precision, the common mistake : "I much fear if your definition of Usury be correct, which is to the effect that it is a sin to derive money from the possession of capital, or otherwise than

by our own personal work.   Should we follow this proposition
to its final logical conclusion, we must preach communism
pure and simple, and contend that property is theft,—which
God forbid."

To this correspondent I answered briefly, "Is my house
not my property unless I let it for lodgings, or my wife not
my property unless I prostitute her ?"

But I believe it will be well, though I intended to enter on
other matters this month, to repeat instead once more, in the
shortest and strongest terms I can find, what I have now
stated at least a hundred times respecting the eternal nature
and sanctity of ' Property.'

A man's ' Property,' the possession ' proper ' to him, his
own, rightly so called, and no one else's on any pretence of
theirs—consists of,

A. The good things,

B. Which he has honestly got,

C. And can skilfully use.

That is the A B C of Property.

A. It must consist of good things—not bad ones.   It is
rightly called therefore a man's ' Goods,' not a man's ' Bads.'

If you have got a quantity of dung lodged in your drains,
a quantity of fleas lodged in your bed, or a quantity of non-
sense lodged in your brains,—that is not ' Property,' but the
reverse thereof ; the value to you of your drains, bed, and
brains being thereby diminished, not increased.

Can you understand *that* much, my practical friend ? *

B. It must be a good thing, honestly got.   Nothing that
you have stolen or taken by force, nor anything that your
fathers stole or took by force, is your property.   Nevertheless, the benignant law of nature concerning any such holding, has always been quite manifestly that you may keep it
—if you can,—so only that you acknowledge that and none
other to be the condition of tenure.†

---

* I suppose myself, in the rest of this letter, to be addressing a " business man of the nineteenth century."

† Thus, in the earlier numbers of *Fors*, I have observed more than
once, to the present landholders of England, that they may keep their

Can you understand that much more, my practical friend ?

C. It must be not only something good, and not only honestly got, but also something you can skilfully use.

For, as the old proverb, " You can't eat your pudding and have it," is utterly true in its bearing against Usury,—so also this reverse of it is true in confirmation of property—that you can't ' have ' your pudding unless you *can* eat it. It may be composed for you of the finest plums, and paid for wholly out of your own pocket ; but if you can't stomach it—the pudding is not for *you.* Buy the finest horse on four legs, he is not ' proper ' to you if you can't ride him. Buy the best book between boards,—Horace, or Homer, or Dante,— and if you don't know Latin, nor Greek, nor Christianity, the paper and boards are yours indeed, but the books—by no means.

You doubt this, my practical friend ?

Try a child with a stick of barley-sugar ;—tell him it is his, but he mustn't eat it ; his face will express to you the fallaciousness of that principle of property in an unmistakable manner. But by the time he grows as old and stupid as you, perhaps he will buy barley-sugar that he can't taste, to please the public.

" I've no pleasure in that picture of Holman Hunt's," said a highly practical man of business to a friend of mine the other day, " nor my wife neither, for that matter ; but I always buy under good advice as to market value ; and one's collection isn't complete without one."

I am very doubtful, my stupid practical friend, whether you have wit enough to understand a word more of what I have got to say this month. However, I must say it on the chance. And don't think I am talking sentiment or metaphysics to you. This is the practicallest piece of lessoning you ever had in your days, if you can but make it out ;— that you can only possess wealth according to your own capacity of it. An ape can only have wealth of nuts, and a dog

lands—if they can ! Only let them understand that trial will soon be made, by the Laws of Nature, of such capacity in them.

of bones,* an earth-worm of earth, a charnel-worm of flesh, a
west-end harlot of silk and champagne, an east-end harlot of
gauze and gin, a modern average fine lady of such meat and
drink, dress, jewels, and furniture, as the vile tradesmen of
the day can provide, being limited even in the enjoyment
of these,—for the greater part of what she calls ' hers,' she
wears or keeps, either for the pleasure of others, if she is
good, or for their mortification, if she is wicked,—but assuredly not for herself. When I buy a missal, or a picture,
I buy it for myself, and expect everybody to say to me,
What a selfish brute you are. But when a lady walks about
town with three or four yards of silk tied in a bundle behind
her, she doesn't see it herself, or benefit by it herself. She
carries it for the benefit of beholders. When she has put all
her diamonds on in the evening, tell her to stay at home and
enjoy them in radiant solitude ; and the child, with his forbidden barley-sugar, will not look more blank. She carries
her caparison either for the pleasure or for the mortification of society ; and can no more enjoy its brilliancy by herself than a chandelier can enjoy having its gas lighted.

We must leave out of the question, for the moment, the
element of benevolence which may be latent in toilette†;
for the main economical result of the action of the great law
that we can only have wealth according to our capacity, in
modern Europe at this hour, is that the greater part of its
so-called wealth is composed of things suited to the capacity
of harlots and their keepers,—(including in the general term
harlot, or daughter of Babylon, both the unmarried ones,
and the married ones who have sold themselves for money,)
—as of watches, timepieces, tapestries, china, and any
kind of pictures or toys good for bedrooms and boudoirs ;
but that, of any wealth which harlots and keepers of harlots

---

* A *masterless* dog. I should have written, but wanted to keep my
sentence short and down to my practical friend's capacity. For if the
dog have the good fortune to find a master, he has a possession thenceforth, better than bones ; and which, indeed, he will, at any moment,
leave, not his meat only, but his life for.

† It is a very subtle and lovely one, not to be discussed hurriedly.

have no mind to, Europe at present takes no cognizance whatsoever.

Now what the difference may be in the quality of property which honest and dishonest women like is—for you, my practical friend—quite an unfathomable question ; but you can at least understand that all the china, timepieces, and lewd pictures, which form the main 'property' of Paris and her imitators, are verily, in the *commercial* sense of the word, property ; and would be estimated as such by any Jew in any bankruptcy court ; yet the harlots don't lend their china, or timepieces, on usury, nor make an income out of their bed-*hangings*,—do they ? So that you see it is perfectly possible to have property, and a very costly quantity of it, without making any profit of such capital ?

But the harlots have another kind of capital which you, my blind practical friend, don't call 'Property' ; but which I, having the use of my eyes as well as of my hands, do. They have beauty of body ;—many of them, also, wit of mind. And on these two articles of property, you observe, my friend, being much *more* their own, and much more valuable things, if they knew it, than china and timepieces—on these they do make an annual income, and turn them over, as you call it, several times perhaps in the year.

Now if beauty of body and wit of tongue can be thus made sources of income, you will rank them perhaps, even as I do, among articles of wealth.

But, in old usury, there was yet another kind of treasure held account of, namely—Beauty of Heart, and Wit of Brains ;—or what was shortly called by the Greek usurers, Psyche—(you may have heard the word before, my practical friend ; but I do not expect you to follow me further). And this Psyche, or Soul, was held by the two great old masters of economy—that is to say, by Plato and David—the best property of all that a man had ; except only one thing, which the soul itself must be starved without, yet which you would never guess, my practical friend, if you guessed yourself into your grave, to be an article of property at all ! The Law of God, of which David says, " My *soul fainteth* for the

longing that it hath unto thy judgments," or in terms which
you can perhaps better understand, "The law of thy mouth
is dearer unto me than thousands of gold and silver."

But indeed the market value of this commodity has greatly
fallen in these times. "Damn the Laws of God," answered
a City merchant of standing to a personal friend of mine,
who was advising him the other day to take a little of that
capital into his business.

Then, finally, there is just one article of property more to be
catalogued, and I have done. The Law-giver Himself,
namely ; the Master of masters, whom, when, as human dogs,
we discover, and can call our own Master, we are thenceforth
ready to die for, if need be. Which Mr. Harrison and the
other English gentlemen who are at present discussing, in
various magazines, the meaning of the word 'religion' * (appearing never to have heard in the course of their education,
of either the word 'lictor' or 'ligature') will find, is, was,
and will be, among all educated scholars, the perfectly simple
meaning of that ancient word ; and that there can be no
such thing, even for sentimental Mr. Harrison, as a religion of
Manity, nor for the most orthodox hunting parson, as a religion of Dogity ; nor for modern European civilization as a
religion of Bitchity, without such submission of spirit to the
worshipped Power as shall in the most literal sense 'bind' and
chain us to it for ever.

And now, to make all matters as clear as may be, I will
put down in the manner of a Dutch auction—proceeding to
the lower valuation,—the articles of property, rightly so
called, which belong to any human creature.

I. The Master, or Father, in the old Latin phrase, 'Pater
Noster ;' of whom David wrote, "Whom have I in heaven
but thee, and there is none upon earth that I desire beside
thee ; " but this possession, includes in Plato's catalogue the
attendant spirits, " θεοὺς, ὄντας δεσπότας, καὶ τοὺς τούτοις
ἑπομένους "—" the Gods being Masters and those next to

* See 'definition' quoted as satisfactory in *Anthropological Magazine*,
" the belief in spiritual beings," which would make the devil a religious
person, inasmuch as he both believes—and fears.

them," specially signified in another place as the "Gods, and the Angels, and the Heroes, and the Spirits of our Home, and our Ancestors."

II. The Law or Word of God, which the Bible Society professes to furnish for eighteenpence. But which, indeed, as often heretofore stated in *Fors Clavigera*, is by no means to be had at that low figure ; the whole long hundred and nineteenth Psalm being little more than one agonizing prayer for the gift of it : and a man's life well spent if he has truly received and learned to read ever so little a part of it.

III. The Psyche, in its sanity, and beauty (of which, when I have finished my inventory, I will give Plato's estimate in his own words). Some curious practical results have followed from the denial of its existence by modern philosophers ; for the true and divine distinction between 'genera' of animals, and quite the principal 'origin of species' in them, is in their Psyche : but modern naturalists, not being able to vivisect the Psyche, have on the whole resolved that animals are to be classed by their bones ; and whereas, for instance, by divine distinction of Psyche, the Dog and Wolf are precisely opposite creatures in their function to the sheepfold ; and, spiritually, the Dominican, or Dog of the Lord, is for ever in like manner opposed to the Wolf of the Devil, modern science, finding Dog and Wolf indistinguishable in their Bones, declares them to be virtually one and the same animal.*

IV. The Body, in its sanity and beauty : strength of it being the first simple meaning of what the Greeks called virtue : and the eternity of it being the special doctrine of

---

* See the last results of modern enlightenment on this subject in Mr. Waterhouse Hawkins's directions for the scientific representation of Dogs, illustrated by the charming drawings of that great artist ;—especially compare the learned outlines of head and paw in Plate II., and the delineation of head without Psyche in Plate III., with the ignorant efforts of Velasquez in such extremities and features in our fourth photograph. Perhaps Mr. Waterhouse Hawkins will have the goodness, in his next edition, to show us how Velasquez ought to have expressed the Scapholinear, Cuneiform, Pisiform, Trapezium, Trapezoid, Magnum, and Unciform bones in those miserably drawn fore-paws.

the form of religion professed in Christendom under the name of Christianity.

V. The things good and pleasing to the Psyche ; as the visible things of creation,—sky, water, flowers, and the like ; and the treasured-up words or feats of other Spirits.

VI. The things good and pleasing to the Body ; summed under the two heads of Bread and Wine, brought forth by the Amorite King of Salem.

VII. The documents giving claim to the possession of these things, when not in actual possession ; or 'money.'

This catalogue will be found virtually to include all the articles of wealth which man can either possess or lend, (for the fourth, fully understood, means the entire treasure of domestic and social affection ;) and the law of their tenure is that a man shall neither sell nor lend that which is indeed his *own ;* neither his God, his conscience, his soul, his body, or his wife's ; his country, his house, nor his tools.   But that things which are not ' his own,' but over which he has charge or authority, (as of more land than he can plough, or more books than he can read,) these he is bound to lend or give, as he sees they may be made serviceable to others ; and not for farther gain to himself.   Thus his Grace the Archbishop of Canterbury is, under penalties, bound to make his very excellent library at Lambeth serviceable to other scholars ; but it is not at all permitted to his Grace, by the laws of God, to use any part of the income derived from his pretty estate on the slope of the Addington Hills, for the purchase of books, by the loan of which, in the manner of Mr. Mudie, to the ignorant inhabitants of the village of Croydon, his Grace may at once add to his income (not more than) five per cent. on the capital thus laid out in literature ; and to his dignity as a Christian pastor.   I know, as it happens, more about the heather than the rents of his Grace's estate at Addington ; my father and I having taken much pleasure in its bloom, and the gleaming of blue-bells amongst it—when he, in broken health, sought any English ground that Scottish flowers grew on, and I was but a child ;—so that I thought it would please him to be laid in his last rest at the feet of those brown hills. And thus, as I say, I know somewhat of their flowers, but never inquired into their rents ; and perhaps, as I rather hope, the sweet wood and garden ground serve only for his Grace's entertainment—not emolument : but even if only so, in these hard times his Grace must permit me to observe that he has quite as much earthly ground and lodging as any angel of the Lord can be supposed to require ; and is under no necessity of adding to his possessions by the practice of usury. I do not know if the Archbishop has in his library the works of Mr. Thackeray ; but he probably has sometimes relieved his studies of the Christian Fathers with modern literature, and may remember a figure of an amiable and economical little schoolboy who begins life by lending three halfpence, early in the week, to the boys who had outrun their income, for four halfpence at the week's end. The figure of the same little boy grown into an Archbishop, and making a few pence extra on his episcopal income by the loan of his old school books, did not, it appears, suggest itself to the lamented author ; but here it is, in relief, for us :—

East Surrey Hall, Museum and Library Company

(LIMITED).

Registered under the Companies Acts, 1862 *and* 1867.

President.

. HIS GRACE THE ARCHBISHOP OF CANTERBURY.

Vice-Presidents.

GRANVILLE LEVESON GOWER, ESQ., *High Sheriff of Surrey.*
S. BIRCH, ESQ., LL.D., etc., *British Museum.*
REV. DR. MOFFAT, *late African Missionary.*
THE HIGH BAILIFF OF THE BOROUGH OF SOUTHWARK.
THE MAYOR OF REIGATE.

IT is proposed to found at Croydon * an Institution to be called the *East Surrey Hall, Museum and Library.* This Institution, to be placed in the largest town of Surrey, is intended for the benefit and use of the whole county.

* Being somewhat interested in Croydon, as readers of past *Fors* know, and in Museums also, I give large print to these proposals.

The Hall will be adapted for public meetings of every description, and it is hoped that it will also be an ornament to the town.

In the Museum it is intended to form a collection of objects of historic, scientific, and artistic interest, particularly of such as may be found in the County of Surrey. The Museum will be free.

The Library will consist of standard works of reference, arranged in rooms suitably furnished for the purposes of reading and study. In addition to works on general literature, it is intended to place in this Library, Books, Maps, and everything of the like nature, tending to elucidate the History, Topography, etc., of the County of Surrey, and especially of the Parish of Croydon. In the Company's Memorandum of Association it is expressly stipulated that one department of this Library shall be Free.

Other parts of the building will be so arranged as to be suitable for occupation, or for letting as offices to Friendly Societies and other Public Bodies.

The Capital required to found this Institution will be raised by means of Donations and One Pound Shares.

The Donations will be applied to carrying out all or any of the above objects, according as the Donor may desire.

The Articles of Association provide that "no dividend shall be declared in any one year exceeding in amount £5 per cent. per annum upon the amount of the Capital of the Company for the time being called up. If, in any one year, the net earnings of the Company would allow of a dividend exceeding in amount the said dividend of £5 per cent. per annum being declared, the Directors shall employ the surplus earnings in improving the buildings of the Company, or in the purchase of additional stock or effects, or otherwise, for the benefit of the Company, as the Directors for the time being shall from time to time determine."

VENICE, *16th September*, 1876.

I am weary, this morning, with vainly trying to draw the Madonna-herb clustered on the capitals of St. Mark's porch; and mingling its fresh life with the marble acanthus leaves which saw Barbarossa receive the foot of the Primate of Christendom on his neck;—wondering within myself all the while, which did not further my painting, how far the existing Primate of Canterbury, in modestly declining to set his

foot upon the lion and the adder, was bettering the temper
of the third Alexander ; and wondering yet more whether
the appointment—as vice-defender of the Faith for Her
Majesty—of Lord Lonsdale to be curator of Lancashire souls,
in the number implied by the catalogue of livings in his patronage, given in our fourth article of Correspondence, gave
to the Lord of the Dales of Lune more of the character of the
Pope, or the Lion ?

What may be the real value of the Lancashire souls as a
property in trust, we may, perhaps, as clearly gather from
the following passage of Plato as from any Christian political
economist.

" And now, whosoever has been content to hear me speaking of the Gods, and of our dear ancestors, let him yet hear
me in this. For next to the Gods, of all his possessions his
soul is the mightiest, being the most his own.

" And the nature of it is in all things twofold ; the part
that is stronger and better, ruling, and the part that is weaker
and worse, serving ; and the part of it that rules is always
to be held in honour before that that serves. I command,
therefore, every man that he should rightly honour his soul,
calling it sacred, next to the Gods and the higher Powers
attendant on them.

" And indeed, to speak simply, none of us honours his soul
rightly, but thinks he does. For Honour is a divine good,
nor can any evil thing bring it,[a] or receive ; and he who
thinks to magnify his soul by any gifts to it, or sayings, or
submittings, which yet do not make it better, from less
good, seems indeed to himself to honour it, but does so in
nowise.

" For example, the boy just become man thinks himself
able to judge of all things ; and thinks that he honours his
own soul in praising it ; and eagerly commits to its doing
whatsoever it chooses to do.

" But according to what has been just said, in doing this
he injures and does not honour his soul, which, second to the
Gods, he is bound to honour.

[a] I have no doubt of the mingled active sense of τίμιος in this sentence, necessary by the context ; while also the phrase would be a mere
flat truism, if the word were used only in its ordinary passive meaning.

" Neither when a man holds himself not guilty of his own errors, nor the cause of the most and the greatest evils that befall him [b] ; but holds others to be guilty of them, and himself guiltless, always ;—honouring his own soul, as it seems ; but far away is he from doing this, for he injures it ; neither when he indulges it with delights beyond the word and the praise of the Lawgiver [c] ;—then he in nowise honours it, but disgraces, filling it with weaknesses and repentances ; neither when he does not toil through, and endure patiently, the contraries of these pleasures, the divinely praised Pains, and Fears, and Griefs, and Mournings, but yields under them ; then he does not honour it in yielding ; but, in doing all these things, accomplishes his soul in dishonour ; neither (even if living honourably) [d] when he thinks that life is wholly good, does he honour it, but shames it, then also weakly allowing his soul in the thought that all things in the invisible world are evil ; and not resisting it, nor teaching it that it does not know but that, so far from being evil, the things that belong to the Gods of that world may be for us the best of all things. Neither when we esteem beauty of body more than beauty of soul, for nothing born of the Earth is more honourable than what is born of Heaven ; and he who thinks so of his soul knows not that he is despising his marvellous possession : neither when one desires to obtain money in any dishonourable way, or having so obtained it, is not indignant and unhappy therefore—does he honour his soul with gifts ; far otherwise ; he has given away the glory and honour of it for a spangle of gold ; and all the gold that is on the earth, and under the earth, is not a price for virtue."

That is as much of Plato's opinions concerning the Psyche as I can write out for you to-day ; in next *Fors*, I may find you some parallel ones of Carpaccio's : meantime I have to correct a mistake in *Fors*, which it will be great delight to

[b] To see clearly that whatever our fates may have been, the heaviest calamity of them—and, in a sort, the only real calamity—is our own causing, is the true humility which indeed we profess with our lips, when our heart is far from it.

[c] Pleasures which the Word of God, or of the earthly Lawgiver speaking in His Name, does not allow, nor *praise ;* for all right pleasures it praises, and forbids sadness as a grievous sin.

[d] This parenthesis is in Plato's mind, visibly, though not in his words.

all Amorites to discover; namely, that the Princess, whom I judged to be industrious because she went on working while she talked to her father about her marriage, cannot, on this ground, be praised beyond Princesses in general; for, indeed, the little mischief, instead of working, as I thought, —while her father is leaning his head on his hand in the greatest distress at the thought of parting with her,—is trying on her marriage ring!

NOTES AND CORRESPONDENCE.

I. Affairs of the Company.

I am sending in gifts to the men at Sheffield, wealth of various kinds, in small instalments—but in secure forms. Five bits of opal; the market value of one, just paid to Mr. Wright, of Great Russell Street, £3; a beryl, of unusual shape, ditto, £2; a group of emeralds, from the mine of Holy Faith of Bogota, and two pieces of moss gold,—market value £2 10s.,—just paid to Mr. Tennant. Also, the first volume of the Sheffield Library; an English Bible of the thirteenth century,—market value £50,—just paid to Mr. Ellis. I tell these prices only to secure the men's attention, because I am not sure what acceptant capacity they have for them. When once they recognize the things themselves to be wealth,—when they can see the opals, know the wonderfulness of the beryl, enjoy the loveliness of the golden fibres, read the illuminations of the Bible page,—they will not ask what they cost, nor consider what they can get for them. I don't believe they will think even of lending their Bible out on usury.

I have no subscriptions, or other progress of the Society, to announce this month.

II. Affairs of the Master.

I am a little ashamed of my accounts this time, having bought a missal worth £320 for myself, and only given one worth £50 to Sheffield. I might state several reasons, more or less excusing this selfishness; one being that the £50 Bible is entirely perfect in every leaf, but mine wants the first leaf of Genesis; and is not, therefore, with all its beauty, fit for the first volume of the library. But it is one of my present principles of action not at all to set myself up for a reformer, and it must be always one not to set up for a saint; and I must beg my severely judging readers, in the meantime, rather to look at what I have done, than at what I have left undone, of the things I ask others to do. To the St. George's Fund I have given a tenth of my living,—and much more than the tenth of the rest was before, and is still given to the poor. And if any of the rich people whom we all know will do as much as this, I believe you may safely trust them to discern and do what is right with the portion they keep, (if kept openly, and not Ananias-fashion,) and if you press them farther, the want of grace is more likely on your part than theirs. I have never, myself, felt so much contempt for any

living creature as for a miserable Scotch woman—curiously enough of
Burns' country, and of the Holy Willy breed,—whom I once by mis-
chance allowed to come and stay in my house; and who, asking, when
I had stated some general truths of the above nature, "why I kept
my own pictures;" and being answered that I kept them partly as a
national property, in my charge, and partly as my tools of work,—said
"she liked to see how people reasoned when their own interests were
touched;"—the wretch herself evidently never in all her days having
had one generous thought which could not have been smothered if it
had touched 'her own interests,' and being therefore totally unable to
conceive any such thought in others.

Farther, as to the price I ask for my books, and my continuing to
take rent for my house property, and interest from the Bank, I must
request my readers still for a time to withhold their judgment;—
though I willingly insert the following remonstrance addressed to my
publisher on the subject by an American Quaker gentleman, whose
benevolent satisfaction in sending Mr. Sillar's three shillings to St.
George's Fund, has induced him farther to take this personal interest
in the full carrying out of all my principles.

33, OAK STREET, ROCHESTER, N.Y., U.S.A.,
11*th mo.* 4*th,* 1875.

GEORGE ALLEN.

Respected Friend,—I have paid to the Post Office here, to be
paid to thee in London, the equivalent of three shillings, which I have
been requested to forward to thee for the St. George's Fund, in payment for W. C. Sillar's pamphlets on Usury.

Thy friend,
EDWARD RUSHMORE.

P.S.—I am a constant reader of *Fors Clavigera*, and was by it put
in the way to obtain W. C. Sillar's pamphlets. I have abandoned the
practice of usury, and take pleasure in the thought that the payment
for the pamphlets, though trifling, goes to St. George's Fund. I sincerely wish Mr. Ruskin could feel it his duty to act promptly in withdrawing his money from usury. I think it would increase tenfold the
force of his teaching on the subject. Please show this to him, if
convenient.—E. RUSHMORE.

I am partly, indeed, of my correspondent's way of thinking in this
matter; but I must not allow myself to be dazzled by his munificence
into an undue respect for his opinion; and I beg to assure him, and
one or two other religious gentlemen who have had the goodness to
concern themselves about my inconsistency, that the change in my
mode of life which they wish me to carry out, while it would cause no
inconvenience to *me,* seeing that I have before now lived in perfect
comfort, and could now live in what is much more to me than comfort

—peace—on a couple of guineas a week; plaguing myself no more
either with authorship or philanthropy, and asking only so much charity
from the Bursar of Corpus as to take charge for me of the sum of
£2,000 sterling, and dole me out my guineas from that dead capital
monthly,—the surplus, less burial expenses, to be spent in MSS. for
Corpus library at my death;—while, I say, this would be an entirely
satisfactory arrangement, and serenely joyful release from care, to
myself, it would be an exceedingly inconvenient arrangement to a
number of persons who are at present dependent on me for daily bread,
and who, not sharing my views about Interest, would have no consolation in their martyrdom. For which, and sundry valid reasons besides,
I once for all assure my conscientious correspondents that the time is
not yet come for me to do more than I have done already, and that I
shall receive without cavilling, or asking for more, the tenth part of
their own fortunes for St. George, with extreme pleasure.

The Master's Accounts.

			£	s.	d.
Aug.	21.	Crawley (a)	30	0	0
"		George Inn, Aylesbury (b)	30	0	0
	23.	Circular notes (c)	200	0	0
"		Down's	50	0	0
	25.	Annie Brickland	10	0	0
Sept.	1.	Raffaelle	10	0	0
"		Bernard Quaritch	320	0	0
			£655	0	0
		Balance, Aug. 15th	596	12	8
		Sale of £500 Bank Stock	1279	8	0
			1876	0	8
			655	0	0
		Balance Sept. 15th	£1221	0	8

(a) Quarterly wages.

(b) Representing some dinners to friends ; also exploring drives in
the neighbourhood.

(c) Fast melting away in expensive inns, the only ones in which I can
be quiet. If some pious young English boys and girls, instead of setting
up for clergymen and clergywomen, would set up, on their marriage,
for publicans, and keep clean parlours, lavendered sheets, and honest
fare, all for honest price, for poor wanderers like myself, I doubt not
their reward would be great in Heaven.

III. From *Carlisle Journal.*

"The deceased nobleman was the third Earl of the second creation
of the title. He was born on the 27th of March, 1818, and was consequently fifty-eight years of age when he died. He was educated at

Westminster and Trinity College, Cambridge, taking the degree of M.A. in 1838. In 1841, he entered the Life Guards as Cornet, and retired as Captain in 1854. From 1847 to 1872 he represented West Cumberland in Parliament in the Conservative interest, and succeeded to the title of Earl of Lonsdale upon the death of his uncle in 1872. He was Lord-Lieutenant and Custos Rotulorum of Cumberland and Westmoreland, Hon. Colonel of the Royal Cumberland Militia, and of Cumberland Rifle Volunteers, and Lieutenant-Colonel of Westmoreland and Cumberland Yeomanry Cavalry.

"The Earl was patron of more than forty church livings in this diocese. The following, forty-three in number, were, for the most part, wholly at his disposal, and of course descend to his successor :—Aikton, Armathwaite, Bootle, Bolton, Bowness, Brigham, Buttermere, Cockermouth, Cleator, Corney, Distington, Embleton, Gosforth, Hensingham, Haile, Kirkandrews-upon-Eden, Kirkbride, Lorton, Loweswater, Morseby, Mosser, St. Bees, Threlkeld, Whicham, Whitbeck; St. James, Christ Church, St. Nicholas, and Holy Trinity, Whitehaven ; Askham, Bampton, Barton, Kirkby Stephen, Lowther, Patterdale, Clifton, Ravenstondale, Shap, Startforth (Yorkshire), Bampton Kirk, Orton, St. John's-in-the-Vale, and Crosthwaite.

"The late Lord Lonsdale never took a prominent public part in political life, although he had a seat in the House of Commons for twenty-five years; but he had won much personal popularity as a country gentleman. In agriculture he was naturally interested, the rental of his landed estates in Cumberland alone being over £40,000 a year, and in Westmoreland nearly as much more ; but it was that department concerning the breeding of horses to which he turned most attention. In the development of this taste he became an active member of the Turf. His horse 'King Lud' won the Cesarewitch Stakes in 1873, and it was its noble owner's ambition to win the Cumberland Plate with it the following year. An unfortunate accident, however, lost him the race, and as in the previous year the breakdown of 'The Preacher' had also proved a disappointment, he did not try again. But horse-racing was not the only kind of sport with which the late Earl was closely connected. In the hunting-field he was a popular M.F.H., but only the other day it was announced that failing health had compelled him to say that he could not after next season hunt the Cottesmore hounds, of which he has held the mastership for six years.

"The remains of the deceased peer were removed to Lowther Castle on Tuesday evening, and several members of the Town and Harbour Board accompanied them from Whitehaven Castle to the railway station. The hearse was followed by two mourning coaches, containing the Viscount Lowther and Colonel Williams; Mr. R. A. Robinson, Mr. Mawson, and Mr. Borthwick. After these followed servants in the employ of the late lord, the trustees, and other inhabitants.

"The funeral will probably take place to-morrow or on Monday, at the family mausoleum at Lowther.

"The flags on the public buildings of Whitehaven and Carlisle have since Tuesday been displayed half-mast high."—*Carlisle Journal,* August 18th, 1876

The *Sportsman* contains the following memoir of the late Lord Lonsdale as a patron of the Turf :—"When he succeeded his uncle to the title of Earl of Lonsdale in 1872, he relinquished his Parliamentary duties. It was then that the observance of a very ancient custom de volved upon him—that of giving a cup to be raced for on Burgh Marsh, the contest to be confined to horses bred in the barony. The only occasions of race meetings being held on the Marsh, or foreshores of the Solway, are when there is a new Lord-Lieutenant of Cumberland, and from having assisted at the meeting—the management of which was entrusted to Mr. Lawley—I can well remember with what zeal his lordship entered into the rural sports, and the graceful speech he made when he presented the cup to Major Browne, who won with 'The Crow,' a son of 'Grand Secret,' that had been travelling the county. It was the especial delight of Lord Lonsdale that the winner was ridden by Jem Snowdon—a native of Carlisle; and he presented the jockey with a handsome whip, and complimented the Cumberland horseman on his riding. There were not less than sixty thousand people present, and within almost a stone's throw of the Grand Stand was the monument put up to mark the spot where died King Edward, who was on his way to Scotland when death overtook him. Lord Lonsdale acted as steward of Carlisle Races for years, and he took a great deal of interest in the meeting, as he also did in the local gathering on Harras Moor, close to Whitehaven."

IV. I am very grateful for the following piece of letter, (as for all other kindness from the Companion to whom I owe it;) and really I think it is "enough to make one give up wearing Valenciennes."

"August 9th, 1876.

"My dear Master,—I have tried in vain to resist those words in the August *Fors,*—'*some one tell me,*' but at last resolve to say my say, trusting to your indulgence if it is in vain.

"Some years ago, a friend of mine visiting Brussels went over the Royal Lace Manufactory, and seeing a woman busily at work on a very fine, and, according to the then fashion, large, collar, went up to her, and inquired how long she had been over this one piece. The woman answered, four years; and handed the work for my friend to examine more closely, but without changing her position, or lifting her eyes from the spot on which they were fixed; and on being asked the reason of this, said it would take too long time to have again to *fix* her eyes, so she kept them to the *one* spot through all the working hours. This is quite true. But the women were working in a large, light room—I doubt the correctness of the dark cellar, and do not see the reason for it—but all who have ever done any fine work can understand the loss of time in moving the eyes. But, after all, is lace-making worse for women than the ceaseless treadle movement of the sewing-machine? Lace-making hurts eyes only; the machine injures the whole woman—so I am told."

V. A letter from a Methodist minister, though written on the 14th, only reaches me here at Venice on the 28th. It will appear in next *Fors.* The gist of it is contradiction of Mr. Sillar's statement that the Wesleyans altered John Wesley's rules. "The alterations, whether good or bad," (says my new correspondent,) "were made by himself." I am not surprised to hear this; for had Wesley been a wise Christian, there would no more now, have been Wesleyan than Apollosian ministers.

LETTER LXXI.

VENICE, *4th October*, 1876.

I AM able at last to give you some of the long-promised opinions of Carpaccio on practical subjects ; not that, except ironically, I ever call them ' opinions.' There are certain men who *know* the truths necessary to human life ; they do not ' opine ' them ; and nobody's ' opinions,' on any subject, are of any consequence opposed to them. Hesiod is one of these, Plato another, Dante another, Carpaccio is another. He speaks little, and among the inspired painters may be thought of as one of the lesser prophets ; but his brief book is of extreme value.

I have been happy enough to get two of my faithful scholars to work upon it for me ; and they have deciphered it nearly all—much more, at all events, than I can tell you either in this *Fors*, or in several to come.

His message is written in the Venetian manner, by painting the myths of the saints, in his own way.

If you will look into the introduction to the *Queen of the Air*, you will find it explained that a great myth *can* only be written in the central time of a nation's power. This prophecy of Carpaccio's may be thought of by you as the sweetest, *because* the truest, of all that Venice was born to utter : the painted syllabling of it is nearly the last work and word of hers in true life. She speaks it, and virtually, thereafter, dies, or begins to die.

It is written in a series of some eighteen to twenty pictures, chiefly representing the stories of St. Ursula, St. George, and St. Jerome.

The first, in thoughtful order, of these, the dream of St. Ursula, has been already partly described. The authorities of the Venetian Academy have been kind enough to take the picture down and give it me to myself, in a quiet room, where I am making studies which I hope will be of use in Oxford, and elsewhere.

But there is this to be noted before we begin ; that of these three saints, whose stories Carpaccio tells, one is a quite real one, on whose penman's work we depend for our daily Bible-bread. Another, St. George, is a very dimly real one,—very disputable by American faith, and we owe to him, only in England, certain sentiments ;—the Order of the Garter, and sundry sign-boards of the George and Dragon. Venice supposed herself to owe more to him ; but he is nevertheless, in her mind also, a very ghostly saint,—armour and all too light to sink a gondola.

Of the third, St. Ursula, by no industry of my good scholars, and none has been refused, can I find the slightest material trace. Under scholarly investigation, she vanishes utterly into the stars and the æther,—and literally, as you will hear, and see, into moonshine, and the modern German meaning of everything,—the Dawn.* Not a relic, not a word, remains of her, as what Mr. John Stuart Mill calls " a utility embodied in a material object."

The whole of her utility is Immaterial—to us in England, immaterial, of late years, in every conceivable sense. But the strange thing is that Carpaccio paints, of the substantial and indisputable saint—only three small pictures ; of the disputable saint, three more important ones ; but of the entirely aërial saint, a splendid series, the chief labour of his life.

The chief labour ;—and chief rest, or play, it seems also ; questionable in the extreme as to the temper of Faith in which it is done.

We will suppose, however, at first, for your better satisfac-

---

* The primary form in which the legend shows itself is a Nature myth, in which Ursula is the Bud of flowers, enclosed in its rough or hairy calyx, and her husband, Æther—the air of spring. She opens into lovely life with ' eleven' thousand other flowers, their fading is their sudden martyrdom. And—says your modern philosopher— ' That's all ! '

tion, that in composing the pictures he no more believed there ever had been a Princess Ursula than Shakspeare, when he wrote Midsummer Night's Dream, believed there had been a Queen Hippolyta : and that Carpaccio had just as much faith in angels as Shakspeare in fairies—and no more. Both these artists, nevertheless, set themselves to paint, the one fairies, the other angels and saints, for popular—entertainment, (say your modern sages,) or popular—instruction, it may yet appear. But take it your own way ; and let it be for popular amusement. This play, this picture which I am copying for you, were, both of them we will say, toys, for the English and Venetian people.

Well, the next question is, whether the English and Venetians, when they *could* be amused with these toys, were more foolish than now, when they can only be amused with steam merry-go-rounds.

Below St. George's land at Barmouth, large numbers of the English populace now go to bathe. Of the Venetians, beyond St. George's island, many go now to bathe on the sands of Lido. But nobody thinks of playing a play about queens and fairies, to the bathers on the Welsh beach. The modern intellectual teacher erects swings upon the beach. There the suspended population oscillate between sea and sky, and are amused. Similarly in Venice, no decorative painter at Lido thinks of painting pictures of St. Nicholas of the Lido to amuse the modern Venetian. The white-necktied orchestra plays them a ' pot-pourri,' and their steamer squeaks to them, and they are amused.

And so sufficiently amused, that I, hearing with sudden surprise and delight the voice of native Venetian Punch last night from an English ship, and instantly inquiring, with impatience, why I had not had the happiness of meeting him before, found that he was obliged to take refuge as a runaway, or exile, under the British Flag, being forbidden in his own Venice, for evermore—such the fiat of liberty towards the first Apostolic Vicar thereof.

I am willing, however, for my own part, to take Carpaccio a step farther down in the moral scale still. Suppose that he painted this picture, not even to amuse his public—but to amuse himself !

To a great extent I *know* that this is true. I know,—(you needn't ask how, because you can't be shown how,—but I *do* know, trust me,) that he painted this picture greatly to amuse himself, and had extreme delight in the doing of it ; and if he did not actually believe that the princess and angels ever were, at least he heartily wished there had been such persons, and could be.

Now this is the first step to real faith. There may never have been saints : there may be no angels,—there may be no God. Professors Huxley and Tyndall are of opinion that there is no God : they have never found one in a bottle. Well : possibly there isn't ; but, my good Sheffield friends, do you wish there was ? or are you of the French Republican opinion—" If there were a God, we should have to shoot him " as the first great step towards the " abolition of caste " proposed by our American friends ? *

You will say, perhaps,—It is not a proper intellectual state to approach such a question in, to wish anything about it. No, assuredly not,—and I have told you so myself, many a time. But it is an entirely proper state to fit you for being approached by the Spirits that you wish for, if there are such. And if there are not, it can do you no harm.

Nor, so long as you distinctly understand it to be a wish, will it warp your intellect. " Oh, if I had but Aladdin's lamp, or Prince Houssain's carpet ! " thinks the rightly-minded child, reading its *Arabian Nights*. But he does not take to rubbing his mother's lamps, nor to squatting on scraps of carpet, hopefully.

Well—concerning these Arabian nights of Venice and the Catholic Church. Carpaccio thinks,—" Oh, if there had but been such a Princess as this—if there could but be ! At least I can paint one, and delight myself in the image of her ! "

Now, can you follow him so far as this ? Do you really wish there were such a Princess ? Do you so much as want **any** kind of Princess ? Or are your aims fixed on the attain-

* Correspondence, Article VI.

ment of a world so constituted that there shall be no Princesses in it any more,—but only Helps in the kitchen, who shall " come upstairs to play the piano," according to the more detailed views of the American Socialist, displayed in our correspondence.

I believe you can scarcely so much as propose this question to yourselves, not knowing clearly what a Princess is. For a Princess is truly one of the members of that Feudal System which, I hear on all hands, is finally ended. If it be so, it is needful that I should explain to you specifically what the Feudal System was, before you can wisʜ for a Princess, or any other part of it, back again.

The Feudal System begins in the existence of a Master, or Mister ; and a Mistress,—or, as you call her, Missis,—who have deputed authority over a piece of land, hereditarily theirs ; and absolute authority in their own house, or home, standing on such land : authority essentially dual, and not by any means admitting two masters, or two missises, still less our American friend's calculated desirable quantity of 150, mixed. And the office of a Master implies the office of Servants ; and of a Mistress, the office of Maids. These are the first Four Chemical Elements of the Feudal System.

The next members of it in order of rank are the Master of the Masters, and Mistress of the Mistresses ; of whom they hold their land in fee, and who are recognized still, in a sort, as landlord and landlady, though for the most part now degenerate into mere tax-gatherers ; but, in their true office, the administrators of law concerning land, and magistrates, and hearers of appeal between household and household : * their duty involving perfect acquaintance and friendship with all the households under their rule ; and their dominion, therefore, not by any possibility extending over very large space of territory,—what is commonly called in England an 'estate' being usually of approximately convenient space.

The next members of the Feudal System in order of rank, are the Lord of the Landlords, and Lady of the Landladies ; commonly called their Duke, Doge, or leader, and Duchess

* Compare the last page of *Fors*, October 1875.

or Dogaressa : the authority of this fourth member of the Feudal System being to enforce law and hear appeal between Lord and Lord ; and to consult with them respecting the harmonious government of their estates over such extent of land as may from some specialty of character be managed by common law referring to some united interest,—as, for instance, Cumberland, by a law having reference to pastoral life, Cornwall by laws involving the inspection of mines of tin, and the like,—these provinces, or shires, having each naturally a capital city, cathedral, town hall, and municipality of merchants.

As examples of which Fourth Order * in the Feudal System, the Dukes and Dukedoms of York, Lancaster, Venice, Milan, Florence, Orleans, and Burgundy, may be remembered by you as having taken very practical part in the government, or, it may be, misgovernment, of the former world.

Then the persons of the Fifth Order, in the Feudal System, are the Duke of the Dukes, and Duchess of the Duchesses, commonly called the King and Queen, having authority and magistracy over the Dukes of the provinces, to the extent in which such provinces may be harmoniously joined in a country or kingdom, separated from other portions of the world by interests, manners, and dialect.

Then the Sixth Order in the Feudal System, much, of late years, misunderstood, and even forgotten, is that of the Commander or Imperator of the Kings ; having the same authority and office of hearing appeal among the Kings of kingdoms, as they among the Dukes of provinces.

The systems of all human civilized governments resolve themselves finally into the balance of the Semitic and Iapetic powers under the anointed Cyrus of the East and Karl of the West.†

The practical power of the office has been necessarily lost since the Reformation ; and in recent debates in an English

---

* I. Servant. II. Master. III. Lord. IV. Duke.

† I want to write a long note on Byzantine empire,—Commanders of the Faithful,—Grand Turks,—and the " Eastern question." But can't: and perhaps the reader will be thankful.

Parliament on this subject, it appeared that neither the Prime Minister of England, nor any of her Parliamentary representatives, had the slightest notion of the meaning of the word.

The reason that the power of the office has been lost since the Reformation, is that all these temporal offices are only perfected, in the Feudal System, by their relative spiritual offices. Now, though the Squire and the Rector still in England occupy their proper symmetrical position, the equally balanced authority of the Duke and Bishop has been greatly confused : that of the King and Cardinal was so even during the fully animated action of both ; and all conception of that of the Emperor and Pope is of course dead in Protestant minds.

But there was yet, in the Feudal System, one Seventh and Final Authority, of which the imagination is like to be also lost to Protestant minds. That of the King of Kings, and Ruler of Empires ; in whose ordinances and everlasting laws, and in 'feudom' or faith and covenant with whom, as the Giver of Land and Bread, all these subordinate powers lived, and moved, and had their being.

And truly if, since we cannot find this King of Kings in the most carefully digested residuum, we are sure that we cannot find Him anywhere ; and if, since by no fineness of stopper we can secure His essence in a bottle, we are sure that we cannot stay Him anywhere, truly what I hear on all hands is correct ; and the Feudal System, with all consequences and members thereof, is verily at an end.

In the meantime, however, you can now clearly understand the significance, in that system, of the word Princess, meaning a King's daughter, bred in such ways and knowledges as may fit her for dominion over nations. And thus you can enjoy, if otherwise in a humour for its enjoyment, the story of the Princess Ursula, here following,—though for the present you may be somewhat at a loss to discern the practical bearings of it ; which, however, if you will note that the chief work of the Princess is to convert the savage minds of the 'English,' or people of Over-sea, from the worship of

their god ' Malcometto,' to the 'rule of St. John the Baptist,'
—you may guess to be in some close connection with the
proposed ' practice ' of St. George's Company ; not less, indeed, than the functions of Carpaccio's other two chiefly
worshipped saints.

The legends of St. Ursula, which were followed by him,
have been collated here at Venice, and reduced to this
pleasant harmony, in true help to me, by my good scholar
James Reddie Anderson. For whose spirit thus active with
us, no less than for the spirit, at rest, of the monk who preserved the story for us, I am myself well inclined to say
another Pater and Ave.

THE STORY OF ST. URSULA.*

There was once a just and most Christian King of Britain,
called Maurus. To him and to his wife Daria was born a
little girl, the fairest creature that this earth ever saw. She
came into the world wrapped in a hairy mantle, and all men
wondered greatly what this might mean. Then the King
gathered together his wise men to inquire of them. But
they could not make known the thing to him, for only God
in Heaven knew how the rough robe signified that she should
follow holiness and purity all her days, and the wisdom of
St. John the Baptist. And because of the mantle, they
called her ' Ursula,' ' Little Bear.'

Now Ursula grew day by day in grace and loveliness, and
in such wisdom that all men marvelled. Yet should they
not have marvelled, since with God all things are possible.
And when she was fifteen years old she was a light of all
wisdom, and a glass of all beauty, and a fountain of scripture
and of sweet ways. Lovelier woman there was not alive.
Her speech was so full of all delight that it seemed as though
an angel of Paradise had taken human flesh. And in all the
kingdom no weighty thing was done without counsel of
Ursula.

So her fame was carried through the earth, and a King of

---

* This Life of St. Ursula has been gathered from some of the stories
concerning her which were current through Italy in the time of Carpaccio. The northern form of the legend, localized at Cologne, is
neither so lovely nor so ancient.

England, a heathen of over-seas, hearing, was taken with the love of her. And he set all his heart on having her for wife to his son Æther, and for daughter in his home. So he sent a mighty and honourable embassy, of earls and marquesses, with goodly company of knights, and ladies, and philosophers; bidding them, with all courtesy and discretion, pray King Maurus to give Ursula in marriage to Æther. "But," he said, "if Maurus will not hear your gentle words, open to him all my heart, and tell him that I will ravage his land with fire, and slay his people, and make himself die a cruel death, and will, after, lead Ursula away with me. Give him but three days to answer, for I am wasted with desire to finish the matter, and hold Ursula in my ward."

But when the ambassadors came to King Maurus, he would not have his daughter wed a heathen ; so, since prayers and gifts did not move him, they spoke out all the threats. Now the land of Britain was little, and its soldiers few, while the heathen was a mighty King and a conqueror ; so Maurus, and his Queen, and his councillors, and all the people, were in sore distress.

But on the evening of the second day, Ursula went into her chamber, and shut close the doors ; and before the image of the Father, who is very pitiful, prayed all night with tears, telling how she had vowed in her heart to live a holy maiden all her days, having Christ alone for spouse. But, if His will were that she should wed the son of the heathen King, she prayed that wisdom might be given her, to turn the hearts of all that people who knew not faith or holiness ; and power to comfort her father and mother, and all the people of her fatherland.

And when the clear light of dawn was in the air, she fell asleep. And the Angel of the Lord appeared to her in a dream, saying, "Ursula, your prayer is heard. At the sunrising you shall go boldly before the ambassadors of the King of Over-sea, for the God of Heaven shall give you wisdom, and teach your tongue what it should speak." When it was day, Ursula rose to bless and glorify the name of God. She put on for covering and for beauty an enwrought mantle like the starry sky, and was crowned with a coronet of gems. Then, straightway passing to her father's chamber, she told him what grace had been done to her that night, and all that now was in her heart to answer to the ambassadors of Over-sea. So, though long he would not, she persuaded her father.

Then Maurus, and his lords and councillors, and the ambassadors of the heathen King, were gathered in the Hall of Council. And when Ursula entered the place where these lords were, one said to the other, " Who is this that comes from Paradise ? " For she moved in all noble gentleness, with eyes inclined to earth, learned, and frank, and fair, delightful above all women upon earth. Behind her came a hundred maidens, clothed in white silk, fair and lovely. They shone brightly as the stars, but Ursula shone as the moon and the evening star.

Now this was the answer Ursula made, which the King caused to be written, and sealed with the royal seal, and gave to the ambassadors of the King of Over-sea.

" I will take," she said, ." for spouse, Æther, the son of my lord the King of Over-sea. But I ask of my lord three graces, and with heart and soul * pray of him to grant them.

" The first grace I ask is this, that he, and the Queen, and their son, my spouse, be baptized in the name of the Father, and of the Son, and of the Holy Spirit.

" The second grace is that three years may be given me, before the bridal, in which to go to and fro upon the sea, that I may visit the bodies of the Saints in Rome, and the blessed places of the Holy Land.

"And for the last grace, I ask that he choose ten fair maidens of his kingdom, and with each of these a thousand more, all of gentle blood, who shall come to me here, in Britain, and go with me in gladness upon the sea, following this my holy pilgrimage."

Then spake one of the nobles of the land to Maurus, saying, " My lord the King, this your daughter is the Dove of Peace come from Paradise, the same that in the days of the Flood brought to the Ark of Noah the olive-branch of good news." And at the answer, were the ambassadors so full of joy that they wellnigh could not speak, and with praise and triumph they went their way, and told their master all the sweet answer of Ursula.

Then my lord the King said, " Praised and blessed be the name of our God Malcometto, who has given my soul for comfort that which it desired. Truly there is not a franker lady under the wheel of the sun ; and by the body of my mother I swear there is nothing she can ask that I will not freely give. First of the maidens she desires shall be my

* Molto incarnalmente.

daughter Florence." Then all his lords rose, man by man, and gladly named, each, his child.

So the will of Ursula was done ; and that King, and all his folk, were baptized into the Holy Faith. And Æther, with the English maidens, in number above ten thousand, came to the land of Britain.

Then Ursula chose her own four sisters, Habila, and Julia, and Victoria, and Aurea, and a thousand daughters of her people, with certain holy bishops, and great lords, and grave councillors, and an abbot of the order of St. Benedict, men full of all wisdom, and friends of God.

So all that company set sail in eleven ships, and passing this way and that upon the sea, rejoiced in it, and in this their maiden pilgrimage. And those who dwelt by the shores of the sea came forth in multitudes to gaze upon them as they passed, and to each man it appeared a delightful vision. For the ships sailed in fair order, side by side, with sound of sweet psalms and murmur of the waters. And the maidens were clad, some in scarlet and some in pure samite, some in rich silk of Damascus, some in cloth of gold, and some in the purple robe that is woven in Judea. Some wore crowns, others garlands of flowers. Upon the shoulder of each was the visible cross, in the hands of each a pilgrim's staff, by their sides were pilgrims' scrips, and each ship's company sailed under the gonfalon of the Holy Cross. Ursula in the midst was like a ray of sunlight, and the Angel of the Lord was ever with them for guide.

So in the holy time of Lent they came to Rome. And when my Lord the Pope came forth, under the Castle of St. Angelo, with great state, to greet them, seeing their blessed assembly, he put off the mantle of Peter, and with many bishops, priests, and brothers, and certain cardinals, set himself to go with them on their blessed pilgrimage.

At length they came to the land of Slavonia, whose ruler was friend and liegeman to the Soldan of Babylon. Then the Lord of the Saracens sent straightway to the Soldan, telling what a mighty company had come to his land, and how they were Christian folk. And the Soldan gathered all his men of war, and with great rage the host of the heathen made against the company of Ursula.

And when they were nigh, the Soldan cried and said, " What folk are ye?" And Ursula spake in answer, " We are Christian folk : our feet are turned to the blessed tomb of our Lord Jesus Christ, for the saving of our souls, and that we may win grace to pass into eternal life, in the blessed Paradise." And the Soldan answered, "Either deny your God, or I will slay you all with the sword. So shall ye die a dolorous death, and see your land no more." And Ursula answered, "Even so we desire to be sure witnesses for the name of God, declaring and preaching the glory of His name; because He has made heaven and earth and the sea by His Word; and afterward all living things; and afterward has willed, Himself, to die, for our salvation and glory. And who follows Him shall go to rejoice in *His* Fatherland and in His Kingdom."

Then she turned to her people : " My sisters and my brothers, in this place God has given us great grace. Embrace and make it sure, for our death in this place will be life perpetual, and joy, and sweetness never-ending. And there, above, we shall be with the Majesty and the angels of Paradise." Then she called her spouse to comfort and teach him. And he answered her with these words, "To me it appears three thousand years that death is a-coming, so much have I already tasted of the sweetness of Paradise."

Then the Soldan gave commandment that they should all be slain with the sword. And so was it done.

Yet when he saw Ursula standing, in the midst of all that slaughter, like the fairest stalk of corn in harvest, and how she was exceeding lovely, beyond the tongues of this earth to tell, he would have saved her alive, and taken her for wife. But when she would not, and rebuked him, he was moved with anger. Now there was a bow in his hand, and he set an arrow on the string, and drew it with all his strength, and it pierced the heart of the glorious maiden. So she went to God.

And one maiden only, whose name was Corbula, through fear hid herself in the ship. But God, who had chosen all that company, gave her heart, and with the dawn of the next day she came forth willingly, and received the martyr's crown.

Thus all were slain, and all are gone to Paradise, and sing the glad and sweet songs of Paradise.

Whosoever reads this holy history, let him not think it a great thing to say an Our Father, and a Hail Mary, for the soul of him who has written it.

Thus far the old myth. You shall hear now in what man-

ner such a myth is re-written by a great man, born in **the**
days of a nation's strength.

Carpaccio begins his story with what the myth calls **a**
dream. But he wishes to tell you that it was no dream,—
but a vision ;—that a real angel came, and was seen by
Ursula's soul, when her mortal eyes were closed.

" The Angel of the Lord," says the legend. What !—
thinks Carpaccio ;—to this little maid of fifteen, the angel
that came to Moses and Joshua ? Not so, but her own guardian angel.

Guardian, and to tell her that God will guide her heart to-
morrow, and put His own answer on her lips, concerning her
marriage. Shall not such angel be crowned with light, and
strew her chamber with lilies ?

There is no glory round his head ; there is no gold on his
robes ; they are of subdued purple and gray. His wings are
colourless—his face calm, but sorrowful,—wholly in shade.
In his right hand he bears the martyr's palm ; in his left,
the fillet borne by the Greek angels of victory, and, together
with it, gathers up, knotted in his hand, the folds of shroud*
with which the Etrurians veil the tomb.

---

* I could not see this symbol at the height at which the picture hung
from the ground, when I described it in 1872. The folds of the drapery
in the *hand* are all but invisible, even when the picture is seen close ;
and so neutral in their gray-green colour that they pass imperceptibly
into violet, as the faint green of evening sky fades into its purple. But
the folds are continued under the wrist in the alternate waves which the
reader may see on the Etruscan tomb in the first room of the British
Museum, with a sculpturesque severity which I could not then understand, and could only account for by supposing that Carpaccio had
meant the Princess to "dream out the angel's dress so particularly" !
I mistook the fillet of victory also for a scroll ; and could not make out
the flowers in the window. They are pinks, the favourite ones in
Italian windows to this day, and having a particular relation to St.
Ursula in the way they rend their calyx ; and I believe also in their
peculiar relation to the grasses (of which more in *Proserpina*). St.
Ursula is not meant, herself, to recognize the angel. He enters under
the door over which she has put her little statue of Venus ; and
through that door the room is filled with light, so that it will not seem
to her strange that his own form, as he enters, should be in shade : and

He comes to her, " in the clear light of morning ; " the Angel of Death.

You see it is written in the legend that she had shut close the doors of her chamber.

They have opened as the angel enters,—not one only, but all in the room,—all in the house. He enters by one at the foot of her bed ; but beyond it is another—open into the passage ; out of that another into some luminous hall or street. All the window-shutters are wide open ; they are made dark that you may notice them,—nay, all the press doors are open ! No treasure bars shall hold, where *this* angel enters.

Carpaccio has been intent to mark that he comes in the light of dawn. The blue-green sky glows between the dark leaves of the olive and dianthus in the open window. But its light is low compared to that which enters *behind* the angel, falling full on Ursula's face, in divine rest.

In the last picture but one, of this story, he has painted her lying in the rest which the angel came to bring ; and in the last, is her rising in the eternal Morning.

For this is the first lesson which Carpaccio wrote in his Venetian words for the creatures of this restless world,—that Death is better than *their* life ; and that not bridegroom rejoices over bride as they rejoice who marry not, nor are given in marriage, but are as the angels of God, in Heaven.

she cannot see his dark wings. On the tassel of her pillow, (Etrurian also,) is written " Infantia " ; and above her head, the carving of the bed ends in a spiral flame, typical of the finally ascending Spirit. She lies on her bier, in the last picture but one, exactly as here on her bed ; only the coverlid is there changed from scarlet to pale violet. See notes on the meaning of these colours in third *Deucalion.*

NOTES AND CORRESPONDENCE.

I. Affairs of the Company.

Venice, October 20th.—I have sent for press, to-day, the fourth number of *Deucalion*, in which will be found a statement of the system on which I begin the arrangement of the Sheffield Museum.

There are no new subscriptions to announce. Another donation, of fifty pounds, by Mrs. Talbot, makes me sadly ashamed of the apathy of all my older friends. I believe, in a little while now, it will be well for me to throw them all aside, and refuse to know any one but my own Companions, and the workmen who are willing to listen to me. I have spoken enough to the upper classes, and they mock me ;—in the seventh year of *Fors* I will speak more clearly than hitherto,—but not to *them.*

Meantime, my Sheffield friends must not think I am neglecting them, because I am at work here in Venice, instead of among them. They will know in a little while the use of my work here. The following portions of letter from the Curator of our Museum, with a piece of biography in it, which I venture to print, in haste, assuming permission, will be of good service to good workers everywhere.

"H. Swan to J. Ruskin.

"WALKLEY, SHEFFIELD, *October* 18, 1876.

"Dear Master,—The interest in the Museum seems still increasing. Yesterday (Sunday), in addition to our usual allotment of casual calls at the Museum, we had a visit from a party of working men; two or three of them from Barnsley, but the most Sheffielders, among which last were several of those who came to meet thee on the last occasion. Their object was a double one; first, to see what progress we were making with the Museum ; and, secondly, to discuss the subject of Usury, the unlawfulness of which, in its ordinary aspects, being (unlike the land question) a perfectly new notion to all except one or two. The objection generally takes this shape : 'If I have worked hard to earn twenty pounds, and it is an advantage to another to have the use of that twenty pounds, why should he get that advantage without paying me for it ?' To which my reply has been, there may, or may not, be reasons why the lender should be placed in a better position for using his powers of body or mind ; but the special question for you, with your twenty pounds, now is, not what right has he to use the money without payment—(he has every right, if you give him leave; and none, if you don't ;)—the question *you* have to propose to yourself is this. 'Why should I, as a man and a Christian, after having been paid for what I have earned, expect or desire to make an agreement by which

I may get, from the labour of others, money I have not earned?'
Suppose, too, bail for a hundred pounds to be required for a prisoner
in whose innocence you believed, would you say I will be bail for the
hundred pounds, but I shall expect five pounds from him for the advantage he will thereby get? No ; the just man would weigh well
whether it be right or no to undertake the bail ; but, having determined, he would shrink from receiving the unearned money, as I believe the first unwarped instinct of a good man does still'in the case of
a loan.

"Although, as I have said, all question as to the right of what is
called a moderate rate of interest was new to most of our visitors, yet
I found a greater degree of openness to the truth than might have been
expected. One of the most interesting parts of the discussion was the
relation by one of the party of his own experiences, in years past, as a
money-lender. 'In the place where I used to work at that time,' said
he, ' there was a very many of a good sort of fellows who were not so
careful of their money as I was, and they used often to run out of cash
before the time came for them to take more. Well, knowing I was one
that always had a bit by me, they used to come to me to borrow a bit
to carry them through to pay-day. When they paid me, some would
ask if I wanted aught for the use of it. But I only lent to pleasure
them, and I always said, No, I wanted naught. One day, however,
Jack —— came to me, and said, "Now, my lad, dost want to get
more brass for thyself, and lay by money? because I can put thee in
the way of doing it." I said that was a great object for me. "Well,"
said he, "thou must do as I tell thee. I know thou'rt often lending
thy brass to them as want a lift. Now thou must make them pay for
using thy money, and if thou works as I tell thee, it'll grow and grow.
And by-and-by they'll be paying and paying for the use of their own
money over and over again." Well, I thought it would be a good thing
for me to have the bits of cash come in and in, to help along with what
I earned myself. So I told each of the men, as they came, that I
couldn't go on lending for nothing, and they must pay me a bit more
when they got their pay. And so they did. After a time, Jack ——
came again, and said, "Well how'rt getting on?" So I told him what
I was doing, and that seemed all right. After a time, he came again, and
said, "Now thou finds what I said was right. The men can spare thee
a bit for thy money, and it makes things a deal more comfortable for
thyself. Now I can show thee how a hundred of thy money shall bring
another hundred in." "Nay," said I, "thou canst not do that. That
can't be done." "Nay, but it can," said Jack. And he told me how to
manage ; and that when I hadn't the cash, he would find it, and we'd
halve the profits. [Say a man wants to borrow twenty pounds, and is
to pay back at three shillings a week. The interest is first deducted
for the whole time, so that if he agrees to pay only five per cent. he
will receive but nineteen pounds; then the interest is more than five
per cent. on the money actually out during the very first week, while
the rate gradually rises as the weekly payments come,—slowly at first,
but at the last more and more rapidly, till, during the last month, the
money-lender is obtaining two hundred per cent. for the amount (now,
however, very small) still unpaid.]

" ' Well, it grew and grew. Hundreds and hundreds I paid and received every week, (and we found that among the poorest little shops

it worked the best for us). At last it took such hold of me that I became a regular bloodsucker—a bloodsucker of poor folk, and nothing else. I was always reckoning up, night and day, how to get more and more, till I got so thin and ill I had to go to the doctor. It was old Dr Sike, and he said, " Young man, you must give up your present way of work and life, or I can do nothing for you. You'll get worse and worse."

" 'So I thought and thought, and at last I made up my mind to give it all up, though I was then getting rich. But there was no blessing on what I'd got, and I lost it every farthing, and had to begin again as poor as I was when I first left the workhouse to learn a trade. And now, I've prospered and prospered in my little way till I've no cause to worry anyways about money, and I've a few men at work with me in my shop.

" 'Still, for all that, I don't see why I shouldn't have interest on the little capital I've saved up *honestly ;* or how am I to live in my old age ?'

" Another workman suggested, 'Wouldn't he be able to live on his capital?' 'Aye, but I want to leave that to somebody else,' was the answer. [Yes, good friend, and the same excuse might be made for any form of theft.—J. R.]

" I will merely add, that if there were enforced and public account of the amount of moneys advanced on loan, and if the true conditions and workings of those loans could be shown, there would be revealed such an amount of cruel stress upon the foolish, weak, and poor of the small tradesmen (a class far more numerous than are needed) as would render it very intelligible why so many faces are seamed with lines of suffering and anxiety. I think it possible that the fungus growth and increasing mischief of these loan establishments may reach such a pitch as to necessitate legislative interference, as has been the case with gambling. But there will never fail modes of evading the law, and the sufficient cure will be found only when men shall consider it a dishonour to have it imputed to them that *any* portion of their income is derived from usury."

THE UNION BANK OF LONDON (CHANCERY LANE BRANCH) IN ACCOUNT WITH THE ST. GEORGE'S FUND.

1876.		*Dr.*	£	s.	d.
Aug.	16.	To Balance...............................	94	3	4
Oct.	12.	" Draft at Bridgewater (per Mr. Ruskin)...	50	0	0
	24.	" (J. P. Stilwell)........................	25	0	0
			£169	3	4

		Cr.	£	s.	d.
Oct.	12.	By postage of Pass Book....................	0	0	3
	25.	Balance....................................	169	3	1
			£169	3	4

II. **Affairs of the Master.**

		£	s.	d.	£	s.	d
Sept. 15.	Balance (*a*).....................				1221	0	8
20.	Kate...........................	100	0	0			
26.	—— at Venice, Antonio (*b*)......	50	0	0			
Oct. 1.	Secretary......................	25	0	0			
3.	Downs.........................	50	0	0			
5.	Gift (*c*)........................	20	0	0			
10.	Loan...........................	200	0	0			
"	Jackson.......................	50	0	0			
					495	0	0
Oct. 15.	Balance.................................				£726	0	8

III. I print the following letter with little comment, because I have
no wish to discuss the question of the uses of Dissent with a Dissenting Minister ; nor do I choose at present to enter on the subject at all.
St. George, taking cognizance only of the postscript, thanks the Dissenting Minister for his sympathy ; but encourages his own servant to
persist in believing that the "more excellent way" (of Charity,) which
St. Paul showed, in the 13th of Corinthians, is quite as truly followed
in devoting the funds at his said servant's disposal to the relief of the
poor, as in the maintenance of Ruskinian Preachers, for the dissemina-
tion of Ruskinian opinions, in a Ruskinian Society, with the especial
object of saving Mr. Ruskin's and the Society's souls.

"September 14th, 1876.

"Dear Mr. Ruskin,—Mr. Sillar's 'valuable letter' in last month's
Fors, (*a*) would have been more valuable if he had understood what he
was writing about. Mr. Tyerman (in his 'Life and Times of Wesley,'
p. 431,) gives the trifling differences between the present Rules of the
Methodist Societies and the first edition issued in 1743. Instead of
'*interested persons* having altered old John Wesley's rules' (he was
forty years old when he drew them up) 'to suit *modern ideas*'—the
alterations, whether good or bad, were made by himself.

"The first contributions in the 'Classes' were made for the express
purpose of discharging a debt on a preaching house. Then they were
devoted '*to the relief of the poor*,' there being at the time no preachers
dependent on the Society for support. *After* 1743, when circuits had
been formed and preachers stationed in certain localities, their maintenance gradually became the principal charge upon the Society's
funds. (See Smith's 'History of Methodism, vol. i., p. 669.) In 1771
Wesley says expressly that the contributions are applied '*towards the
expenses of the Society*.' (*b*) ('Journal,' vol. iii., p. 205.) Certainly
Methodism, thus supported, has done far more to benefit the poor and

(*a*) By report from Bank ; but the 'repayments' named in it should not have been
added to the cash account, being on separate account with the Company. I will make
all clear in December.

(*b*) For Signora Caldara (Venetian botany).

(*c*) Nominally loan, to poor relation, but I do not suppose he will ever be able to pay
me. The following £200 I do not doubt receiving again.

raise them, than any amount of mere almsgiving could have done. Methodist preachers have at least one sign of being in the apostolical succession. They can say, with Paul, ' as poor, yet making many rich.' (c)

" 'Going to law ' was altered by Mr. Wesley to ' brother going to law with brother,' in order, no doubt, to bring the rule into verbal agreement with I. Cor. vi. 6. (d)

" ' Usury ' was defined by Mr. Wesley to be · unlawful interest, (e) in accordance with the ordinary notions of his day. He was greatly in advance of his age, yet he could scarcely have been expected to anticipate the definition of Usury, given as far as I know. (f) for the first time in *Fors* for August, 1876. I don't see why we Methodists should be charged with breaking the laws of Moses, David, and Christ (*Fors*, p. 253), if we consider ' old John Wesley's ' definition to be as good as the ' modern idea.'

" Of course St. George, for whom I have the greatest respect and admiration, will correct Mr. Sillar's mistake.

" I am, Sir,

" ANOTHER READER OF·FORS (which I wish you would sell a little cheaper), and

" A METHODIST PREACHER."

" P. S.—Why should you not copy old John Wesley, and establish your St. George's Company on a legal basis ? In 1784 he drew up a Deed of Declaration, which was duly enrolled in Chancery. It stated the purposes for which his Society was formed, and the mode in which it was to be governed. A Deed of Trust was afterwards drawn up for *one* of our chapels, reciting at length this Deed of Declaration, and all the purposes for which the property was to be used. All our other property is settled on the same trusts. A single line in each subsequent chapel deed—stating that all the trusts are to be the same as those of the ' Model Deed,' as we call the first one—obviates the necessity and expense of *repeating* a very long legal document.

' Success to St. George,—yet there is, I think, ' a more excellent way.' "

a. Mr. Sillar's letter did not appear in the last month's *Fors.* A small portion of it appeared, in which I regret that Mr. Sillar so far misunderstood John Wesley as to imagine him incapable of altering his own rules so as to make them useless.

b. I wish the Wesleyans were the only Society whose contributions are applied to no better purpose.

c. I envy my correspondent's complacency in his own and his Society's munificence, too sorrowfully to endeavour to dispel it.

d. The ' *verbal* ' agreement is indeed secured by the alteration. But as St. Paul, by a ' brother,' meant any Christian, I shall be glad to learn from my correspondent whether the Wesleyans understand their rule in that significance.

e. Many thanks to Mr. Wesley. Doubtless his disciples know what rate of interest is lawful, and what not ; and also by what law it was made so ; and always pause with pious accuracy at the decimal point whereat the excellence of an investment begins to make it criminal. St. George will be grateful to their representative for information on these—not unimportant—particulars.

f. How far that *is*, my correspondent's duly dissenting scorn of the wisdom of the Greeks, and legality of the Jews, has doubtless prevented his thinking it necessary to discover. I must not waste the time of other readers in assisting his elementary investigations; but have merely to point out to him that definitions either of theft, adultery, usury, or murder, have only become *necessary* in modern times : and that Methodists, and any other persons, are charged by me with breaking the law of Moses, David, and Christ, in so far only as they do accept Mr. John Wesley's, or any other person's, definition instead of *their* utterly unquestionable meaning. (Would T. S. of North Tyne, reprint his letters for me from the Sunderland paper to be sent out with December *Fors?*)

IV. I reprint the following paragraph chiefly as an example of our ineffable British absurdity. It is perfectly right to compel fathers to send their children to school ; but, once sent, it is the schoolmaster's business to keep hold of them. In St. George's schools, it would have been the little runaway gentleman who would have got sent to prison; and kept, sotto piombi, on bread and water, until he could be trusted with more liberty. The fate of the father, under the present application of British law, leaves the problem, it seems to me, still insoluble but in that manner. But I should like to know more of the previous history of parent and child.

" The story of George Widowson, aged fifty-seven, told at the inquest held on his remains at Mile End Old Town on Wednesday, is worth recording. Widowson was, as appears by the evidence of his daughter, a sober, hard-working man until he was sent to prison for three days in last December in default of paying a fine for not sending his son, a boy eleven years of age, to school. The deceased, as several witnesses deposed, constantly endeavoured to make the child go to school, and had frequently taken him there himself ; but it was all in vain. Young Widowson when taken to school invariably ran away, the result being that his father was driven to distraction. His imprisonment in December had preyed on his mind, and he took to drinking. He frequently threatened to destroy himself rather than be imprisoned again. Hearing that another summons was about to be issued against him, he broke up his home, and on the night of the 30th ultimo solved the educational problem by throwing himself into the Regent's Canal. Fear of being again sent to prison by the School Board was, his daughter believed, the cause of his committing this act. The jury returned a verdict in accordance of this opinion ; and although George Widowson was wrong to escape from the clutches of the friends of humanity by putting an end to his life, those who blame him should remember that imprisonment to a *bonâ fide* working man of irreproachable character is simply torture. He loses all that in his own eyes makes life worth preservation."—*Pall Mall Gazette, July 7th,* 1876.

V. The next extract contains some wholesome comments on our more advanced system of modern education.

" INDIAN CIVIL SERVICE.—At a meeting of the Indian section of the Society of Arts, under the presidency of Mr. Andrew Cassels, a paper on 'Competition and its Effects upon Education' was read by Dr. George Birdwood. In the course of his remarks, he commented at length upon the India Office despatch of Feb. 24, regarding 'the selection and training of candidates for the Indian Civil Service,' and feared that it would but serve to confirm and aggravate and rapidly extend the very worst evil of the old system of competition—namely, the degeneration of secondary education throughout England. . . . . The despatch tended to make over all the secondary schooling of the country to the crammers, or to reduce it to the crammers' system. They were making the entrance examinations year by year more and more difficult —as their first object must necessarily now be, not the moral and intellectual discipline of the boyhood of England, but to show an ever-growing percentage of success at the various competitive examinations always going on for public services. 'The devil take the hindermost' was fast becoming the ideal of education, even in the public schools. If they seriously took to cramming little fellows from twelve to fourteen for entrance into public schools, the rising generation would be used up before it reached manhood. A well-known physician, of great experience, told him that the competition for all sorts of scholarships and appointments was showing its evil fruits in the increase of insanity, epilepsy, and other nervous diseases amongst young people of the age from seventeen to nineteen, and especially amongst pupil-teachers ; and if admission into the public schools of England was for the future to be regulated by competition, St. Vitus's dance would soon take the place of gout, as the fashionable disease of the upper classes. This was the inevitable result of the ill-digested and ill-regulated system of competition for the public services, and especially the Indian Civil Service, which had prevailed ; and he feared that the recent despatch would only be to hasten the threatened revolution in their national secondary schools, and the last state of cramming under the despatch would be worse than the first. . . . . The best of examiners was the examiner of his own pupils ; for no man could measure real knowledge like the teacher. What should be aimed at was regular moderate study and sound and continuous discipline to start the growing man in life in the healthiest bodily and moral condition possible. He objected to children striving for prizes, whether in games or in studies. The fewer prizes won at school, the more would probably be won in life. Let their only anxiety be to educate their children well, and suffer no temptation to betray them into cramming, and the whole world was open to them."—*Daily Telegraph.*

VI. The development of 'humanity' in America is so brilliantly illustrated in the following paragraphs, that I have thought them worth preserving :—

From ' The American Socialist, devoted to the Enlargement and Perfection of Home.'

"THE FUTURE OF SOCIETY.

"An American, visiting Europe, notices how completely there the various functions of the social body are performed. He finds a servant, an officer, a skilled workman, at every place. From the position of the stone-breaker on the highway, up to that of the highest Government official, every post is filled; every personal want of the traveller or the citizen is attended to. Policemen guard him in the streets, lackeys watch for his bidding at the hotels, railroad officials with almost superfluous care forward him on his way. As compared with American 'railroad management, the great English roads probably have four *employés* to our one. This plenitude of service results from three things —viz., density of population, which gives an abundant working class ; cheapness of labour; and the aristocratic formation of society that tends to fix persons in the caste to which they were born. The effect is to produce a smoothness in the social movement—an absence of jar and friction, and a release in many cases from anxious, personal outlook, that are very agreeable. The difference between English and American life in respect to the supply of service is like that between riding on a highly-finished macadamized way, where every rut is filled and every stone is removed, and picking one's way over our common country roads.

"Another thing that the traveller observes in Europe is the abundance everywhere of works of art. One's sense of beauty is continually gratified : now with a finished landscape, now with a noble building, now with statues, monuments, and paintings. This immense accumulation of art springs in part of course from the age of the nations where it is found ; but it is also due in a very great degree to the employment given to artists by persons of wealth and leisure. Painting, sculpture, and architecture have always had constant, and sometimes munificent, patrons in the nobility and the Established Church.

"Observing these things abroad, the American asks himself whether the institutions of this country are likely to produce in time any similar result here. Shall we have the finished organization, the mutual service, and the wealth of art that characterize European society ? Before answering this, let us first ask ourselves whether it is desirable that we should have them in the same manner that they exist abroad ? Certainly not. No American would be willing to pay the price which England pays for her system of service. The most painful thing which one sees abroad is the utter absence of ambition in the class of household servants. Men who in this country would be looking to a seat in the legislature, (*a*) and who would qualify themselves for it, there dawdle away life in the livery of some noble, in smiling, aimless, donothing content, and beget children to follow in their steps. On seeing these servile figures, the American thanks heaven that the ocean rolls between his country and such a system. Rather rudeness, discomfort, self-service, and poverty, with freedom and the fire of aspiration, than luxury purchased by the enervation of man !

a May St. George be informed of how many members the American Legislature is finally to be composed ; and over whom it is to exercise the proud function of legislation, which is to be the reward of heroic and rightly-minded flunkeys ?

" Still, cannot we have the good without the bad ? Cannot we match Europe in culture and polish without sacrificing for it our manhood ? And if so, what are the influences in this country that are working in that direction ? In answering this question, we have to say frankly that we see nothing in democracy alone that promises to produce the result under consideration. In a country where every one is taught to disdain a situation of dependence, where the hostler and the chambermaid see the way open for them to stand even with the best in the land, if they will but exercise their privilege of ' getting on,' there will be no permanent or perfect service. And so long as every man's possessions are divided and scattered at his death, there will be no class having the secured leisure and the inducement to form galleries of art. Why should John Smith take pains to decorate his house with works of art, when he knows that within a year after his death it will be administered upon by the Probate Court, and sold with its furniture for the benefit of his ten children ? " (Well put,—republican sage.)

" In a word, looking at the æsthetic side of things, our American system must be confessed to be not yet quite perfect." (You don't say so !) " Invaluable as it is for schooling men to independence and aspiration, it requires, to complete its usefulness, another element. The Republic has a sequel. That completing element, that sequel, is Communism. Communism supplies exactly the conditions that are wanting in the social life of America, and which it must have if it would compete with foreign lands in the development of those things which give ease and grace to existence.

" For instance, in respect to service : Communism, by extinguishing caste and honouring labour, makes every man at once a servant and lord. It fills up, by its capacity of minute organization, all the social functions as completely as the European system does; while, unlike that, it provides for each individual sufficient leisure, and frequent and improving changes of occupation. The person who serves in the kitchen this hour may be experimenting with a microscope or giving lessons on the piano the next. Applying its combined ingenuity to social needs, Communism will find means to consign all repulsive and injurious labour to machinery. It is continually interested to promote labour-saving improvements. The service that is performed by brothers and equals from motives of love will be more perfect than that of hired lackeys, while the constantly varying round of occupation granted to all will form the most perfect school for breadth of culture and true politeness. Thus Communism achieves through friendship and freedom that which the Old World secures only through a system little better than slavery.

" In the interest of art and the cultivation of the beautiful, Communism again supplies the place of a hereditary aristocracy and a wealthy church. A Community family, unlike the ephemeral households of ordinary society, is a permanent thing. Its edifice is not liable to be sold at the end of every generation, but like a cathedral descends by unbroken inheritance. Whatever is committed to it remains, and is the care of the society from century to century. With a home thus established, all the members of a community are at once interested to gather about it objects of art. It becomes a picture-gallery and a museum, by the natural accretion of time, and by the zeal of persons who know that every embellishment added to their home will not only be a pleasure to them personally, but will remain to associate them with the pleasure of future beholders in all time to come.

"Thus in communism we have the conditions that are necessary to carry this country to the summit of artistic and social culture. By this route, we may at one bound outstrip the laboured attainments of the aristocracies of the Old World. The New York Central Park shows what can be achieved by combination on the democratic plan, for a public pleasure-ground. No other park is equal to it. Let this principle of combination be extended to the formation of homes as well as to municipal affairs, and we shall simply dot this country over with establishments (_b_) as much better than those of the nobles of England as they are better than those of a day-labourer. We say better, for they will make art and luxury minister to universal education, and they will replace menial service with downright brotherhood. Such must be the future of American society."

" _To the Editor of the ' American Socialist.'_

" In your first issue you raise the question, ' _How large ought a Home to be ?_ ' This is a question of great interest to all; and I trust the accumulated answers you will receive will aid in its solution.

" I have lived in homes varying in numbers from one (the bachelor's home) to several hundred; and my experience and observation lead me to regard one hundred and twenty-five as about the right number to form a complete home. I would not have less than seventy-five nor more than one hundred and fifty. In my opinion a Home should minister to all the needs of its members, spiritual, intellectual, social, and physical. This ordinary monogamic homes cannot do; hence resort is had to churches, colleges, club-rooms, theatres, etc.; and in sparsely settled regions of country, people are put to great inconvenience and compelled to go great distances to supply cravings as imperative as the hunger for bread. This view alone would not limit the number of persons constituting a Home; but I take the ground that in a perfect Home there will be a perfect blending of all interests and perfect vibration in unison of all hearts; and of course thorough mutual acquaintance. My experience and observation convince me that it is exceedingly difficult, if not impossible, to secure these results in a family of over one hundred and fifty members.

"In simply a monetary view it is undoubtedly best to have large Homes of a thousand or more; but money should not have great weight in comparison with a man's spiritual, intellectual and social needs.— D. E. S.

_b._ As a painter, no less than a philanthropist, I am curious to see the effect of scenery, in these ' polite' terms of description, "dotted over with establishments."

LETTER LXXII.

VENICE, *9th November*, 1876, 7 *morning.*

I HAVE set my writing-table close to the pillars of the great window of the Ca' Ferro, which I drew, in 1841, carefully, with those of the next palace, Ca' Contarini Fasan. Samuel Prout was so pleased with the sketch that he borrowed it, and made the upright drawing from it of the palace with the rich balconies, which now represents his work very widely as a chromolithotint.*

Between the shafts of the pillars, the morning sky is seen pure and pale, relieving the grey dome of the church of the Salute ; but beside that vault, and like it, vast thunderclouds heap themselves above the horizon, catching the light of dawn upon them where they rise, far westward, over the dark roof of the ruined Badia ;—but all so massive, that, half an hour ago, in the dawn, I scarcely knew the Salute dome and towers from theirs ; while the sea-gulls, rising and falling hither and thither in clusters above the green water beyond my balcony, tell me that the south wind is wild on Adria.

"Dux inquieti turbidus Adriæ."—The Sea has her Lord, and the sea-birds are prescient of the storm ; but my own England, ruler of the waves in her own proud thoughts, can she rule the tumult of her people, or, pilotless, even so much as discern the thunderclouds heaped over her Galilean lake of life ?

Here is a little grey cockle-shell, lying beside me, which I gathered, the other evening, out of the dust of the Island of St. Helena ; and a brightly-spotted snail-shell, from the thistly sands of Lido ; and I want to set myself to draw these, and describe them, in peace.

* My original sketch is now in the Schools of Oxford.

'Yes,' all my friends say, 'that is my business ; why can't I mind it, and be happy ?'

Well, good friends, I would fain please you, and myself with you ; and live here in my Venetian palace, luxurious ; scrutinant of dome, cloud, and cockle-shell. I could even sell my books for not inconsiderable sums of money if I chose to bribe the reviewers, pay half of all I got to the booksellers, stick bills on the lampposts, and say nothing but what would please the Bishop of Peterborough.

I could say a great deal that would please him, and yet be very good and useful ; I should like much again to be on terms with my old publisher, and hear him telling me nice stories over our walnuts, this Christmas, after dividing his year's spoil with me in Christmas charity. And little enough mind have I for any work, in this seventy-seventh year that's coming of our glorious century, wider than I could find in the compass of my cockle-shell.

But alas ! my prudent friends, little enough of all that I have a mind to may be permitted me. For this green tide that eddies by my threshold is full of floating corpses, and I must leave my dinner to bury them, since I cannot save ; and put my cockle-shell in cap, and take my staff in hand, to seek an unimcumbered shore. This green sea-tide !—yes, and if you knew it, your black aud sulphurous tides also— Yarrow, and Teviot, and Clyde, and the stream, for ever now drumly and dark as it rolls on its way, at the ford of Melrose.

Yes, and the fair lakes and running waters in your English park pleasure-grounds,—nay, also the great and wide sea, that gnaws your cliffs,—yes, and Death, and Hell also, more cruel than cliff or sea ; and a more neutral episcopal person than even my Lord of Peterborough * stands, level-barred balance in hand,—waiting (how long ?) till the Sea shall give up the dead which are in it, and Death, and Hell, give up the dead which are in them.

Have you ever thought of, or desired to know, the real meaning of that sign, seen with the human eyes of his soul by the disciple whom the Lord loved ? Yes, of course you

* See terminal Article of Correspondence.

have ! and what a grand and noble verse you always thought
it. "And the Sea—— " Softly, good friend,—I know you
can say it off glibly and pompously enough, as you have
heard it read a thousand times ; but is it, then, merely a piece
of pomp ? mere drumming and trumpeting, to tell you—what
might have been said in three words—that all the dead rose
again, whether they had been bedridden, or drowned, or slain ?
If it means no more than that, is it not, to speak frankly,
bombast, and even bad and half unintelligible bombast ?—
for what does ' Death ' mean, as distinguished from the Sea,
the American lakes ? or Hell as distinguished from Death,—
a family vault instead of a grave ?

But suppose it is not bombast, and does mean something
that it would be well you should think of,—have you yet
understood it,—much less, thought of it ? Read the whole
passage from the beginning : 'I saw the Dead, small and
great, stand before God. And the Books were opened ; "—
and so to the end.

' *Stand* ' in renewed perfectness of body and soul—each
redeemed from its own manner of Death.

For have not they each their own manner ? As the seed
by the drought, or the thorn,—so the soul by the soul's hunger, and the soul's pang ;—athirst in the springless sand ;
choked in the return-wave of Edom ; grasped by the chasm
of the earth : some, yet "calling out of the depths ; " but
some—" Thou didst blow with Thy wind, and the sea covered
them ; they sank as lead in the mighty waters." But *now*
the natural grave, in which the gentle saints resigned their
perfect body to the dust, and perfect spirit to Him who gave
it ;—and now the wide sea of the world, that drifted with its
weeds so many breasts that heaved but with the heaving
deep ;—and now the Death that overtook the lingering step,
and closed the lustful eyes ;—and now the Hell, that hid with
its shade and scourged with its agony ; the fierce and foul
spirits that had forced its gates in flesh ;*—all these the
Loved Apostle saw compelled to restore their ruin ; and all
these, their prey, stand once again, renewed, as their Maker

* *Conf. Inferno,* xxiii. 123.

made them, before their Maker. " And the Sea gave up the Dead which were in it, and Death, and Hell, the Dead which were in them."

Not bombast, good reader, in any wise ; nor a merely soothing melody of charming English, to be mouthed for a ' second lesson.'

But is it worse than bombast, then ? Is it, perchance, pure Lie ?

Carpaccio, at all events, thought not ; and this, as I have told you, is the first practical opinion of his I want you to be well informed of.

Since that last *Fors* was written, one of my friends found for me the most beautiful of all the symbols in the picture of the Dream ; one of those which leap to the eyes when they are understood, yet which, in the sweet enigma, I had deliberately twice painted, without understanding.

At the head of the princess's bed is embroidered her shield ; (of which elsewhere)—but on a dark blue-green space in the cornice above it is another very little and bright shield, it seemed,—but with no bearing. I painted it, thinking it was meant merely for a minute repetition of the escutcheon below, and that the painter had not taken the trouble to blazon the bearings again. (I might have known Carpaccio never would even *omit* without meaning.) And I never noticed that it was not in a line above the escutcheon, but exactly above the princess's head. It gleams with bright silver edges out of the dark-blue ground—the point of the mortal Arrow !

At the time it was painted the sign would necessarily have been recognised in a moment ; and it completes the meaning of the vision without any chance of mistake.

And it seems to me, guided by such arrow-point, the purpose of *Fors* that I should make clear the meaning of what I have myself said on this matter, throughout the six years in which I have been permitted to carry on the writing of these letters, and to preface their series for the seventh year, with the interpretation of this Myth of Venice.

I have told you that all Carpaccio's sayings are of knowledge, not of opinion. And I mean by knowledge, *com-*

municable knowledge. Not merely personal, however certain —like Job's 'I know that my Redeemer liveth,' but discovered truth, which can be shown to all men who are willing to receive it. No great truth is allowed by nature to be demonstrable to any person who, foreseeing its consequences, desires to refuse it. He has put himself into the power of the Great Deceiver ; and will in every effort be only further deceived, and place more fastened faith in his error.

This, then, is the truth which Carpaccio knows, and would teach :—

That the world is divided into two groups of men ; the first, those whose God is their God, and whose glory is their glory, who mind heavenly things ; and the second, men whose God is their belly, and whose glory is in their shame,* who mind earthly things. That is just as demonstrable a scientific fact as the separation of land from water. There may be any quantity of intermediate mind, in various conditions of bog ;—some, wholesome Scotch peat,—some, Pontine marsh,—some, sulphurous slime, like what people call water in English manufacturing towns ; but the elements of Croyance and Mescroyance are always chemically separable out of the putrescent mess : by the faith that is in it, what life or good it can still keep, or do, is possible ; by the miscreance in it, what mischief it can do, or annihilation it can suffer, is appointed for its work and fate. All strong character curdles itself out of the scum into its own place and power, or impotence : and they that sow to the Flesh do of the Flesh reap corruption ; and they that sow to the Spirit, do of the Spirit reap Life.

I pause, without writing 'everlasting,' as perhaps you expected. Neither Carpaccio nor I know anything about Duration of life, or what the word translated 'everlasting' means. Nay, the first sign of noble trust in God and man, is to be able to act without any such hope. All the heroic deeds, all the purely unselfish passions of our existence,

* Mr. Darwin's last discoveries of the gestures of honour and courtesy among baboons are a singular completion of the types of this truth in the natural world.

depend on our being able to live, if need be, through the shadow of death : and the daily heroism of simply brave men consists in fronting and accepting Death as such, trusting that what their Maker decrees for them shall be well.

But what Carpaccio knows, and what I know also, are precisely the things which your wiseacre apothecaries, and their apprentices, and too often your wiseacre rectors and vicars, and *their* apprentices, tell you that you can't know, because " eye hath not seen nor ear heard them," the things which God hath prepared for them that love Him. But God has revealed them to *us*,—to Carpaccio, and Angelico, and Dante, and Giotto, and Filippo Lippi, and Sandro Botticelli, and me, and to every child that has been taught to know its Father in Heaven,—by the Spirit : because we have minded, or do mind, the things of the Spirit in some measure, and in such measure have entered into our rest.

" The things which God *hath prepared* for them that love Him." Hereafter, and up there, above the clouds, you have been taught to think ;—until you were informed by your land-surveyors that there was neither up nor down ; but only an axis of x and an axis of y ; and by aspiring aeronauts that there was nothing in the blue but damp and azote. And now you don't believe these things are prepared *any*where ? They are prepared just as much as ever, when and where they used to be : just now, and here, close at your hand. All things are prepared,—come ye to the marriage. Up and down on the old highways which your fathers trod, and under the hedges of virgin's bower and wild rose which your fathers planted, there are the messengers crying to you to come. Nay, at your very doors, though one is just like the other in your model lodging houses,—there is One knocking, if you would open, with something better than tracts in His basket ;—supper, and very material supper, if you will only condescend to eat of angel's food first. There are meats for the belly, and the belly for meats ; doth not your Father know that ye have need of these things ? But if you make your belly your only love, and your meats your only masters, God shall destroy both it and them.

Truly it is hard for you to hear the low knocking in the hubbub of your Vanity Fair. You are living in the midst of the most perfectly miscreant crowd that ever blasphemed creation. Not with the old snap-finger blasphemy of the wantonly profane, but the deliberate blasphemy of Adam Smith : ' Thou shalt hate the Lord thy God, damn His laws, and covet thy neighbour's goods.' Here's one of my own boys getting up that lesson beside me for his next Oxford examination. For Adam Smith is accepted as the outcome of Practical Philosophy, at our universities ; and their youth urged to come out high in competitive blasphemy. Not the old snap-finger sort,* I repeat, but that momentary sentiment, deliberately adopted for a national law.' I must turn aside for a minute or two to explain this to you.

The eighth circle of Dante's Hell (compare vol. i., p. 331), is the circle of Fraud, divided into ten gulphs ; in the seventh of these gulphs are the Thieves, by Fraud,—brilliantly now represented by the men who covet their neighbours' goods and take them in any way they think safe, by high finance, sham companies, cheap goods, or any other of our popular modern ways.

Now there is not in all the *Inferno* quite so studied a piece of descriptive work as Dante's relation of the infection of one cursed soul of this crew by another. They change alternately into the forms of men and serpents, each biting the other into this change—

> " Ivy ne'er clasped
> A doddered oak, as round the other's limbs
> The hideous monster intertwined his own ;
> Then, as they both had been of burning wax,
> Each melted into other."

Read the story of the three transformations for yourself (Cantos xxiv., xxv.), and then note the main point of all, that

* In old English illuminated Psalters, of which I hope soon to send a perfect example to Sheffield to companion our Bible, the vignette of the Fool saying in his heart, ' There is no God,' nearly always represents him in this action. Vanni Fucci makes the Italian sign of the Fig,— 'A fig for you ! '

the spirit of such theft is especially indicated by its intense
and direct manner of blasphemy :—

> " I did not mark,
> Through all the gloomy circle of the abyss,
> Spirit that swelled so proudly 'gainst its God,
> Not him who headlong fell from Thebes."

The soul is Vanni Fucci's, who rifled the sacristy of St.
James of Pistoja, and charged Vanni della Nona with the
sacrilege, whereupon the latter suffered death.   For in those
days, death was still the reward of sacrilege by the Law of
State ; whereas, while I write this *Fors*, I receive notice of
the conjunction of the sacred and profane civic powers of
London to de-consecrate, and restore to the definitely pronounced ' unholy' spaces of this world, the church of All-
Hallows, wherein Milton was christened.

A Bishop was there to read, as it were, the Lord's Prayer
backwards, or at least address it to the Devil instead of to
God, to pray that over this portion of British Metropolitan
territory *His* Kingdom might again come.

A notable sign of the times,—completed, in the mythical
detail of it, by the defiance of the sacred name of the Church,
and the desecration of good men's graves,* lest, perchance, the St. Ursulas of other lands should ever come on
pilgrimage, rejoicing, over the sea, hopeful to see such holy
graves among the sights of London.

Infinitely ridiculous, such travelling as St. Ursula's, you
think,—to see dead bodies, forsooth, and ask, with every
poor, bewildered, Campagna peasant, " Dov' è San Paolo ? "
Not at all such the object of modern English and American
tourists !—nay, sagacious Mr. Spurgeon came home from his
foreign tour, and who more proud than he to have scorned,
in a rational manner, all relics and old bones ?   I have some
notes by me, ready for February, concerning the unrejoicing

---

* My friend Mr. W. C. Sillar rose in the church, and protested, in the
name of God, against the proceedings. He was taken into custody as disorderly.—the press charitably suggested, only drunk ;—and was I believe discharged without fine or inprisonment, for we live in liberal
days.

manner of travel adopted by the sagacious modern tourist, and his objects of contemplation, for due comparison with St. Ursula's ; but must to-day bring her lesson close home to your own thoughts.

Look back to the 103d and 124th pages of vol. i. The first tells you, what this last sign of Church desecration now confirms, that you are in the midst of men who, *if* there be truth in Christianity at all, must be punished for their open defiance of Heaven by the withdrawal of the Holy Spirit, and the triumph of the Evil One. And you are told in the last page that by the service of God only you can recover the presence of the Holy Ghost of Life and Health—the Comforter.

This—vaguely and imperfectly, during the last six years, proclaimed to you, as it was granted me—in this coming seventh year I trust to make more simply manifest ; and to show you how every earthly good and possession will be given you, if you seek first the Kingdom of God and His Justice. If, in the assurance of Faith, you can ask and strive that such kingdom may be with you, though it is not meat and drink, but Justice, Peace, and Joy in the Holy Ghost,—if, in the first terms I put to you for oath,* you will do good work, whether you live or die, and so lie down at night, whether hungry or weary, at least in peace of heart and surety of honour ;—then, you shall rejoice, in your native land, and on your nursing sea, in all fulness of temporary possessions ; —then, for you the earth shall bring forth her increase, and for you the floods clap their hands ;—throughout your sacred pilgrimage, strangers here and sojourners with God, yet His word shall be with you,—"the land shall not be sold for ever, for the land is Mine," and after your numbered days of happy loyalty, you shall go to rejoice in His Fatherland, and with His people.

* Compare vol. ii., p. 277, observing especially the sentence out of 2nd Esdras, "before *they* were sealed, that have gathered Faith for a Treasure."

NOTES AND CORRESPONDENCE.

I. Affairs of the Company.

There is no occasion to put our small account again in print till the end of the year: we are not more than ten pounds ahead, since last month. I certainly would not have believed, six years ago, that I had so few friends who had any trust in me; or that the British public would have entirely declined to promote such an object as the purchase of land for national freehold.

Next year I shall urge the operatives whom any words of mine may reach, to begin some organization with a view to this object among themselves. They have already combined to build co-operative mills; they would find common land a more secure investment.

I am very anxious to support, with a view to the determination of a standard of material in dress, the wool manufacture among the old-fashioned cottagers of the Isle of Man; and I shall be especially grateful to any readers of *Fors* who will communicate with Mr. Egbert Rydings (Laxey, Isle of Man,) on this subject. In the island itself, Mr. Rydings tells me, the stuffs are now little worn by the better classes, because they 'wear too long,'—a fault which I hope there may be yet found English housewives who will forgive. At all events, I mean the square yard of Laxey homespun of a given weight, to be one of the standards of value in St. George's currency.

The cheque of £25, sent to Mr. Rydings for the encouragement of some of the older and feebler workers, is the only expenditure, beyond those for fittings slowly proceeded with in our museum at Sheffield, to which I shall have to call attention at the year's end.

II. Affairs of the Master.

Though my readers, by this time, will scarcely be disposed to believe it, I really *can* keep accounts, if I set myself to do so: and even greatly enjoy keeping them, when I do them the first thing after my Exodus or Plato every morning; and keep them to the uttermost farthing. I *have* examples of such in past diaries; one in particular, great in its exhibition of the prices of jargonel and Queen Louise pears at Abbeville. And my days always go best when they are thus begun, as far as pleasant feeling and general prosperity of work are concerned. But there is a great deal of work, and especially such as I am now set on, which does not admit of accounts in the morning; but imperatively requires the fastening down forthwith of what first comes into one's mind after waking. Then the accounts get put off; tangle their thread—(so the Fates always instantly then ordain)—in some eightpenny matter, and without Œdipus to help on the right hand and Ariadne on the left, **there's** no bringing them right again. With due invocation to both, I

think I have got my own accounts, for the past year, stated clearly
below.

	RECEIPTS.			EXPENDITURE.			BALANCE.		
	£	s.	d.	£	s.	d.	£	s.	d.
February	1344	17	9	817	0	0	527	17	9
March	67	10	0	370	2	3	225	5	6
April	1522	12	4	276	10	0	1471	7	10
May	484	18	3	444	16	3	1511	9	10
June	179	0	0	464	11	0	1225	18	10
July..............	0	0	0	460	0	0	765	18	10
August	180	11	8	328	19	6	617	11	0
September	0	0	0	427	5	0	190	6	0
October............	1279	8	0	655	0	0	814	14	0
November..........	0	0	0	495	0	0	784	8	0
December	592	15	4	242	0	0	1135	3	4

In the first column are the receipts for each month; in the second, the
expenditure; in the third, the balance, which is to be tested by adding
the previous balance to the receipts in the first column, and deducting
the expenditure from the sum.

The months named are those in which the number of *Fors* was published in which the reader will find the detailed statements : a grotesque
double mistake, in March, first in the addition and then in the subtraction, concludes in a total error of threepence; the real balance being
£225 5s. 6d. instead of £225 5s. 9d. I find no error in the following accounts beyond the inheritance of this excessive threepence : (in October,
the entry under September 1, is misprinted 10 for 15; but the sum
is right), until the confusion caused by my having given the banker's
balance in September, which includes several receipts and disbursements
not in my own accounts, but to be printed in the final yearly estimate in
Fors of next February. My own estimate, happily less than theirs,
brings my balance for last month to £784 8s.; taking up which result,
the present month's accounts are as follows :—

	RECEIPTS.	£	s.	d.		£	s.	d.
Oct. 15.	Balance	784	8	0				
	Dividend on £6,500 Stock .	292	10	0				
	Rents, Marylebone . .	90	15	4				
	Rents, Herne Hill . .	30	0	0				
	Oxford, Half-year's Salary .	179	10	0	—	1377	3	4

	EXPENDITURE.							
Oct. 15 to *Nov.* 15.	Self at Venice .	150	0	0				
Oct. 24.	Burgess	42	0	0				
Nov. 1.	Raffaelle	15	0	0				
" 7.	Downs . . .	25	0	0				
" 11.	Crawley	10	0	0	—	242	0	0

Balance, Nov. 15 . . .	£1135	3	4

III. I have lost the reference to a number of the *Monetary Gazette* of three or four weeks back, containing an excellent article on the Bishop of Peterborough's declaration, referred to in the text, that the disputes between masters and men respecting wages were a question of Political Economy, in which the clergy must remain 'strictly neutral.' Of the Bishop's Christian spirit, in the adoption of his Master's "Who made me a divider?" rather than of the earthly wisdom of John the Baptist, "Exact no more than that which is appointed you," the exacting public will not doubt. I must find out, however, accurately what the Bishop *did* say; and then we will ask Little Bear's opinion on the matter. For indeed, in the years to come, I think it will be well that nothing should be done without counsel of Ursula.

IV. The following is, I hope, the true translation of Job xxii. 24, 25. I greatly thank my correspondent for it.

" Cast the brass to the dust, and the gold of Ophir to the rocks of the brooks.

" So, will the Almighty be thy gold and thy shining silver.*

"Yes, then wilt thou rejoice in the Almighty and raise thy countenance to God."

V. The following letter from a Companion may fitly close the correspondence for this year. I print it without suppression of any part, believing it may encourage many of my helpers, as it does myself : —

" My dear Master,—I have learnt a few facts about Humber keels. You know you were interested in my little keel scholars, because their vessels were so fine, and because they themselves were once simple bodies, almost guiltless of reading and writing. And it seems as if even the mud gives testimony to your words. So if you don't mind the bother of one of my tiresome letters, I'll tell you all I know about them.

" The Humber keels are, in nearly all cases, the property of the men who go in them. They are house and home to the keel family, who never live on shore like other sailors. It is very easy work navigating the rivers. There's only the worry of loading and unloading,—and then their voyages are full of leisure.

" Keelmen are rural sailors, passing for days and days between cornfields and poppy banks, meadows and orchards, through low moist lands, where skies are grand at sunrise and sunset.

" Now all this evidently makes a happy joyous life, and the smart colours and decoration of the boats are signs of it. Shouldn't you say so ? Well, then, independence, home, leisure and nature are right conditions of life—and that's a bit of St. George's doctrine I've verified nearly all by myself ; and there are things I know about keel folks besides, which quite warrant my conclusions. But to see these very lowly craft stranded low on the mud at low tide, or squeezed in among other ships—big and grimy things—in the docks, you would think they were too low in the scale of shipping to have any pride or pleasure in life ; yet I really think they are little arks, dressed in rainbows. Remember

* Silver of strength.

please, Humber keels are quite different things to barges of any kind. And now keels are off my mind—except that if I can ever get anybody to paint me a gorgeous one, I shall send it to you.

" My dear Master, I have thought so often of the things you said about yourself, in relation to St. George's work ; and I feel sure that you are disheartened, and too anxious about it—that you have some sort of feeling about not being sufficient for all of it. Forgive me, but it is so painful to think that the Master is anxious about things which do not need consideration. You said, I think, the good of you was, that you collected teaching and laws for us. But is that just right ? Think of your first impulse and purpose. Was not that your commission ? Be true to it. To me it seems that the good of you (as you say it) is that you have a heart to feel the sorrows of the world—that you have courage and power to speak against injustice and falsehood, and more than all, that you act out what you say. Everybody else seems asleep or dead— wrapped up in their own comfort or satisfaction,—and utterly deaf to any appeal. Do not think your work is less than it is, and let all un-worthy anxieties go. The work is God's, if ever any work was, and He will look after its success. Fitness or unfitness is no question, for you are chosen. Mistakes do not matter. Much work does not matter. It only really matters that the Master stays with us, true to first appoint-ment ; that his hand guides all first beginnings of things, sets the pat-terns for us,—and that we are loyal.

" Your affectionate servant."

LETTER LXXIII.

VENICE, *20th November*, 1876.

THE day on which this letter will be published will, I trust, be the first of the seventh year of the time during which I have been permitted, month by month, to continue the series of *Fors Clavigera.* In which seventh year I hope to gather into quite clear form the contents of all the former work ; closing the seventh volume with accurate index of the whole. These seven volumes, if I thus complete them, will then be incorporated as a single work in the consecutive series of my books.

If I am spared to continue the letters beyond the seventh year, their second series will take a directly practical character, giving account of, and directing, the actual operations of St. George's Company ; and containing elements of instruction for its schools, the scheme of which shall be, I will answer for it, plainly enough, by the end of this year, understood. For, in the present volume, I intend speaking directly, in every letter, to the Yorkshire operatives, and answering every question they choose to put to me,—being very sure that they will omit few relevant ones.

And first they must understand one more meaning I have in the title of the book. By calling it the ' Nail bearer,' I mean not only that it fastens in sure place the truths it has to teach, (see vol. i., p. 175,) but also, that it nails down, as on the barn-door of our future homestead, for permanent and picturesque exposition, the extreme follies of which it has to give warning : so that in expanded heraldry of beak and claw, the spread, or split, harpies and owls of modern philosophy may be for evermore studied, by the curious, in the parched skins of them.

For instance, at once, and also for beginning of some

such at present needful study, look back to vol. ii., p. 236, wherein you will find a paragraph thus nailed fast out of the *Pall Mall Gazette*—a paragraph which I must now spend a little more space of barn-door in delicately expanding. It is to the following effect, (I repeat, for the sake of readers who cannot refer to the earlier volumes): "The wealth of this world may be 'practically' regarded as infinitely great. It is not true that what one man appropriates becomes thereby useless to others ; and it is also untrue that force or fraud, direct or indirect, are the principal, or indeed that they are at all common or important, modes of acquiring wealth."

You will find this paragraph partly answered, though but with a sneer, in the following page, vol. ii., p. 237 ; but I now take it up more seriously, for it is needful you should see the full depth of its lying.

The 'wealth of this world' consists broadly in its healthy food-giving land, its convenient building land, its useful animals, its useful minerals, its books, and works of art.

The healthy food-giving land, so far from being infinite, is, in fine quality, limited to narrow belts of the globe. What properly belongs to you as Yorkshiremen is only Yorkshire. You by appropriating Yorkshire keep other people from living in Yorkshire. The Yorkshire squires say the whole of Yorkshire belongs to them, and will not let any part of Yorkshire become useful to anybody else, but by enforcing payment of rent for the use of it ; nor will the farmers who rent it allow its produce to become useful to anybody else but by demanding the highest price they can get for the same.

The convenient building land of the world is so far from being infinite, that, in London, you find a woman of eight-and-twenty paying one-and-ninepence a week for a room in which she dies of suffocation with her child in her arms ; see vol. i., p. 333 ; and, in Edinburgh, you find people paying two pounds twelve shillings a year for a space nine feet long, five broad, and six high, ventilated only by the chimney ; see vol. ii., p. 187 ; and compare vol. i., p. 399.

The useful animals of the world are not infinite : the finest horses are very rare ; and the squires who ride them, by appropriating them, prevent you and me from riding them. If you and I and the rest of the mob took them from the squires, we could not at present probably ride them ; and unless we cut them up and ate them, we could not divide them among us, because they are not infinite.

The useful minerals of Yorkshire are iron, coal, and marble,—in large quantities, but not infinite quantities by any means; and the masters and managers of the coal mines, spending their coal on making useless things out of the iron, prevent the poor all over England from having fires, so that they can now only afford close stoves, (if those !) *Fors,* vol. i., p. 403.

The books and works of art in Yorkshire are not infinite, nor even in England. Mr. Fawkes' Turners are many, but not infinite at all, and as long as they are at Farnley they can't be at Sheffield. My own thirty Turners are not infinite, and as long as they are at Oxford, can't be at Sheffield. You won't find, I believe, another such thirteenth-century Bible as I have given you, in all Yorkshire ; and so far from other books being infinite, there's hardly a woman in England, now, who reads a clean one, because she can't afford to have one but by borrowing.

So much for the infinitude of wealth. For the mode of obtaining it, all the land in England was first taken by force, and is now kept by force. Some day, I do not doubt, you will yourselves seize it by force. Land never has been, nor can be, got, nor kept, otherwise, when the population on it was as large as it could maintain. The establishment of laws respecting its possession merely define and direct the force by which it is held : and fraud, so far from being an unimportant mode of acquiring wealth, is now the only possible one ; our merchants say openly that no man *can* become rich by honest dealing. And it is precisely because fraud and force *are* the chief means of becoming rich, that a writer for the *Pall Mall Gazette* was found capable of writing this passage. No man could by mere overflow of his natural folly have written it. Only in the settled purpose of maintaining the interests of Fraud and Force ; only in fraudfully writing for the concealment of Fraud, and frantically writing for the help of unjust Force, do literary men become so senseless.

The wealth of the world is not infinite, then, my Sheffield friends ; and moreover, it is most of it unjustly divided, because it has been gathered by fraud, or by dishonest force, and distributed at the will, or lavished by the neglect, of such iniquitous gatherers. And you have to ascertain definitely, if you will be wise Yorkshiremen, how much of it is actually within your reach in Yorkshire, and may be got without fraud, by *honest* force. Compare propositions 5 and 6, pages 294 and 295, vol. i.

It ought to be a very pleasant task to you, this ascertaining how much wealth is within your reach in Yorkshire, if, as I see it stated in the article of the *Times* on Lord Beaconsfield's speech at the Lord Mayor's dinner, quoted in *Galignani* of the 10th of November, 1876 : "The immense accession of wealth which this country has received through the development of the railway system and the establishment of free trade, makes the present war expenditure," etc., etc., etc. What it does in the way of begetting and feeding Woolwich Infants is not at present your affair ; your business is to find out what it does, and what you can help it to do, in making it prudent for you to beget, and easy for you to feed, Yorkshire infants.

But are you quite sure the *Times* is right ? Are we indeed, to begin with, richer than we were ? How is anybody to know ? Is there a man in Sheffield who can,—I do not say, tell you what the country is worth,—but even show you how to set about ascertaining what it is worth ?

The *Times* way, *Morning Post* way, and *Daily News* way, of finding out, is an easy one enough, if only it be exact.

Look back to *Fors* of December, 1871, and you will find the *Times* telling you that "by every kind of measure, and on every principle of calculation, the growth of our prosperity is established," because we drink twice as much beer, and smoke three times as many pipes, as we used to. But it is quite conceivable to *me* that a man may drink twice as much beer, and smoke three times as many pipes, as he used to do, yet not be the richer man for it, nor his wife or children materially better off for it.

Again, the *Morning Post* tells you (*Fors*, October, 1872,) that because the country is at present in a state of unexampled prosperity, coals and meat are at famine prices ; and the *Daily News* tells you (*Fors*, vol. i., p. 411) that because coals are at famine prices, the capital of the country is increased. By the same rule, when everything else is at famine prices, the capital of the country will be at its maximum, and you will all starve in the proud moral consciousness of an affluence unprecedented in the history of the universe. In the meantime your wealth and prosperity have only advanced you to the moderately enviable point of not being able to indulge in what the *Cornhill Magazine* (*Fors*, vol. i., p. 404) calls the " luxury of a wife," till you are forty-five—unless you choose to sacrifice all your prospects in life for that unjustifiable piece of extravagance ;—and your young women (*Fors*, vol. i., p. 419) are applying, two thousand at a time, for places in the Post Office !

All this is doubtless very practical, and businesslike, and comfortable, and truly English. But suppose you set your wits to work for once in a Florentine or Venetian manner, and ask, as a merchant of Venice would have asked, or a ' good man ' of the trades of Florence, *how much money there is in the town,*—who has got it, and what is becoming of it ? These, my Sheffield friends, are the first of economical problems for *you*, depend upon it ; perfectly soluble when you set straightforwardly about them ; or, so far as insoluble, instantly indicating the places where the roguery is. Of money honestly got, and honourably in use, you can get account : of money ill got, and used to swindle with, you will get none.

But take account at least of what is countable. Your initial proceeding must be to map out a Sheffield district clearly. Within the border of that, you will hold yourselves Sheffielders ;—outside of it, let the Wakefield and Bradford people look after themselves ; but determine your own limits, and see that things are managed well within them. Your next work is to count heads. You must register every man, woman, and child, in your Sheffield district ; (compare and read carefully the opening of the *Fors* of February last year ;) then register their incomes and expenditure ; it will be a troublesome business, but when you have done it, you will know what you are about, and how much the town is really worth. Then the next business is to establish a commissariat. Knowing how many mouths you have to feed, you know how much food is wanted daily. To get that quantity good ; and to distribute it without letting middlemen steal the half of it, is the first great duty of civic authority in villages, of ducal authority in cities and provinces, and of kingly authority in kingdoms.

Now, for the organization of your commissariat, there are two laws to be carried into effect, as you gain intelligence and unity, very different from anything yet conceived · for your co-operative stores—(which are a good and wise beginning, no less). Of which laws the first is that, till all the mouths in the Sheffield district are fed, no food must be sold to strangers. Make all the ground in your district as productive as possible, both in cattle and vegetables ; and see that such meat and vegetables be distributed swiftly to those who most need them, and eaten fresh. Not a mouthful of anything is to be sold across the border, while any one is hungry within it.

Then the second law is, that as long as any one remains unfed, or barebacked, the wages fund must be in common.* When every man, woman, and child is fed and clothed, the

---

* Don't shriek out at this, for an impossible fancy of St. George's. St. George only cares about, and tells you, the constantly necessary laws in a well-organized state. *This* is a temporarily expedient law in a distressed one. No man of a boat's crew on short allowance in the Atlantic, is allowed to keep provisions in a private locker;—still less must any man of the crew of a *city* on short allowance.

saving men may begin to lay by money, if they like ; but while there is hunger and cold among you, there must be absolutely no purse-feeding, nor coin-wrapping. You have so many bellies to fill ;—so much wages fund (besides the eatable produce of the district) to do it with.* Every man must bring all he earns to the common stock.

"What ! and the industrious feed the idle ? "

Assuredly, my friends ; and the more assuredly, because under that condition you will presently come to regard their idleness as a social offence, and deal with it as such : which is precisely the view God means you to take of it, and the dealing He intends you to measure to it. But if you think yourselves exempted from feeding the idle, you will presently believe yourselves privileged to take advantage of their idleness by lending money to them at usury, raising duties on their dissipation, and buying their stock and furniture cheap when they fail in business. Whereupon you will soon be thankful that your neighbour's shutters are still up, when yours are down ; and gladly promote his vice for your advantage. With no ultimate good to yourself, even at the devil's price, believe me.

Now, therefore, for actual beginning of organization of this Sheffield commissariat, since probably, at present, you won't be able to prevail on the Duke of York to undertake the duty, you must elect a duke of Sheffield for yourselves. Elect a doge, if, for the present, to act only as purveyor-general :—honest doge he must be, with an active and kind duchess. If you can't find a couple of honest and well-meaning married souls in all Sheffield to trust the matter to, I have nothing more to say : for by such persons, and by such virtue in them only, is the thing to be done.

* "But how if other districts refused to sell *us* food, as you say we should refuse to sell food to *them ?* "

You *Sheffielders* are to refuse to sell food only because food is scarce with you, and cutlery plenty. And as you had once a reputation for cutlery, and have yet skill enough left to recover it if you will, the other districts of England (and some abroad) will be glad still to give you some of their dinner in exchange for knives and forks,—which is a perfectly sagacious and expedient arrangement for all concerned.

Once found, you are to give them fixed salary * and fixed authority ; no prince has ever better earned his income, no consul ever needed stronger lictors, than these will, in true doing of their work. Then, by these, the accurately esti-mated demand, and the accurately measured supply, are to be coupled, with the least possible slack of chain ; and the quality of food, and price, absolutely tested and limited.

But what's to become of the middleman ?

If you really saw the middleman at his work, you would not ask that twice. Here's my publisher, Mr. Allen, gets tenpence a dozen for his cabbages ; the consumer pays threepence each. That is to say, you pay for three cabbages and a half, and the middleman keeps two and a half for him-self, and gives you one.

Suppose you saw this financial gentleman, in bodily pres-ence, toll-taking at your door,—that you bought three loaves, and saw him pocket two, and pick the best crust off the third as he handed it in ;—that you paid for a pot of beer, and saw him drink two-thirds of it and hand you over the pot and sops,—would you long ask, then, what was to become of him ?

To my extreme surprise, I find, on looking over my two long-delayed indexes, that there occurs not in either of them the all-important monosyllable ' Beer.' But if you will look out the passages referred to in the index for 1874, under the articles ' Food ' and ' Fish,' and now study them at more leisure, and consecutively, they will give you some clear notion of what the benefit of middlemen is to you ; then, finally, take the *Fors* of March, 1873, and read the 383d and 384th pages carefully,—and you will there see that it has been shown by Professor Kirk, that out of the hundred and fifty-six millions of pounds which you prove your

---

* The idea of fixed salary, I thankfully perceive, is beginning to be taken up by philanthropic persons, (see notice of the traffic in intoxi-cating liquors in *Pall Mall Budget* for December 1, 1876,) but still con-nected with the entirely fatal notion that they are all to have a fixed salary themselves for doing nothing but lend money, which, till they wholly quit themselves of, they will be helpless for good.

prosperity by spending annually on beer and tobacco, you pay a hundred millions to the rich middlemen, and thirty millions to the middling middlemen, and for every two shillings you pay, get threepence-halfpenny worth of beer to swallow!

Meantime, the Bishop, and the Rector, and the Rector's lady, and the dear old Quaker spinster who lives in Sweetbriar Cottage, are *so* shocked that you drink so much, and that you are such horrid wretches that nothing can be done for you! and you mustn't have your wages raised, because you *will* spend them in nothing but drink. And to-morrow they are all going to dine at Drayton Park, with the brewer who is your member of Parliament, and is building a public-house at the railway station, and another in the High Street, and another at the corner of Philpott's Lane, and another by the stables at the back of Tunstall Terrace, outside the town, where he has just bricked over the Dovesbourne, and filled Buttercup Meadow with broken bottles; and, by every measure, and on every principle of calculation, the growth of your prosperity is established!

You helpless sots and simpletons! Can't you at least manage to set your wives—what you have got of them—to brew your beer, and give you an honest pint of it for your money? Let *them* have the halfpence first, anyhow, if they must have the kicks afterwards.

Read carefully over, then, thirsty and hungry friends, concerning these questions of meat and drink, that whole *Fors* of March, 1873; but chiefly Sir Walter's letter, and what it says of Education, as useless, unless you limit your tippling-houses.

Yet some kind of education is instantly necessary to give you the courage and sense to limit them. If I were in your place, I should drink myself to death in six months, because I had nothing to amuse me; and such education, therefore, as may teach you how to be rightly amused I am trying with all speed to provide for you. For, indeed, all real education, though it begins in the wisdom of John the Baptist—(quite *literally* so; first in washing with pure water,) goes on into an entirely merry and amused life, like St. Ursula's; and ends in a delightsome death. But to be amused like St. Ursula you must feel like her, and become interested in the distinct nature of Bad and Good. Above all, you must learn to know faithful and good men from miscreants. Then you will be amused by knowing the histories of the good ones—and very greatly entertained by visiting their tombs, and seeing their statues. You will even feel yourselves pleased, some day, in walking considerable distances, with that and other objects, and so truly seeing foreign countries, and the shrines of the holy men who are alive in them, as well as the shrines of the dead. You will even, should a voyage be necessary, learn to rejoice upon the sea, provided you know first how to row upon it, and to catch the winds that rule it with bright sails. You will be amused by seeing pretty people wear beautiful dresses when you are not kept yourselves in rags, to pay for them; you will be amused by hearing beautiful music, when you can get your steam-devil's tongues, and throats, and wind-holes anywhere else, stopped, that you may hear it; and take enough pains yourselves to learn to know it, when you do. All which sciences and arts St. George will teach you, in good time, if you are obedient to him:—without obedience, neither he nor any saint in heaven can help you. Touching which, now of all men hated and abused, virtue,—and the connection more especially of the arts of the Muse with its universal necessity,—I have translated a piece of Plato for you, which, here following, I leave you to meditate on, till next month.

The Athenian.—"It is true, my friends, that over certain of the laws, with us, our populace had authority; but it is no less true that there were others to which they were entirely subject."

The Spartan.—"Which mean you?"

The Athenian.—"First, those which in that day related to music, if indeed we are to trace up to its root the change which has issued in our now too licentious life."

For, at that time, music was divided according to certain ideas and forms necessarily inherent in it; and one kind of songs consisted of prayers to the gods, and were called hymns ; and another kind, contrary to these, for the most part were called laments,* and another, songs of resolute strength and triumph, were sacred to Apollo ; and a fourth, springing out of the frank joy of life, were sacred to Dionusos, and called 'dithyrambs.' † And these modes of music they called laws as they did laws respecting other matters ; but the laws of music for distinction's sake were called Harplaws.

And these four principal methods, and certain other subordinate ones, having been determined, it was not permitted to use one kind of melody for the purpose of another ; and the authority to judge of these, and to punish all who disobeyed the laws concerning them, was not, as now, the hissing, or the museless ‡ cry of the multitude in dispraise, neither their clapping for praise : but it was the function of men trained in the offices of education to hear all in silence ; and to the children and their tutors, and the most of the multitude, the indication of order was given with the staff ; §

* The Coronach of the Highlanders represents this form of music down to nearly our own days. It is to be defined as the sacredly ordered expression of the sorrow permitted to human frailty, but contrary to prayer, according to Plato's words, because expressing will contrary to the will of God.

† "The origin of this word is unknown" (Liddell and Scott). But there must have been an idea connected with a word in so constant use, and spoken of matters so intimately interesting ; and I have myself no doubt that a sense of the doubling and redoubling caused by instinctive and artless pleasure in sound, as in nursery rhymes, extended itself gradually in the Greek mind into a conception of the universal value of what may be summed in our short English word 'reply'; as, first, in the republication of its notes of rapture by the nightingale, —then, in the entire system of adjusted accents, rhythms, strophes, antistrophes, and echoes of burden ; and, to the Greek, most practically in the balanced or interchanged song of answering bodies of chorus entering from opposite doors on the stage : continuing down to our own days in the alternate chant of the singers on each side of the choir.

‡ 'Museless,' as one says 'shepherdless,' unprotected or helped by the muse.

§ I do not positively understand this, but the word used by Plato signifies properly, ' putting in mind,' or rather putting in the notion, or ' nous'; and I believe the wand of the master of the theatre was used for a guide to the whole audience, as that of the leader of the orchestra is to the band,—not merely, nor even in any principal degree, for timekeeping. (which a pendulum in his place would do perfectly),—but for exhortation and encouragement. Supposing an audience thoroughly bent on listening and understanding, one can conceive the suggestion of parts requiring attention, the indication of subtle rhythm which would have escaped uncultivated ears, and the claim for sympathy in

and in all these matters the multitude of the citizens was willing to be governed, and did not dare to judge by tumult ; but after these things, as time went on, there were born, beginners of the museless libertinage,—poets, who were indeed poetical by nature, but incapable of recognizing what is just and lawful for the Muse ; exciting themselves in passion, and possessed, more than is due, by the love of pleasure : and these mingling laments with hymns, and pæans with dithyrambs, and mimicking the pipe with the harp, and dragging together everything into everything else, involuntarily and by their want of natural instinct * led men into the false thought that there is no positive rightness whatsoever in music, but that one may judge rightly of it by the pleasure of those who enjoy it, whether their own character be good or bad. And constructing such poems as these, and saying, concerning them, such words as these, they led the multitude into rebellion against the laws of music, and the daring of trust in their own capacity to judge of it. Whence the theatric audiences, that once were voiceless, became clamorous, as having professed knowledge, in the things belonging to the Muses, of what was beautiful and not ; and instead of aristocracy in that knowledge, rose up a certain polluted theatrocracy. For if indeed the democracy had been itself composed of more or less well-educated persons, there would not have been so much harm ; but, from this beginning in music, sprang up general disloyalty, and *pronouncing of their own opinion by everybody about everything ;* and on this followed mere licentiousnesss, for, having no fear of speaking, supposing themselves to know, fearlessness begot shamelessness. For, in our audacity, to have no fear of the opinion of the better person, is in itself a corrupt impudence, ending in extremity of license. And on this will always follow the resolve no more to obey established authorities ; then, beyond

parts of singular force and beauty, expressed by a master of the theatre, with great help and pleasure to the audience ;—we can imagine it best by supposing some great, acknowledged, and popular master, conducting his own opera, secure of the people's sympathy. A people not generous enough to give sympathy, nor modest enough to be grateful for leading, is not capable of hearing or understanding music. In our own schools, however, all that is needful is the early training of children under true musical law ; and the performance, under excellent masters, of appointed courses of beautiful music, as an essential part of all popular instruction, no less important than the placing of classical books and of noble pictures, within the daily reach and sight of the people.

* Literally, ' want of notion or conception.'

this, men are fain to refuse the service and reject the teach-ing of father and mother, and of all old age,—and so one is close to the end of refusing to obey the national laws, and at last to think no more of oath, or faith, or of the gods them-selves : thus at last likening themselves to the ancient and monstrous nature of the Titans, and filling their lives full of ceaseless misery.

NOTES AND CORRESPONDENCE.

I. Affairs of the Company.

Our accounts to the end of the year will be given in the February *Fors.* The entire pause in subscriptions, and cessation of all serviceable offers of Companionship,* during the last six months, may perhaps be owing in some measure to the continued delay in the determination of our legal position. I am sure that Mr. Somervell, who has communicated with the rest of the Companions on the subject, is doing all that is possible to give our property a simply workable form of tenure; and then, I trust, things will progress faster; but, whether they do or not, at the close of this seventh year, if I live, I will act with all the funds then at my disposal.

II. Affairs of the Master.

		£	s.	d.
Paid—				
Nov. 18.	The Bursar of Corpus	13	0	0
"	Henry Swan; engraving for 'Laws of Fésole'............................	5	0	0
29.	Jackson	25	0	0
Dec. 7.	C. F. Murray, for sketch of Princess Ursula and her Father, from Carpaccio..	10	0	0
10.	Oxford Secretary	100	0	0
11.	Self at Venice†	150	0	0
12.	Downs	50	0	0
15.	Burgess	42	0	0
		£395	0	0

	£	s.	d.
Balance, November 15th	£1135	3	4
	395	0	0
Balance, December 15th........................	£740	3	4

---

* I have refused several which were made without clear understanding of the nature of the Companionship; and especially such as I could perceive to be made, though unconsciously, more in the thought of the honour attaching to the name of Companions, than of the self-denial and humility necessary in their duties.

† Includes the putting up of scaffolds at St. Mark's and the Ducal Palace to cast some of their sculptures; and countless other expenses, mythologically definable as the opening of Danae's brazen tower: besides enormous bills at the "Grand Hotel," and sundry inexcusable "indiscriminate charities."

III. The mingled impertinence and good feeling of the following letter makes it difficult to deal with. I should be unjust to the writer in suppressing it, and to myself, (much more to Mr. Sillar,) in noticing it. The reader may answer it for himself : the only passage respecting which I think it necessary to say anything is the writer's mistake in applying the rule of doing as you would be done by to the degree in which your neighbour may expect or desire you to violate an absolute law of God. It may often be proper, if civil to your neighbour, to drink more than is good for you ; but not to commit the moderate quantity of theft or adultery which you may perceive would be in polite accordance with his principles, or in graceful compliance with his wishes.

" *November* 14*th*, 1876.

" Dear Mr. Ruskin,—Why so cross ? *I* don't want to discuss with you the ' uses of Dissent.' I am no more a Dissenting minister than you are, and not nearly as much of a Dissenter; and where you find my ' duly dissenting scorn of the wisdom of the Greeks and the legality of the Jews ' I don't know.

" Mr. Sillar backbites with his pen, and does evil to his neighbour. He does it quite inadvertently, misled by a passage in a book he has just read. Mr. Ruskin, forgetting his own clear exposition of Psalm xv., takes up the reproach against his neighbour, believes the evil, and won't even pray for the sinner. I correct the mistake ; whereupon Mr. Ruskin, instead of saying he is sorry for printing a slander, or that he is glad to find Mr. Sillar was mistaken, calls him an ass, ('unwise Christian—altering rules so as to make them useless,' are his words, but the meaning is the same,) and sneers at Methodism, evidently without having made even an ' elementary investigation ' of its principles, or having heard one sermon from a Methodist preacher,—so at least I judge from *Fors* XXXVI., (vol. ii., p. 120).

" If you wanted information—which you don't—about our rules, I would point out that our rules are only three :—1, ' To do no harm; ' 2, ' To do all the good we can to men's bodies and souls;' and 3, ' To attend upon all the ordinances of God.' A Methodist, according to Mr Wesley's definition, (pardon me for quoting another of his definitions; unfortunately, in this case it does not express what *is*, but what ought to be,) is, ' One who lives after the method laid down in the Bible.'

" In answer to your questions, we don't approve of *going to law*, yet sometimes it may be necessary to appeal unto Cæsar ; and in making a reference to a Christian magistrate in a Christian country, we don't think we should be doing what St. Paul condemns,—' going to law before the unjust, before unbelievers, and not before saints.'

" As to usury and interest. Hitherto, perhaps wrongly, we have been satisfied with the ordinary ideas of men—including, apparently, some of your most esteemed friends—on the subject. You yourself did not find out the wrong of taking interest until Mr. Sillar showed you how to judge of it (*Fors* for 1874, vol. ii., p. 250) ; and your investigations are still, like mine, so elementary that they have not influenced your practice.

" I cannot tell you with ' pious accuracy ' the exact number of glasses of wine you may properly take, giving God thanks ; but pray don't take too many. Personally, I fancy the rule, ' Do unto others as you would be done by,' would keep me on the right side if I had any capital to invest, which I haven't. My good mother, eighty-three years of age, has a small sum, and since reading *Fors* I have just calculated that she has already received the entire amount in interest ; and of course she must now, if your ideas are correct, give up the principal, and ' go and work for more.'

" As for my postscript, I really thought, from *Fors* (vol. III., pages 225–234), that you were bothered with lawyers, and did not know what to do with sums of money given to you for a definite purpose, and which apparently could not be legally applied to that purpose. A plan that has answered well for John Wesley's Society would, I thought, answer equally well for another company, in which I feel considerable interest. The objects of the two societies are not very dissimilar : our rules are substantially yours, only they go a little further. But whilst aiming at remodelling the world, we begin by trying to mend ourselves, and to ' save our own souls,' in which I hope there is nothing to raise your ire, or bring upon us the vials of your scorn. Referring to *Fors* (vol. III., pages 113–120), I think I may say that ' we agree with most of your directions for private life.' In our plain and simple way,—assuredly not with your eloquence and rigour,—' we promulgate and recommend your principles,' without an idea that they are to be considered distinctively yours. We find them in the Bible; and if we don't ' aid your plans by sending you money,' it is because not one of us in a hundred thousand ever heard of them ; and besides, it is possible for us to think that, whilst your plans are good, our own are better. For myself, I have for some time wished and intended to send something, however trifling it might seem to you, towards the funds of St. George's Company. Will you kindly accept 20*s.* from a *Methodist Preacher ?* * I was going to send it before you referred to us, but spent the money in your photographs and Xenophon ; and sovereigns are so scarce with me that I had to wait a little before I could afford another.

" And now, if you have read as far as this, will you allow me to thank you most sincerely for all that I have learnt from you. I could say much on this subject, but forbear. More intelligent readers you may have, but none more grateful than

" Yours very truly,
" A METHODIST PREACHER."

* With St. George's thanks.

LETTER LXXIV.

VENICE, *Christmas Day,* 1876.*

LAST night, St. Ursula sent me her dianthus "out of her
bedroom window, with her love," and, as I was standing
beside it, this morning,—(ten minutes ago only,—it has just
struck eight,) watching the sun rise out of a low line of cloud,
just midway between the domes of St. George, and the
Madonna of Safety, there came into my mind the cause of
our difficulties about the Eastern question : with considerable amazement to myself that I had not thought of it before ;
but, on the contrary, in what I had intended to say, been
misled, hitherto, into quite vain collection of the little I
knew about either Turkey or Russia ; and entirely lost sight,
(though actually at this time chiefly employed with it !) of
what Little Bear has thus sent me the flower out of the dawn
in her window, to put me in mind of,—the religious mean-
ings of the matter.

I must explain her sign to you more clearly before I can
tell you these.

She sent me the living dianthus, (with a little personal
message besides, of great importance to *me,* but of none to
the matter in hand,) by the hands of an Irish friend now
staying here : but she had sent me also, in the morning, from
England, a dried sprig of the other flower in her window,
the sacred vervain,† by the hands of the friend who is helping me in all I want for *Proserpina,*—Mr. Oliver.

* I believe the following entry to be of considerable importance to
our future work ; and I leave it, uncorrected, as it was written at the
time, for that reason.

† I had carelessly and very stupidly taken the vervain for a decorative
modification of olive. It is painted with entire veracity, so that my
good friend Signor Coldara, who is painting Venetian flowers for us,
knew it for the " Erba Luisa " at the first glance,) went to the Botani-

Now the vervain is the ancient flower sacred to domestic purity ; and one of the chief pieces of teaching which showed me the real nature of classic life, came to me ten years ago, in learning by heart one of Horace's house-songs, in which he especially associates this herb with the *cheerful* service— yet sacrificial service—of the household Gods.

"The whole house laughs in silver ;—maid and boy in happy confusion run hither and thither ; the altar, wreathed with chaste vervain, asks for its sprinkling with the blood of the lamb."

Again, the Dianthus, of which I told you more was to be learned, means, translating that Greek name, " Flower of God, " or especially of the Greek Father of the Gods ; and it is of all wild flowers in Greece the brightest and richest in its divine beauty. (In *Proserpina,* note classification.*)

Now, see the use of myths, when they are living.

You have the Domestic flower, and the Wild flower.

You have the Christian sacrifice of the Passover, for the Household ; and the universal worship of Allah, the Father of all,—our Father which art in Heaven, made of specialty to you by the light of the crimson wild flower on the mountains ; and all this by specialty of sign sent to you in Venice, by the Saint whose mission it was to convert the savage people of " England, over-sea."

I am here interrupted by a gift, from another friend, of a little painting of the 'pitcher' (Venetian water-carrier's) of holy water, with the sprinkling thing in it,—I don't know its name,—but it reminds me of the " Tu asperges " in Lethe, in the Purgatorio, and of other matters useful to me : but mainly observe from it, in its bearing on our work, that the blood of Sprinkling, common to the household of the Greek, Roman, and the Jew,—and water of Sprinkling, common to all nations on earth, in the Baptism to which Christ submit-

cal Gardens here, and painted it from the life. I will send his painting, with my own drawing of the plant from the Carpaccio picture, to the Sheffield museum. They can there be photographed for any readers of *Fors* who care to see such likeness of them.

* All left as written, in confusion : I will make it clear presently.

ted,—the one, speaketh better things than that of Abel, and the other than that unto Moses in the cloud and in the sea, in so far as they give *joy* together with their purity ; so that the Lamb of the Passover itself, and the Pitcher of Water borne by him who showed the place of it, alike are turned, the one, by the last Miracle, into sacramental wine which immortally in the sacred Spirit makes glad the Heart of Man, and the other, by the first Miracle, into the Marriage wine, which here, and immortally in the sacred, because purified Body, makes glad the Life of Man.

2nd January, 1877.

Thus far I wrote in the morning and forenoon of Christmas Day : and leave it so, noting only that the reference to the classification in *Proserpina* is to the name there given for the whole order of the pinks, including the dianthus,—namely, Clarissa. It struck me afterwards that it would be better to have made it simply ' Clara,'—which, accordingly, I have now determined it shall be. The Dianthus will be the first sub-species ; but note that this Greek name is modern, and bad Greek also ; yet to be retained, for it is *our* modern contribution to the perfectness of the myth. Carpaccio meant it, first and practically, for a balcony window-flower—as the vervain is also : and what more, I can't say, or seek, to-day, for I must turn now to the business for this month, the regulation of our Sheffield vegetable market :—yet for *that*, even you will have to put up with another page or two of myth, before we can get rightly at it.

I must ask you to look back to *Fors* of August, 1872, and to hear why the boy with his basket of figs was so impressive a sign to me.

He was selling them before the south façade of the Ducal Palace ; which, built in the fourteenth century, has two notable sculptures on its corner-stones. Now, that palace is the perfect type of such a building as should be made the seat of a civic government exercising all needful powers.*

* State prisoners were kept in the palace, instead of in a separate tower, as was our practice in London. that none might be in bonds more than a month before they were brought up for judgment.

How soon you may wish to build such an one at Sheffield depends on the perfection of the government you can develop there, and the dignity of state which you desire it should assume. For the men who took counsel in that palace "considered the poor," and heard the requests of the poorest citizens, in a manner of which you have had as yet no idea given you by any government visible in Europe.

This palace being, as I said, built in the fourteenth century, when the nation liked to express its thoughts in sculpture, and being essentially the national palace, its builder, speaking as it were the mind of the whole people, signed first, on its corner-stones, their consent in the scriptural definition of worldly happiness,—" Every man shall dwell under his vine and under his fig tree." And out of one corner-stone he carved a fig tree ; out of the other, a vine. But to show upon what conditions, only, such happiness was to be secured, he thought proper also on each stone to represent the temptations which it involved, and the danger of yielding to them. Under the fig tree he carved Adam and Eve, unwisely gathering figs : under the vine, Noah, unwisely gathering grapes.

'*Gathering*,' observe ;—in both instances the hand is on the fruit ; the sculpture of the drunkenness of Noah differing in this from the usual treatment of the subject.

These two sculptures represent broadly the two great divisions of the sins of men ; those of Disobedience, or sins against known command,—Presumptuous sins—and therefore, against Faith and Love ; and those of Error, or sins against unknown command, sins of Ignorance—or, it may be, of Weakness, but not against Faith, nor against Love.

These corner-stones form the chief decoration or grace of its strength—meaning, if you read them in their national lesson, "Let him that thinketh he standeth, take heed lest he fall." Then, next above these stones of warning, come the stones of Judgment and Help.

3rd January, 1877.

Above the sculpture of Presumptuous Sin is carved the Angel Michael, with the lifted sword. Above the sculpture of Erring Sin, is carved the angel Raphael, leading Tobias, and his dog.

Not *Tobit,* and his dog, observe. It is very needful for us to understand the separate stories of the father and son, which gave this subject so deep a meaning to the mediæval Church. Read the opening chapter of Tobit, to the end of his prayer. That prayer, you will find, is the seeking of death rather than life, in entirely noble despair. Erring, but innocent ; blind, but *not thinking that he saw,*—therefore without sin.

To him the angel of all beautiful life is sent, hidden in simplicity of human duty, taking a servant's place for hire, to lead his son in all right and happy ways of life, explaining to him, and showing to all of us who read, in faith, for ever, what is the root of all the material evil in the world, the great error of seeking pleasure before use. This is the dreadfulness which brings the true horror of death into the world, which hides God in death, and which makes all the lower creatures of God—even the happiest, suffer with us,—even the most innocent, injure us.*

But the young man's dog went with them—and returned, to show that all the lower creatures, who can love, have passed, through their love, into the guardianship and guidance of angels.

And now you will understand why I told you in the last *Fors* for last year that you must eat angel's food before you could eat material food.

Tobit got leave at last, you see, to go back to his dinner.

Now, I have two pretty stories to tell you, (though I must not to-day,) of a Venetian dog, which were told to me on Christmas Day last, by Little Bear's special order. Her own dog, at the foot of her bed, is indeed unconscious of the angel with the palm ; but is taking care of his mistress's earthly crown ; and St. Jerome's dog, in his study, is seriously and admiringly interested in the progress of his

---

* Measure,—who can,—the evil that the Horse and Dog, worshipped before God, have done to England.

master's literary work, though not, of course, understanding the full import of it.

The dog in the vision to the shepherds, and the cattle in the Nativity, are always essential to these myths, for the same reason ; and in next *Fors*, you shall have with the stories of the Venetian dog, the somewhat more important one of St. Theodore's horse,—God willing. Finally, here are four of the grandest lines of an English prophet, sincere as Carpaccio, which you will please remember :

> ' The bat that flits at close of eve,
> Hath left the brain that won't believe.'

> ' Hurt not the moth, nor butterfly,
> For the Last Judgment draweth nigh.'

And now, Tobit having got back to his dinner, we may think of ours : only Little Bear *will* have us hear a little reading still, in the refectory. Take patience but a minute or two more.

Long ago, in *Modern Painters*, I dwelt on the, to me, utter marvellousness, of that saying of Christ, (when "on this wise showed He Himself ")—

"Come and dine. . . . .
. . . . So when they had dined," etc.

I understand it now, with the "Children, have ye here any meat ?" of the vision in the chamber. My hungry and thirsty friends, do not you also begin to understand the sacredness of your daily bread ; nor the divinity of the great story of the world's beginning ;—the infinite truth of its "Touch not—taste not—handle not, of the things that perish in the using, but only of things which, whether ye eat or drink, are to the glory of God "?

But a few more words about Venice, and we come straight to Sheffield.

My boy with his basket of rotten figs *could* only sell them in front of the sculpture of Noah, because all the nobles had perished from Venice, and he was there, poor little costermonger, stooping to cry fighiaie between his legs, where the

stateliest lords in Europe were wont to walk, erect enough,
and in no disordered haste. (Curiously, as I write this very
page, one of the present authorities in progressive Italy,
progressive without either legs or arms, has gone whizzing
by, up the canal, in a steam propeller, like a large darting
water beetle.) He *could* only sell them in that place, because
the Lords of Venice were fallen, as a fig tree casteth her untimely figs ; and the sentence is spoken against them, " No
man eat fruit of thee, hereafter." And he could only sell
them in Venice at all, because the laws of the greater Lords
of Venice who *built* her palaces are disobeyed in her modern
liberties. Hear this, from the Venetian Laws of State respecting " Frutti e Fruttaroli," preserved in the Correr
Museum.

19th June, 1516.*—" It is forbidden to all and sundry to
sell bad fruits. Figs, especially, must not be kept in the
shop from one day to another, on pain of fine of twenty-five
lire."
30th June, 1518.—" The sale of squeezed figs and preserved
figs is forbidden. They are to be sold ripe."
10th June, 1523.—" Figs cannot be preserved nor packed.
They are to be sold in the same day that they are brought
into this city."

The intent of these laws is to supply the people largely
and cheaply with ripe fresh figs from the mainland, and to
prevent their ever being eaten in a state injurious to health,
on the one side, or kept, to raise the price, on the other.
Note the continual connection between Shakspeare's ideal,
both of commerce and fairyland, with Greece, and Venice :
" Feed him with apricocks and dewberries,—with purple
grapes, *green* figs, and mulberries " ; the laws of Venice
respecting this particular fruit being originally Greek ;
(Athenian ; see derivation of word ' sycophant,' in any good
dictionary).

But the next law, 7th July, 1523, introduces question of a
fruit still more important to Venetians.

* Innibito a chiunque il vendere frutti cattivi." *Before* 1516, observe,
nobody *thought* of doing so.

"On pain of fine (ut supra), let no spoiled or decaying melons or bottle-gourds be sold, nor any yellow cucumbers."

9th June, 1524.—"The sale of fruits which are not good and nourishing is forbidden to every one, both on the canals and lands of this city. Similarly, it is forbidden to keep them in baskets more than a day ; and, similarly, to keep bad mixed with the good."

On the 15th July, 1545, a slight relaxation is granted of this law, as follows : "Sellers of melons cannot sell them either unripe or decayed (crudi o marci), without putting a ticket on them, to certify them as such."

And to ensure obedience to these most wholesome ordinances of state, the life of the Venetian greengrocer was rendered (according to Mr. John Bright,*) a burden to him, by the following regulations :—

* (*Fors*, Vol. II., p. 131.)

I observe that, in his recent speech at Rochdale, Mr. Bright makes mention of me which he " hopes I shall forgive." There is no question of forgiveness in the matter ; Mr. Bright speaks of me what he believes to be true, and what, to the best of his knowledge, is so: he quotes a useful passage from the part of my books which he understands ; and a notable stanza from the great song of Sheffield, whose final purport, nevertheless, Mr. Bright himself reaches only the third part of the way to understanding. He has left to me the duty of expressing the ultimate force of it, in such rude additional rhyme as came to me yesterday, while walking to and fro in St. Mark's porch, beside the grave of the Duke Marino Morosini ; a man who knew more of the East than Mr. Bright, and than most of his Rochdale audience ; but who nevertheless shared the incapacity of Socrates, Plato, and Epaminondas, to conceive the grandeur of the ceremony " which took place yesterday in Northern India."

Here is Ebenezer's stanza, then, with its sequence, taught me by Duke Morocen :—

> " What shall Bread-Tax do for thee
> Venerable Monarchy ?
> Dreams of evil,—sparing sight,
> Let that horror rest in night."

> What shall Drink-Tax do for thee,
> Faith-Defending Monarchy ?
> Priestly King,—is *this* thy sign,
> Sale of Blessing,—Bread,—and Wine ?

> What shall Roof-Tax do for thee,
> Life-Defending Monarchy ?

6th July, 1559.—" The superintendents of fruits shall be confined to the number of eight, of whom two every week, (thus securing a monthly service of the whole octave,) shall stand at the barrier, to the end that no fruits may pass, of any kind, that are not good."

More special regulations follow, for completeness of examination ; the refusal to obey the law becoming gradually, it is evident, more frequent as the moral temper of the people declined, until, just two centuries after the issuing of the first simple order, that no bad fruit is to be sold, the attempts at evasion have become both cunning and resolute, to the point of requiring greater power to be given to the officers, as follows :—

28th April, 1725.—" The superintendents of the fruits may go through the shops, and seek in every place for fruits of bad quality, and they shall not be impeded by whomsoever it may be. They shall mount upon the boats of melons and other fruits, and shall prohibit the sale of bad ones, and shall denounce transgressors to the magistracy."

Nor did the government once relax its insistance, or fail to carry its laws into effect, as long as there was a Duke in Venice. Her people are now Free, and all the glorious liberties of British trade are achieved by them. And having been here through the entire autumn, I have not once been able to taste wall-fruit from the Rialto market, which was not *both* unripe and rotten, it being invariably gathered hard, to last as long as possible in the baskets ; and of course the rottenest sold first, and the rest as it duly attains that desirable state.

The Persian fruits, however, which, with pears and cherries, fill the baskets on the Ducal Palace capitals, are to the

---

Find'st thou rest for England's head,
Only free among the Dead ?

Loosing still the stranger's slave,—
Sealing still thy Garden-Grave ?
Kneel thou there ; and trembling pray,
" Angels, roll the stone away."

(Venice, 11th January, 1877.)

people of far less importance than the gourd and melon. The
' melon boats,' as late as 1845, were still so splendid in beauty
of fruit, that my then companion, J. D. Harding, always
spent with me the first hour of our day in drawing at the Rialto
market. Of these fruits, being a staple article in constant
domestic consumption, not only the quality, but the price,
became an object of anxious care to the government ; and
the view taken by the Venetian Senate on the question I
proposed to you in last *Fors*, the function of the middle-man
in raising prices, is fortunately preserved at length in the following decree of 8th July, 1577 :—

Decree of the Most Illustrious Lords, the Five of the Mariegole.*

"It is manifestly seen that Melons in this City have reached
a price at which scarcely anybody is bold enough to buy
them ; a condition of things discontenting to everybody, and
little according with the dignity of the persons whose duty it
is to take such precautionary measures as may be needful,"
(the Five most Illustrious, to wit,) "and although our Pre-
sessors † and other Magistrates, who from time to time have
had special regard to this difficulty, have made many and di-
vers provisional decrees, yet it is seen manifestly that they
have always been vain, nor have ever brought forth the
good effect which was desired : and the cause of this is
seen expressly to be a great number of buyers-to-sell-again
who find themselves in this city, and in whose presence it is
impossible so quickly to make public anything relating to the
import or export of food, but this worst sort of men pounce
on it,‡ and buy it, before it is born ; in this, using all the in-
telligences, cunnings, and frauds which it is possible to imagine ; so that the people of this city cannot any more buy
anything, for their living, of the proper Garden-master of it ;
but only from the buyers-to-sell-again, through whose hands
such things will pass two or three times before they are sold,

* A Mariegola. Madre-Regola, or Mother-Law, is the written code of
the religious and secular laws either of a club of Venetian gentlemen, or
a guild of Venetian tradesmen. With my old friend Mr. Edward Cheney's
help, I shall let you hear something of these, in next *Fors*.

† Those who before us sat on this Seat of Judgment.

‡ Most illustrious, a little better grammar might here have been advisable ;—had indignation permitted.

which notable disorder is not by any manner of means to be
put up with.   Wherefore, both for the universal benefit of
all the City, and for the dignity of our Magistracy, the great
and illustrious Lords, the Five Wise Men, and Foreseers upon
the Mariegole, make it publicly known that henceforward
there may be no one so presumptuous as to dare, whether as
Fruiterer, Green-grocer, Buyer-to-sell-again, or under name
of any other kind of person of what condition soever, to sell
melons of any sort, whether in the shops or on the shore of
our island of Rialto, beginning from the bridge of Rialto
as far as the bridge of the Beccaria ; and similarly in any
part of the piazza of St. Mark, the Pescaria, or the Tèra
Nuova,* under penalty to whosoever such person shall sell
or cause to be sold contrary to the present order, of 120
ducats for each time ; to lose the melons, and to be whipped
round the Piazza of the Rialto, or of San Marco, wheresoever he has done contrary to the law ; " but the Garden-
masters and gardeners may sell where they like, and nobody
shall hinder them.

5th January, Morning.

I will give the rest of this decree in next *Fors* ; but I must
pause to-day, for you have enough before you to judge of
the methods taken by the Duke and the statesmen of Venice
for the ordering of her merchandize, and the aid of her poor.

I say, for the ordering of her merchandize ; other merchandize than this she had ;—pure gold, and ductile crystal,
and inlaid marble,—various as the flowers in mountain
turf.   But her first care was the food of the poor ; she knew
her first duty was to see that they had each day their daily
bread.   Their corn and pomegranate ; crystal, not of flint,
but life ; manna, not of the desert, but the home—"Thou
shalt let none of it stay until the morning."

" To *see* that they had their daily bread ; " yes—but how
to make such vision sure ?   My friends, there is yet one
more thing, and the most practical of all, to be observed by
you as to the management of your commissariat.   Whatever
laws you make about your bread—however wise and brave,

---

* These limitations referring to the Rialto market and piazza, leave the
town greengrocers free to sell, they being under vowed discipline of the
Mariegola of Greengrocers.

you will not get it, unless you pray for it. If you would not be fed with stones, by a Father Devil, you must ask for bread from your Father, God. In a word, you must understand the Lord's Prayer—and *pray it;* knowing, and desiring, the Good you ask ; knowing also, and abhorring, the Evil you ask to be delivered from. Knowing and obeying your Father who is in Heaven ; knowing and wrestling with ' your Destroyer' who is come down to Earth ; and praying and striving also, that your Father's will may be done there,—not his ; and your Father's kingdom come there, and not his.

And finally, therefore, in St. George's name, I tell you, you cannot know God, unless also you know His and your adversary, and have no fellowship with the works of that Living Darkness, and put upon you the armour of that Living Light.

' Phrases, still phrases,' think you? My friends, the Evil spirit indeed exists ; and in so exact contrary power to God's, that as men go straight to God by believing in Him, they go straight to the Devil by disbelieving in him. Do but fairly rise to fight him, and you will feel him fast enough, and have as much on your hands as you are good for. Act, then. Act—yourselves, waiting for no one. Feed the hungry, clothe the naked, to the last farthing in your own power. Whatever the State does with its money, do you that with yours. Bring order into your own accounts, whatever disorder there is in the Chancellor of the Exchequer's ; then, when you have got the Devil well under foot in Sheffield, you may begin to stop him from persuading my Lords of the Admiralty that they want a new grant, etc., etc., to make his machines with ; and from illuminating Parliament with new and ingenious suggestions concerning the liquor laws. For observe, as the outcome of all that is told you in this *Fors,* all taxes put by the rich on the meat or drink of the poor, are *precise* Devil's laws. That is why they are so loud in their talk of national prosperity, indicated by the Excise, because the fiend, who blinds them, sees that he can also blind you, through your lust for drink, into quietly allowing yourselves to pay fifty millions a year, that the rich may make their machines of blood with, and play at shedding blood.*

But patience, my good fellows. Everything must be confirmed by the last, as founded on the first, of the three resolutions I asked of you in the beginning,—" Be sure you can obey good laws before you seek to alter bad ones." No rattening, if you please ; no pulling down of park railings ; no rioting in the streets. It is the Devil who sets you on that sort of work. Your Father's Servant does not strive, nor cry, nor lift up his voice in the streets. But He will bring forth judgment unto victory ; and, doing as He bids you do, you may pray as He bids you pray, sure of answer, because in His Father's gift are all order, strength, and honour, from age to age, for ever.

Of the Eastern question, these four little myths contain all I am able yet to say :—

    I. St. George of England and Venice does not bear his sword for his own interests ; nor in vain.

    II. St. George of Christendom becomes the Captain of her Knights in putting off his armour.

    III. When armour is put off, pebbles serve.

    IV. Read the psalm 'In Exitu.'

* See third article in Correspondence, showing how the game of our nobles becomes the gain of our usurers.

NOTES AND CORRESPONDENCE.

I. Affairs of the Company.

Our accounts I leave wholly in the hands of our Companion, Mr.
Rydings, and our kind helper, Mr. Walker. I believe their statement
will be ready for publication in this article.

[For accounts of the St. George's Fund and Sheffield Museum see
five following pages.]

Our legal affairs are in the hands of our Companion, Mr. Somervell,
and in the claws of the English faculty of Law : we must wait the result of the contest patiently.

I have given directions for the design of a library for study connected
with the St. George's Museum at Sheffield, and am gradually sending
down books and drawings for it, which will be specified in *Fors* from
time to time, with my reasons for choosing them. I have just presented the library with another thirteenth-century Bible,—that from
which the letter R was engraved at page 215 of vol. I. ; and two drawings from Filippo Lippi and Carpaccio, by Mr. C. F. Murray.

II. Affairs of the Master.

I am bound to state, in the first place,—now beginning a new and
very important year, in which I still propose myself for the Master of
the St. George's Company,—that my head certainly does not serve me
as it did once, in many respects. The other day, for instance, in a
frosty morning at Verona, I put on my dressing-gown (which is of
bright Indian shawl stuff) by mistake for my great coat; and walked
through the full market-place, and half-way down the principal street,
in that costume, proceeding in perfect tranquillity until the repeated
glances of unusual admiration bestowed on me by the passengers led
me to investigation of the possible cause. And I begin to find it no
longer in my power to keep my attention fixed on things that have little
interest for me, so as to avoid mechanical mistakes. It is assuredly true,
as I have said in the December *Fors*, that I *can* keep accounts ; but, it
seems, not of my own revenues, while I am busy with the history of those
of Venice. In page 359, vol. III., the November expenses were deducted
from the sum in the first column instead of from that in the third, and
the balance in that page should have been £670 9s. 4d. ; and in last *Fors*,
£275 9s. 4d. My Greenwich pottery usually brings me in £60 ; but I remitted most of the rent, this year, to the tenant, who has been forced
into expenses by the Street Commissioners. He pays me £24 16s. 9d.,
bringing my resources for Christmas to the total of £300 6s. 1d.

JOHN RUSKIN, Esq., IN ACCOUNT WITH THE ST. GEORGE'S FUND.

Dr.

1876.	£	s.	d.
Subscription to March 14th, see April *Fors*..	1023	11	10
Addition to end of year:—			
May..........	8	6	1
June..........	10	10	0
July..........	102	0	6
September..........	16	16	0
November..........	50	0	0
December..........	10	0	0
Cheques { £300 / £500 / £330 }	1130	0	0
	2351	4	5
To Balance..........	108	8	0
	£2459	12	5

Cr.

1876.	£	s.	d.
Paid to Bankers, see April *Fors*..........	977	12	1
" " May, less 3d. charges..	52	9	3
" " June..........	95	12	6
" " October..........	50	0	0
" " December..........	10	0	0
Purchase of land and house at Sheffield for Museum..........	930	0	0
Law expenses, ditto..........	26	15	11
Chemicals at Museum..........	5	0	0
Prints, Colnaghi..........	29	10	0
Law Expenses, Tarrant and Mackrill..........	20	17	5
Repairs of Cottages at Barmonth..........	27	0	0
Cheque to H. Swan, Sheffield, see Feb. *Fors*	50	0	0
Ditto ditto	44	0	0
Ditto ditto see Aug. *Fors*	55	15	3
Ditto ditto see Nov. *Fors*	60	0	0
Mr. Rydings, for feeble workers at Laxey, Isle of Man,	25	0	0
	£2459	12	5

THE UNION BANK OF LONDON (CHANCERY LANE BRANCH) IN ACCOUNT WITH THE ST. GEORGE'S FUND.

Dr.

1876.			£	s.	d.
Jan.	1.	To Balance	14	1	10
"	6.	" Dividend on £8000 Consols	119	0	0
"	13.	" Per George Allen	24	11	1
Feb.	15.	" Per John Ruskin, Esq.	25	0	0
"		" Draft at Sheffield	8	0	0
"		" Ditto at Amblesile	6	0	0
"		" Ditto at Bridgewater	100	0	0
"		" Ditto at Birmingham	5	0	0
"	22.	" Per John Ruskin, Esq.	35	0	0
Mar.	4.	" Draft at Windsor	20	0	0
"	7.	" Per John Ruskin, Esq.	25	0	0
"		" Draft at Oxford	50	0	0
"	14.	" Per John Ruskin, Esq.	6	0	0
"		" Draft at Sheffield	20	0	0
May	3.	" Per John Ruskin, Esq.	17	11	11
"	6.	" Draft at Bridgwater	9	19	3
"	9.	" Ditto at Douglas, £25, less charges	24	18	9
June	9.	" Per John Ruskin, Esq.	5	0	0
"	18.	" Draft at Bridgwater	20	12	6
"		" Ditto at Bilston	50	0	0
"	17.	" Cash per John Ruskin, Esq.	20	0	0
July	6.	" Dividend on £8000 Consols	118	10	0
Oct.	12.	" Draft at Bridgwater	50	0	0
"	24.	" Per J. P. Stilwell	25	0	0
Dec.	4.	" Draft at Bridgwater	10	0	0
"	23.	" Per George Allen	12	6	0
			£821	10	5

Cr.

1876.			£	s.	d.
Feb.	22.	By charges on two local notes	0	0	10
"	25.	" Postage of pass book	0	0	3
Mar.	3.	" John Ruskin, Esq.	300	0	0
July	28.	" Ditto	330	0	0
Oct.	12.	" Postage of pass book	0	0	3
Dec.	31.	By Balance	191	9	1
			£821	10	5

Dr.   CASH STATEMENT OF ST. GEORGE'S COMPANY TO 31ST DECEMBER, 1876.   **Cr.**

RECEIPTS.	£	s.	d.
Subscriptions to beginning of year, see April *Fors*	785	1	10
Ditto to end of year, see *Fors,* April to July, Sept., Nov., and Dec.	461	2	7
Ditto from Mr. George Allen, viz.:			
Miss Kate Bradley ..£1 1 0			
F. Somerscales 5 0 0			
Miss Guest 2 2 0			
Mona 1 1 0			
Miss Guest 2 2 0			
'Methodist Preacher' 1 0 0			
	12	6	0
Ditto from Mr. Rydings, Dec. 14. 33 15 0			
	1292	5	5
Interest on £7000 Consols to Jan., 1875, and on £8000 from July, 1875, to July, 1876.	1007	17	6
Interest from balance at bankers'	9	18	0
Balance remaining due to Mr. Ruskin for sums advanced at various times	108	8	0
	£2418	8	11

PAYMENTS.	£	s.	d.
Purchase of £1000 Consols	918	15	0
Power of attorney for dividends	0	5	0
Cheque book and other small charges at bankers'	0	6	3
Purchase of land and house at Sheffield for Museum	930	0	0
Law expenses on the above	26	15	11
F. D. Acland, for chemicals at Museum	5	0	0
Fittings, salary, taxes, etc., at ditto, per separate accounts to Dec. 31	193	12	2
Repairs of cottages at Barmouth	27	0	0
Colnaghi and Co., for prints	29	10	0
Law charges for the Company	20	17	5
Mr. Rydings, for feeble "home spun" workers at Laxey	25	0	0
Mr. Rydings, cheque sent to Italy and not yet returned £33 15 0			
Cash at bankers' 191 9 1			
Ditto at Museum 16 3 1			
	241	7	2
	£2418	8	11

EGBERT RYDINGS IN ACCOUNT WITH ST. GEORGE'S COMPANY

(From June 29th, 1876, to January 16, 1877).

Dr.

1876.		£	s.	d.
June 29.	To Mrs. Jane Lisle	1	1	0
" 30.	" Charles Firth	1	1	0
Aug. 7.	" G. No. 50	10	10	0
" 12.	" Miss Sargood	2	2	0
" 12.	" Miss Christina Allan	2	2	0
Sept. 1.	" John Morgan, for 1871, No. 6	1	1	0
" 5.	" Geo. Thomson	5	0	0
Nov. 8.	" John Morgan, for 1876, No. 6	1	1	0
" 9.	" B. B., No. 26	1	10	0
Dec. 7.	" J. D., No. 49	0	5	0
" 9.	" Josiah Gittins	1	0	0
" 9.	" Miss M. Guest	2	2	0
" 12.	" A. H., No. 37	5	5	0
" 16.	" Wm. Smither	5	5	0
July 1.	" Miss M. Guest (received by Mr. Ruskin, omitted in his account)	2	2	0
Dec. 23.	" Miss Dora Livesey	5	0	0
" 29.	" John E. Fowler	3	0	0
1877.				
Jan. 1.	" Miss Julia Firth	7	0	0
" 1.	" John and Mary Gay	1	1	0
" 3.	" Miss Sarah A. Gimson	1	1	0
" 16.	" Miss F. B.	2	0	0
		£59	18	0

Cr.

1876.		£	s.	d.
Dec. 14.	By Cash paid to the Union Bank to the St. George's Fund	33	15	0
1877.				
Jan. 16.	" Balance in E. Ryding's hands	26	3	0
		£59	18	0

SHEFFIELD MUSEUM ACCOUNT.

Dr.		£	s.	d.
1876.				
July 1. To Balance in hand............		38	17	2
Nov. 22. " J. Ruskin, Esq, by cheque........		60	0	0
		£98	17	2

Cr.		£	s.	d.	£	s.	d.
1876.	*Current Expenses.*						
July 1.	H. Swan (salary)..........	10	0	0			
" 17.	Gas..........	0	6	2			
Sept. 11.	Water	0	5	7			
Oct. 1.	H. Swan (salary)	10	0	0			
Nov. 16.	Water..........	0	8	8			
Dec. 13.	Gas........	0	7	3			
" 23.	Poor-rate	0	15	4			
					22	3	0
	Repairs and Building Expenses.						
Oct. 14.	J. Tunnard, for two gates...	3	15	0			
Dec. 20.	Silicate Paint Company...	0	17	1			
" 21.	Gravel and cartage........	0	13	6			
					5	5	7
	Fittings and Cases.						
Sept. 6.	Jones, for cloth	0	3	6			
" 6.	Cockayne, ditto	0	3	4			
" 7.	Jackson, ditto......	0	7	8			
Oct. 12.	C. H. Griffiths, safe	6	0	0			
Nov. 22.	Leaf and Co., velvets......	3	7	4			
Dec. 1.	Smithson and Dale, cabinet cases...	40	0	0			
" 12.	Cockayne, velvet........	0	2	3			
					50	4	1
	Cartage of goods........	3	13	2			
	Petty expenses........	1	8	3			
					5	1	5
	Balance in hand........				16	3	1
					£98	17	2

Examined, and found correct, WM. WALKER, Jan. 9th, 1877.

My expenses to the end of the year are as follows:—

			£	s.	d.
Dec.	18.	Raffaelle (a)	15	0	0
"	22.	A. Giordani (b)	20	0	0
"	23.	Self	50	0	0
"	25.	Gift to relation	60	0	0
"		Paul Huret (c)	5	0	0
"	27.	Downs	10	0	0
			£160	0	0

Thus leaving me, according to my own views, (I don't vouch for the banker's concurrence in all particulars,) £140 6s. 1d. to begin the year with, after spending, between last New Year's Day, and this, the total sum of——I won't venture to cast it till next month ; but I consider this rather an economical year than otherwise. It will serve, however, when fairly nailed down in exposition, as a sufficient specimen of my way of living for the last twelve years, resulting in an expenditure during that period of some sixty thousand, odd pounds. I leave, for the present, my Companions to meditate on the sort of Master they have got, begging them also to remember that I possess also the great official qualification of Dogberry, and am indeed "one that hath had losses." In the appropriate month of April, they shall know precisely to what extent, and how much—or little—I have left, of the money my father left me. With the action I mean to take in the circumstances.

III. I reprint the following admirable letter with all joy in its sturdy statements of principle ; but I wish the writer would look at Mr. D. Urquhart's ' Spirit of the East.' He is a little too hard upon the Turk, though it is not in Venice that one should say so.

" TURKISH LOANS AND BULGARIAN ATROCITIES.

" *To the Editor of the Carlisle Journal.*

" Sir,—There appears to be one probable cause of the present Eastern imbroglio which has escaped the notice of most of those who have written or spoken on the subject, viz., the various Turkish loans which have been floated on the London Stock Exchange.

" At first sight, few would be inclined to regard these as the root of the present mischief, but investigation may reveal that Turkish loans at high rates of interest, and Bulgarian atrocities follow each other simply as cause and effect.

" Of course few of the Christian investors in these loans would ever

(a) In advance, because he goes home to Assisi at Christmas.
(b) The old Venetian sculptor who cast the Colleone statue for the Crystal Palace. Payment for casting Noah's vine on the Ducal Palace.
(c) My godson at Boulogne. (His father, a pilot, now dead, taught me to steer a lugger.) Christmas gift for books and instruments.

think, when lending their spare capital to the Turk, that they were aiding and abetting him in his brutalities, or sowing the seed which was to produce the harvest of blood and other abominations in the Christian provinces under his sway. But such, nevertheless, may be the fact, and the lenders of the sinews of war to tyrannical and bloodthirsty governments should be warned that they are responsible for the sanguinary results which may ensue.

"The horrors to which our world has been subjected, through this system of lending and borrowing, are beyond possibility of computation. But let us simply inquire how much misery, destitution, and death lie at the door of our own national debt.

"If our ecclesiastical leaders could take up this subject during the present mission, and preach sermons upon it (as Christ Himself would have done), from such texts as these,—'For they bind burdens upon men's shoulders, grievous to be borne, and will not touch them themselves with one of their fingers,' and 'For ye devour widows' houses,' they would not find it necessary to refer so much to empty or appropriated pews, or to lament that only five per cent. of our working men are in attendance at church.

"One can fancy the effect which could be produced by a few sermons on these texts. Our own debt is a 'burden' which takes nearly one pound annually from every man, woman, and child in the kingdom, and our war armaments take nearly another pound. How many ' widows' houses' must these 'burdens' be literally devouring? And yet when do we find the professed followers of 'the Prince of Peace' imitating their Master, and crying out boldly against those who lay these heavy burdens upon the shoulders of the people?

"Few would think, when investing in the Turkish loans, that they were laying the train which has just exploded in the Turkish provinces with such disastrous effects, scattering so much ruin and desolation amongst the poor inhabitants there. No, they would only think what a good investment it was, and what a large interest the Turkish Government had engaged to pay for the accommodation. This is as far as borrower and lender usually look. The child wishes to hold the razor, the maniac wants the revolver; let them have them; it is their lookout, not ours, what use they make of them; and in this same spirit we callously hand over the wealth which the labour of England and its laws have put under our control, to a race of homicides, and sit supinely by while they, having transformed part of it into powder and shot, shower these relentlessly over their Christian subjects, till the heart of Europe turns sick at the sight.

"Now, let us follow the consequences, as they crop out in natural sequence. The Turk obtains his loan from Englishmen, and doubtless intends to pay the large interest he promised; but how has he to accomplish this? If he had had a Fortunatus' purse he would not have had to borrow. He has no such purse, but he has provinces, where a population of Christians are faithfully cultivating the soil, and in one way or another providing themselves with the means of existence. These have to be the Fortunatus' purse, out of which he will abstract the cash to pay the English lenders the promised interest on their loan. The principal he spends in luxurious living, and in providing the arguments (gunpowder and steel) which may be required to convince his Christian subjects that they owe the English lenders the interest he has engaged to pay for the loan. The loan itself, of course, had been con-tracted for their protection and defence !

" Here, then, we come to the old story. His tax-farming agents have to apply the screw of higher taxes to the people, demanding more and still more, to pay these English lenders their interest, till human pa-tience reaches its limit ; and the provinces revolt, resolved to be free from those unjust and cruel exactions, or to perish in the attempt. The rest is all too well known to need recapitulation. Every one knows how the Turkish hordes rushed down upon the patient people whom they had despoiled for centuries, like an avalanche of fire and steel, and the horrors and abominations that ensued. Yet, when a neigh-bouring monarch, of kindred faith to the suffering provinces, demanded (with an

> ' Avenge, O Lord, Thy slaughtered Saints, whose bones
> Lie scattered o'er Bulgaria's mountains cold ')

that these oppressions and atrocities should cease, as our Oliver Crom-well did effectually two centuries ago, when similar atrocities were be-ing perpetrated in Piedmont, what did we see ?

" To the everlasting shame of England, we saw its fleet despatched to Besika Bay, as a menace to Russia not to put an end to these iniquities, and as a hint to Turkey to stamp out the revolt as quickly as possible, and by whatever means it might see fit to employ.

" Now to what have we to attribute this degradation of the British flag and British influence ? Is it to secure British interests, the inter-est of a beggarly fifty millions, or thereabouts, of foolishly invested money, that our jolly tars have to be despatched to give at least moral support and countenance to the murderers of women and children ?

" Why, take it on this mercenary ground, and calculate what those Christians, if freed from their thraldom to the Turk, might make out of this ' fairest part of God's creation ' in a year or two, and the result will be astonishing. An agricultural race like the French, in a year, would raise ten times fifty millions' worth of produce from the ground which Turkish rule is only cumbering. Then is it not time this cum-berer were cut down ? It has been let alone for centuries, and we, as its special husbandman, with a zeal worthy of a better cause, have been digging about it and dunging it (to our cost), and all to no purpose, and yet we have statesmen who think this fruitless—Heaven's lightning-struck—old trunk must still be nourished as a shelter and protection to our interests in the East.

" These Turks, whom a few are so anxious to protect, have been a curse to Europe ever since they entered it. Their first generally known atrocities upon Christians were the massacres and outrages on the pil-grims who, in the middle ages, were visiting the Holy Sepulchre. Serve them right for their folly, say many. But call it our ' ancient muni-ments,' and how then ? What would be said if a party from London, visiting Stonehenge, had to get their heads broken by the people of Salisbury for their folly ? These atrocities roused the chivalry of the Christian nations of Europe, and gave rise to the Crusades. These eventually led to the Turks' entrance into Europe, which they were likely to overrun, when Sobieski, ' a man sent from God, whose name was John,' came to the front and drove them back again. Ever since their appearance, they have been a thorn in the side of Europe—a thorn which should long ere this have been extracted.

" Should Europe extract this thorn now, and send this man of the sword back to his native deserts, and place a guard of Christian knights in charge of Constantinople, to teach him, should he attempt to return, that ' all they that take the sword shall perish with the sword,' then the nations of Europe, too long crushed under the weight of ' bloated armaments' and standing armies, might begin to study the art of peace.

" Then might we begin to regard ironclads and Woolwich infants as demons from the pit, which some of our bishops might venture to exorcise as monsters that were devouring widows' houses every day they floated, or every time they were discharged ; and which had no right to exist in a Christian or sane community. Then, too, we might find that Russia was, after all, no more a bear than England was a lion ; and that, though peopled with men with passions like our own, they had them not less bridled than we, and could prove themselves to be men of honour, men to be trusted, and men who desired to stand by the principles of right and justice, be the consequences what they might, even though the heavens should fall and earthly patronisers of the angels be dissatisfied.—I am, etc., COSMOPOLITAN."

IV. I am grieved to leave my Scottish correspondent's letter still without reply. But it is unconnected with the subjects on which I wish to lay stress in this letter ; and I want to give its own most important subject a distinct place.

ERRATUM.—In *Fors* of December last, p. 351, *for* XXIII., *read* XXXIII.

LETTER LXXV.

VENICE, 1*st February*, 1877.

I AM told that some of my "most intelligent readers" can make nothing of what I related in last *Fors*, about St. Ursula's messages to me. What is their difficulty? Is it (1), that they do not believe in guardian angels,—or (2), that they do not think me good enough to have so great an angel to guard me,—or (3), that knowing the beginning of her myth, they do not believe in St. Ursula's personality?

If the first, I have nothing more to say ;—if the second, I can assure them, they are not more surprised than I was myself ;—if the third, they are to remember that all great myths are conditions of slow manifestation to human imperfect intelligence ; and that whatever spiritual powers are in true personality appointed to go to and fro in the earth, to trouble the waters of healing, or bear the salutations of peace, can only be revealed, in their reality, by the gradual confirmation in the matured soul of what at first were only its instinctive desires, and figurative perceptions.

Oh me ! I had so much to tell you in this *Fors*, if I could but get a minute's peace ;—my stories of the Venetian doggie, and others of the greater dog and the lesser dog—in Heaven ; and more stories of Little bear in Venice, and of the Greater bear and Lesser bear in Heaven ; and more of the horses of St. Mark's, in Venice, and of Pegasus and the chivalry of Heaven ;—ever so much more of the selling of lemons in Venice, and of the twelve manner of fruits in Heaven for the healing of the nations. And here's an infernal paragraph about you, in your own Sheffield, sent me in a Lincoln paper by some people zealous for schools of art, —poor fools !—which is like to put it all out of my head. Of that presently. I *must* try to keep to my business.

Well, the beginning of all must be, as quickly as I can, to

VOL. III.—26

show you the full meaning of the nineteenth Psalm. "Cœli enarrant ; " the heavens declare—or make clear—the honour of God ; which I suppose, in many a windy oratorio, this spring, will be loudly declared by basses and tenors, to tickle the ears of the public, who don't believe one word of the song all the while !

But it is a true song, none the less ; and you must try to understand it before we come to anything else ; for these Heavens, so please you, are the real roof, as the earth is the real floor, of God's house for you here, rentless, by His Law. That word 'cœli,' in the first words of the Latin psalm, means the 'hollow place.' It is the great space, or, as we conceive it, vault, of Heaven. It shows the glory of God in the existence of the light by which we live. All force is from the sun.

The firmament is the ordinance of the clouds and sky of the world.* It shows the handiwork of God. He daily paints that for you ; constructs, as He paints,—beautiful things, if you will look,—terrible things, if you will think. Fire and hail, snow and vapour, stormy wind, (cyclone and other) fulfilling His Word. The Word of God, printed in very legible type of gold on lapis-lazuli, needing no translation of yours, no colporteurship. There is no speech nor language where *their* voice is not heard. Their sound is gone out into all lands, and their word to the ends of the world. In them hath He set a tabernacle for the Sun, the Lord of Physical Life ; in them also, a tabernacle for the Sun of Justice, the Lord of Spiritual Life. And the light of this Sun of the Spirit is divided into this measured Iris of colours :—

I. The Law of the Lord. Which is perfect, converting the soul.

That is the constant law of creation, which breathes life into matter, soul into life.

II. The testimonies of the Lord. Which are sure, —making wise the simple.

These are what He has told us of His law, by the lips of

* See *Modern Painters*, in various places.

the prophets,—from Enoch, the seventh from Adam, by Moses, by Hesiod, by David, by Elijah, by Isaiah, by the Delphic Sibyl, by Dante, by Chaucer, by Giotto. Sure testimonies all ; their witness agreeing together, making wise the simple—that is to say, all holy and humble men of heart.

III. THE STATUTES OF THE LORD. Which are right, and rejoice the heart.

These are the appointed conditions that govern human life ;—that reward virtue, infallibly ; punish vice, infallibly ; —gladsome to see in operation. The righteous shall be glad when he seeth the vengeance—how much more in the mercy to thousands ?

IV. THE COMMANDMENT OF THE LORD. Which is pure, enlightening the eyes.

This is the written law—under (as we count) ten articles, but in many more, if you will read. Teaching us, in so many words, when we cannot discern it unless we are told, what the will of our Master is.

V. THE FEAR OF THE LORD. Which is clean, enduring for ever.

Fear, or faith,—in this sense one : the human faculty that purifies, and enables us to see this sunshine ; and to be warmed by it, and made to live for ever in it.

VI. THE JUDGMENTS OF THE LORD. Which are true, and righteous altogether.

These are His searchings out and chastisements of our sins ; His praise and reward of our battle ; the fiery trial that tries us, but is "no strange thing"; the crown that is laid up for all that love His appearing. More to be desired are they than gold ;—(David thinks first of these special judgments)—Sweeter than honey, or the honeycomb ;— moreover by them is Thy servant warned, and in keeping of them there is great reward. Then—pausing—"Who can understand his errors? Cleanse Thou me from the faults I know not, and keep me from those I know ; and let the

words of my lips, and the thoughts of my brain, be acceptable in thy open sight—oh Lord my strength, who hast made
me,—my Redeemer, who hast saved."

That is the natural and the spiritual astronomy of the
nineteenth Psalm ; and now you must turn back at once to
the analysis given you of the eighth, in *Fors*, May, 1875.

For as, in the one, David looking at the sun in his light,
passes on to the thought of the Light of God, which is His
law, so in the eighth Psalm, looking at the sun on his throne,
as the ruler and guide of the state of Heaven, he passes on
to the thoughts of the throne and state of man, as the ruler
and light of the World : Thou hast made him a little lower
than the angels,—Thou hast put all things under his feet,—
beasts and all cattle, creeping things and flying fowl.

It is of this dominion in love over the lower creatures that
I have to speak to-day : but I must pause a moment to point
out to you the difference between David's astronomy with
his eyes, and modern astronomy with telescopes.*

David's astronomy with the eyes, first rightly humbles
him,—then rightly exalts ;—What is man that Thou so
regardest him—yet, how Thou hast regarded ! But modern
astronomy with telescope first wrongly exalts us, then
wrongly humbles.

First, it wrongly exalts. Lo and behold—we can see a
dozen stars where David saw but one ; we know how far
they are from each other ; nay, we know where they will all
be, the day after to-morrow, and can make almanacks. What
wise people are we ! Solomon, and all the Seven Sages of
Greece,—where are they ? Socrates, Plato, and Epaminondas—what talk you to us of them ! Did they know, poor
wretches, what the Dog Star smelt of ?

We are generally content to pause at this pleasant stage
of self-congratulation ; by no means to ask further what the
general conclusions of the telescope may be, concerning ourselves. It might, to some people, perhaps seem a deficiency
in the telescope that it could discern no Gods in heaven ;
that, for all we could make out, it saw through the Gods,

* Compare the whole of the lecture on Light, in *Eagle's Nest.*

and out at the other side of them. Mere transparent space, where we thought there were houses, and gardens, and rivers, and angels, and what not. The British public does not concern itself about losses of that nature : behold, there is the Universe ; and here are we, the British public, in the exact middle of it, and scientific of it in the accuratest manner. What a fine state of things ! Oh, proud British public, have you ever taken this telescopic information well into your minds ; and considered what it verily comes to?

Go out on the seashore when the tide is down, on some flat sand ; and take a little sand up into your palm, and separate one grain of it from the rest. Then try to fancy the relation between that single grain and the number in all the shining fields of the far distant shore, and onward shores immeasurable. Your astronomer tells you, your world is such a grain compared with the worlds that are, but that he can see no inhabitants on them, no sign of habitation, or of beneficence. Terror and chance, cold and fire, light struck forth by collision, desolateness of exploding orb and flying meteor. Meantime—you, on your grain of sand—what are you ? The little grain is itself mostly uninhabitable ; has a damp green belt in the midst of it. In that,—poor small vermin,—you live your span, fighting with each other for food, most of the time ; or building—if perchance you are at peace—filthy nests, in which you perish of starvation, phthisis, profligate diseases, or despair. There is a history of civilization for you ! briefer than Mr. Buckle's, and more true—when you see the Heavens and Earth without their God.

It is a fearful sight, and a false one. In what manner or way I neither know nor ask ; this I know, that if a prophet touched your eyes, you might in an instant see all those eternal spaces filled with the heavenly host ; and this also I know, that if you will begin to watch these stars with your human eyes, and learn what noble men have thought of them, and use their light to noble purposes, you will enter into a better joy and better science then ever eye hath seen.

" Take stars for money—stars, not to be told
By any art,—yet to be purchased."

I have nothing to do, nor have you, with what is happening in space, (or possibly may happen in time,) we have only to attend to what is happening here—and now. Yonder stars are rising. Have you ever noticed their order, heard their ancient names, thought of what they were, as teachers, 'lecturers,' in that large public hall of the night, to the wisest men of old? Have you ever thought of the direct promise to you yourselves, that you may be like them if you will? "They that be wise, shall shine as the brightness of the firmament; and they that turn many to righteousness, as the stars, for ever and ever."

They that be *wise.* Don't think that means knowing how big the moon is. It means knowing what you ought to do, as man or woman; what your duty to your father is, to your child, to your neighbour, to nations your neighbours. A wise head of the English Government for instance, (Oliver, had he been alive,) would have sent word, a year ago, to the Grand Signior, that if he heard a word more of 'atrocities' in Bulgaria after next week, he would blow his best palace into the Bosphorus. Irrespective of all other considerations, that was the first thing to be wisely said, and done, if needful. What *has* been said and *not* done, since,—the quantities of print printed, and talk talked, by every conceivable manner of fool,—not an honest syllable in all the lot of it, (for even Mr. Bright's true and rational statement— the only *quite* right word, as far as I can judge, I've seen written on the business,* that Russians had as much right to the sea, everywhere, as anybody else, was tainted by his party spirit), I only wish I could show, in a heap of waste paper, to be made a bonfire of on Snowdon top.

That, I repeat, was the one simple, knightly, English-

---

* I do not venture to speak of the general statements in my master Carlyle's letter; but it seemed to me to dwell too much on the idea of total destruction to the Turk, and to involve considerations respecting the character of Turk and Russian not properly bearing on the business. It is not, surely, 'the Eastern Question' whether Turkey shall exist, or Russia triumph, but whether we shall or shall not stop a man in a turban from murdering a Christian.

hearted thing to be done ; and so far as the 'Interests of England' are concerned, her first interest was in this, to *be* England ; and not a filthy nest of tax-gatherers and horse-dealers. For the horse-dealer and the man-dealer are alike ignoble persons, and their interests are of little consequence. But the horse-rider and the man-ruler, which was England's ancient notion of a man, and Venice's also, (of which, in abrupt haste, but true sequence, I must now speak,) have interests of a higher kind. But, if you would well understand what I have next to tell you, you must first read the opening chapter of my little Venetian guide, *St. Mark's Rest*, which will tell you something of the two piazzetta shafts, of which Mr. Swan has now photographs to show you at St. George's Museum ; and my Venetian readers, on the other hand, must have this *Fors* to tell them the meaning of the statues on the top of said pillars.

These are, in a manner, her Jacob's pillars, set up for a sign that God was with her. And she put on one of them, the symbol of her standard-bearer, St. Mark ; and on the other, the statue of 'St. Theodore,' whose body, like St. Mark's, she had brought home as one of her articles of commercial wealth ; and whose legend—what was it, think you ? —What Evangel or Gospel is this, to be put level with St. Mark's, as the banner on the other wing of the Venetian Host ?

Well, briefly, St. Mark is their standard-bearer in the war of their spirit against all spiritual evil ; St. Theodore, their standard-bearer in the war of their body against material and fleshly evil :—not the evil of sin, but of *material malignant force*. St. Michael is the angel of war against the dragon of sin ; but St. Theodore, who also is not merely a saint, but an angel, is the angel of noble fleshly life in man and animals, leading both against base and malignant life in men and animals. He is the Chevalier, or Cavalier, of Venice,—her first of loving knights, in war against all baseness, all malignity ; in the deepest sense, St. Theodore, literally 'God gift,' is Divine life in nature ; Divine Life in the flesh of the animal, and in the substance of the wood and

of the stone, contending with poison and death in the animal,—with rottenness in the tree, and in the stone. He is first seen, (I can find no account of his birth,) in the form of a youth of extreme beauty ; and his first contest is with a dragon very different from St. George's ; and it is fought in another manner. So much of the legend I must give you in Venice's own words, from her Mother-Rule of St. Theodore, —the Rule, from the thirteenth century down, of her chief Club, or School, of knights and gentlemen. But meditate a little while first on that Venetian word, "Mother-Law." You were told, some time since, in *Fors*, by an English lawyer, that it was not a lawyer's business to make laws. He spoke truth—not knowing what he said. It is only God's business to make laws. None other's than His ever were made, or will be. And it is lawyers' business to read and enforce the same ; however laughable such notion of this function may be to the persons bearing present name of lawyer.*
I walked with one of these—the Recorder of London—to and fro beside a sweet river bank in South England, a year ago ; he discoursing of his work for public benefit. He was employed, at that time, in bringing before Parliament, in an acceptably moderate form, the demand of the Railroad Companies to tax the English people to the extent of six millions, as payment for work they had expected to have to do ; and were *not* to do.

A motherly piece of law, truly ! many such Mariegolas your blessed English liberties provide you with ! All the while, more than mother, "for she *may* forget, yet will I not forget thee "—your loving Lord in Heaven pleads with you in the everlasting law, of which all earthly law, that shall ever stand, is part ; lovable, infinitely ; binding, as the bracelet upon the arm—as the shield upon the neck ; covering, as the hen gathereth her brood under her wings ; guiding, as the nurse's hand the tottering step ; ever watchful, merciful,

---

* Compare *Unto this Last*, in the note, significant of all my future work, at page 78. (I am about to republish this book page for page in its first form.)

life-giving ; Mariegola to the souls,—and to the dust,—of all the world.

This of St. Theodore's was first written, in visible letters for men's reading, here at Venice, in the year 1258. " At which time we all, whose names are written below, with a gracious courage, with a joyful mind, with a perfect will, and with a single spirit,* to the honour of the most holy sav-

---

* " Cum gratiosæ mente, cum alegro anemo, cum sincera voluntate, et cum uno spirito, ad honor de lo santissimo salvador et signor nostro, misier Jesucristo et de la gloriosa verghene madona senta maria soa mare."

So much of the dialect of Venice, in mid-thirteenth century, the reader may bear with; the ' mens ' being kept in the Homeric sense still, of fixed purpose, as of Achilles. It is pretty to see the word ' Mother ' passing upon the Venetian lips into ' sea.'

The precious mariegola from which these passages are taken was first, I believe, described by Mr. Edward Cheney, *Remarks on the Illuminated Manuscripts of the early Venetian Republic*, page 13. Of the manuscript written in 1258 there remain however only two leaves, both illuminated : (see notes on them in fifth chapter of *St. Mark's Rest*,) the text is the copy of the original one, written after 1400. Mr. Cheney's following account of the nature of the ' Schools ' of Venice, of which this was the earliest, sums all that the general reader need learn on this subject :—

" Though religious confraternities are supposed to have existed at a much earlier period, their first *historical* mention at Venice dates from the middle of the thirteenth century. They were of various sorts some were confined to particular guilds and callings, while others included persons of every rank and profession.

" The first object of all these societies was religious and charitable. Good works were to be performed, and the practices of piety cherished. In all, the members were entitled to receive assistance from the society in times of need, sickness, or any other adversity.

" The ' Confraternita Grandi,' (though all had the same object,) were distinguished by the quantity, as well as by the quality, of their members, by their superior wealth, and by the magnificence of the buildings in which they assembled : buildings which still exist, and still excite the admiration of posterity, though the societies to which they owed their existence have been dispossessed and suppressed.

" The ' Confraternità Piccole,' less wealthy, and less magnificently lodged, were not the less constituted societies, with their own rules and charters, and having their own chapel, or altar, in the church of their patron-saint, in the sacristy of which their ' mariegola ' was usually pre-

iour and lord sir Jesus christ, and of the glorious virgin madonna saint mary his mother, and of the happy and blessed sir saint theodore, martyr and cavalier of God,— ('martir et cavalier de dio')—and of all the other saints and saintesses of God," (have set our names,—understood) " to the end that the abovesaid sir, sir saint theodore, who stands continually before the throne of God, with the other saints, may pray to our Lord Jesus christ that we all, brothers and sisters, whose names are underwritten, may have by his most sacred pity and mercy, remission of our minds, and pardon of our sins."

"Remission of mind" is what we now profess to ask for in our common prayer, " Create in me a clean heart, oh Lord, and renew a right spirit within me." Whereupon follow the stories of the contest and martyrdom of St. Theodore, and of the bringing his body to Venice. Of which tradition, this is the passage for the sake of which I have been thus tedious to you.

"For in that place there was a most impious dragon, which, when it moved, the earth trembled ; when it came forth of its cave, whatsoever it met, it devoured.

"Then St. Theodore said in his heart, ' I will go, and of my Father's substance,* will strive with the most impious dragon.' So he came into the very place, and found there grass with flowers, and lighted down off his horse, and slept, not knowing that in that place was the cave of the dragon. And a kind woman, whose name was Eusebia, a Christian, and fearing God, while she past, saw St. Theodore sleeping, and went with fear, and 'took him by the hand, and raised him up, saying, ' Rise, my brother, and leave this place, for, being a youth, you know not, as I see, the fear that is in

served. Many of the confraternities had a temporal as well as a spiritual object, and those which were composed exclusively of members of the same trade regulated their worldly concerns, and established the rules by which the Brothers of the Guild should be bound. Their byelaws were subject to the approval of the Government ; they were stringent and exclusive, and were strictly enforced. No competition was allowed."

* " Litor paterne substantie mee."

this place. A great fear is here. But rise quickly, and go thy way.' Then the martyr of Christ rose and said, ' Tell me, woman, what fear is in this place.' The maidservant of God answered, saying, 'Son, a most impious dragon inhabits this place, and no one can pass through it.' Then St. Theodore made for himself the sign of the cross, and smiting on his breast, and looking up to heaven, prayed, saying, 'Jesus, the Son of the living God, who of the substance of the Father didst shine forth for our salvation, do not slack my prayer which I pray of thee, (because thou in battle hast always helped me and given me victory) that I may conquer this explorer of the Devil.' Thus saying, he turned to his horse, and speaking to him as to a man, said, 'I know that in all things I have sinned against thee, oh God, who, whether in man or beast, hast always fought with me. Oh thou horse of Christ, comfort thee, be strong like a man, and come, that we may conquer the contrary enemy.' And as the horse heard his master saying prayerful words, (rogalia verba,) he stood, looking forth as with human aspect, here and there ; expecting the motion of the dragon. Then the blessed Theodore with a far-sent voice cried, and said, ' Dragon, I say to thee, and give precept to thee in the name of my Lord Jesus Christ, who is crucified for the human race, that thou shouldest come out of thy place, and come to me.' Instantly as he heard the voice of St. Theodore, he prepared himself that he should go out to him. And he moving himself and raging, presently in that place the stones were moved, and the earth trembled . . . . Then the blessed Theodore, as he saw him moving himself in his fury, mounted his horse, and trampled him down, and the horse, giving a leap, rose over the most impious dragon, trampling it down with all its four feet. Then the most strong martyr of Christ, St. Theodore, extending his lance, struck it through the heart, and it lay stretched out dead."

VENICE, *Purification of the Virgin*, 1877.

Oh me, again, how am I ever to tell you the infinite of meaning in this all-but-forgotten story. It is eleven years to-day since the 2nd of February became a great festival to me : now, like all the days of all the years, a shadow ; deeper, this, in beautiful shade. The sun has risen cloudless, and I have been looking at the light of it on the edges of St. Ursula's flower, which is happy with me, and has four buds bursting, and one newly open flower, which the first sunbeams filled with crimson light down under every film of petal ; whose jagged edges of paler rose broke over and over each other, tossed here and there into crested flakes of petal foam, as if the Adriatic breakers had all been changed into crimson leaves at the feet of Venice-Aphrodite. And my dear old Chamouni guide, Joseph Contet, is dead ; he who said of me, " le pauvre enfant,—il ne sait pas vivre " and (another time) he would give me nine sous a day, to keep cows, as that was all I was worth, for aught he could see. Captain of Mont Blanc, in his time,—eleven times up it, before Alpine clubs began ; like to have been left in a crevasse of the Grand Plateau, where three of his mates were left, indeed ; he, fourth of the line, under Dr. Hamel, just brought out of the avalanche-snow breathing. Many a merry walk he took me in his onward years—fifty-five or so, thirty years ago. Clear in heart and mind to the last, if you let him talk ; wandering a little if you wanted him to listen ;—I have known younger people with somewhat of that weakness. And so, he took to his bed, and—ten days ago, as I hear, said, one evening, to his daughter Judith, "Bon soir, je pars pour l'autre monde," and so went. And thinking of him, and of others now in that other world, this story of St. Theodore, which is only of the Life in this, seems partly comfortless. 'Life in nature.' There's another dead friend, now, to think of, who could have taught us much, James Hinton ; gone, he also, and we are here with guides of the newest, mostly blind, and proud of finding their way always with a stick. If they trusted in their dogs, one would love them a little for their dogs' sakes. But they only vivisect their dogs.

If I don't tell you my tale of the Venetian doggie at once, it's all over with it. How so much love and life can be got into a little tangle of floss silk, St. Theodore knows ; not I ; and its master is one of the best servants in this world, to one of the best masters. It was to be drowned, soon after its eyes had opened to the light of sea and sky,—a poor worthless wet flake of floss silk it had like to have been, presently. Toni pitied it, pulled it out of the water, bought it for certain sous, brought it home under his arms. What it learned out of his heart in that half-hour, again, St. Theodore knows ;—but the mute spiritual creature has been his own, verily, from that day, and only lives for him. Toni, being a pious Toni as well as a pitiful, went this last autumn, in his holiday, to see the Pope ; but did not think of taking the doggie with him, (who, St. Theodore would surely have said, ought to have seen the Pope too.) Whereupon, the little silken mystery wholly refused to eat. No coaxing, no tempting, no nursing, would cheer the desolate-minded thing from that sincere fast. It would drink a little, and was warmed and medicined as best might be. Toni came back from Rome in time to save it ; but it was not its gay self again for many and many a day after ; the terror of such loss, as yet again possible, weighing on the reviving mind, (stomach, supposably, much out of order also). It greatly dislikes getting itself wet ; for, indeed, the tangle of its mortal body takes half a day to dry ; some terror and thrill of uncomprehended death, perhaps, remaining on it, also,—who knows ; but once, after this terrible Roman grief, running along the quay cheerfully beside rowing Toni, it saw him turn the gondola's head six feet aside, as if going away. The dog dashed into the water like a mad thing. " See, now, if aught but death part thee and me."

Indistinguishable, doubtless, in its bones from a small wolf : according to Mr. Waterhouse Hawkins ; but much distinguishable, by St. Theodore's theology, telling of God, down, thus far at least, in nature. Emmanuel,—with us ; in Raphael, in Tobias, in all loving and lowly things ; "the young man's dog went with them."

And in those Adriatic breakers, anger-fringed, is He also ?

—Effice queso, fretum, Raphael reverende, quietum.* And in the Dragons also, as in the deeps? Where is the battle to begin? How far down in the darkness lies this enemy, for whom Hell beneath is moved at the sound of his coming?

I must not keep you longer with mythic teaching to-day; but may briefly tell you that this dragon is the ' Rahab ' which I mistook in the 86th Psalm; the crocodile, spiritually named for the power of Egypt, with that of Babylon. Look in the indices of *Fors* for the word "Crocodile," and remember that the lifted cobra is the crest of the Egyptian Kings, as the living crocodile their idol. Make what you can out of that, till I have more time to tell you of Egyptian animal and herb gods; meantime, for the practical issue of all this.

I have told you the wealth of the world consists, for one great article, in its useful animals.

How to get the most you can of those, and the most serviceable?

"Rob the squires' stables, to begin with?"

No, good friends,—no. Their stables have been to them as the first wards of Hell, locked on them in this life, for these three hundred years. But you must not open them that way, even for their own sakes.

"Poach the squires' game?"

No, good friends,—no. Down among the wild en'mies, the dust of many a true English keeper forbids you that form of theft, for ever.

"Poison the squires' hounds, and keep a blood bull terrier?"

Worse and worse—merry men, all.

No—here's the beginning. Box your own lad's ears the first time you see him shy a stone at a sparrow; and heartily, too: but put up, you and mother—(and thank God for the blessed persecution,)—with every conceivable form of vermin the boy likes to bring into the house,†—and go hungry yourselves rather than not feed his rat or his rabbit.

* Engraved above the statute of Raphael on the Ducal Palace.

† See the life of Thomas Edwards: (abstract given in *Times* of January 22nd of this year).

Then, secondly,—you want to be a gentleman yourself, I suppose ?

Well, you can't be, as I have told you before, nor I neither ; and there's an end, neither of us being born in the caste : but you may get some pieces of gentlemen's education, which will lead the way to you son's being a better man than you.

And of all essential things in a gentleman's bodily and mortal training, this is really the beginning—that he should have close companionship with the horse, the dog, and the eagle. Of all birthrights and bookrights—this is his first. He needn't be a Christian,—there have been millions of Pagan gentlemen ; he needn't be kind—there have been millions of cruel gentlemen ; he needn't be honest,—there have been millions of crafty gentlemen. He needn't know how to read, or to write his own name. But he *must* have horse, dog, and eagle for friends. If then he has also Man for his friend, he is a noble gentleman ; and if God for his Friend, a king. And if, being honest, being kind, and having God and Man for his friends, he *then* gets these three brutal friends, besides his angelic ones, he is perfect in earth, as for heaven. For, to be his friends, these must be brought up with him, and he with them. Falcon on fist, hound at foot, and horse part of himself—Eques, Ritter, Cavalier, Chevalier.

Yes ;—horse and dog you understand the good of ; but what's the good of the falcon, think you ?

To be friends with the falcon must mean that you love to see it soar ; that is to say, you love fresh air and the fields. Farther, when the Law of God is understood, you will like better to see the eagle free than the jessed hawk. And to preserve your eagles' nests, is to be a great nation. It means keeping everything that is noble ; mountains, and floods, and forests, and the glory and honour of them, and all the birds that haunt them. If the eagle takes more than his share, you may shoot him,—(but with the knight's arrow, not the blackguard's gun)—and not till then.

Meantime, for you are of course by no means on the direct way to the accomplishment of all this, your way to such

wealth, so far as in your present power, is this : first, acknowledgment of the mystery of divine life, kindly and
dreadful, throughout creation ; then the taking up your own
part as the Lord of this life ; to protect, assist, or extinguish,
as it is commanded you. Understand that a mad dog is to be
slain ; though with pity—infinitude of pity,—(and much
more, a mad *man*, of an injurious kind ; for a mad dog only
bites flesh ; but a mad man, spirit : get your rogue, the
supremely maddest of men, with supreme pity always, but
inexorably, hanged). But to all good and sane men and
beasts, be true brother ; and as it is best, perhaps, to begin
with all things in the lowest place, begin with true brotherhood to the beast : in pure simplicity of practical help, I
should like a squad of you to stand always harnessed, at the
bottom of any hills you know of in Sheffield, where the
horses strain ;—ready there at given hours ; carts ordered not
to pass at any others : at the low level, hook yourselves on
before the horses ; pull them up too, if need be ; and dismiss
them at the top with a pat and a mouthful of hay. Here's
a beginning of chivalry, and gentlemanly life for you, my
masters.

Then next, take *canal* life as a form of 'university' education.

Your present system of education is to get a rascal of an
architect to order a rascal of a clerk-of-the-works to order a
parcel of rascally bricklayers to build you a bestially stupid
building in the middle of the town, poisoned with gas, and
with an iron floor which will drop you all through it some
frosty evening ; wherein you will bring a puppet of a cockney lecturer in a dress coat and a white tie, to tell you
smuggly there's no God, and how many messes he can make
of a lump of sugar. Much the better you are for all that,
when you get home again, aren't you ?

I was going here to follow up what our Companion had told
us (Fors, December, 1876, Art. V. of Corr.), about the Hull
'keels' ; and to show you how an entirely refined life was
conceivable in these water cottages, with gardens all along
the shore of them, and every possible form of wholesome ex-

ercise and teaching for the children, in management of boat and horse, and other helpfulness by land and water ; but as I was beginning again to walk in happy thought beside the courses of quiet water that wind round the low hill-sides above our English fields,—behold, the *Lincoln Gazette*, triumphant in report of Art-exhibitions and competitions, is put into my hand,—with this notable paragraph in it, which Fors points me to, scornful of all else :—

"A steam engine was used for the first time on Wednesday," (January 24th), "in drawing tram-cars through the crowded streets of Sheffield. The tramways there are about to dispense with the whole of their horses, and to adopt steam as the motive power."

And doubtless the Queen will soon have a tramway to Parliament, and a kettle to carry her there, and steam-horse guards to escort her. Meantime, my pet cousin's three little children have just had a Christmas present made to them of a real live Donkey ; and are happier, I fancy, than either the Queen or you. I must write to congratulate them ; so good-bye for this time, and pleasant drives to you.

NOTES AND CORRESPONDENCE.

I. Affairs of the Company.

I hope the accounts last month, with their present supplement, will be satisfactory. The sense of steady gain, little by little indeed, but infallible, will become pleasant, and even triumphant, as time goes on.

The present accounts supply some omissions in the general ones, but henceforward I think we need not give Mr. Walker or Mr. Ryding the trouble of sending in other than half-yearly accounts.

The best news for this month is the accession of three nice Companions; one sending us two hundred pounds for a first tithe; and the others, earnest and experienced mistresses of schools, having long worked under St. George's orders in their hearts, are now happy in acknowledging him, and being acknowledged. Many a young creature will have her life made happy and noble by their ministry.

THE UNION BANK OF LONDON (CHANCERY LANE BRANCH) IN ACCOUNT WITH ST. GEORGE'S COMPANY.

				£	s.	d.
Dr.						
1877.	Jan. 1.	To Balance.......................		191	9	1
	23.	" Per Mr. John Ruskin, cheque at				
		Bridgwater (Talbot)..	£50 0 0			
		Ditto ditto	26 11 3			
		Sheffield (Fowler)..	20 0 0			
				96	11	3
	25.	" Per ditto, draft at Brighton (Moss)		200	0	0
	26.	" Per Mrs. Bradley...............		7	0	0
	29.	" Per Mr. John Ruskin (Mr. Ryding's				
		cheque)		33	13	4
	Feb. 15.	" Per ditto, draft at Bridgwater				
		(Browne)		100	0	0
				£628	13	8
Cr.						
1877.	Feb. 15.	By Balance		£628	13	8

II. Affairs of the Master.

I believe I have enough exhibited my simplicities to the public,—the more that, for my own part, I rather enjoy talking about myself, even in my follies. But my expenses here in Venice require more illustration than I have time for, or think *Fors* should give space to ; the Companions will be content in knowing that my banker's balance, February 5, was £1030 14*s.* 7*d.* ; but that includes £118 10*s.*, dividend on St. George's Consols, now paid by the trustees to my account for current expenses. The complete exposition of my present standing in the world I reserve for the Month of Opening.

III.
"EDINBURGH, *November* 2, 1876.

" I have been for some time a pupil of yours, at first in art, where I am only a beginner, but later in those things which belong to my profession, (of minister). Will you allow this to be my excuse for addressing you ?—the subject of my letter will excuse the rest.

" I write to direct your attention to an evil which is as yet unattacked, in hopes that you may be moved to lift your hand against it; one that is gaining virulence among us in Scotland. I know no way so good by which its destruction may be compassed as to ask your help, and I know no other way.

" I shall state the mere facts as barely as I can, being sure that whatever my feelings about them may be, they will affect you more powerfully." (Alas, good friend—you have no notion yet what a stony heart I've got !) " I know you say that letters need not ask you to *do* anything ; but that you should be asked for help in this case, and not give it, I believe to be impossible. Please read this letter, and see if that is not true ; the next four pages may be missed, if the recent regulations made to carry out the Anti-Patronage Act have engaged your attention. The evil I speak of has to do with them.

" This Act made the congregation the electors of their pastor, the Government leaving the General Assembly to regulate the process of election. It has enacted that the congregation meet and choose a committee to make inquiries, to select and submit to a second meeting of voters the names of one or more clergymen, whom they (the committee) are agreed to recommend. It is then in the power of the congregation to approve or disapprove the report ; if the latter, a new committee is appointed ; if the former, they proceed to elect ; then if one name only is submitted, they accept it, and call the clergyman named to be their pastor ; if more than one, to choose between them by voting.

" But the Assembly did not venture to take precautions against an abuse of which every one knew there was danger, or rather certainty. Everyone knew that the congregations would not consent to choose without greater knowledge of the men to be chosen from, than could be obtained by means of the committee ; and every one knew also of what sort was the morality popular on the subject. And what has happened is this : between the first meeting (to elect a committee), and the second meeting (to elect a minister), the church is turned into a theatre for the display and enjoyment of the powers—physical, mental, and devotional —of the several candidates.

" On a vacancy being declared, and the committee appointed, these latter *find that they do not need to exert themselves to seek fit men!* " (Italics and note of admiration mine ;—this appearing to me a most wonderful discovery on the part of the committee, and indeed the tap-root of the mischief in the whole business.) " They are inundated with letters of application and testimonials from men who are seeking, not the appointment, but permission to preach before the congregation.

" The duties of the committee are practically confined to sifting " (with what aperture of sieve ?) "these applications, and selecting a certain number, from twelve to three, who are on successive Sundays to conduct public worship before the electors, who may thus compare and choose.

" When all the ' leet' (as it is called) have exhibited themselves, a second meeting is called, and the committee recommend two or three of those who are understood to be most ' popular,' and the vote is duly taken. At first it was only unordained licentiates who were asked to ' preach on the leet' (as they call it), and they only for parishes ; but nowadays—*i.e.*, this year—they ask and get men long ordained to do it ; men long ordained lay themselves out for it ; and for most assistantships (curacies) the same is required and given ; that is to say, that before a man can obtain leave to work he must shame himself, and everything which it is to be the labour of his life to sanctify. He is to be the minister of Christ, and begin that by being the devil's. I suppose his desire is to win the world for Christ : as he takes his first step forward to do so, there meets him the old Satan with the old offer (there is small question here of whether he appears visible or not), ' Some of this will I give thee, if thou wilt bow down and worship me.' You see how it is. He is to conduct a service which is a sham ; he is to pray, but not to Him he addresses ; to preach, but as a candidate, not as an ambassador for Christ. The prayer is a performance, his preaching a performance. It is just the devil laughing at Christ, and trying to make us join him in the mockery." (No, dear friend, not quite that. It is the Devil *acting* Christ ; a very different matter. The religious state which the Devil must attack by pretending religious zeal, is a very different one from that which he can attack—as our modern political economists, —by open scorn of it.)

" They are not consistent. There should be a mock baptism, a mock communion, a mock sick woman, to allow of more mock prayer and more mock comfort. Then they would see what the man could do— for a pastor's work is not confined to the usual Sunday service,—and could mark all the gestures and voice-modulations, and movements of legs and arms properly. I once was present as elector at one of these election-services, and can give my judgment of this people's ' privilege.' It simply made me writhe to see the man trying his best with face, figure, and voice to make an impression ; to listen to the competition sermon and the competition prayer : to look at him and think of George Eliot's ' Sold but not paid for.' The poor *people*,—will twenty years of faithful ministry afterwards so much as undo the evil done them in the one day ? They are forced to assemble in God's house for the purpose of making that house a theatre, and divine service a play, with themselves as actors. They are to listen to the sermon, but as critics : for them to join in the prayers they stand up or kneel to offer, would be unfaithfulness to the purpose of their gathering. They are then to listen and criticise—to enjoy, if they can. On future Sundays will not they find themselves doing the same ?

" I have not spoken to many about it, but what they say is this: 1. How else can the people know whom to choose ? (But that is not the question.) 2. The clergyman is doing so great a thing that he should forget himself in what he does—*id est*, he is to throw himself down (having gone to the temple to do it), and trust to the angels. Supposing that were right, it could make little difference: the actor may forget himself in 'Macbeth,' but he is not the less an actor; and it is not a case of forgetting or remembering, but of doing. Yet this has been urged to me by a leading ecclesiastic and by other good men; who, besides, ignored the two facts, that all clergymen are not Christians," (is this an *acknowledged* fact, then, in our Reformed Churches, and is it wholly impossible to ascertain whether the candidates do, or do not, possess so desirable a qualification?) "far less exalted Christians, and that the Church has no right to lead its clergy into temptation. 3. The people ought to listen as sinners, and worship as believers, even at such exhibitions; judging of the minister's abilities from their own impression afterwards. (This is met by the two facts stated above as applied to the lay members of the Church and congregation; and by this, that they are unfaithful to the main purpose of their meeting, if they lose sight of that purpose to listen and pray.) 4. That certainly a poor assistantship is not worth preaching and praying for, but that a good one, or a parish, is. 5. That one must conform to the spirit of the age. (Spirit of God at a discount.)

"To this long letter I add one remark: that the reasons why the Church submits to this state of things seem to be the desire of the ecclesiastical party in power to do nothing which may hinder the influx of Dissenters (who in Scotland enjoy the same privileges); and the fact that our feelings on the subject, never fine, are already coarsened still more by custom.

"Dear sir (if you will allow me to call you so), I have expressed myself ill, and not so that you can, from what I have written, put yourself in our place. But if you were among us, and could see how this is hurting everybody and everything, and corrupting all our better and more heavenward feelings,—how it is taking the heart out of our higher life, and making even our best things a matter of self-seeking and 'supply and demand,'—then you could not help coming to our rescue. I know the great and good works you have planned and wish to finish; but still, do this before it is too late for us. I seem to ask you as Cornelius did Peter. All Scotland is the worse for it, and it will spread to England. And after all you are one of us, one of the great army of Christ—I think a commander; and I claim your help, and beseech it, believing no one else can give what I ask.

"Ever your faithful servant to command,
"A LICENTIATE OF THE CHURCH OF SCOTLAND."

I can only answer provisionally this able and earnest letter, for the evils which my correspondent so acutely feels, and so closely describes, are indeed merely a minor consequence of the corruption of the motives, no less than the modes, of ordination, through the entire body of the Christian Churches. No way will ever be discovered of rightly ordaining men who have taken up the trade of preaching as a means of livelihood, and to whom it is matter of personal interest whether they preach in one place or another. Only those who have *left* their means of living, that they may preach, and whose peace follows them as they wander, and abides where they enter in, are of God's ordaining : and, practically, until the Church insists that every one of her ministers shall either have an independent income, or support himself, for his ministry on Sunday, by true bodily toil during the week, no word of the living Gospel will ever be spoken from her pulpits. How many of those who now occupy them have verily been invited to such office by the Holy Ghost, may be easily judged by observing how many the Holy Ghost has similarly invited, of religious persons already in prosperous business, or desirable position.

But, in themselves, the practices which my correspondent thinks so fatal, do not seem to me much more than ludicrous and indecorous. If a young clergyman's entire prospects in life depend, or seem to depend, on the issue of his candidature, he may be pardoned for en- deavouring to satisfy his audience by elocution and gesture, without suspicion, because of such efforts, of less sincerity in his purpose to fulfill to the best of his power the real duties of a Christian pastor : nor can I understand my correspondent's meaning when he asks, " Can twenty years undo the mischief of a day ? " I should have thought a quarter of an hour's honest preaching next Sunday quite enough to undo it.

And, as respects the direct sin in the anxious heart of the poor gesticulant orator, it seems to me that the wanderings of thought, or assumptions of fervour, in a discourse delivered at such a crisis, would be far more innocent in the eyes of the Judge of all, than the consistent deference to the opinions, or appeals to the taste, of his congregation, which may be daily observed, in any pulpit of Christendom, to warp the preacher's conscience, and indulge his pride.

And, although unacquainted with the existing organization of the Free Church of Scotland, I am so sure of the piety, fidelity, and good sense of many of her members, that I cannot conceive any serious diffi- culty in remedying whatever may be conspicuously indecorous in her present modes of Pastor-selection. Instead of choosing their clergymen by universal dispute, and victorious acclaim, might not the congregation appoint a certain number of—(may I venture to use the most signifi- cant word without offence ?)—*cardinal*-elders, to such solemn office ? Surely, a knot of sagacious old Scotchmen, accustomed to the temper, and agreeing in the theology, of their neighbours, might with satisfac- tion to the general flock adjudge the prize of Pastorship among the supplicant shepherds, without requiring the candidates to engage in competitive prayer, or exhibit from the pulpit prepared samples of polite exhortation, and agreeable reproof.

Perhaps, also, under such conditions, the former tenor of the young minister's life, and the judgment formed by his masters at school and college, of his character and capacity, might have more weight with the jury than the music of his voice or the majesty of his action ; and, in a church entirely desirous to do what was right in so grave a matter, another Elector might reverently be asked for His casting vote ; and the judgment of elders, no less than the wishes of youth, be subdued to the final and faithful petition,

"Show whether of these two, *Thou* hast chosen."

IV. The following noble letter will not eventually be among the least important of the writings of my Master. Its occasion, (I do not say its subject, for the real gist of it lies in that sentence concerning the Catechism,) is closely connected with that of the preceding letter. My ecclesiastical correspondent should observe that the Apostles of the Gospel of Dirt have no need to submit themselves to the ordeal of congregational Election. They depend for their influence wholly on the sweetness of the living waters to which they lead their flocks.

The *Androssan and Saltcoats Herald* publishes the following extract of a letter written to a friend by Mr. Carlyle : " A good sort of man is this Darwin, and well-meaning, but with very little intellect. Ah, it is a sad, a terrible thing to see nigh a whole generation of men and women, professing to be cultivated, looking round in a purblind fashion, and finding no God in this universe. I suppose it is a reaction from the reign of cant and hollow pretence, professing to believe what, in fact, they do not believe. And this is what we have got to. All things from frog-spawn ; the gospel of dirt the order of the day. The older I grow—and I now stand upon the brink of eternity—the more comes back to me the sentence in the Catechism which I learned when a child, and the fuller and deeper its meaning becomes, 'What is the chief end of man ?—To glorify God, and enjoy Him for ever.' No gospel of dirt, teaching that men have descended from frogs through monkeys, can ever set that aside."

V. The following admirable letter contains nearly all I have to affirm as to the tap-root of economy, namely, house-building :—

"TO THE EDITOR OF THE SPECTATOR.
"CARSHALTON, *Jan.* 27, 1877.

" Sir,—Some seven or eight years ago you permitted me to give you an account of a small house which I had recently built for my own occupation. After the ample experience which I have had, more particularly during the wet of this winter, you may like to know what my convictions now are about houses and house-building. You will remember that I was driven to house-building because of my sufferings in villas. I had wanted warmth and quiet, more particularly the latter, as I had a good deal of work to do which could not be done in a noise. I will not recount my miseries in my search after what to me were primal necessities of life. Suffice to say, at last I managed to buy a little piece of ground, and to put on it a detached cottage, one story high, with four good bedrooms, two sitting-rooms, and a study. I got what

I desired, and never once during these seven years have I regretted building. There are some things which I should like altered, and for the benefit of those who may be intending to follow my example, I will say what they are, and get rid of them. In the first place, the house ought to have one room in the roof, and that room should have been the study, away from all household hubbub, and with a good view of the stars. I could easily have kept out both cold and heat. In the next place, what is called a kitchener is a miserable contrivance for wasting coals, and, what is worse, for poisoning the soft water and spoiling the flowers with the soot which the great draught blows out of the chimney. At the same time, I would earnestly advise an oven in which bread can be baked. No dyspeptic person can well overrate the blessing of bread made simply from flour, yeast, water, and salt; and it is absolutely impossible to procure such bread from ordinary bakers. Thirdly, as I have a garden, I would use earth-closets, and save the expense of manure, and the chance of bursting pipes in frosty weather. Lastly, the cellar ought to have been treble the size it now is, and should have had a stove in it, for warming the house through gratings in the ceiling. I cannot recollect anything else I should like changed, except that I should like to have had a little more money to spend upon making the rooms loftier and larger.

"Now for what I have gained. We have been perfectly dry during all this winter, for the walls are solid, and impervious even to horizontal rain. They are jacketed from the top of the ground-floor upwards with red tiles, which are the best waterproof covering I know, infinitely preferable to the unhealthy looking suburban stucco. Peace has been secured. Not altogether because a man must have a very large domain if he is to protect himself utterly against neighbours who will keep peacocks, or yelping curs which are loose in the garden all night. But the anguish of the piano next door fitting into the recess next to my wall,— worse still, the anguish of expectation when the piano was not playing, are gone. I go to bed when I like, without having to wait till my neighbours go to bed also. All these, however, are obvious advantages. There is one, not quite so obvious, on which I wish particularly to insist. I have got a home. The people about me inhabit houses, but they have no homes, and I observe that they invite one another to their 'places.' Their houses are certain portions of infinite space, in which they are placed for the time being, and they feel it would be slightly absurd to call them 'homes.' I can hardly reckon up the advantages which arise from living in a home, rather than a villa, or a shed, or whatever you like to call it, on a three years' agreement, or as an annual tenant. The sacredness of the family bond is strengthened. The house becomes the outward and visible sign of it, the sacramental sign of it. All sorts of associations cluster round it, of birth, of death, of sorrow, and of joy. Furthermore, there seems to be an addition of permanence to existence. One reason why people generally like castles and cathedrals is because they abide, and contradict that sense of transitoriness which is so painful to us. The house teaches carefulness. A man loves his house, and does not brutally damage plaster or paint. He takes pains to decorate it as far as he can, and is not selfishly anxious to spend nothing on what he cannot take away when he moves. My counsel, therefore, to everybody who can scrape together enough money to make a beginning is to build. Those who are not particularly sensitive, will at least gain solid benefits, for which they will be thankful ; and those with a little more soul in them will become aware of subtle pleasures and the growth of sweet and subtle virtues, which, to say the least, are not promoted by villas. Of course I know it will be urged that estimates will be exceeded, and that house-building leads to extravagance. People who are likely to be led into extravagance, and can never say 'No,' should not build. They may live anywhere, and I have nothing to say to them. But really the temptation to spend money foolishly in house-building is not greater than the tempation to walk past shop windows.

"I am, Sir, etc.,

"W. HALE WHITE."

VI.

" Pardon the correction, but I think you were not quite right in saying in a recent *Fors* that the spiral line could be drawn by the hand and eye only. Mr. F C. Penrose, whose work on the Parthenon you referred to in one of your earlier books, showed me some time ago a double spiral he had drawn with a machine of his own devising, and also a number of other curves (cycloidal, conchoidal, and cissoidal, I think) drawn in the same way, and which latter, he said he believed, had never been drawn with absolute accuracy before."

My correspondent has misunderstood me. I never said 'the spiral' but *this* spiral, under discussion.

I have no doubt the machines are very ingenious. But they will never draw a snail-shell, nor any other organic form. All beautiful lines are drawn under mathematical laws organically *transgressed*, and nothing can ever draw these but the human hand. If Mr. Penrose would make a few pots with his own hand on a potter's wheel, he would learn more of Greek art than all his measurements of the Parthenon have taught him.